9TH April

My Dear Sophie,

The inform about to share with you I have been sitting on for a considerable amount of time, and for a number of reasons I have decided to share it with you now. The sad part for me is that my Father never knew.

Through this mans son, also called Edward, the three of us, you, Kirsty and I are all direct Descendants, Blood line of this man. I kid you not. Fact. The potrait on the front of this book is of your Fifteenth Great Grandfather. In addition of course his younger sister was Jane Seymour, Queen of England for Eighteen months and also gave birth to a King of England King Edword VI

So Jane Seymour was your fifteenth Great Aunt, Blood line Now I don't expect you to read this book, probably not your scene, But I do expect

P.T.O

you to keep it and sometime in the future, when I am long gone and no longer around you might reach up to this book, open it up and think of me and smile

lots of love
Dad xx

EDWARD SEYMOUR

EDWARD SEYMOUR

LORD PROTECTOR

TUDOR KING IN ALL BUT NAME

MARGARET SCARD

Also by Margaret Scard

Tudor Survivor: The Life and Times of William Paulet

First published 2016

The History Press
The Mill, Brimscombe Port
Stroud, Gloucestershire, GL5 2QG
www.thehistorypress.co.uk

© Margaret Scard, 2016

The right of Margaret Scard to be identified as the Author
of this work has been asserted in accordance with the
Copyright, Designs and Patents Act 1988.

British Library Cataloguing in Publication Data.
A catalogue record for this book is available from the British Library.

ISBN 978 0 7509 6243 8

Typesetting and origination by The History Press
Printed and bound by CPI Group (UK) Ltd

Contents

Acknowledgements

Edward Seymour has been a part of my life for many years, sometimes to the exclusion of all else, and I owe an enormous debt of gratitude to my husband, Geoffrey, for enabling me to dedicate so much time and effort to this biography. To both him and to Valery Rose I also give heartfelt thanks for their many hours of proof-reading and for their invaluable comments and encouragement. The research for this work has taken me to many libraries and archives, but I would especially like to thank the staff of the Bodleian Libraries for their patience and assistance. Finally, although only the author's name appears on the cover, a book such as this has involved many people and I express my grateful thanks to them all.

Dramatis Personae

Thomas Cranmer: Archbishop of Canterbury (1533–56). The leading proponent of religious reform during Edward VI's reign.

John Dudley: Viscount Lisle (1542–47), Earl of Warwick (1547–51), Duke of Northumberland (1551–53). Appointed Lord Admiral (1543–47, 1549–50), Lord Great Chamberlain (1547–50), Lord Great Master and president of the privy council (1550–53). The strongest opponent of the Duke of Somerset and leader of two coups against him.

Henry Fitzalan: Earl of Arundel. Appointed Lord Chamberlain (1546–50). A Catholic who sided with Somerset against Dudley.

Stephen Gardiner: Bishop of Winchester (1531–51). An outspoken opponent of religious reform.

William Herbert: Earl of Pembroke. Distantly related to Somerset by marriage. Supported Dudley and refused to bring military aid to Somerset during the 1549 coup.

William Paget: Baron Paget. Principal secretary (1543–47), Comptroller of the Royal Household (1547–49). Secretary and chief ally to Somerset.

Katherine Parr: Queen of England (1543–47), wife of Thomas Seymour (1547–48).

William Parr: Earl of Essex (1543–47), Marquis of Northampton (1547–71). Appointed Lord Great Chamberlain (1550–53). Brother of Katherine Parr. Supported Dudley against Somerset.

William Paulet: Lord St John (1539–50), Earl of Wiltshire (1550–51), Marquis of Winchester (1551–72). Appointed Lord Chamberlain (1543–45), Lord Great Master (1545–50), Lord High Treasurer (1550–72). Supported Dudley against Somerset.

Richard Rich: Baron Rich (1547–67). Appointed Lord Chancellor (1547–51). Despite his support for Somerset's appointment as Lord Protector, Rich later helped to bring him down.

John Russell: Baron Russell (1539–50), Earl of Bedford (1550–55). Appointed Lord Privy Seal (1542–55). A military commander who incurred Somerset's displeasure and refused to support him during the 1549 coup.

Anne Seymour: Duchess of Somerset. Wife of the Duke of Somerset.

Edward Seymour: Viscount Beauchamp (1536–37), Earl of Hertford (1537–47), Duke of Somerset (1547–52). Appointed Lord Great Chamberlain (1543–47), Lord High Treasurer (1547–49), Lord Protector of England (1547–49).

Edward Seymour: Earl of Hertford (1547–52). Son and heir of the Duke of Somerset.

Jane Seymour: Queen of England (1536–37). Sister of the Duke of Somerset.

Thomas Seymour: Baron Seymour of Sudeley (1547–49). Appointed Lord Admiral (1547–49). Brother of the Duke of Somerset. Envious of his brother's superior position.

Sir John Thynne: steward and close associate of the Duke of Somerset.

Thomas Wriothesley: Baron Wriothesley (1544–47), Earl of Southampton (1547–50). Appointed principal secretary (1540–44), Lord Chancellor (1544–47). Opposed Somerset's assumption of power. Removed from office by Somerset and later helped to bring down the Lord Protector.

Ambassadors

Eustace Chapuys: Imperial ambassador for Charles V (1529–45).

François van der Delft: Imperial ambassador (1545–50).

Jehan Scheyfve: Imperial ambassador (1550–53).

Odet de Selve: French ambassador (1546–49).

Seymour Family Tree

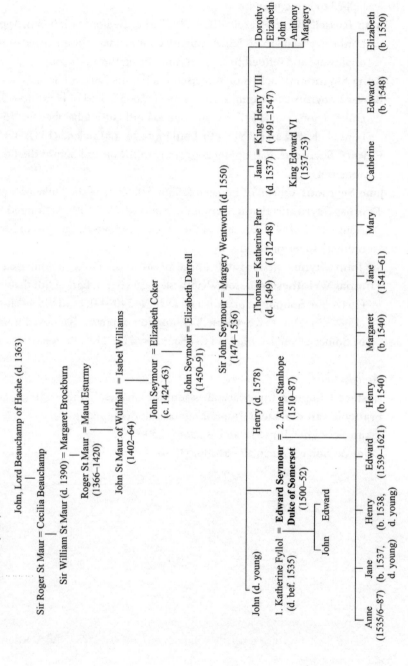

1

Family and Early Years

For nearly three years Edward Seymour was the most powerful man in England. During the sixteenth century only the four renowned Tudor monarchs – Henry VII, Henry VIII, Mary and Elizabeth – wielded greater power. Yet such authority was not his by right. It came about only because of a stroke of good fortune – his sister, Jane, married Henry VIII and then gave birth to a son. It was his kinship to this boy, Edward VI, that gave Seymour an advantage over other men. Seymour had many good qualities that fitted him for high office, but they were undermined by personality traits that would ultimately leave him isolated and vulnerable. Ambition and luck would take him far but when he lost the support of the people around him he would have to fight to maintain his pre-eminence.

Edward Seymour's rise to greatness began with an execution. In 1536, George Boleyn knelt on the scaffold at Tower Hill. Within the Tower his sister, Queen Anne, awaited the same fate. As the executioner's axe fell upon George, Edward Seymour prepared for the future; just eleven days later the king married Jane Seymour and Edward became the monarch's new brother-in-law. Through his six marriages Henry VIII acquired numerous brothers-in-law. Four of these – George Boleyn, Edward Seymour, Thomas Seymour and William Parr – were to leave their mark upon the annals of England's history. They were ambitious and keen to make their way at court, but despite their achievements three of them were to die upon the scaffold. Only one would live to die of old age.

Being the king's brother-in-law did not guarantee a successful career at the royal court but it was certainly a step along the way. Patronage and advancement came from the king and, with a sister to speak on their behalf, the royal brothers-in-law were in a favoured position. But the court of Henry VIII was a bear-pit where only the skilful survived and those closest to the king were in the most danger. Some men gained the enmity of the king; others, including Cardinal Wolsey and Thomas Cromwell, were brought down by the machinations of their enemies. George Boleyn fell because the king had tired of Anne. Edward Seymour was stepping into a precarious situation.

The story of Henry VIII and Anne Boleyn is well known. After over twenty years of marriage to Catherine of Aragon, Henry still had no male heir. His break with the Roman Catholic Church and the papacy enabled him to marry Anne; it also set England upon a path of religious reform along which Edward Seymour would continue to take the country. The king's sense of elation occasioned by his marriage to Anne in January 1533, after so many years of waiting, was soon followed by disenchantment with her failure to give him the promised son and heir. Their daughter, Elizabeth, was no consolation to Henry, and after Anne had miscarried a boy in early 1536 he was actively seeking a way to annul their marriage. He had put aside one wife, Catherine of Aragon, and could do the same again. Although she was not guilty of the charges of adultery made against her, Anne's behaviour provided the king with the solution he sought. Her over-familiarity with gentlemen of the court and her close relationship with her brother gave the king and her enemies sufficient grounds to destroy her.

Henry needed an heir and he soon chose Jane Seymour to provide this much-wanted son. In 1535 he had visited Wulfhall in Wiltshire, the home of the Seymour family, and this may have been when Jane first made an impression on him. She and her brothers, Edward and Thomas, were the children of a country gentleman, John Seymour. Like many long-established families, the Seymours claimed descent from one of the men who had accompanied William the Conqueror to England in 1066 – in their case, Wido de St Maur. His son acquired land in Wiltshire, Somerset and Gloucestershire and for a time their descendants were settled at Penhow Castle on the Welsh border. It was 300 years after their arrival, however, before the Seymours became people of note. Roger St Maur, following the proven route to fortune, married an heiress, Cecilia, who in 1363 inherited half the estate of her father, John, Lord Beauchamp of Hache in Somerset. Through this marriage the Seymours (as they became known in the fifteenth century) gained both status and property. Their wealth increased further when Roger's grandson, also Roger, married Maud, the younger daughter of Sir William Esturmy. This marked the point at which the family connection with Wulfhall began. Sir William had no male heir and willed a large part of his Savernake property, including Wulfhall, and a house at Elvetham, Hampshire, to Roger and Maud's son, John, who also assumed Sir William's hereditary role as warden of Savernake Forest in 1427.[1]

John was a wealthy gentleman and established himself as a prominent figure in Wiltshire serving as sheriff and on various commissions until his death in 1464.

The family maintained their position in the county and in 1474 John's great-grandson, another John Seymour, was born at Wulfhall. The eldest of eight children, this John was to be Edward Seymour's father. John had not reached his majority when his father died in 1491 and his wardship was granted to Sir Henry Wentworth.[2] Sometime prior to 1499, at which point he succeeded to his father's lands and to the wardenship of Savernake Forest, John married Sir Henry's daughter, Margery, giving his family a distant connection to nobility and a line of descent back to Edward III.[3]

John acquitted himself well in minor appointments at court and proved his worth in battle. He was knighted by Henry VII after the defeat of the Cornish rebels at Blackheath in 1497; further battle honours came in 1513 when he was raised to knight banneret by Henry VIII after the Battle of the Spurs at Therouanne, an honour that entitled him to lead a company of men in battle under his own banner.[4] Like many other gentlemen he was periodically called to attend upon the king, not in any intimate capacity but as part of a large entourage. When Henry VIII met Francis I of France at the Field of the Cloth of Gold in 1520 Sir John was among the company and later, in 1532, he attended the king as a groom of the bedchamber during his meeting with Francis at Boulogne.[5]

Sir John has left his mark on posterity not on account of his own achievements but because he sired three offspring who trod the corridors of power during the turbulent years of Henry VIII and Edward VI. John and Margery had ten children, six sons and four daughters, of whom two sons and one daughter probably died in infancy. The eldest surviving son, John, may have lived until he was about 20 but he appears to have been overshadowed from an early age by his brother Edward. Edward Seymour was born around 1500 and during the following nine years he was joined by brothers Henry and Thomas and sister Jane. Of his other sisters, Dorothy would later marry Sir Clement Smith and Elizabeth would wed, as the second of her three husbands, Gregory, the son of Thomas Cromwell.[6] However, it was Jane's elevation to the position of Queen of England that presented the opportunity for two of her three surviving brothers to shine at court. While Henry Seymour remained in the shadows, marrying Barbara Wolfe and living until 1578, Edward and Thomas were both talented and ambitious. Edward would become the most powerful man in England; Thomas would become his rival.

In the sixteenth century the most successful route to advancement was through the support of an influential patron. Edward Seymour was only 14 when he first came to the attention of Henry VIII and was appointed as a page of honour to the king's sister, Mary, on the occasion of her marriage to Louis XII of France. It placed him in one of the grandest households in Europe. Seymour's father held no great influence at court and there is no obvious reason why Edward was selected for this honour, but it was certainly a small triumph for his family. On 2 October 1514 the young Seymour and the sons of Lords Roos and Cobham, who also served as pages, joined Mary and her entourage sailing from Dover to Calais. A symbolic marriage had already taken place at Greenwich and on 9 October Seymour witnessed the magnificence of a royal wedding in the church at Abbeville, followed a month later by Mary's crowning in the abbey church of St Denis in Paris. To Louis's annoyance, Mary had been accompanied by a large retinue and he soon sent most of her attendants back to England. The three pages were allowed to remain with her but their time in France was cut short: the 52-year old Louis died just twelve weeks later, exhausted by his energetic 18-year-old wife, or so it was said.[7]

A few months before travelling to France, Seymour had been married to Katherine Fyloll. Marriage at such an early age was often an arrangement for the future and was not an impediment to his appointment as Mary's page. He was also expected to continue his education and after his return to England he went to study at Oxford University.[8] University had previously been primarily for the clergy but increasingly the sons of noblemen and gentlemen were attending, not with the intention of gaining education to a scholarly level but rather to prepare themselves for participation in the expanding government administration of the country. Seymour was the first member of his family to be recorded as attending Oxford. There is, however, no record of him completing his degree and he may have been among the many students who attended for only one or two years. The suggestion that he also studied at Cambridge University seems unlikely and it may be that his appointment as chancellor of Cambridge in 1547 caused this confusion.

Since many university lectures and textbooks were in Latin, and proficiency in that language was a prerequisite for entry, his early education must have included Latin alongside the usual subjects of reading, religion and basic arithmetic, no doubt under the guidance of the family priest as was commonplace. University tuition included philosophy, theology, arithmetic, geometry and astronomy; for courtiers and men in positions of authority who needed to be able to express their views clearly and cogently, the lessons in logic and rhetoric and the skill gained in debate might have proved to be the most useful. The ability to influence other men through argument could have momentous outcomes, as Seymour would later experience.

Details of Seymour's early career are sparse but show a young man who was slowly establishing himself on the periphery of the royal court. Early in 1521, while he was employed by Cardinal Wolsey, Seymour had his first exposure to the religion of the new Protestant reformers, whose ideas would later influence his own beliefs and pave the way for the Edwardian Reformation. Between January and May the Holy Roman Emperor, Charles V, presided at the Imperial diet at Worms on the Rhine, an assembly that denounced the views of the Protestant reformer, Martin Luther. That spring, on the recommendation of Henry VIII and Wolsey, Charles admitted Seymour to his service as a gentleman of his court at Worms. There is no record of what Seymour's role entailed but it is certain that Wolsey expected him to act as his eyes and ears, reporting news from the Imperial court. Seymour must have become aware of the issues surrounding Martin Luther and the new evangelical theology during his time at Worms. Could this have been the point at which he began to consider these new ideas?

Seymour and Charles were of a similar age, which may have helped foster friendship between them. Certainly the emperor was 'well pleased' with him, suggesting a good relationship between the two men that may have had some bearing on Seymour's future amity towards Charles.[9] The two men would meet again. After witnessing the English victory over Boulogne in 1544, Seymour visited Charles in Brussels to negotiate his support for Henry VIII against the French.

Seymour's first experience of war came in August 1523 when Charles Brandon, Duke of Suffolk, led an invasion into France. This provided a valuable opportunity to learn about warfare, not least the importance of having a common goal and reliable allies, and the hazards of conducting a campaign as winter started. The venture was a joint assault against Francis I by Henry VIII, Charles V and Charles, Duke of Bourbon. The 14,000 Englishmen were joined by 7,000 men from the Low Countries and a further 10,000 Germans who were to march into France from the east. The expedition proved fruitless. Bourbon's revolt was betrayed and Charles V did little towards the enterprise. The English plan to take Boulogne was abandoned and Suffolk's forces instead marched towards Paris. The army took Montdidier on 28 October and marched to within 50 miles of the capital but by then it was late in the season, the weather was becoming harsh and the Germans were deserting. The invasion was abandoned and the army withdrew, leaving the French to reclaim the towns that the English had taken on their advance. As an invasion it had been a failure but Seymour proved his worth and he was one of fourteen men to be knighted by Suffolk at Roye.[10] In the future, the experience he had gained would be of great value when he led the English army to war.

The following year Seymour received his first appointment at the English court when he was made an esquire of the king's household.[11] It was a relatively minor position and such appointments were often honorary, requiring only occasional attendance at court. However, it further enhanced his social status in Wiltshire where he was establishing himself as a man of authority. In January 1525 he was appointed a justice of the peace in his home county and at a later date also for Somerset. With no standing army or police force, the king was reliant on the local nobility and gentry to maintain order throughout the country. Justices had the power to examine and imprison minor criminals and to send more serious cases to the assizes. As the sixteenth century progressed government involvement in subjects' lives grew. The responsibilities of the justices increased as their judicial and administrative duties widened and they endeavoured to enforce the many regulations issued by the privy council. These covered a myriad of issues from food prices and the maintenance of local highways to the periodic collection of subsidies, and, in the case of the coastal counties, the maintenance of coastal defences and warning beacons.

Seymour's first appointment of note came when, aged 25, he was appointed Master of the Horse to the king's bastard son, Henry Fitzroy.[12] Born in 1519 to the king's mistress, Elizabeth Blount, Fitzroy was at that time the king's only living son and when he was 6 years old Henry chose to acknowledge him as a member of his family. On 18 June 1525 Fitzroy was created both Earl of Nottingham and Duke of Richmond and Somerset, an unprecedented double dukedom that made him the premier duke in the land. A month later he was appointed Lord Admiral of England. There was immediate speculation that the king would make the new 6-year-old duke his heir but Henry had not given up hope of a legitimate son. Although the likelihood of sons with his queen, Catherine of Aragon, was remote (she was then aged 40) there was the possibility that if she should die before the king he might father an heir with a new wife. Nevertheless, a titled son, even one who was illegitimate, could still be useful as a pawn in marriage. So the titles Henry gave to Fitzroy were not the usual royal family titles of Cornwall and York. They were instead connected with the house of Tudor. The king's father had held the title Earl of Richmond and his great-grandfather, John Beaufort, had been Duke of Somerset.

Historically, royal relatives had acted as figureheads and representatives of the monarchy but Henry VIII had no brothers or legitimate sons. When Richmond was also appointed Warden General of the Scottish Marches and president of the newly resurrected Council of the North it became apparent that the king planned to exert his royal authority in the north through his son. At the same time he sent his 9-year-old daughter, Mary, to Ludlow to head the Council for the Marches of Wales. By appointing his children to these posts Henry retained some semblance of control in the extremities of the kingdom and avoided placing extensive power in the hands of local magnates. Richmond took no part in council business although as the king's representative in the north of England he welcomed all visiting noblemen and dignitaries. Much of his time was spent at lessons he shared with his young companions and in riding, hawking and archery.

Richmond was to live at Sheriff Hutton in Yorkshire. He left London with a large retinue in July and after a leisurely progress reached his destination at the end of August. It was intended that he should have a large household appropriate to his position and titles, with kitchen staff, officers and servants for the public chambers and a privy chamber staff as his personal servants. Among them was his Master of the Horse, Edward Seymour.

The office of Master of the Horse had originated in the royal household but a similar post existed in all large houses. With horses as the only means of travel, other than on foot, stables were of vital importance. Seymour was responsible for all aspects of transport and oversaw everything from the management and financing of the stables and staff to the provision of horses for riding, hunting, jousting and even baggage horses for pulling carts when the household moved. It was a privileged position of significant responsibility. Richmond's safety was paramount to the king and Seymour would be expected to ride close by to supervise him, helping him to hone his riding skills while restraining him from attempting any feats that might endanger his life. Given the possibility of Richmond one day becoming king, this appointment in Yorkshire gave Seymour the opportunity to earn the boy's favour. However, it also removed him from court and hence from the king, the immediate source of patronage.

It was during his time at Sheriff Hutton that Seymour came into contact with a young man who would later play a prominent role in his life. For many years the lives of Edward Seymour and William Parr would be intertwined. William, the only son of Thomas Parr and his wife, Maud, was just 12 years old when he joined Richmond as one of his companions. His father had died in 1517 when William was 4, and he and his two sisters, Katherine and Anne, had grown up in the care of their mother. The Parr family were northern gentry who had established themselves as wealthy, influential landowners in Kendal, Westmorland. They were also well connected at court where Maud was a lady-in-waiting to the queen, Catherine of Aragon.

Being part of Richmond's household was a golden opportunity for both Seymour and Parr, offering the chance to become acquainted with boys who might one day become men of influence. Among the young duke's other companions were Henry Grey, who later became Earl of Dorset and father of Lady Jane Grey; Henry Clifford, the future Earl of Cumberland; and Thomas Fiennes, who became Lord Dacre. This period may, too, have been when Seymour first became acquainted with Richard Page, Richmond's vice-chamberlain, who would later become Seymour's stepfather-in-law.

It is unclear how long Seymour remained at Sheriff Hutton but in 1527 he returned to France for a time as a member of Cardinal Wolsey's retinue. Wolsey was to be Henry VIII's representative at a meeting with Francis I and he took it upon himself to act in all ways as king. His cavalcade resembled nothing less than a royal progress. Ahead of the cardinal, Seymour rode among a great number of gentlemen all dressed in coats of black velvet with chains of gold about their necks. Following behind Wolsey came a great array of servants wearing livery coats with an image of a cardinal's hat emblazoned upon them. Although Wolsey may have chosen to ride upon a mule for the image of poverty and modesty it portrayed, this beast was adorned in finest crimson velvet with stirrups of copper and gilt.[13] The company travelled at a sedate pace, taking a week to cover the journey from London to Dover from where they took a ship to Calais and continued on to meet Francis at Amiens on 5 August. A peace treaty was agreed between the two countries. However, other negotiations for a marriage between Princess Mary and Francis's second son, the Duke of Orleans, as well as Wolsey's proposal that he deputise for Pope Clement while he was a captive of Charles V, came to naught.

Henry VIII was sufficiently impressed by Seymour to appoint him as an 'esquire of the body to the King' in September 1531 with an annuity of 50 marks.[14] The position gave unrivalled access to Henry, helping him to dress and undress and attending to his needs, both day and night. Seymour's position at court was sufficiently elevated for him to present a New Year gift to the king a few weeks later – a sword with a gilt handle and the word 'kalendars' upon it – and to receive a gift of money in return. He was among the royal retinue when Henry, accompanied by Anne Boleyn, met Francis I at Calais in 1532 and the following June he served as carver to the Archbishop of Canterbury at the banquet held after Anne's coronation.[15] It was a great honour to be chosen as carver to some great personage and all gentlemen were taught the skills of this complicated ritual where all beasts and birds were carved and presented in a different manner. He was not the only member of his family to be appointed on this occasion; his brother Henry was also chosen to attend at table as a server. Henry never attained the rank or influence of Edward and Thomas. He spent some time at court and served as carver to Queen Katherine Parr but for much of his life he lived in the country. His sister, Jane, appointed him as steward and bailiff of several manors and after her death he continued to manage these properties.[16]

Edward Seymour had begun to acquire land and property that would eventually form part of an enormous portfolio providing him with a large annual income. All land in England belonged to either the Church or the king but much of the crown land and property was granted to people either for their own use or to be managed on behalf of the king. In July 1517 Seymour and his father had been appointed joint constables of Bristol Castle, responsible for maintaining the castle in a fit state. He also received an appointment to be steward of two manors in Somerset and Wiltshire which he administered through a bailiff but which would have provided certain perks. Although the income from the land was intended for the king, stewards received rewards such as the right to fish in the rivers upon the land or to hunt a fixed number of deer each year or to cut a quantity of timber for their own use. Other parcels of land granted to Seymour were managed for his own benefit. In 1528 he received property from several religious houses dissolved by Cardinal Wolsey, and following the downfall of Wolsey he was granted three manors in Yorkshire.[17] When great men fell there were rich pickings for those in favour with the king.

Seymour also began acquiring land from other men, effectively buying the right to use land that had been granted to them by the king. He was aggressive in his land acquisition and adept at trying to manipulate legal loopholes for his own benefit, causing one witness to complain that 'it is hard trusting to his courtesy, for he hath small conscience'.[18] One particular dispute between him and Arthur Plantagenet, Viscount Lisle, which began in 1533 and continued for nearly four years, demonstrates both the complexity of land ownership and Seymour's focused ambition. Lisle had the right to use land that his first wife, Elizabeth Grey, had inherited. Upon Lisle's death the land was to pass to John Dudley, her son by her first marriage to Edmund Dudley. However, John sold his claim on the estate to Seymour who agreed to pay Lisle £140 per year as rent to use the land during Lisle's lifetime. Seymour, though, persevered to gain complete control of the land. Lisle was always short of money and in 1536 he took out a loan using the land as a bond for repayment. Unbeknown to Lisle the loan was secured by Seymour so that, when Lisle was unable to repay the sum by the due date, he was put into Seymour's debt. The king's chief minister, Thomas Cromwell, and the Lord Chancellor, Thomas Audley, who acted as arbitrators between the two men, considered that Seymour had handled Lisle 'very craftily' but were unable to resolve the dispute. Seymour eventually agreed to extend the payment date but Lisle again missed the deadline. Seymour was determined to have the estate and as Cromwell realised, 'this man will be by no means entreated'. When Lisle eventually sent the money three weeks later Seymour refused to accept it and took immediate and complete control of the land.[19]

Seymour was to be involved in a further land dispute with the Lisles in 1538. On that occasion, however, it was Lisle's second wife, Honor Bassett, who opposed him on behalf of John Bassett, her son from her first marriage. Henry Daubeney, who had a claim on land that should rightfully have reverted to John Bassett, transferred his rights to Seymour, preventing Bassett taking ownership.

Lady Lisle appealed to the king to rule in her son's favour and, after Seymour and Daubeney were spoken to by the king and Cromwell, they were so 'shaken up' that they promised to meddle no further. There may, however, have been rather more to this altercation than just land ownership. There is a suggestion that Seymour (who by this time was Earl of Hertford) used his influence to have Daubeney elevated to Earl of Bridgewater. In return Daubeney arranged for Somerset to inherit some of his lands after his death.[20]

By 1535 Seymour's first wife was dead and he was free to marry again. His first marriage to Katherine Fyloll, the daughter of a Dorset landowner, was not a success and had ended years earlier. Seymour had been only 14 when the couple married in the spring of 1514. Until he reached the age of 21 they had lived in his father's household, John Seymour having agreed to provide them with 'as well meat, drink, learning and lodging, as apparel convenient for their degree'. John also gave the couple lands worth £40 a year and Edward was to inherit further land to the value of 100 marks when his father died. With surprising prescience, the marriage agreement drawn up by their respective fathers had foreseen the possibility that the union might fail. If Edward Seymour should 'disagree with the marriage' within three years and the marriage be dissolved, John agreed that he would pay Katherine a dowry of 200 marks to remarry.[21]

In the event the marriage lasted longer than three years but sometime after that Edward Seymour was given cause to question the paternity of his eldest son, John, who was born in 1518. Rumour started that the boy's father was Seymour's own father, John – a possibility since Katherine lived in the same house as her father-in-law and Edward had been away at university. Certainly, there was a child called John who was recognised as being Edward Seymour's illegitimate brother and who later served as a gentleman-pensioner for Queen Elizabeth. However, there is no firm evidence that the two children were one and the same.[22] Edward chose not to divorce Katherine but to put her into a convent. It was a decision apparently supported by her father, William Fyloll, who gave her £40 a year for life 'as long as she shall live virtuously and abide in some honest house of religion of women'. William also decreed that Seymour was to have no part of the £40.

There was a serious estrangement between William Fyloll and Katherine and Edward Seymour. William stipulated that 'for many diverse causes and considerations' neither Katherine, Edward nor their two sons, John and Edward, should receive any land or property from his estate. In his will, made on 14 May 1527, he left most of his estate to his nephew, Sir Thomas Trenchard. However, in expectation that his two daughters and their husbands would challenge this, he left strict instructions that his executors were to pay no attention to them. There was serious concern about the state of the old man's mind. In 1530, on account of his 'having many sundry and inconstant fantasies in his latter days', his will was set aside by an Act of Parliament. Sir William's Fyloll's land and manors were then shared between Katherine, her sister Anne, their mother and their husbands.[23]

Seymour's second wife, Anne, was the daughter of Sir Edward Stanhope, of Rampton in Nottinghamshire. Through her mother, Elizabeth Bourchier, Anne was descended from Edward III. Considering the young age at which he entered into his first marriage, Seymour's first bride had been chosen by his family. However, as a man in his 30s, his second bride was undoubtedly his own choice. Anne was about ten years younger than Seymour who, by the time of their marriage, was well established at court. Although not handsome, later portraits depict his face as serious and refined; however, the firm set of his mouth suggests a man not to be trifled with. His marriage to Anne appears to have been successful although in 1549 Anne was shaken when her husband lost his temper with her. For the first time she experienced the full extent of his wrath. Seymour had mistakenly believed that Anne had betrayed secrets to Lady Fitzwilliam; he was furious and 'she had never so much displeasure of her husband since she was first Sir Edward Seymour's wife'.[24]

The couple had married by 9 March 1535 and had eleven children: Anne, who had been born by early 1536; Jane, born in 1537, and Henry in 1538 (both of whom died in infancy); Edward in 1539, who became Earl of Hertford; Henry and Margaret, born in 1540; Jane, in 1541; Mary and Catherine. Two more children were born after Seymour became Lord Protector: a son born in 1548 was also named Edward, probably in honour of his godfather, the king; and finally, in 1550, at the age of about 40, Anne Seymour gave birth to Elizabeth.[25] Four of the children died unmarried but through the remainder, and the two sons by his first marriage, Seymour left a long progeny.

Uncertainty about the paternity of the eldest son from his first marriage raised the possibility of disputes over the inheritance of his estates. To resolve this issue Seymour was granted an Act of Parliament in 1540 by which he disinherited John.[26] All his property was to be inherited by the heirs from his marriage with Anne or any future wife. However, in the event that there were no such living male heirs, the property was to pass in the first instance to Edward, his second son from his first marriage, and secondly to his two brothers, Henry and Thomas and finally to his daughters. Anne Seymour has been much maligned throughout the centuries as being proud, haughty and controlling but the assertion that it was at her insistence that Seymour established such an inheritance is unfounded. Ensuring the future of large estates was not an unusual activity and Seymour was trying to protect the interests of his new family.

2

Brother of the Queen

At the beginning of 1536 there was nothing to set Seymour apart from the other ambitious men close to the king. Suddenly this all changed and his star was in the ascendant, not through his own actions but because his sister, Jane, caught the eye of the king. Jane had joined the court at some time around 1529 as a lady-in-waiting, first to Catherine of Aragon and then to Anne Boleyn. There is no record of when Henry first considered her to be a potential amour. He would undoubtedly have seen her at court among the queen's ladies and Jane could have been at Wulfhall when Henry visited the house during his progress in September 1535, either among Anne's retinue or helping her parents to host the royal visitors. The king unexpectedly visited the Seymours again the following month. As the progress neared its end, an outbreak of plague near Guildford caused him to change his itinerary and spend one night at their house at Elvetham. It was an enormous undertaking to accommodate the king with his huge entourage and the Seymour family had just five days to prepare for this visit.[1]

Henry had quickly become disillusioned with his second bride and still needed an heir. As early as October 1534 the Imperial ambassador, Eustace Chapuys, wrote of a young lady at court favoured by the king, although he did not name her.[2] In January 1536, soon after Catherine of Aragon died, Anne miscarried a boy child. The news was devastating for the royal couple, and for Anne it was the beginning of her downfall. She might have survived as queen if she had retained the support of the king's chief minister, Thomas Cromwell, but the two had disagreed over how the assets from dissolved monasteries should be used. The refusal of the emperor to recognise her as queen was also hampering Cromwell's efforts to strengthen Henry's relationship with Charles V.

Anne had failed to deliver the only thing Henry wanted – a son – and he took this second miscarriage to be a sign of God's disfavour with their marriage. Once again he convinced himself that if he was to have a son, he must take a new wife. To remove a second queen from the throne would not be easy, but in the meantime Jane proved to be a useful distraction. In early February, Chapuys identified her as the lady who had captured the king's attention and in March Henry sent her a letter with a purse full of sovereigns. Jane responded in a most modest manner – or was it a scheming response? – by kissing the letter and returning it unopened with the purse and a message to the king. Falling to her knees she implored the messenger to tell Henry that she was:

> a gentlewoman of good and honourable parents, without reproach, and that she had no greater riches in the world than her honour, which she would not injure for a thousand deaths, and that if he wished to make her some present in money she begged it might be when God enabled her to make some honourable match.[3]

It was a clever reply leaving the real meaning of Jane's response unclear. Was she referring to some future husband other than the king or had she set her sights on the crown? If her intent was the latter it was a perfect response and the effect upon the king was that his love and desire for her was 'wonderfully increased'. Henry did not want a mistress; he needed a new wife, and to prove that his intentions were honourable he declared that henceforth he would only speak with her in the presence of one of her relatives. With this in mind, and as a means of meeting with Jane in secret away from the eyes of the court, the king moved Cromwell from his chamber close to the royal apartments at Greenwich Palace and lodged Edward Seymour and his wife there. Henry could reach this chamber unobserved from the privy apartments and meet Jane chaperoned by her family.

Jane has been portrayed as meek and virtuous but there is a sense of almost Machiavellian scheming by her and her family as she waited to oust the crowned Queen of England. They had seen what the Boleyns had achieved; all the Seymours needed to do was bide their time. Henry had married one commoner, why should he not marry a second? Was Jane planning her own course or was she being guided? She undoubtedly favoured the idea of marriage to the king – it is difficult to believe she would have gone along with the scheme if she had been truly against the idea. However, when Edward Seymour and his family realised there was a possibility of Jane wearing a crown they supported, guided and encouraged her. The opportunities and rewards for her family would be enormous. Chapuys believed, too, that Jane was being guided by certain members of the court. For example, Sir Nicholas Carew, the Master of the Horse, was one of a number of Catholics who wanted to see Anne removed, Mary restored to her position as a princess of England and heir to the crown and the return of England to the papacy. They believed that, as queen, Jane could bring this about and they encouraged her not to give in to the king's advances except in marriage.[4]

Their hope of restoring Mary was futile, though, and later caused Jane to make a serious mistake. Mary had been declared illegitimate when Henry divorced Catherine of Aragon and her title changed to Lady Mary. Shortly before they were married Jane suggested to the king that Mary should be restored as princess and hence recognised as Henry's daughter and heir to the crown. The request was met with the rebuttal that she was a fool and should look to the future of the children they would have together, not to any others; a reminder, perhaps, to her family and friends that Jane did not have unbridled influence with the king.[5]

Seymour was reaping the benefits of his sister's success. On 3 March 1536 he was made a gentleman of the privy chamber.[6] The gentlemen worked in shifts and when he was on duty Seymour was expected to be in the privy chambers by 7 a.m. each morning to dress the king. He waited upon him and kept Henry company during the day and then at night he took his turn at sleeping on a pallet in the king's chamber, ready to answer his monarch's summons at any time. His easy access to the king provided countless opportunities to praise his sister's virtues.

By the end of April Cromwell was ready to move against Queen Anne after gathering evidence that she had been overly familiar with members of the court. Anne was well practised in the game of courtly love, of flattery and flirting, and it was easy for her enemies to concoct accusations of unseemly behaviour. On 2 May Anne and her brother George, Viscount Rochford, were arrested and taken to the Tower. Although she was probably unprepared for the seriousness of the charges against her, Anne knew she had been ousted from her husband's affections. While she waited in the Tower for her trial, she wrote to Henry that if she was proven to be guilty he would be at liberty 'to follow your affection already settled on that party, for whose sake I am now as I am; whose name I could some good while since, have pointed unto, your grace being not ignorant of my suspicion therein'.[7] On 15 May, she and her brother were tried and found guilty of treason on the grounds of their supposed incest together. Anne was similarly found guilty of adultery with Henry Norris, Francis Weston, William Brereton and Mark Smeaton. Rochford was beheaded at Tower Hill two days later and on 19 May Anne was executed at Tower Green. The way was clear for Jane and her brother to step into their shoes.

Events moved quickly for Jane. On 17 May the Archbishop of Canterbury, Thomas Cranmer, had pronounced the marriage of Henry and Anne to be null and void. Two days later he granted a dispensation for Henry and Jane to marry because they were fifth cousins and on 20 May the couple were betrothed. On Tuesday 30 May the king married his third wife privately in the small queen's closet at Whitehall. Seymour was now the king's brother-in-law and three days later, as the king and his court made a stately procession along the Thames to Greenwich, Seymour watched from the royal barge as his sister made her first journey as queen, travelling in her own barge, surrounded by her ladies.[8]

On 4 June, the great religious festival day of Whitsunday, Jane was proclaimed queen at Greenwich and began what was to be her very short reign.[9] One of her first engagements was to receive Chapuys, after which the ambassador met with Seymour. One can only wonder at the latter's thoughts as Chapuys explained to him the benefits for England and all Christendom if Mary were to be restored to her rightful position. Chapuys left the meeting believing that Seymour would do all in his power to achieve such an end but it is more likely that Seymour had expectations of a future nephew of his, rather than an ardent Catholic, being heir to the throne of England.[10]

There was concern at the speed with which the king had divested himself of one wife and acquired another. For many, though, the news was greeted with joy because the marriage had brought the king 'out of hell into heaven'. Sir John Russell praised Jane: 'she is as gentle a lady as ever I knew, and as fair a Queen as any in Christendom'. This was rather at odds with Chapuys's description of Jane as 'of middle stature and no great beauty, so fair that one would call her rather pale than otherwise'. A portrait of Jane by Holbein depicts a composed young woman with fair skin and hair, a little plumpness about her chin, a tight mouth and a slightly over-large nose. The picture shows her wearing a gown with gold embroidery and a kirtle and sleeves made of cloth of silver. She is adorned with jewels, including an IHS pendant, and sets herself apart from her predecessor by wearing a traditional English hood rather than the fashionable French style introduced by Anne Boleyn. She was not as clever as Anne, being of no 'great wit' although she had 'good understanding', but then Henry had no desire to have another wife who would argue and dispute with him.[11]

Edward Seymour's future looked assured – his sister was Queen of England and he was related to Henry VIII. Just a week after the marriage he received his greatest recognition so far when he was created Viscount Beauchamp of Hache in Somerset, granted for service 'done and to be done; as also of his circumspection, valour and loyalty'.[12] The honour, a reward for past efforts and an incentive for future service, was undoubtedly allied to his sister's elevation and was accompanied by an annuity of 20 marks a year and a sizeable grant of land and manors in Wiltshire. Seymour's choice of Beauchamp resurrected the title that had died out nearly 200 years earlier, when his ancestor, Lord John Beauchamp, had died without an heir, and added an element of ancient lineage to his new position. The attribute of 'circumspection' foreshadowed the cautious approach he displayed during his early years as a military commander although it was a quality that eluded him during his final years in power.[13]

Seymour's brother, Thomas, was not faring as well in achieving recognition at court, although it was a general principle that the older sibling should have primacy. In 1530 he had accompanied Sir Francis Bryan, who served as ambassador at the French court, and acted as his courier carrying despatches across the Channel to and from the king.[14] When Jane married Henry, Thomas followed his brother in being appointed a gentleman of the privy chamber but there was to be no title for him yet.

In the pecking order of precedence Beauchamp (as we shall now know him) ranked above the barons, not only at court but also in Parliament where he soon made his first appearance. On 7 June, in readiness for the opening of Parliament, the court travelled from Greenwich to Whitehall. It was a magnificent spectacle as the long procession of barges made its way up the Thames. Along the river ships fired their guns and as the flotilla came close to the city it was met by two barges of musicians blowing trumpets and playing shawms and sackbutts. The barges passed by the Tower, where the walls were hung with streamers and banners, to the accompaniment of 400 guns fired in celebration to mark the triumphant arrival of a new queen. It was in stark contrast to the day, less than three weeks earlier, when the old queen had been beheaded. On through London Bridge the boats continued, the musicians still playing, until they reached the steps of Whitehall.

The following day Jane stood in the gatehouse at the palace to watch her husband and brother ride out with the other lords to the opening of Parliament. Preceding the king and bearing his cap of maintenance was the Duke of Richmond.[15] This was possibly the last time the young man was seen in public for within seven weeks the king's only son had died from a lung infection. Although Henry had not declared Richmond to be his heir there had always been the option to do so; with him gone the king's need for Jane to give birth to a son was even greater.

Beauchamp's status continued to rise. He was appointed Chancellor of North Wales and he purchased the office of Captain and Governor of Jersey from Lord Thomas Vaux for £150.[16] This was a royal appointment but occasionally the king would allow such posts to be sold. For the English, Jersey was an important defensive position, close to the French coast, and a trading centre that could prove lucrative for the governor. Among Beauchamp's predecessors in the post was his brother-in-law, Sir Anthony Ughtred, who had died in 1534. Beauchamp's sister, Elizabeth, and Ughtred had lived at Mont Orgueil Castle in

Jersey but Beauchamp chose to govern through a lieutenant. With his sister as queen he had no wish to be isolated in Jersey, away from the opportunities that the court offered. His new intimacy with the king created tensions between himself and some members of the court and being absent would have left the way clear for his enemies to talk against him. Rivalry was intense and there were always men who resented the success of others. In particular, Beauchamp had attracted the antipathy of Anne Boleyn's relations, the Howards. After years of being the premier family at court while Anne was the royal favourite they now saw their place usurped by the Seymours.

Plans were made for Jane to be crowned queen. James Nedam, the king's surveyor, arranged for work to be carried out during September 'against the Coronation of Queen Jane Seymour'. The great hall and kitchens at Westminster Palace underwent alterations; railings were made to stop the people pressing forward as the procession moved along King's Street between the palace and Westminster Abbey. Inside the abbey a raised walkway and platform were constructed so the watching people could more easily see the ceremony.[17] Letters were ready to be delivered, informing the recipients that they would receive the Knighthood of the Bath in honour of the event. The coronation was planned for 29 October – the Sunday before All Hallows' Day – but at the end of September it was postponed because of plague at Westminster where people at the abbey had been infected. Jane never was crowned queen. Any plans for a coronation the following year were overtaken when she became pregnant. However, the people were treated to another grand spectacle just before Christmas when the court moved from Westminster to spend the festive season at Greenwich. The Thames was frozen solid; no boats could sail so the royal party travelled on horseback through the city. People came out to watch as Henry and Jane, attended by a great company, passed along streets hung with 'rich gold and arras'. Along the route stood abbots, priests and friars wearing copes of gold and holding crosses, candlesticks or censors to cense the king and queen as they rode by.[18]

Yet even as they stood there, the way of life of these churchmen was under threat. Henry's struggle to divorce Catherine of Aragon and marry Anne Boleyn had set him on a path that would lead to the reformation of the Church in England. The Act in Restraint of Appeals in 1533 had allowed for the royal divorce to be settled in England rather than in the papal courts. The following year Henry had declared himself Supreme Head of the Church in England, removing himself and his subjects from the control of the pope. Further statutes increasingly brought the clergy under royal authority and gave the king power to reform Church doctrine. In 1536 the 'Ten Articles' maintained that only three sacraments – the Eucharist, baptism and penance – were necessary for salvation.

The abolition of less important holy days had the effect of reducing the number of holidays the people could enjoy, and a move to diminish the value of images in worship was followed by the dissolution of the smaller monasteries. Although this was ostensibly because these communities were corrupt and their monks could provide much-needed members for the larger religious houses, the real reason was because the king needed money. The Church owned vast wealth in both land and valuable items of plate and jewels.

The monasteries were important centres of local life providing succour when necessary, employment and education. Their closure would be sure to affect the lives of local people. Some religious communities were spared with the help of patrons and by the outlay of cash. St Mary's convent in Winchester secured reprieve by paying the king 500 marks and giving Beauchamp a manor to enlist his support in their cause.[19] Over the next few years, however, Beauchamp's sympathy for the monasteries would wane.

Many people believed these changes to their Church and religion threatened their lives and even their future in heaven. The Church was a major part of their world. The services, festivals and holy days dictated the daily and annual rhythm of their lives. Life was hard and people lived constantly under the shadow of death. The Church offered eventual salvation from all the troubles of life. As the king soon found out, many of his subjects were determined to protect their religion.

At some point during 1536 Beauchamp was among a group of seventeen peers summoned to Westminster to a 'council' meeting.[20] No reason for this gathering is given in the records. However, it was an unusually large number of noblemen to be summoned and it is possible this was a 'great council', called because of a threat of rebellion. Historically, when medieval kings of England needed advice they had called together many of the peers of the realm as a great council. However, by the sixteenth century the monarch relied increasingly upon a small group of trusted advisers, only some of whom were nobles. In October 1536, as rebellion spread through the northern counties, the king may have felt it necessary to revert to a monarch's traditional advisers and seek counsel from his noblemen. They were the men upon whom he depended to re-establish order throughout the kingdom.

In Lincolnshire, as the populace suffered from poor harvests, tax collection and the loss of the monasteries, the people and priests rebelled amid rumours that visiting commissioners would confiscate church plate. The commissioners were seized and riots spread throughout the county as the local gentry joined the revolt. However, with the king's refusal to consider the rebel demands, his threat of extreme punishment and the approach of the royal army, within a few days the rebels were persuaded to beg for pardon and disband. But by then trouble had spread to Yorkshire. This Pilgrimage of Grace, as the rebels termed it, was a well-organised revolt led by a lawyer, Robert Aske, and involved over 30,000 men including members of the nobility. The rebels never sought open warfare. Their complaint was not directly against the king, to whom they professed undying loyalty, but against his policies – the recent measures of taxation, dissolution of the monasteries and the changes to the Church and their religion. The Dukes of Suffolk and Norfolk and the Marquis of Exeter, Henry Courtenay, were sent to settle the rising. However, their armies were heavily outnumbered and all the king could do was agree to negotiate on the rebels' demands. The rebel forces dispersed with the promise of a pardon and expectations of their grievances being addressed. However, Henry waited and in early 1537 after minor riots broke out in the north he used these as an excuse to retaliate. Nearly 200 rebels, including some of the leaders, were executed.

During all this trouble Jane asked a favour of the king. The effect of her request upon Henry must have caused a sense of alarm in both her and Beauchamp and made them realise the fragility of her position. One day she went down on her knees before her husband and begged him to restore the abbeys. His response was reminiscent of the earlier warning he had given her regarding Princess Mary. She should not meddle in affairs of state, he said, and should remember the fate of her predecessor, 'which was enough to frighten a woman who is not very secure'.[21] Until Jane had produced the son that Henry craved, Beauchamp knew that his sister's position – and his own – was tenuous.

So it must have been a great relief when, in early 1537, he learned that Jane was expecting a child. On 27 May a *Te Deum* was sung in St Paul's Cathedral to celebrate the 'quickening' of the child – Jane had felt the future prince or princess move inside her. In the streets bonfires were lit and hogsheads of wine were provided for the people to join in the celebrations. Beauchamp and the rest of England prayed for a boy. As Charles Wriothesley, one of the heralds, recorded in his Chronicle: 'I pray Jesus, and it be his will, send us a prince'.[22] It was a time of concern and excitement for Beauchamp as well as his sister – concern that the pregnancy should have a happy conclusion and excitement at what the birth of this baby would mean for him. Earlier that year he had celebrated the birth of his second daughter, Jane, who had been baptised in the chapel at Chester Place in February. Such events were accompanied by a magnificent display of pomp and wealth and his status was now so high that it was rumoured the king had lent him the royal font for that occasion. The baby's position as the queen's niece was also reflected in the selection of prestigious godparents – Queen Jane, Princess Mary and the King's right-hand man, Cromwell – and the choice of the name Jane.[23]

Beauchamp's elation at his family's progress at court had been heightened further by his own appointment on 22 May to the king's council.[24] He was to be one of the handful of men on whom Henry relied for advice and who were responsible for effecting his instructions for governing the country. This was Beauchamp's most prestigious appointment so far and was undoubtedly due to his relationship to the king. Council appointments usually accompanied specific offices at court, but at that time Beauchamp held no official position.

The Seymour family had become people of consequence and any connection with them was highly sought. After her husband, Sir Anthony Ughtred, died in 1534 Beauchamp's sister, Elizabeth, had returned to England from Jersey. She had little money and was reliant on her friends for accommodation. However, by 1537, her position as the queen's sister made her a very desirable match, causing Sir Arthur Darcy, who lived in the north of the country and may have considered asking her to be his wife, to comment that 'some southern lord shall make you forget the north'. That was, indeed, what happened. In March Elizabeth wrote to the king's chief minister, Thomas Cromwell, asking for help. This may have prompted the proposal that she take Cromwell's son, Gregory, as her second husband. At the beginning of August she and Gregory were married.[25] It was a good match for both sides, allying Gregory and his father with the queen's family and the future King of England while relating the Seymours to the king's right-hand man.

On Sunday 16 September Jane took to her chambers at Hampton Court Palace to await the birth. As was the custom, she was closeted away from the world in a darkened room attended only by women. Beauchamp, like the king, could only wait in ignorance of what was taking place in the chamber, aware that the outcome could determine the future of his sister, himself and his family. If Jane and the child should die, as was all too common in the sixteenth century, his family's hopes and his elevated status at court would be at risk.

After a long and difficult labour which lasted for two days and three nights, Jane gave birth to a son at 2 a.m. on Friday 12 October. Beauchamp was uncle to the next King of England and the future of the Tudor dynasty was secure. Jane's position as Henry's wife was assured and her brother could expect further honours from the king. Beauchamp's elation at hearing the news was evident in the generous payment of 20s that he gave to Robert Moulsey, who brought him word of the birth.[26] The baby prince was named Edward to celebrate his birth on the eve of the feast day of St Edward the Confessor, King of England five centuries earlier. Heralds were despatched and letters sent out announcing the birth of a son 'conceived in lawful matrimony' between the king and queen.[27]

England erupted in celebration. At 8 a.m. a *Te Deum* was sung in every parish church in London, all the bells were rung and fires were lit in the streets. Members of the king's council, the French ambassador, judges, the Lord Mayor and aldermen and city craftsmen all joined in the celebrations at St Paul's Cathedral to praise

God 'for joy of our prince'. A great fusillade of guns was fired from the Tower. In the evening, festivities began again. New fires were lit around which the people banqueted on fruit, drinking from the hogsheads of wine that had been set around the city for 'poor people to drink as long as they listed'. There was a cacophony of sound as musicians played, two thousand shots were fired from the Tower and all the church bells rang out until 10 p.m.[28]

Three days later, on 15 October, the baby was baptised in the chapel at Hampton Court. It was an elaborate piece of court ceremonial. A great procession moved from the prince's apartments along the gallery to the great watching chamber and great hall and down to the chapel. The route was lit by torches and at the door of the chapel a porch covered in cloth of gold had been constructed. Gentlemen, clerics and the choir led the way, two by two, followed by knights, councillors, ambassadors and nobles in ascending order of status. Beauchamp and his brother Thomas both took part in the ceremony but again it was Beauchamp who took the place of honour. Thomas was among the gentlemen supporting a canopy held aloft over the Marchioness of Exeter as she carried the young prince. Beauchamp carried the 4-year-old Lady Elizabeth (as the young princess was titled after her mother's execution) who held the richly garnished chrysom. As was the custom, the king and queen did not attend the baptism. When the ceremony was finished and the congregation had enjoyed spices, wafers and wine the procession re-formed and made its way to the queen's chamber where Jane was still recovering. Here the baby received the blessings of his parents.[29] Henry VIII would never know that this son, for whom he had striven so hard, would not be the progenitor of a long Tudor dynasty or that this would be the last baptism of a Tudor baby.

The following Thursday, Beauchamp received his reward for his sister's success when he was created Earl of Hertford in the presence chamber at Hampton Court. The award was accompanied by a grant of £20 per annum to help him live in a manner befitting an earl.[30] In 1539, when he next took his seat in Parliament, Hertford was one of only fifteen earls, with just two dukes and one marquis holding more senior rank. He was among the premier nobles of England, a fact that may have rankled with his brother Thomas, who, on the day of Hertford's creation, was made a knight by the king. Throughout their respective careers Hertford was to outrank his brother substantially in both title and position. Ultimately Thomas's resentment of this would lead to his downfall and death. But that was in the future. For a short time everything was perfect for the Seymour family … until disaster struck.

The queen was still recovering from the birth when, on Tuesday 23 October, she had a 'natural lax'; she seemed to improve, but that night she took a turn for the worse. The king had intended to ride to Esher on the Wednesday but delayed his journey due to the queen's condition. The physicians hoped that if she slept through the following night she would be past danger but by 8 a.m. Jane's confessor was with her to administer the last rites.[31] For Hertford and his family it was a catastrophe. All their hopes for the future were dashed. If the king remarried they could be supplanted. Suddenly their privileged position was at risk.

Jane died late at night on 24 October, having been queen for less than seventeen months. However, she had achieved what neither of her predecessors had done – she had left a prince of England. Some people believed her death was caused by her attendants allowing her to take cold and to eat such 'things that her fantasies in sickness called for'. In reality, the probable cause was septicaemia following either puerperal fever or a massive haemorrhage.[32] The king had displayed no sadness at the loss of his previous wives but after Jane's death he moved to Westminster where he 'mourned and kept himself close and secret a great while'.[33]

Jane's body went through elaborate preparation before her funeral. The wax chandler removed the entrails, which were interred in the chapel at Hampton Court, and treated the body 'with searing, balming, spicing and trammeling in cloth' before it was sealed in a lead chest encased in a wooden coffin. For five days a watch was kept around the coffin as it lay beneath a hearse in the presence chamber. On 31 October, accompanied by a long procession, it was carried through the great watching chamber and galleries, all hung with black cloth, to the chapel where it was laid beneath another hearse. The hearse, a large wooden frame, was adorned with wax candles, and banners and pennants declaring Jane's rank as queen. Here, each day, masses were said and at night priests and gentlemen ushers kept watch by the coffin before being replaced by the queen's ladies early each morning.

On Monday 12 November Jane's body was carried to the chapel at Windsor Castle on a chariot draped with black velvet and drawn by six horses, accompanied by a long procession of heralds, noblemen, gentlemen, ladies, clerics and servants. On the coffin lay an effigy of Jane 'richly apparelled like a queen' with a gold crown. In her right hand was placed a gold sceptre, on her fingers were rings set with precious stones and upon her feet were shoes of cloth of gold. That night the mourners stayed at Windsor and the following morning Jane was buried in St George's Chapel. As was traditional, the king did not attend the funeral; the chief mourner was his daughter, Mary, and although Hertford was summoned to Hampton Court to join the cortege neither he nor his brother played any part in the ceremony. After the funeral, as everyone moved to the castle for a sumptuous banquet, in London a bell was tolled in every parish church for six hours starting at noon.[34]

Jane was dead but she had served her purpose. Henry VIII had a son and heir. In the future he would exchange marriage vows with three more wives but at his death it was Jane beside whom he chose to spend eternity.

3

The Quiet Years

With Jane gone, Hertford's position at court changed. His meteoric rise came to an abrupt halt and he received no further honours or rewards on account of his late sister's position. He remained a prominent figure but from now on advancement would come through his own merit. For the next five years, with no opportunities to prove his worth, his progress at court slowed. Following his sister's death he was described by one correspondent as 'young and wise, of small power' but he was still considered to be a man of influence and some people went to great lengths to maintain a friendship with him.[1] Viscount Lisle was deputy governor of Calais, an important appointment but one that placed the holder far from court and the prospect of advancement. It was useful to have contacts at court from whom help could be sought and, in spite of their earlier disagreements over land, Lisle's wife was desperate to maintain a good relationship with Hertford. On one occasion Lady Lisle had sent him a gift of a caged bird from Calais but before the bird could be delivered it was killed by a cat. Hertford apparently took the loss 'right grievously' whereupon Lady Lisle sent her own bird although she 'would not do the same for any lord in England, except the King'. However, the amity between the two families was not shared by Lisle's steward, John Husee. He mistakenly believed that Hertford might be made governor of Calais and informed his master that he would never wish to see Lisle serving as deputy to Hertford. Lady Lisle's daughter, Katherine Bassett, also preferred to keep her distance from the Hertfords, refusing the offer that her mother had sought for her to serve in their household.[2]

Importantly, Hertford was favoured by the people who really mattered and he remained high in royal esteem. In 1538 Husee reported to Lisle that Hertford had accompanied the king during the presentation of New Year gifts in the presence chamber. That year, for the first time, the courtiers also presented gifts to Prince Edward and Hertford gave his new nephew a piece of gilt plate. His wife, too, joined in the traditional exchange of gifts and one year she gave the king a shirt that cost 100s.[3] This enormous sum suggests that the shirt was intricately embroidered, perhaps in 'black-work' or even in gold thread. The king reciprocated, sending New Year gifts in return.

In the March 1538 the king and Cromwell stood as godfathers at the baptism of Hertford and Anne's first son, Henry. They each gave a cup as a gift for the baby, and Cromwell paid 30s as the customary reward to the midwife and nurse. The child died during infancy, however, and it was the earl's second son, Edward, who later became his heir. Edward was baptised at Beauchamp Place in London, with the dukes of Norfolk and Suffolk as his godfathers.[4] He had been born at night and it appears the family were caught unawares without a midwife close by. The gates of the city were always locked at night and a messenger, John Smith, paid the keepers at both Ludgate and Aldgate to open the gates so that he could pass through the city to collect the midwife rather than riding the slower route around the outside of the city wall.[5]

Hertford's life was relatively uneventful. He continued as a councillor, attended Parliament when it was in session and carried out his duties as a courtier. The routine was broken by occasional appointments to commissions, several of which involved sitting in judgement on people with whom he was familiar. When a nobleman was accused of treason he was tried by a panel of his peers, and, since the number of nobles was small, the accused man was often known personally by his examiners. In 1538, only a year after the Marquis of Exeter had supported Hertford at his creation as an earl, Hertford was one of the judges who tried him for treason. Exeter; Henry Pole, Lord Montagu; Sir Geoffrey Pole and Sir Edward Neville were accused of wanting to overthrow the king and conspiring with Cardinal Reginald Pole, who had been encouraging Francis I and Charles V to invade England. Geoffrey was pardoned after giving evidence against the others, all of whom were executed. However, this trial also provided the king with an opportunity to rid himself of members of the house of York whose real 'crime' was to be heirs of the Plantagenet line and, hence, claimants to the throne of England. Henry VIII was removing a threat to the Tudor dynasty. Two years later Sir Nicholas Carew was arrested for allegedly being implicated in the same plot and again Hertford was one of the commissioners who sent him to the block.[6]

In 1541 Hertford had the difficult task of trying Thomas Fiennes, Lord Dacre, for murder. Dacre had carried the canopy at Queen Jane's funeral and had served with Hertford at the trial of Lords Darcy and Hussey, who were found guilty of supporting the rebels during the Pilgrimage of Grace.[7] Dacre and a group of friends were accused of murdering a gamekeeper they encountered while poaching on a neighbouring estate. Despite his companions' confessions, Dacre claimed he had never intended to murder the man. It was a difficult decision for the jury of peers: they did not want to find him guilty – he was, after all, only 25 – but his companions had admitted guilt. It would have eased their task if Dacre had confessed to the crime. Hertford and several other jury members met to discuss the case before the trial in an attempt to convince themselves of his guilt. On 27 June, seventeen noblemen met in Star Chamber to hear the case. There was great disagreement over the verdict. The raised voices of the lords could be heard through two closed doors before 'suddenly and softly' they agreed he was guilty. Dacre changed his plea, perhaps in the hope of clemency, but was sentenced to be hanged.[8]

Hertford turned some of his attention towards his role as governor of Jersey. It was not an easy command, exacerbated by the Jersey men's preference for their own customs and laws over those imposed by England and by the ever-changing relationship between England and France. His lieutenant, William Cornish, kept him well-informed of events and Hertford seems to have responded promptly, albeit sometimes against his lieutenant's advice. There were occasions when Cornish's ability to act was hampered by his lack of authority; his regular appeals for instruction suggest that Hertford may already have been exhibiting a failure to delegate responsibility. With the French casting covetous eyes on Jersey, the defence of the island was paramount and Hertford authorised improvements to the fortifications, the most substantial of which was an 85ft high D-shaped bastion at Mont Orgueil Castle. Known today as Somerset Tower, it provided a solid base upon which six large cannon were positioned and helped turn the castle into a near-impregnable fortress.[9]

During 1541 Hertford had an opportunity to hone his diplomatic skills. On 16 January he visited France for two months to investigate a dispute between the French and English over the boundary of the Pale at Calais. Despite the French ambassador, Charles de Marillac, considering Hertford to be 'much esteemed here for his goodness, sweetness and grace rather than experience of affairs', the king chose to send him rather than use local men because he would bring a fresh mind to the discussion. As was commonplace in boundary disputes with the French, after their final meeting on 13 February the two sides parted amicably but without coming to an agreement. Two years earlier Hertford had recommended improvements to the fortifications at Calais and Guisnes and he now took the opportunity to examine the new works and to check local food and coal supplies. But he also had a secret, more delicate objective. There had been reports from Calais of heretics making seditious comments and he was to search for any evidence that might incriminate, in particular, Sir John Wallop, the captain of Guisnes. Hertford had to use great subterfuge without arousing suspicion to entice several men, including Wallop, back to England where they could be questioned. His mission was successful and by mid-March he had returned to England.[10]

For several years Hertford had been proposed for election as a Knight of the Garter but had always been passed over. Finally, in 1541, the members of the order supported his nomination.[11] The Order of the Garter had been founded in 1348 by Edward III and was held concurrently by the king, the Prince of Wales and twenty-four knights. Each knight was installed at St George's Chapel at Windsor Castle where his banner of arms, helmet, crest and sword were displayed above a stall bearing a plate depicting the recipient's coat of arms.

Hertford was becoming a wealthy man, primarily through his acquisition of land and property. The king rewarded his servants with little in the way of monetary payments; their rewards generally came in the form of grants of land and manors from which income was derived. In August 1537 he had received land worth nearly £160 per annum for which he paid the king an annual rent of £16. This increased his annual income from land and property grants to £604, which, together with the value of his inherited lands and annuities, amounted to an income of £1,107 6s 8d each year.[12] He was especially keen to secure a good bargain. John Berwick, who negotiated Hertford's land purchases, was very quick to agree one deal for him after he had persuaded the valuer to rate a parcel of land at £40 rather than its true value of £160. At the same time he advised Hertford against a further purchase that he believed was over-valued.[13]

Hertford continued to add to his property portfolio. In 1537 the king had supported his bid to exchange a house with Roland Lee, Bishop of Coventry and Lichfield. Hertford wanted Chester Place, the bishop's residence on the Strand, just outside Temple Bar and close to Westminster. In exchange he offered a house at Kew that the king had granted him a year earlier after it was forfeited by Henry Norris, one of the men brought down with Anne Boleyn. Lee objected on the grounds that Kew was too far from London and he needed Chester Place to be close to the court (which, presumably, was why Hertford wanted the property himself). Lee eventually agreed but later regretted that he had given the house 'to him that will never do me good'. He wished that, instead, he had given it to Cromwell as an inducement to favour him in securing a benefice. Lee had no expectations of favours from Hertford.[14]

Further property came as a result of the Dissolution. In 1538 Hertford had acquired the site of Muchelney Abbey in Somerset together with eighteen manors and other properties. Two years later he succeeded to his cousin Sir William Sturmy's estate that adjoined his own.[15] It was preferable to own neighbouring properties that could be joined together to form large estates, rather than to have many isolated smaller pieces of land. In 1541 Hertford made an exchange with the king, receiving land close to his estate at Wulfhall and in Somerset in return for property in Middlesex and Hampshire. He was also granted the dissolved priory of Sheen in Surrey which, being near the Thames, was ideally placed for access to London.[16]

His Wiltshire home, Wulfhall, was 5 miles south-east of Marlborough and 60 miles from London, a journey he could make in two days with an overnight stop at his house at Elvetham near Fleet in Hampshire. Although the house is often referred to as Wolf Hall, the spelling in the Domesday Record was Ulfela. This was probably the name of an early owner and has nothing to do with an animal. The present house on the site is of later date and includes little of the original building.

During his summer progress in August 1539 the king visited Wulfhall again. Hertford had inherited the property when his father died just before Christmas in 1536, having lived long enough to see his daughter become Queen of England.[17] The estate was a good size – over 1,260 acres, most of which was pasture. Much of the land was enclosed, creating smaller parks: 'Horse', 'Red Deer', 'Topenhays' and 'Soden' Parks. The timber-framed house was of a fair size built around two courtyards and sufficiently large to have a long gallery (a relatively new innovation), a 'broad' chamber and a chapel. Close to the house were productive gardens – an orchard and a half-acre walled garden where the family could grow vegetables. 'The Great Palyd Gardyne' was probably a large fenced area and there were two gardens whose names suggest they may have been for recreation – 'My Olde Lady's Gardyne' and 'My Young Lady's Gardyne'. Hertford employed over forty men, and seven women including two nurses for the children. One man was employed to catch foxes and others to catch the wild boar in the forest. Hertford enjoyed the hunting at Wulfhall and kept deer, hounds, spaniels and hawks for entertainment. In September 1537 he had written to Cromwell wishing the chief minister was with him to enjoy 'the best sport with bows, hounds and hawks' as they hunted partridges.[18]

For the king's visit in 1539 Hertford decided the building was not sufficiently large to house Henry and his court. So he moved into his massive barn – 172ft long and 26ft wide – that was converted into living accommodation for the occasion. Accounts for the visit refer to pieces of painted canvas that were probably hung to cover the walls of the barn. Meanwhile, his mother and his children moved into Tottenham Lodge, a house on the estate, leaving Wulfhall free for the king. Wulfhall was not large enough to house all the 200 people who accompanied Henry and some were housed in Burbage and other nearby villages.

The king arrived on the afternoon of Saturday 9 August and stayed until after dinner on Tuesday morning. Henry had no queen at that time so the royal retinue was smaller than it had been on his previous visit with Anne Boleyn, but hosting the royal visitor was still a mammoth undertaking involving vast quantities of food. The household accounts refer to around 230 'messes' being served to the royal entourage at each meal. A 'mess' was a quantity of food usually intended for four people to share but on this occasion it seems more likely the numbers referred to actual meals served. With a further seventy members of his own household and visiting friends to feed, Hertford's kitchen staff, aided by the king's master cook and many of the royal household servants, were providing in excess of 600 meals a day.

It was unreasonable to expect his hosts to source such a vast quantity of food so the royal visitor travelled with wagons of food supplies to supplement what was available locally. Hertford provided as much as he could with help from his friends and neighbours. However, it appears that the king expected his host to foot the bill for the visit by buying supplies from his royal guest. On the day of the king's arrival Hertford paid £1 12s 3d for flour and meal for the twenty dozen (240) loaves of bread which the royal bakers made that day. Over £7 was spent on beer, ale and wine and £6 on exotic foodstuffs – spices including cloves, ginger, cinnamon and turnsole (a purple food colour for jellies and confectionery) – together with 8lb of sugar and 600 pears, which all suggests a dish of spiced pears.

Because Saturday was one of the days on which the Church and government ordered men to eat no meat, the menu for supper contained only fish. Hertford was able to provide nearly half of this himself, and eighteen different types of fish were prepared that day. Sea fish such as lobster and plaice came from the king's stocks but much of the freshwater fish – pike, trout, bream, tench, roach and perch – came from local rivers and out of Hertford's own fishponds that supplied fresh fish all year round.

Entertaining the king was an enormous drain on his courtiers' purses and Hertford's expenses for the complete week, including the royal visit, amounted to £288 19s 10d. On the Sunday there were two meals to provide and vast quantities of meat were eaten. The options on the tables included 6 cows, 24 sheep, 12 calves, 242 chickens and capons of various quality, 38 quails, 7 swans, 2 storks, 24 larks and 28 gulls, alongside venison and game birds provided by Hertford's friends and neighbours.[19] The visit appears to have been a success and the following December the king visited Hertford again, accompanied by a large retinue that included Norfolk, Suffolk, Parr, Russell and Surrey. On that occasion, however, the visit was only for supper and was probably held at his London house. Entertainment was reciprocated. In November 1538 Hertford and his wife had joined a small gathering at Westminster for a banquet after which the king had taken his guests on a guided tour of the palace.[20]

Wulfhall was in Savernake Forest and it was Hertford's duty as warden to manage and protect the woodland for the king. Timber was a vital part of the Tudor economy. It was used as fuel for heating and cooking, for building houses and making furniture, for carts and shipbuilding and for fencing. Careful husbandry of the trees ensured that timber was a renewable resource, so replanting followed felling. Selected trees were left to mature for use in buildings and ships while others were coppiced every few years to provide smaller lengths for fencing, fuel and even basket-making. Hertford was too busy in London to give much time to forest matters and the day-to-day management was undertaken by a lieutenant and a ranger. They also conducted the forest courts to settle disputes between local tenants and to try poachers and men caught stealing wood. As warden Hertford was entitled to certain perquisites, or perks, as payment for his efforts. These included permission to carry out activities such as collecting firewood and timber, to fish in local ponds and to hunt the 'lesser' beasts. It was illegal to hunt deer – they were the preserve of the king – but it is likely that as part of his payment Hertford was allowed to take a certain number of deer each year.

By the time of the king's visit to Wulfhall in 1539 negotiations were already in hand for Henry to take a fourth wife. In October 1538 Thomas Seymour had been part of an English delegation to France negotiating for a marriage between Henry and Christina of Denmark but nothing had come of the proposal.[21] The following year the king decided it would be more advantageous to make an alliance with the Protestant German states. England was fearful of an invasion after the pope had called upon Charles V and Francis I to attack England and return the country to the Catholic faith. Henry needed allies.

The king's choice of bride settled upon Anne of Cleves. It was a decision welcomed by Hertford, who thought it the best thing to happen since the birth of Prince Edward, because he believed a connection with the House of Cleves would be advantageous for the succession.[22] No doubt he was rejoicing at the prospect of a Protestant queen rather than a Catholic one from France or Spain. Hertford's brother, Thomas, was part of the advance party to welcome Anne at Calais, and on 13 December he and his brother-in-law Gregory Cromwell were among the gentlemen who dined with her before she sailed for England.[23] Hertford and his wife joined the enormous entourage of nobles, knights, gentlemen, esquires and ladies that attended the king when he received Anne at Shooters Hill near Greenwich on 3 January 1540. Three days later the royal couple were married but the marriage was short-lived. The king was horrified by the appearance and bearing of his new wife. After just six months, when the threat of invasion had passed, the marriage was annulled on the grounds of an earlier betrothal between Anne and François, heir to the Duke of Lorraine. Anne took the title of 'sister to the king' and spent the rest of her life living in comfort in England.

For Cromwell, who had proposed and arranged the marriage, the outcome was a disaster; on 28 July he was executed on unproven charges of treason and heresy. He had been a loyal and valuable servant to Henry but he had made a grave error in encouraging the king into the Cleves match. He had also aroused enmity at court, not only on account of some of his policies but because of his lowly birth. His recent investiture as Earl of Essex had annoyed men like the Duke of Norfolk who resented the success of a man who was the son of a blacksmith.

Hertford was unaffected by the fall of Cromwell. However, his sister Elizabeth, who had served as a lady-in-waiting to Anne of Cleves, was thrown into great despair fearing that she and her husband would be affected by her father-in-law's demise. In the hope of royal clemency, Elizabeth wrote to the king craving his favour and assistance, despite her father-in-law's 'most detestable offence'. Before his death Cromwell, too, had written to the king. In the knowledge that all his property and goods would be confiscated, he had beseeched Henry to be a 'good and gracious lord to my poor son, the good and virtuous lady his wife and their poor children'. The king took their pleas to heart and Gregory's creation as Baron Cromwell the following December replaced the courtesy title of Lord Cromwell that had been forfeited after his father's attainder.[24]

On the day of Cromwell's execution the king married his fifth wife, Catherine Howard. She was still in her late teens and the marriage was destined for disaster. Less than two years later she was executed on charges of adultery and unchaste living before her marriage. For three months from August until the end of October 1541 the king, Catherine and the court had been on progress to York. During this period Hertford stayed in London; when the king was away from the capital it was usual for some of the councillors to travel with him while the remainder stayed in the city to attend to government business. Instructions and messages were sent daily between the two parts of the council. In October Archbishop Cranmer was given information about the queen's relationship (before her marriage) with two men, Francis Dereham and Henry Manox. It was a dangerous revelation and Cranmer, unsure how to tell the king, sought advice from Hertford and Thomas Audley, the Lord Chancellor. Henry was passionately in love with Catherine and no one was prepared to face him with such news for fear of his anger. The two men advised Cranmer to write the details in a letter to give to the king on his return to court. Further inquiries revealed that, while Catherine may not have been adulterous since becoming queen, she had had a liaison with Thomas Culpeper, a gentleman of the king's privy chamber. Throughout November and December Hertford was one of the councillors who examined Catherine's servants and family, including the Dowager Duchess of Norfolk, in whose house the indiscretions with Dereham and Manox had taken place. He was also one of the commissioners to try Culpeper and Dereham.[25] The two men were found guilty and executed. Two months later, in February 1542, Catherine was beheaded.

As the king turned his mind to other matters, for Hertford the quiet years were nearly over. Henry was about to embark on a succession of wars that would present Hertford with the opportunity to show his real qualities and to establish himself on his own merits, not just as the brother of a Queen of England.

4

Fighting the Scots

For the next few years England was at war with both France and Scotland; at last Hertford would have an opportunity to prove himself. Traditionally, prowess in war had been a sure way to win royal favour and advancement at court but for the previous twenty years there had been little opportunity for courtiers to demonstrate their abilities in this way. Indeed, the men who had increasingly established themselves at court were administrators, men such as Wolsey, Cromwell, Russell, Paulet and Paget. Hertford would finally be able to establish himself as a worthy member of Henry's court.

In 1542 Henry VIII was negotiating for an alliance with either Francis I or Charles V, whichever would be of most benefit to England. However, he knew that whomever he chose would involve the country in war. A truce between France and Spain was failing and each side was seeking the English king's support. Francis wanted Henry to wage war against the emperor, Charles sought his help in defending his territories against advances by both the French and the Turks. Charles was in a difficult position. His empire was too extensive for him to control alone so while he governed Spain his brother, Ferdinand, ruled as king of Hungary in the east; his sister, Mary, acted as regent of the Netherlands; and he relied upon the co-operation of the princes of the German states. Recent attempts had failed to reconcile the growing differences in religion between the Catholic emperor and the Schmalkaldic League, a defensive alliance of Lutheran princes who were set on establishing Protestantism in their states. In 1542 Charles's empire was under attack on two fronts: to the west, Francis was increasing his army on the Luxembourg border and encouraging the religious disunity between the emperor and the German Protestant princes by offering them support; and on his eastern borders Charles was threatened by Suleiman the Magnificent, Sultan of the Ottoman Empire, who was intent on invading Hungary, from where he could advance into Germany.

Henry chose England's old ally, Spain, and came to an agreement with Charles that together they would invade France. No date was set and in the meantime he sent Thomas Seymour to observe the Imperial forces in action against the Turks. For four months Thomas accompanied the emperor's troops as an observer as they besieged and made repeated assaults upon the Turkish-occupied town of Pest. It was an unsuccessful campaign for the emperor and Henry decided not to support Charles in this war. For Thomas, though, it proved to be valuable experience in siege warfare and battle tactics.

Meanwhile, Henry turned his attention to Scotland. By the summer of 1542, as French troops threatened the emperor's lands in the Low Countries, Henry decided to attack the Scots while Francis was thus occupied with another enemy and unable to send aid to Scotland. The English king's claim that he was not attempting to establish sovereignty over the country but only retaliating because Scotsmen were making raids over the border was a little hollow. Henry still harboured ambition to conquer his northern neighbour. He also intended to assert his authority over his nephew, James V of Scotland, who had broken a promise to meet with him at York the previous year. Talks in September to establish a long-term peace failed to reach a conclusion and even while they were taking place Henry was making preparations to attack Scotland. He intended to send an army across the border to capture Edinburgh but it was an enterprise that would be blighted by poor logistics and the difficulty of finding suitable commanders. It did, though, give Hertford his first experience of fighting in the border country.

The Duke of Norfolk, an accomplished military leader, was assigned to lead the army towards Edinburgh. On 13 October he reported that one of his commanders, William Fitzwilliam, Earl of Southampton, was sick and unlikely to recover. As a replacement he proposed Hertford because of his earlier experience in battle, his position as Prince Edward's uncle and because 'he is my near kinsman and shall be very welcome'.[1]

With no time for preparation, Hertford left London on 16 October and rode quickly to join Norfolk at Berwick, arriving late on 21 October.[2] The following morning he marched out at the head of the vanguard (the forward part of the formation), leading the army into Scotland. For a week the force moved through the borderlands to Kelso, burning towns and destroying crops, but the muddy travelling conditions were appalling. The terrain was poor and although they had planned to travel 7 or 8 miles each day the furthest they achieved was 5 miles.

Norfolk and Hertford were forced to give up and return with the troops to Berwick because of a lack of food. Even before they had set out, the two men knew of the supply difficulties and had complained to the council that 'the great enterprise is not feasible, for lack of victuals'. They had been short of wheat for bread, biscuits, beer, malt and oats and lacked sufficient strong carriages to transport the goods. Some small ships had brought beer into Berwick but this was rationed. The larger ships which carried further supplies were too big to enter the harbour and had been forced to anchor off Holy Island. During the campaign soldiers had died from lack of food and from drinking 'puddle water'. Norfolk, though, had only praise for his men, telling the council that he 'never thought Englishmen could endure with so little and yet be willing to go forward'.[3]

When Hertford reached Berwick on 29 October he received a commission appointing him Warden General of the Scottish Marches. The warden was the king's representative on the borders, responsible for the safety of local Englishmen and for securing the border against raids by the Scots. It was his duty to maintain a force to keep watch and carry out reprisal raids into Scotland. It was a daunting command and one for which Hertford thought he was not the right man. He quickly sent the privy council a list of his objections to the appointment. He was a stranger to these northern Englishmen, he wrote, and he believed they would be more willing to serve a warden who was known to them. He feared, too, that having travelled north with little warning, bringing with him only three or four servants and little in the way of belongings, he was not suitably equipped to live in the manner expected of the king's representative. He had expected to find everything he needed ready on his arrival but all that had awaited him was an empty tent. To remain there in such condition, he maintained, would be to dishonour both the king and himself.[4]

The warden general's post was unlikely to be a popular appointment except, perhaps, with noblemen who lived in the north of England. For men who lived in the south the prospect of the weather in northern climes and the constant threat from marauding Scotsmen may have made them reluctant to seek such preferment. Norfolk, knowing the post was vacant, had made it clear that he did not want it. He was not well, suffering from a bowel complaint, and he feared that at his old age (69) the winter would kill him. Escaping the cold countries of the north would, he trusted, 'somewhat lengthen his life'.[5]

The king agreed with Hertford's own objections and released him from the position for lack of servants and furniture. Thomas Manners, Earl of Rutland, who had held the post briefly in August, was reappointed but his appointment did not last long. Just days later Rutland reported that he was in poor health and by 8 November John Dudley, who had been created Viscount Lisle following his stepfather's death the previous March, had been given the post.

Despite being poorly attended and no better accommodated than the rest of his men, Hertford agreed to remain until Lisle had arrived even if he had to 'lie in his clothes, and have but bread and drink'.[6] He moved to Alnwick, probably into the relative comfort of the castle, and set about overseeing the wardenship of the north. He was very methodical in his work, paying great attention to detail, writing long memoranda of matters to be dealt with and then striking out points that he, presumably, had resolved.[7] While some of his commanders continued to make small raids into Scotland, Hertford set to work planning a large assault across the border.

He explained to the council on 13 November why he was slow to carry out any exploits. 'A man', he said, 'must know where and what his forces are before he attempts anything'. He had spent the previous week assessing the garrison strength at just over 2,500 but he reckoned they were the worst supplied soldiers to have ever attempted such feats on the border. No garrison, he warned, could continue at Alnwick unless supplies were soon sent from the south. Maintaining sufficient food for both men and horses was a constant difficulty. Supplies of hay and oats were so low that horses were soon being fed on straw. Many of the horses were only strong enough to carry a man for 8 or 10 miles at walking pace. Hertford complained that he would rather have 2,000 willing footmen than these horsemen who wanted to return home. A suggestion from the Duke of Norfolk that, despite his lack of men, Hertford should take troops into an area of Scotland where the Scots had a powerful force earned a strong rebuke from Hertford. He would not risk the lives of himself and his men.[8]

By 15 November Hertford was ready and 800 men carried out a successful raid to destroy Coldingham, 12 miles from Berwick, which the Scots had been planning to garrison. Three days later 2,000 more troops rode through the snow burning many villages and destroying crops. Hertford was learning the tactics that he would use to great effect in the future.

Information about the Scots intentions was brought in by espials (spies). Good information could be expensive – as much as £10 – but was vital for Hertford's planning.[9] As November passed, intelligence reached him that James V was gathering his gentlemen and their servants near the border at Lauder, about 20 miles from Coldstream, with sufficient supplies for forty days. Hertford ordered his border-men to be alert. It was a tense time. Preparations were made to send warning via beacons of any invasion. Each man was to be ready at an hour's notice with sufficient food for four days. If the Scots did invade, stores of English corn were to be burnt and the cattle driven away so that the Scotsmen could not use them

Hertford's orders had some success. The spies had reported that the Scots intended to enter England at two places on the border but one force turned back when it was realised that the English were prepared for them. However, on 24 November a Scottish force, possibly in excess of 14,000 men, met the English at Solway Moss on the border with Cumberland. Although opposed by only 3,000 Englishmen the Scots were routed. Twelve hundred prisoners were taken including two earls, five barons and 500 lairds and gentlemen, while only seven Englishmen were reportedly slain. It was a noteworthy victory for Hertford and was quickly followed by another success when 1,000 horsemen travelled overnight to Coldstream and next day burnt the town and abbey. For James V and the Scots, Solway Moss was a devastating defeat but worse was to come for the country. On 14 December James died, probably of disease, leaving his 6-day-old daughter, Mary, as queen of Scotland. For a time hostilities stopped along the borders while the Scots established a new government. The English ceased their raids for, as Lisle remarked, it would not be to Henry VIII's honour 'to make war upon a dead body, or a widow, or a suckling his daughter'.[10]

Within days of Lisle's arrival at Alnwick, Hertford was on his way south, travelling through Newcastle and viewing the fortifications at Hull en route. He was back in London on 18 December, no doubt to the relief of his wife. Anne had been missing him, writing that 'she will not be merry till she hears from him' and 'beseeching him for speedy answer'. However, some of their letters to each other may have gone astray causing Hertford, perhaps unreasonably, to chastise Anne for being 'slack in writing'.[11]

Shortly before the campaign in Scotland Hertford had been appointed Lord Admiral of England but the honour was short-lived. In January 1543 he was advanced further to be Lord Great Chamberlain, a primarily ceremonial role and one of the great offices of state, and Lisle replaced him as Lord Admiral.[12] Lisle was the son of Edmund Dudley, a man renowned for the rapaciousness with which he had extracted money for Henry VII from his subjects and who had been executed early in Henry VIII's reign. Four years younger than Hertford, Lisle, too, had been knighted by Suffolk in France in 1523 and had served as an esquire of the body to Henry. Prior to his posting to the north his only appointment of note had been as vice-admiral in 1537 when, with England at peace, much of his effort had been directed against pirates. He was a talented man and would prove himself to be a good soldier and sailor but he was ambitious and ruthless. During the next few years the lives of Hertford and Lisle were to become increasingly entwined as Lisle became Hertford's most prominent enemy.

Hertford was to make several more forays into Scotland in the future but during 1543 he spent his time at court, attending to the routine business of a courtier and privy councillor. Two events in July, though, were noteworthy. On 12 July the king married his sixth wife, Katherine Parr. The new queen's brother, William, missed the ceremony because he was serving on the Scottish borders as Lord Warden of the Western Marches. Considering the extent to which Hertford had benefitted from his relationship as brother-in-law to the king, Katherine's marriage could have presented a golden opportunity for Parr. However, he lacked the drive and ambition of Hertford who had already established himself at court before his sister became queen. Parr was politically naïve and argumentative, and within six months of travelling north he was removed from his post as warden. Handsome, charming and educated at Cambridge, Parr was 'not crafty nor involved' and in character was perhaps the antithesis of Hertford and his brother Thomas. Henry VIII called him 'his integrity' and Edward VI knew him as 'his honest uncle'.[13] He would not, though, be a good friend to Hertford.

The second event was to have far-reaching consequences for Hertford. On 1 July the king signed a marriage treaty with the Scottish ambassador, sealing an agreement that Prince Edward should marry Mary, Queen of Scots. It was a momentous alliance, one that would bring Scotland under English control and remove the long-standing enmity between the two countries. However, the elation at the English court was short-lived. Many powerful Scots refused to agree to this union of crowns and the treaty collapsed the following December when it was annulled by the Scottish Parliament. The Scots soon paid the price for this *volte face* as first the king and later Hertford resolved to bring them to heel.

At the beginning of 1544 Henry VIII decided to invade Scotland again. He was furious that the Scots had abandoned the marriage treaty, ending his hope of uniting the two countries, and his response was to destroy Edinburgh. There was, however, another more pressing reason for attacking his great-niece's country: he planned to make war against France later in the year. He therefore needed to devastate the Scottish border areas to prevent the Scots invading England while the English army was in France.

In March Hertford was appointed to replace the Duke of Suffolk as lieutenant-general in the north, releasing Suffolk for service in France.[14] The invasion force was to gather at Newcastle from where an army of 12,000 soldiers and 3,000 sailors were to sail to Leith on the Firth of Forth, close to Edinburgh. There was no standing army in England. When the king went to war all the nobility, gentlemen and courtiers accompanied him, bringing with them their own servants and tenants. All men between the ages of 16 and 60 could be called up for service and the king relied upon the noblemen to act as commanders. Soldiers for war against Scotland were raised in the north of England. Those for defence or war against the French were from the south.

England had not been involved in war for nearly twenty years and, excepting the men on the Scottish borders, the average Englishman's martial skills were not well honed. One of the most effective means of attack for the ordinary footman was the longbow. A skilled archer could loose six arrows a minute at an effective range of 200 yards but it was a weapon that needed regular practice to maintain the strength necessary to pull the bow. Although all Englishmen were ordered to practise weekly at the archery butts provided in each town, as memories of battle faded there was little incentive to do so. In an attempt to boost the declining number of men able to pull a bow, the use of handguns and crossbows was discouraged and local commissioners were instructed to enforce longbow practice.

Hertford reached Newcastle by 13 March. His entry into the town was a more impressive event than his arrival in the north two years earlier. At the head of a great procession rode 3,000 northern horsemen followed by 160 noblemen and gentlemen in coats of black velvet with gold chains. Three trumpeters and three clarions, three officers of arms and a gentleman carrying an unsheathed sword preceded Hertford who was dressed in rich and expensive clothes. Behind him followed three pages, 160 servants wearing his livery and, lastly, 5,000 men on foot.[15] This was a display of his status and authority as the king's representative and on this occasion he could have no complaint about a lack of attendants.

For defensive purposes the English borderland with Scotland was divided into three marches. One of Hertford's first actions was to appoint lords William Eure and Thomas Wharton as wardens of the east and west marches and Sir Ralph Eure (William's son) as warden of the middle march. Hertford had planned carefully. As the ships sailed towards Leith, the wardens and their men were to make raids across the border to 'waste' the country and distract the Scots' attention from the approaching main invasion force. However, remembering the difficulties caused by having unfit horses in 1542, Hertford ordered that the raids should cease after 28 March so that the horses were well rested before the invasion.[16]

Victualling the army was a major difficulty compounded by a dearth of corn and other foods in the area. Hertford had witnessed in 1542 how a shortage of victuals could ruin plans for an invasion. Supplies were sourced in advance by 'purveyors', preferably in the local area to maximise the freshness of the food and to avoid the difficulties of transportation but much was still sent from the south. The staple diet was bread, biscuits, salt beef, herrings, cheese and beer. Bakers, brewers and butchers travelled with the army and, once on the march, the soldiers sought to capture foodstuff from the enemy. Acquiring sufficient carts and hundreds of horses to transport both men and food, drink, tents and other supplies for an invading army was a daunting task. Horses and carriages were commandeered from throughout the country. By the Duke of Suffolk's calculations, an army of 16,000 men would need at least 500 carts, each carrying a ton, to move supplies and munitions. The transport problems were further exacerbated by the timing of this campaign. With little forage available in the fields early in the year, much of the fodder for the horses had to be sent north.[17] For the victuallers, 1544 was to be a logistical nightmare as they sourced food and supplies for armies in both Scotland and France.

Hertford had a long wait for the ships and supplies to arrive. The first vessels reached Tynemouth, the port for Newcastle, on 30 March but others sailed more slowly. By 18 April, when over 100 'sail' had reached the port, Admiral Lisle was still at sea. Hertford became impatient and prepared the troops to start boarding in the hope that the remainder of the fleet would arrive the following day. He warned the privy council that he needed more money because he had insufficient to pay the wages of 5,000 captains, soldiers and sailors. They had used a month's wages while waiting for the fleet and he was 'spending treasure in vain' as the soldiers consumed vital food supplies. It was an inauspicious start to the campaign. Finally, on 20 April, Lisle arrived with the rest of the ships and the remainder of the provisions. All haste was made to put to sea. Within a few days the army was on board waiting for a wind to blow them out of harbour but it was not until 1 May that the winds veered and the ships were finally able to leave Tynemouth.[18]

During his enforced delay at Newcastle, Hertford had finalised his plans for the invasion. It was decided that as the troops were landing at Leith Sir Ralph Eure and his father would lead the men of the east and middle marches to burn Haddington, 12 miles from the port, as a diversion and would then join the army at Edinburgh. Hertford believed they should capture and fortify Leith, rather than destroy the port. It would give the king a good foothold in Scotland and prevent the Scots using it to bring in supplies or the French from landing there. It could easily be re-victualled from Berwick and he thought that if the king held a stronghold many Scots might be encouraged to join the English cause. Fire and sword, he maintained, would cause anger and resentment against the English. It was a maxim which would later be proved correct. However, the king and council would not rely on his judgement, arguing that there was insufficient time to fortify because of the need to move the army to France in the summer.[19]

Hertford was convinced that garrisons in Scotland were the best way forward but he would have to wait until the next reign to put his idea to the test.

With a favourable wind, ships could be a quick means of transporting troops and their use often left the enemy uncertain as to where the assault would be. On 4 May the fleet reached Leith and within four hours Hertford and the whole army had landed 2 miles west of the port. However, the Scots were ready for them and as the English marched towards Leith they soon encountered 6,000 horsemen and footsoldiers; but after a short, sharp engagement the Scotsmen fled, leaving the English to take the town. The following day, with the stores and munitions unloaded from the ships, Hertford marched the army to their objective – Edinburgh. The townspeople knew what to expect. In the hope of avoiding the forthcoming destruction, the Edinburgh provost offered up the keys of the town, on condition that the inhabitants might leave with their baggage and that Edinburgh would be saved from fire. They were to be disappointed. Hertford 'was not sent to treat but to take vengeance' and he was not prepared to accept any conditions. Only unconditional surrender would do.[20]

The army attacked the town on 6 May. The principal town gate was well defended but the English archers shot so well that no Scotsman dared show himself to return fire. The English gunners pulled a cannon up to the gate and broke through after three or four shots. The castle, however, was not such an easy prospect. There was no cover to give the attackers protection and the rock on which it was built was too hard to mine. After a short and unsuccessful assault against the walls of the fortress it was declared to be impregnable. Hertford decided not to waste time and munitions besieging it but instead to completely destroy the town.

They burnt part of the town that day but when they returned the following morning new defences had been built. The army set to work and soon broke them down to re-take the town leaving 400 or 500 Scots dead with the reported loss of only seven Englishmen. Over the next three days the devastation of Edinburgh and of Holyrood abbey and palace continued while outside the town 4,000 border-men laid waste to an area reaching up to 5 miles around the town. The enterprise was such a success that, before leaving Leith, Hertford knighted nearly fifty gentlemen for their exploits and a further eleven on reaching Berwick.

Hertford planned to devastate southern Scotland as a demonstration of what happened to those who broke their promise to Henry VIII. He also intended to ensure that, with no local food supplies, the Scots would be unable to assemble an army near the border that year. He returned to Leith to destroy the town and the pier and on 15 May, as the fleet set sail for England taking with it a number of Scottish ships, the army turned south to continue its devastation. Having arrived by sea, the company was short of carts and carriage horses to transport the food, drink and other goods they would need. One thousand of the English horsemen were ordered to walk while their horses, and any available cattle, were used to pull whatever carts they could find. For three days Hertford led the army through the Scottish lowlands, burning castles, towns and villages and destroying orchards, gardens and crops. The English assault on the Scots was sometimes brutal. At Dunbar the troops waited until the inhabitants thought they were safe and had gone to bed, before burning the town and the people in their sleep. The following day the army found its way blocked by a force of 10,000 Scots defending a narrow valley but after a few shots from the English they fled to the nearby hills. When Hertford led his men back into Berwick it was reported that fewer than forty Englishmen had been killed.[21]

The army had been in Scotland for only two weeks but it had been a gruelling campaign and the troops were exhausted. The king ordered that 4,000 of the soldiers should embark at Berwick and sail directly to Calais but Hertford was concerned about the condition of the men. Although the gentlemen, he explained, were willing to go to France, their 'necessity' was evident. During the expedition they had spent all their money and they had no tents or pavilions. For two months the soldiers had lain in their clothes each night and for the past two weeks had spent every night in the field without covering. Most of them had disease and swollen legs and were so wearied that few were fit to serve. Their clothes were worn out and they had no money to buy more. The gentlemen and their men needed time to go home to recover, regain their health and equip themselves.[22]

Although the king's attention was turned towards France, Hertford had not finished with Scotland. He planned that once the horses were rested the wardens should make a raid on Jedburgh town and abbey. He moved back to Newcastle and then at the end of May to Darlington as he waited for the raid. His departure from Newcastle was not as grand as his arrival. On 27 May he wrote that he could not yet leave the town because of a lack of money, servants, apparel and horses.[23]

Lord Eure and his son led 4,000 men into Scotland early in June and, after Jedburgh refused to surrender, attacked and destroyed the town. Just days before the raid several border families had made pledges before Sir Ralph to become Henry's subjects. After marking red crosses on their coats, forty Scotsmen joined the border-men in raiding their own country in return for protection for their homes. Hertford believed the support of Scotsmen was vital for English success north of the border but he examined closely the claims of these men who professed allegiance to Henry VIII to establish whether their claims were true or a ploy to prevent the destruction of their property.

Hertford's leadership of this campaign had been a significant success. Sir Ralph Eure heaped praise upon him, saying that he had won as much honour for 'annoying' the Scots as any previous northern lieutenant and that the raid to burn Jedburgh would increase it even further. Hertford had proved his skill at leading a large force and ensured that the king could sail to France without fear of an attack against England's northern border. He was now a seasoned commander against the Scots, who would not forget him. Henry VIII was confident that in future 'the terror of his visage' would be sufficient to cause Scotsmen to surrender.[24]

Military and Diplomatic Affairs

During the following two years, although Hertford made one more foray into Scotland, it was France which demanded much of his attention. Henry VIII still craved a military victory and his final opportunity to lead an army to war came during 1544. As Hertford finished his northern campaign in June, plans were well advanced for the invasion of France. The previous year the king had agreed to send 5,000 men, commanded by Sir John Wallop and Thomas Seymour, to support the emperor in the Low Countries on the condition that Charles V would later join him in war against the French. At the end of December 1543 Hertford had been one of the signatories to a treaty whereby England and Spain would make a joint attack on France in 1544 with the intention of taking Paris.[1]

During June the English army of 40,000 men was shipped to Calais where the king joined them the following month. The queen, Katherine Parr, had been appointed to act as regent in Henry's absence. Hertford was ordered to return from Scotland to London to act as one of her councillors with Cranmer, Lord Chancellor Wriothesley, Thomas Thirlby the Bishop of Westminster, and the king's secretary William Petre. One of Hertford's first duties was to travel to Hampton Court Palace and re-establish Prince Edward's household. The young prince was nearly 7 years old and it was time for him to be treated as a young man rather than as a child. Hertford discharged all the prince's ladies and gentlemen and swore in new gentlemen into what was to be a predominantly male household. John Cheke was appointed to join Richard Cox as a tutor to Edward and his young companions.[2] Eighteen boys, all sons of noblemen, were appointed at various times to be the young prince's playmates. Among these were Hertford's sons, Edward, who was later described as being 'the living image of his father', and Henry.[3] It was an unrivalled opportunity for the two boys to forge a long-term relationship with their cousin, the future King of England.

In France, Henry VIII was suffering poor health due to ulcers on his leg. Unable to ride, he cancelled the proposed march to Paris and instead ordered the English army to besiege and capture Boulogne and Montreuil. The assault against them proved to be lengthy. On 13 August, after six weeks at court, Hertford joined the king at Boulogne.[4] On this occasion, though, Henry did not need his services as a general but as a diplomat. On 9 September Hertford and the Bishop of Winchester, Stephen Gardiner, travelled to Hardelot Castle, south of Boulogne, to negotiate terms for peace with the French ambassadors, Cardinal du Bellay and Claude de l'Aubespine. They supped together that night; the following day, after the Duke of Suffolk, Richard Rich and the king's principal secretary, William Paget, had arrived, they began what was to become a long series of discussions. Negotiations did not go well, especially after Boulogne Castle was mined by the English engineers and the town surrendered on 14 September. A meeting of the two ambassadors with Henry VIII at Boulogne made no further progress and the Frenchmen returned to King Francis.[5] No doubt they were relieved to depart. With Boulogne scarred by cannon fire, and the battle site around the town resembling a place of desolation, it was a miserable place. Ambassador Chapuys, suffering from gout, had been with the king at Boulogne throughout the campaign and by the end of September he was begging for someone to replace him and 'get him out of this purgatory'.[6]

Elation at taking Boulogne was tempered by the news that the emperor had made peace with Francis. England stood alone and, with the French now able to turn all their forces against him, Henry lifted the siege at Montreuil and fortified and garrisoned Boulogne. The rest of the army began the journey home and on 30 September the king, accompanied by Hertford and other members of the court, sailed for England. However, only ten days later Hertford and Paget arrived back in Calais late at night to resume negotiations.[7] The two French ambassadors had returned with their master's response to Henry's demands: Francis agreed to pay the pension that Henry claimed if the English king would give up some of his territorial claims in France. He would also pay part of the pension arrears and some reparation towards the costs of the war. Francis, however, refused to break his alliance with Scotland although he was prepared to encourage the Scots into a treaty with the English. The main disagreement over Boulogne remained unresolvable. Henry intended to keep it but Francis refused to give up a single foot of his kingdom.

It was stalemate and the two sides turned to the emperor to act as arbitrator. Francis, though, still hoped he would recover Boulogne by force and thus be quit of all the pensions and other claims against him. Early on 18 October Hertford, Gardiner, Sir John Gage, Paget and Rich met du Bellay and l'Aubespine with the emperor's representatives, Antoine Perrenot de Granvelle and Jean de Montmorency, in the council chamber at Calais. Neither side was prepared to give ground on their differences and the emperor's men refused to take sides, saying they were there to act as mediators. When the French reiterated their master's resolution to have Boulogne, even if by force, matters became heated and the meeting came to an abrupt end.

Henry had decided that if no resolution could be reached, Hertford and Gardiner were to travel to Brussels and declare his views directly to the emperor. A further meeting with the ambassadors proved equally unfruitful and on 24 October Hertford and Gardiner left Calais for Brussels. Their instructions were simple. If Francis would not agree to Henry's conditions for peace, the emperor should be encouraged to join the English king and declare himself the French king's enemy.[8]

The two men and their attendants rode fast and covered the 110 miles to Brussels in three days. It was an exhausting journey but by the following day they were ready for an audience with the emperor. Sitting in a little chair, keeping warm before the fire in the privy chamber, Charles assured them that his first loyalty was to Henry. However, he still wanted to maintain his friendship with Francis. His suggestion that Henry might start to resolve their differences by forgoing part of his pension was not very constructive. Hertford and Gardiner returned to their chambers knowing that the king would not accept the emperor's proposal.[9]

During the next four weeks further meetings with Charles and his ministers, Louis de Praet and Nicholas de Granvelle, proved to be equally unproductive. The financial terms offered by the French were unsatisfactory to the English but the main sticking point was Henry's claim to Boulogne. This proved to be a major obstacle to peace. The emperor could persuade neither side to lessen their demands. Hertford and Gardiner explained that the king had entered the war against France because of his treaty with Charles. If he was not to keep some prize from the war then it was pointless to have entered into it. Charles should declare himself an enemy of France, they insisted, because by invading English territory at Guisnes, Francis had broken his treaty with the emperor in which they had agreed that neither ruler would invade the land of the other's allies. The emperor prevaricated, trying to find a resolution to the problem while still maintaining his friendship with both parties. After one especially tense meeting 'of many words and small purpose' the emperor's ministers invited Hertford and Gardiner to join them in a glass of wine to 'cheer' them. The English ambassadors did their best to be sociable but were relieved to take their leave.[10]

Hertford and Gardiner quickly realised that negotiations were making little headway and decided to return to Calais as soon as possible. However, before they could leave the king ordered them to remain. Their visit was turning out to be longer than they had expected and living in Brussels was expensive. They were running short of money and were forced to ask Sir Richard Rich to send more funds.[11]

Diplomatic work could be tedious and slow and at one point they waited nearly a fortnight for an opportunity to speak to the emperor. He had been suffering with gout and when Hertford and Gardiner finally gained an audience on 16 November they found him sitting in a very low chair with his legs wrapped in black cloth and propped up as high as his body. The emperor listened as they again recited the argument for him to favour England and then sent them away to await his response. But Charles was in no hurry to make an enemy of Francis. Four days later they were called back to be told he would delay his decision for ten weeks while he dealt with other matters. However, in the meantime he would try to induce Francis to see reason and he suggested that the English could use the time to fortify Boulogne.[12]

For Hertford and Gardiner it had been an unsuccessful and frustrating assignment. No progress had been made and Hertford believed that in ten weeks' time they would still be no further forward. Two days later he and Gardiner set off for Calais to return to England. They spent Christmas at Greenwich with the king, who was greatly disgruntled at the emperor's delay. During a meeting with Chapuys and van der Delft the king's exchanges became so heated that Hertford and Gardiner later apologised for his behaviour.[13] At the end of the ten-week deadline the emperor had still failed to make a decision and negotiations dragged on into the spring.

In January 1545 Hertford returned to France to examine and advise on improvements to the fortifications at Guisnes and Boulogne. However, the routine visit took a dramatic turn early in February when, while Hertford was at Guisnes, 10,000 French soldiers laid siege to Boulogne. Setting their camp across the river from the town, they intended to prevent supplies arriving by sea. Hertford and Lord Gray rode to Boulogne, taking with them 400 horsemen and 1,500 footsoldiers. A mile upstream from the town, where a bridge had been built for the army to cross over to the French, they were joined by 2,000 men from the garrison. The French tried to defend the passage but the English broke through and Hertford put the enemy to flight in a 'noble and valiant' victory. Over 600 Frenchmen were slain or captured and much of their artillery and stores were taken.[14] The French, like the Scots, were experiencing Hertford's skill on the battlefield.

Hertford returned to London but not for long; within weeks he was travelling north again. The king remained infuriated by the Scots' rejection of the marriage treaty and his response was to force them into submission by a military onslaught that became known as the 'Rough Wooing'. The expedition in 1544 had failed to produce the desired result. Scotsmen continued their raids across the border, and after Hertford had left the north English aggression against Scotland continued under the command of Sir Ralph Eure. On 27 February 1545 his army of about 5,000 men, including 700 'assured men' (Scottish borderers who had sworn allegiance to Henry VIII), was confronted by a Scottish force at Ancrum Moor near Jedburgh. The Scots enjoyed a convincing victory, aided by the decision of the 'assured men' to change allegiance part way through the battle. Tearing off the red crosses which identified them, they turned on the English. Eight hundred Englishmen were killed, including Eure.

The king's response was predictable. Upon hearing news that the French, having failed to take Boulogne, planned to send troops to help the Scots invade England, Henry raised an army of 30,000 men from the northern counties. Once again Hertford was appointed lieutenant-general to lead the force. On 15 May he left London accompanied by 200 horsemen and footsoldiers, arriving in Darlington two weeks later.[15] He quickly decided on his course of action – to take a large force into Scotland in late summer, by which time he hoped to have sufficient food supplies, and establish garrisons in the lowlands.

Hertford was soon faced with difficulties. Once again there was a shortage of supplies and equipment. His plan to station large numbers of men along the frontier was hampered because although the English fortresses were nearly ready to withstand assault, they lacked sufficient victuals. A pre-emptive attack against Kelso in June was abandoned because of a lack of basic staples, especially wheat and malt. The army was short of carriages and Hertford made repeated requests for another 2,000 pikes, gunpowder and more money to pay the troops.[16] The privy council continued to prevaricate about sending further funds, saying they did not know how much money to send without knowing how long Hertford would keep the army in Scotland.

On 5 September, leaving behind a large force to protect the border, Hertford led the 'battle' group of the army away from Newcastle with 'fair words' and promises of future pay and marched for four days to the Standing Stone upon Crookham Moor near Coldstream. There the whole invasion army of 16,000 men was to meet, the vanguard being led by Henry Clifford, Earl of Cumberland, and the rearward by Lord William Dacre.[17] The following day, although part of the army had been stranded when the River Tweed rose suddenly and the men had to wait for the water to subside, they reached Kelso Abbey in the afternoon.

The 100 inhabitants of the abbey refused to yield to Hertford but by nightfall the walls of the building had been breached and the Scotsmen chased into the steeple. It was a futile attempt to escape and next day Hertford's men stormed the steeple, killing many of those inside.

Hertford believed that with garrisons at Hume Castle, Kelso Abbey and Wark (on the English side of the border near Coldstream) he could subjugate the south-east lowlands. However, Kelso proved unsuitable so it was razed to the ground and the surrounding villages and crops burnt.[18] On 14 September the English army left Kelso and began three days of burning that culminated at Jedburgh where the abbey, town and surrounding villages were destroyed. By now the troops were short of victuals and forced to return to Wark but on the march back they destroyed the buildings and crops for 4 miles on either side of their column. While the main force remained at Wark, Hertford took 4,000 horsemen to attack Hume Castle, a few miles to the north, but the castle was too well defended. Once again he ordered his men to devastate the surrounding area before disbanding the army and returning to Newcastle.

It was the second time he had laid waste to the lowlands of Scotland but on this occasion the damage was so extensive that the Scots had suffered twice as much as when he had attacked Edinburgh. One estimate named nearly 300 towns, villages, abbeys, castles and hamlets burnt and destroyed. Now that the old guard of military leaders – Norfolk and Suffolk – had left the field, Hertford was the most experienced of the king's generals and he earned praise for his handling of the troops. He was professional and paid great attention to detail. He kept discipline and made good use of artillery, infantry and horsemen while using cavalry and outriders for protection. The cartographer John Elder, who accompanied the army, observed that Hertford's plans could not have been bettered.[19]

It had been a successful assault. The attack on Scotland had been brutal but anything less would have achieved nothing. Hertford left the south-east of the country so devastated that it would be impossible for a Scottish army to travel through the lowlands to England. But as he knew, once his troops had left Scotland, England had no power or influence there. The assaults in 1544 and 1545 caused destruction only in the south of the country and did not further the cause of the marriage between Edward and Mary. When Hertford next invaded across the border he would have a new plan for subjugating the country. For now, though, after five months in the north and with plague in many towns in Northumberland, he was ready to leave. By 24 October he was back with the court at Windsor in readiness to attend Parliament the following month.

Henry VIII was getting old. He was too infirm to go on campaign himself but he still harboured hope of bringing Scotland to heel. He was also determined to keep Boulogne, even though the privy council advised against such action because of the enormous cost of maintaining a garrison there. Aware that the French would not willingly give up their quest to regain Boulogne and would mount a further assault on the town, Henry decided to improve defences. He also proposed further fortifications along the route between Calais and Boulogne. After a visit to the area in February 1546, Hertford and Lisle recommended improving the defences at Ambleteuse, north of Boulogne.[20]

There was regular skirmishing between the French and English around Boulogne. The Earl of Surrey had been in command there since September 1545 but in January 1546 he misjudged an attack on the French which resulted in the death of over 200 English soldiers including ten captains. The king had lost confidence in Surrey's ability as a commander and decided to recall him and install Hertford in his place as lieutenant-general of the army in France.[21] For Surrey this recall was not only a slur on his capabilities as a military commander; to be replaced by a man whose family origins he considered lowly was a slight he would not forget.

Hertford landed at Calais on 23 March with a force of over 5,000 men. As always, the limited supply of victuals and other necessaries hampered their progress. Supply ships were dependent on the tides and winds and when Hertford set out towards Ambleteuse a few days later it was with only limited provisions. The company soon had its first encounter with the French. Riding ahead to view the camp at Ambleteuse, Hertford, accompanied by thirty horsemen, came upon twenty-one Frenchmen. The odds were in Hertford's favour and the skirmish resulted in an easy victory for the English – only one Frenchman escaped, the rest being either captured or killed.[22]

For the first time, Hertford and his brother Thomas were on campaign together and they forged a good working relationship. Thomas was well established as a military man and his experience was by now broader than his brother's. Witnessing the emperor's troops besieging the Turks, fighting in France and the Low Countries, observing the tactics used by foreign armies and his appointment as Master of the Ordnance shortly before serving at the siege of Boulogne in 1544 had prepared him for all aspects of land warfare. Thomas had also gained valuable experience as a sailor. In the autumn of 1544 he had served as vice-admiral in command of the navy upon the Narrow Seas – the English Channel between Dover and Calais – keeping the Channel clear of enemy shipping and seizing French ships. Capturing foreign vessels could be a lucrative business. Like many courtiers, Thomas and Hertford owned their own ships. Hertford's pinnace was named *Phoenix* after the bird his sister, Jane, had chosen as her symbol.[23] Captured ships became the property of the king but Hertford and

Thomas were allowed to keep any booty, such as wine, from vessels that their own ships captured. Thomas was an enthusiastic sailor, keen to get to work against the French. Although his initial assignment as vice-admiral had turned into a fiasco after his fleet was scattered by storms, he had acquitted himself well. Several ships were lost, including one captained by his brother Henry, who had a lucky escape after his ship foundered on rocks with the loss of three lives. [24]

Hertford recognised that Thomas could offer valuable advice for the new fortifications at Ambleteuse and when he viewed the site he was accompanied by his brother and two military engineers, Richard Lee and John Rogers. Work started quickly on taking down the old walls and clearing the ground. On 5 April, twenty-four ships arrived with supplies – ordnance, tents, mattresses, victuals – and Hertford reckoned that once the storms subsided, work on the fortress, a pentagonal shaped earthwork faced in masonry, would proceed quickly. He was enthusiastic about the site and proposed that since the English were unfamiliar with the name Ambleteuse it should be changed to the 'New Haven in Boulogne'. [25]

The king was keen to have a military victory in France and was pushing for an assault on either Etaples or Hardeloe or on Ardres near Calais. Hertford, though, was cautious and warned against such ventures. The towns were too well victualled for a short assault to succeed and at Ardres the defensive ditches around the town were so deep as to need ladders to go down – but then no ladder would be long enough to reach the top of the wall from the bottom of the trench. [26]

There were, however, continual skirmishes between the two sides, one of which went badly for the English. On 25 April the marshal of Boulogne, Sir Ralph Ellerker, and a band of his men were enticed out of the town and across the river to confront a company of Frenchmen. The French force was larger than initially perceived and during the attack on the English the Albanois (Italian) soldiers, who should have supported Ellerker, ran away. Ellerker was among fourteen men taken by the French and his body and those of two horsemen were later retrieved with their hearts cut out. [27]

It was not unusual for Henry VIII to use foreign mercenaries to supplement his own forces, and the Italians, Germans and Spaniards who had served under Hertford in Scotland had been ordered to travel to Boulogne. The mercenaries, being professional soldiers, often had more experience of war than Englishmen who had been drafted into the army for occasional service. However, not everyone was happy about employing them. Paget thought them to be untrustworthy and decried the fact that the king was forced to use foreigners 'who every time leave us in the dirt'. The mercenaries were also expensive to hire, being paid £3 a month rather than the £1 wages of an English soldier; and, to ensure they did not leave, when money was short it was given to them first, leaving nothing for the English soldiers.[28] Paget's solution to avoid using mercenaries was to establish peace and give England time to grow stronger for future wars.

The emperor's failure to resolve the differences between England and France had left the two countries still at war and in April negotiations for peace restarted. The first meeting ended in stalemate. The French would not accept the English demands for payment of the pension owed to Henry VIII and would still not agree that England could keep Boulogne and that the French would abandon their support of Scotland. On 15 May the French proposed their own terms. Francis was willing for Henry to keep Boulogne for eight years after which it would be returned to France in exchange for 2 million gold crowns. He would continue to pay the pensions that had been agreed in former treaties and England was not to make war against the Scots without provocation.

However, Henry was slow to respond to the proposals. The French became fed up with waiting and threatened to leave the discussions. Throughout the proceedings there was concern that the talks might fail and both sides were preparing their navies in case of that eventuality. Skirmishes took place at sea. On one occasion twelve French galleys fired shot into the camp and harbour at Ambleteuse. Hertford had artillery pieces taken to the shore and returned fire which 'for an hour was good pastime' until the galleys retired.[29] On 4 May Hertford had sent his brother to England to explain the local situation to the king. When Thomas returned a few days later his ship was chased closely by three galleys and he had to help row to enable the ship to escape. It is probable that on this occasion he was sailing in a galleasse – an oared warship with light guns on the upper deck, up to sixty oars below and a full rig of sails on three masts – which when rowed had the ability to sail into wind. Van der Delft, the Imperial ambassador, reported to the emperor that Henry had built eight galleasses, which he preferred to galleys, because each could carry up to thirteen guns. The situation must have been desperate for Thomas to have joined the rowers. Service in the galleys was horrific, used as a punishment for criminals and captured prisoners, and was considered to be 'no less a penalty than death'.[30]

Meanwhile Hertford was facing difficulties within the camp. During a muster at Ambleteuse there was talk of a mutiny over pay by some of the mercenaries. Discipline within the army was vital and Hertford's response was swift and decisive. He put the camp on alert and turned the guns towards the mutineers, ordering all the men who were loyal to Henry VIII and had no complaint, to leave the gathering. The mutineers, seeing their fellow men turn upon them, 'ran into the tail of the rest' and departed. Hertford was not prepared to let the matter rest there and intended to identify and punish the guilty soldiers. After each company had been warned that the behaviour of the mutineers brought dishonour upon their own country, the men were encouraged to turn in the perpetrators. It was successful and several of the mutineers were punished while others were banished. Hertford was similarly harsh in his attitude towards the treatment of French prisoners. Since English prisoners taken by the French were 'straightly handled' and put to row in galleys he believed that prisoners taken by his troops should be treated similarly.[31]

After several days of procrastination Henry accepted the French proposals in principle but wanted clarification of the town boundaries proposed by the French. Matters dragged on through May and it looked as if the French were preparing to attack Boulogne if the talks failed. French ships were harrying English vessels near the harbour, even managing to take one ship laden with oxen and sheep. As French soldiers gathered at St Etienne, south of Boulogne, Hertford took a force of 7,000 and skirmished with them, although little damage was done to either side.[32] As discussions reached a conclusion Henry proposed that neither side should start to build any new fortifications after the treaty was agreed. However, in a bid to gain an advantage, he instructed Hertford to secretly begin the proposed fortifications at Cap Gris Nez (or Blackness as the English called it) before the treaty was signed. Hertford wasted no time and immediately ordered his men to start work.[33]

The Treaty of Camp was signed on 7 June. It was a partial victory for Henry. He was to receive the pensions he demanded and to retain possession of Boulogne, but only until 1554. However, he was forced to agree not to start war against Scotland without provocation and both sides did agree that no new fortifications would be started around Boulogne. On 9 June Hertford met the French admiral, Claude d'Annebaut, and peace was proclaimed at 10 a.m. that day. The admiral asked for the return of French prisoners but Hertford refused, saying that men who had risked their lives to take prisoners should benefit from the ransoms.[34]

The terms of the treaty were very acceptable to Paget, who wrote to Petre explaining why. To illustrate his point he recounted the fable of a man condemned to die by a king who had a favourite ass. In a bid to save his life the man undertook to teach the ass to talk within twelve months in the expectation that in the meantime he might die or perhaps the king might die, or the ass might die or the ass might speak. Paget explained that by the time the payment for Boulogne was due they might be able to make some new bargain to keep the town, or the French king might not be able to make the payment and so forfeit the town, or the French king might die and his son not want Boulogne or some other thing might chance.[35] What he did not say, because foretelling the king's death could be construed as treason, was that Henry might die and his successor not want Boulogne.

Paget quickly set sail for England to deliver a copy of the treaty to the king but his journey was slowed when he was forced to spend a day at Dover to recover from sea-sickness. His tendency towards sea-sickness was well known and a cause for some friendly banter between him and Hertford. Later that summer, after having an especially calm sailing to France, Hertford wrote to Paget, teasing him about how the journey would have been a pleasant one for him 'because ye are so good a seaman'.[36]

The two men had established a good working relationship which would be at its most effective during the following reign. Born the son of a 'jack of all trades' in London, Paget's education at Cambridge and the patronage of Bishop Gardiner had prepared him for a career as an administrator and diplomat. So successful was his career in royal service that as Principal Secretary of State he acted as the king's right-hand man. He oversaw royal correspondence, offered advice and served as an intermediary to relay opinions and instructions between the king, his councillors and other royal servants. As Henry VIII grew increasingly infirm and withdrew from court life, Paget became a close confidant. More than anybody else, he was aware of the king's intentions and as his influence with Henry grew, men sought Paget's help and advice. Because of their political roles he and Hertford worked closely together and when Hertford was away from court Paget kept him informed of important news and looked after his interests. Out of sight could definitely mean out of mind and absence left the way clear for men to speak to the king against absentees. When Hertford was on the Scottish borders the two men were in regular contact by letter and on one occasion Paget had advised him against criticising council policy for fear of offending some of the councillors.[37]

Hertford remained at Boulogne until the end of July, overseeing the completion of fortifications. It was high summer and the soldiers wanted to return home to England for harvest-time, but he was skilful in handling the men and used imaginative methods to persuade them to remain and to work hard. At Cap Gris Nez a new stone mole, or breakwater, was to be constructed to create an artificial harbour. To win their goodwill Hertford ordered that if they remained the 1,200 men should each be paid a groat a day on top of their wages and they would receive all their pay and return home within fifteen days. Then, to create an incentive to work quickly, he divided the work on the mole into twelve parts. The captains drew lots for their sections and Hertford promised that those who finished their part first should return to England first. Each morning a trumpet sounded at 4 a.m. and a quarter of an hour later a drum-roll called the men to work. Roll-call was taken and they were expected to work for three hours in the morning and then again from 3 p.m. until 6 p.m., when they received their groat. However, the competition engendered by Hertford's plan and the desire to return home encouraged some men to work both day and night. 'Such a piece of work was never done with such a number in so short a time', Hertford wrote to Paget, and he reckoned that most of the work would be finished in half the time he had expected.[38]

However, finances were still an issue. Hertford was keen to retain the men's trust and respect and he begged Paget to send money so that he could pay them and so keep his promise 'or else I shall never be able to serve hereafter'. He was also concerned for their welfare and pleaded with the king to give each man a crown to buy hose since they had spoilt their clothes in their labour. By 13 July the money had arrived and the men were on their way home. Hertford's somewhat unconventional methods had been so successful – 'never was such a work done so quickly and cheaply' – that he instigated a similar order for work on the hill outside Boulogne.[39]

On campaign in both Scotland and France Hertford had shown himself to be a skilful leader, not only tactically but also in handling the troops. His concern for their welfare and his ability to exact loyalty and effort from his men were commendable. However, his success with them may have given him, and those about him, an overly favourable impression of his ability to handle people. As he would later discover, soldiers accustomed to discipline who obeyed orders were easier to control than the wider populace – or the men who governed England for the king. In the meantime he reaped the rewards of his success. For five years Henry VIII's military ambitions had given Hertford the opportunity to prove his worth and establish himself as an authority to be reckoned with at court.

Hertford's return to England was brief. Despite the treaty there was mutual distrust on each side and within a few weeks he made what would prove to be his final visit to France to investigate rumours that the French were building a fortress across the river opposite Boulogne. His departure was delayed by illness and when he finally arrived on 21 September it appeared that work on the new fortifications had already stopped.[40] Tensions remained and as winter approached Thomas Seymour joined negotiations to identify which sites might be fortified at Boulogne. In England, however, any difficulties with France were soon to become insignificant as another issue became more pressing. The king was dying and his heir was only 9 years old.

6

Prelude to Power

It had become increasingly apparent during 1546 that the king's life was moving towards its close. At court the factions started to jockey for position as the political and religious uncertainties grew. The prize at stake was a great one: whoever was paramount when the old king died could win control of the new king and of the government of England. Court factions were split along religious lines. On one side were the Catholics – Gardiner, Norfolk, Wriothesley and Rich. Opposing them were those who favoured the religious ideas which came to be known as Protestantism – Hertford, Lisle, Cranmer, Parr (who had been created Earl of Essex in 1543) and his sister, the queen. Some people expected Katherine to be made regent and to rule England during Edward's minority, as she had done when Henry went to war against France in 1544. It was a situation that would have given the reformers opportunity to exert great influence. Alternatively the king could appoint one of the privy councillors to be regent, most probably either Hertford, Norfolk or Gardiner, who were the prominent figures at court.

The supporters of Catholicism were worried. While Henry VIII was king, England was still a Catholic country although without allegiance to the pope. Henry had recently shied away from further religious reform after Gardiner warned that Cranmer's proposals to abandon rituals such as creeping to the cross on Good Friday and the use of the Lenten veil to screen the altar during Lent might jeopardise a recent alliance with the emperor.[1] However, Prince Edward had been educated and influenced by tutors who favoured the new religion. The Catholic faith in England would be under serious threat with Edward as king and Katherine as regent.

During the summer of 1546 the queen's enemies saw a way to bring about her downfall and raise the hope of a Catholic regency. It was to be a worrying time not only for the queen but also for the people close to her, including Hertford. Some of the ladies who attended Katherine were threatened by the conspiracy and any threat to them was also a threat to their husbands. Many of these ladies were married to high-ranking, influential courtiers. Among those who shared the queen's religious beliefs were Hertford's wife, Anne; Lisle's wife, Jane; the Countess of Sussex, Anne Radcliffe; Joan Denny, wife of Sir Anthony Denny; and the queen's close friend, Katherine Brandon, Duchess of Suffolk.[2] Together they discussed the new religious ideas and the books Katherine read, some of which were hidden away in her chambers because of their supposedly heretical content.

In June 1546 a Protestant woman, Anne Askew, was charged with denying that consecrated bread and wine became flesh and blood. Anne, who had been thrown out by her husband for her heretical views, had been arrested previously but eventually released. On this occasion her situation was more serious. It was suspected that she had been in contact with ladies of the queen's circle and possibly even with the queen herself. Katherine's enemies saw a way of exposing her as a secret Protestant by establishing a connection between her and this supposed heretic.

In the Tower Anne steadfastly refused to acknowledge the real presence in the consecrated elements. When Wriothesley and Rich questioned her concerning her relationship with Katherine's ladies, she denied any contact with them, admitting only that two men who had brought money to her in the Tower claimed to be from Anne Seymour and Joan Denny. Frustrated by her refusal to incriminate Katherine, Wriothesley and Rich eventually ordered Sir Anthony Knyvett, lieutenant of the Tower, to put Anne on the rack. He obeyed reluctantly – it was against the law to rack a woman of gentle birth – but when they ordered him to stretch her further he refused and the two inquisitors removed their gowns and did the deed themselves. Anne Askew never confessed to anything that could implicate the queen but she was found guilty of heresy. When she was taken to be burnt at Smithfield she had to be carried in a chair, so badly had Wriothesley and Rich damaged her body.

Katherine was safe for now but it was not long before a further attempt was made to entrap her. She had taken to discussing her religious ideas with the king and one day in midsummer, after her religious theorising had annoyed Henry, the king complained of this to Gardiner. The bishop saw his opportunity and warned him that there were 'such treasons cloaked with this cloak of heresy' and the king should realise how dangerous it was to 'cherish a serpent within his own bosom'.[3] Henry took the warning to heart. On 8 July the government banned the possession of all heretical books considered to 'contain pernicious and detestable errors and heresies'. It was expected that such books would be found within Katherine's chambers.

Meanwhile, plans were made for her arrest. However, it appears that Katherine came to learn of her danger after the king confided his intentions to one of his doctors. When Henry visited her and turned their talk towards matters of religion, Katherine cleverly used the opportunity to point out that it was not the place of a woman to instruct her husband in such matters. She had only done so, she claimed, in the hope of taking the king's mind off the pain in his legs, and so that she might become better informed from listening to him. Henry was mollified but the following day, as she and the king walked in the gardens, Wriothesley arrived with a guard of forty men to execute her arrest warrant. Only then did Katherine realise just how close she had been to disaster. Henry, though, turned on the Lord Chancellor, calling him 'Arrant knave! beast! and fool!' and dismissed him. The incident sent a clear message to all.[4] Katherine was still definitely in favour with the king. The Catholics realised that they were losing their hold on power. When Hertford returned from France in July he found the reformers in the ascendancy and matters turning in his favour.

During the autumn the king became increasingly isolated from Catholic influence. In September, when he made a short progress away from London, Gardiner and Wriothesley remained in the capital dealing with council business while Hertford, Russell, Essex and Paget accompanied Henry. It was a heaven-sent opportunity for the reformist faction to use their influence against their opponents. Worse was to come for the Catholics. In October they lost a vital link to the king when the religious conservative, Sir Thomas Heneage, was replaced as chief gentleman of the privy chamber by Sir Anthony Denny, a supporter of religious reform. Heneage's removal left the chamber firmly under the control of the reformers.

Throughout the autumn Hertford was regularly at court and privy council meetings, as tensions between the two religious factions increased and became very public. In early October Lisle was excluded from court for a month after he quarrelled with Gardiner and struck him in the face during a council meeting, causing himself much 'trouble and danger'.[5] Gardiner soon found that he, too, was banned from the royal presence when he declined a request to exchange land with the king. The exclusion was a harsh response to a matter that may well have derived partly from a misunderstanding. His enemies, though, were successful in influencing the king against him and keeping him away from court and any opportunity to plead his case with Henry. On 4 December the king's harsh response to Gardiner – 'we see no cause why you should molest us further' – left no doubt in the bishop's mind as to where he stood in Henry's favour.[6]

With Gardiner excluded, the reformers' next target was Norfolk. The duke had previously been adept at wriggling his way out of serious trouble. When his two nieces, Anne Boleyn and Catherine Howard, had fallen he had saved his neck by decrying their behaviour and dissociating himself from them, but on this occasion the opposition against him was too strong. When circumstances presented an opportunity to bring down Norfolk, Hertford and his supporters seized it. His continued presence at court could cause too many difficulties for them in the future.

Despite his reservations about the Seymours and their attachment to the new religion, the Duke of Norfolk knew the advantages of an alliance with the family of the future King of England. In June 1546 he had once again proposed a match between his daughter Mary Howard, the widowed Duchess of Richmond, and Thomas Seymour. It is surprising that Thomas, who by then was 37, was not already married for he was certainly one of the most eligible men at court. The duke had thought so in 1538 when he had first proposed that the couple should marry. Norfolk had used that occasion to make an oblique comment on what he considered to be the Seymour brothers' lowly origins by remarking that he did not wish his daughter to marry one of 'high blood or degree' since he had seen that often no great good came of joining together 'great bloods' by marriage. Norfolk had, however, commended Thomas 'for that he is so honestly advanced by the King's Majesty, as also for his towardness (promising future) and other his commendable merits'. The king had been agreeable to the match, commenting 'merrily' that if the two should wed Norfolk would 'be sure to couple her with one of such lust and youth, as should be able to please her well at all points'. Thomas had been agreeable to the proposal but the marriage never took place, probably because Mary objected.[7]

In 1546, however, Norfolk's proposal was for even closer ties between the two families than he had suggested previously. His son Henry, Earl of Surrey, had five children and Norfolk also planned that two of them should wed two of Hertford's children.[8] He appealed to the king for help in bringing about his proposals but he had reckoned without the antipathy of his son and daughter towards the Seymours. Mary Howard's 'fantasy would not serve to marry' Thomas and Surrey would never agree to his family being allied with men whom he considered were not truly noble. Surrey was proud and arrogant and had long resented what he considered to be *parvenu* nobility, seeing in the rise of those of 'vile birth ... the destruction of all the nobility of this realm'.[9] Although at one time he had appeared to be on good terms with Hertford, Surrey's resentment of him had grown, especially after Hertford replaced him following his ignominious failure in France.

Surrey was rash and reckless in his behaviour and had been imprisoned on several occasions for violence. In 1543 he had spent time in the Fleet prison after running through the streets of London at night breaking windows by using a crossbow to shoot stones. On that occasion it had been brought to the attention of the authorities that the arms carved upon Surrey's bed were similar to those of the king.[10] Wriothesley and Gardiner had questioned Surrey but, although it was illegal to use the royal arms, the matter had been overlooked. However, when the same assertion was made in December 1546 the king acted with speed. Henry was undoubtedly aware that the accession of his son was fast approaching. Seeing the antagonism between Catholics and reformers, and the factional split in the privy council, the old king realised the difficulties that lay ahead for the young prince. Henry could control these men but Edward would be ruled by them and the divisions between them could threaten the security of the country. Any suggestion that Surrey believed he could assert some claim to the throne was a danger to Prince Edward.

The charge against Surrey came after Sir Richard Southwell, an adherent of the Howards, informed the council on 2 December that he knew of information that questioned the earl's loyalty. His accusation may have been prompted by an ongoing disagreement between the two men but the reformers were quick to turn it to their advantage.[11] For the next week Surrey was held at Wriothesley's house for questioning. As the evidence was examined, the Lord Chancellor had opportunity to consider where his future lay – with the Catholics or the reformers. The situation looked bad for Surrey and on 12 December he was arrested and suffered the humiliation of being led publicly through the streets to the Tower. That same day, when Norfolk arrived in the city he was arrested and deprived of his Garter insignia and his Lord Treasurer's staff of office before being taken to the Tower. It left the Catholic party in disarray.

Throughout December Wriothesley increasingly allied himself with the reformers. Charges were soon brought against the father and son. Surrey confessed to using the arms of Edward the Confessor with 'three labels silver', an annotation used only by the royal heir apparent, but claimed he had the right to do so because it had been awarded to his ancestors. Evidence was presented of how he boasted that his father was the best qualified person to govern Edward and the realm because of his experience and lineage. His sister, Mary, was questioned. She admitted that when Norfolk had suggested the match with Thomas Seymour, Surrey had proposed instead that Mary should become the king's mistress. She had been horrified at the suggestion, replying that 'she would cut her own throat rather than she would consent to such a villainy'.[12] Evidence against Surrey was certainly damning. With the imminent accession of Edward it could not be overlooked this time.

While Henry VIII spent his final Christmas in seclusion at Westminster attended by just a few servants, Katherine was ordered to stay at Greenwich. His health was declining rapidly. Shortly before Christmas he had a fever which lasted for thirty hours and left him looking very ill.[13] The festive season passed quietly as plans were made for the future, both for the removal of the Howards and for the safe accession of Prince Edward. Privy council meetings were held away from court at Wriothesley's house, Ely Place. It was not unusual for council meetings to be held in councillors' houses when the king was away from London. On this occasion, however, even after Henry travelled to Westminster on 23 December the council continued to meet at the Lord Chancellor's house until early in January. It is possible the king was so seriously ill that even these men were being kept away from court.

Surrey's trial was set for 13 January 1547 but any expectation of a reprieve was destroyed the day before by his father's confession. Norfolk admitted that he had known that his son used the arms of Edward the Confessor. He also admitted that he displayed the arms of England in his own arms. Norfolk begged for mercy but his and his son's fate were sealed. Next day, at the Guildhall, Surrey faced his judges, among whom were Hertford and Lisle, and a jury of men from the county of Norfolk.[14] As he walked into the chamber, a guard walked ahead of him holding aloft an axe with the blade turned away from Surrey. The trial was long, starting at 9 a.m. and not finishing until darkness had fallen. Surrey was found guilty of using the arms of the heir apparent and as he was led from the building the axe blade was turned towards him, signifying to all that he was guilty of treason.

The king was merciful and commuted the sentence from being hanged, drawn and quartered to beheading. The penalty was extreme but Surrey's actions were construed as treasonous and his punishment was dictated by the timing of the charge. The king was removing anyone who might cause difficulties at the start of his son's reign. He had been greatly vexed by the antagonism between the factions and earlier, on Christmas Eve 1545, he had pleaded with the bishops and noblemen in Parliament to cast aside their religious disagreements. His appeal for unity had gone unheeded and the discord at court would end only when the leaders of one side were removed. Fear for his son's future forced Henry to take this opportunity of ensuring that one faction was silenced.

Surrey was executed on 19 January, the day after the act of attainder against him and his father had received its first reading in Parliament. It was not until 27 January, however, that Hertford, Wriothesley, St John and Russell delivered the royal assent to the act, finally confirming Norfolk and Surrey guilty of high treason. The king was too ill to attend 'but wished it passed without delay in order that certain offices held by Norfolk might be given to others against the approaching creation of the Prince'.[15] All Norfolk's appointments had been forfeited and, as he waited to learn the date of his own execution, the vultures at court waited for the spoils of death.

During those final days of the reign Hertford received his prize. The king declared his intention to appoint him to Norfolk's old offices of Earl Marshal and Lord Treasurer.[16] Both appointments were great offices of state and carried enormous prestige. While the role of Earl Marshal was primarily ceremonial, with responsibility for organising state funerals and royal coronations, the Lord Treasurer exerted enormous influence and was second in rank only to the Lord Chancellor. The appointment was a sure sign of Henry's confidence in his brother-in-law.

Because of the advantage Hertford gained from the removal of his rivals, there has been suspicion that he was involved in a coup against Norfolk and Gardiner to prevent them being named as executors, or even regent, in the king's final will. However, it is unlikely that he or anybody else instigated a plot to bring about their downfall. The probable explanation is that the reformers took advantage of the opportunities that fate provided. Although Henry was a sick man, as Christmas approached no one knew how soon he would die. They also did not know when, or even if, the king would rewrite his will. Sudden death from a heart attack or stroke would have prevented it. Norfolk and Gardiner were already named as executors in Henry's existing will, written in 1544. If there had been any intention of permanently excluding the two men from inclusion in any future government, their enemies needed to be certain that the will would be rewritten. Alternatively, they needed to find more serious accusations to ensure the two men were permanently excluded from court and would never return to royal favour. The charges against Norfolk originated from his son's behaviour, not his own. He confessed that his arms included those used by the heir apparent but whether there was really a need for a charge of treason is questionable. Even today they are still included in the arms of the Dukes of Norfolk. Until Norfolk's admission of guilt shortly before Surrey's trial there was no guarantee that the latter would be convicted. The charges against Gardiner were insubstantial and not sufficiently serious to exclude him from court and council for long.

With the dominant Catholics removed, the way was clear for Hertford to establish himself as the only credible alternative to the queen to act as regent. The king had ensured that, with the new appointments as Earl Marshal and Lord Treasurer, his brother-in-law would soon be the most powerful and exalted man at court. It certainly strengthened Hertford's position as a candidate for the regency. He and Lisle were in control during the weeks before the king's death and nothing was done at court without their approval. Chapuys believed Hertford and Lisle were the only noblemen who were young enough and had sufficient ability to undertake the government of the country.[17] Van der Delft, though, identified Hertford as the dominant councillor and was confident that the two men would fall out because of the differences in their character. He perceived Lisle to be of 'high courage', unlikely to submit to Hertford and favoured by the people and the nobility because of his 'liberality and splendour'. In his view, Hertford was not so accomplished in this respect and was looked down upon by everyone as a 'dry, sour, opinionated man'.[18]

Despite the speculation, Hertford already knew who the king intended would govern England at the start of the next reign. While action was being taken against the Howards, plans had also been made for Edward's accession. As Christmas began the king became ill again and this was probably the reason why, on 26 December, he had revised his will. Surrounded by Hertford, Lisle, Russell, Sir Anthony Browne, Denny, Sir William Herbert and Paget, the ailing king no doubt discussed his plans with them.[19] Four days later the new will had been copied by the clerks and was ready to be signed by Henry but by this stage he was very ill, too ill to write his own signature. Although it was technically illegal, as an emergency measure to ensure the document was authenticated while the king was still alive, it was signed at the beginning and at the end by 'dry stamp'.[20]

It was usual for the king to sign all important documents by hand. However, in a bid to decrease his burden of administration, during his latter years he had granted three men authority to sign routine documents on his behalf – Sir Anthony Denny and his brother-in-law John Gates (who acted as Denny's deputy in the privy chamber), and William Clerc, a clerk of the privy seal. The procedure was that two of them together used a carved wooden 'dry stamp' to make an impression of the signature in the paper which they then inked in. At the end of each month a list of all such documents was drawn up by Clerc and presented to the king for his counter-signature.[21] The procedure was technically forgery and the men were periodically granted a pardon for their actions.

Over the centuries there has been much controversy about this will, especially concerning when and how the king's signature was added. The use of the stamp has opened the way to speculation that the will was forged and the stamp added at a later date. This would have offered the opportunity for Hertford to change the terms of the will for his own benefit. There is, however, no evidence for this and the facts surrounding the use of the stamp may be relatively straightforward.

Throughout Christmas the king had been isolated from the world outside his privy chambers and little news of his condition had been spread by his attendants. Ambassador de Selve, who had waited several days for an audience with Henry, was instead instructed to speak with Hertford on New Year's Day. Later, on 10 January 1547, de Selve reported that the king had been very ill for over fifteen days, so ill that some people believed him to be dead.[22] It is probable, therefore, that on 30 December, when the will was ready for signing, Henry's condition was so serious that there was concern he might die without validating the document. Hence the unprecedented step was taken to use the stamp. The signing of the will was witnessed by eleven men in the presence of Hertford, Paget, Denny and Herbert. These witnesses were William Clerc, six members of the royal household, three physicians and one apothecary.[23] The presence of the latter four is indicative of just how ill Henry was that day and, importantly, the group included Denny, Gates and Clerc – the three men authorised to use the dry stamp.

After the will had been stamped, and presumably inked, in full view of all the witnesses Henry handed the document to Hertford. What happened next is unclear but may have been just the result of human frailty. The will should have been presented to William Clerc to be entered on to the parchment roll of documents stamped in December but it was not finally listed until the very end of the January 1547 list.[24] On 29 January, after the king's death, Hertford sent a key to Paget with instructions not to declare the full contents of the will until they had consulted together. The most probable scenario is that Hertford had locked the will away securely in a box on 30 December, expecting it to be needed in the very near future. There it remained until the end of January. Only when the will was finally unlocked and perused, sometime between 29 and 31 January, did they realise that it had not been recorded on Clerc's list. It is highly possible that, with the document locked safely away, Hertford forgot that the will needed to be entered on the roll and that, because the will never came into his possession after it was signed, Clerc had failed to add it to the December list. Hertford would have realised that the omission needed to be rectified to verify the will before it was made public and so the will was entered at the end of the January roll by Clerc.

The king rallied and by 17 January he was sufficiently recovered to receive the French and Imperial ambassadors.[25] Outside the privy chambers life continued but tension was mounting and tempers running high. Wriothesley may have sided with the reformers but 'violent and injurious words' which Hertford used against him revealed a strained relationship.[26] Parliament had been re-convened on 14 January and Hertford attended each day. However, little business was done apart from passing the attainders against Norfolk and Surrey. The reign was drawing to a close and the mechanism of government was slowing as the country waited for a new beginning. At the privy council meeting on 23 January Hertford watched as his brother Thomas was sworn in as a member of the privy council. According to the council minutes the king was keen that he should learn the workings of the council. Lisle, though, would later claim that when it was proposed that Thomas should join the council, the ailing monarch had cried out 'No, no' even though his breath was failing.[27] However, before Thomas could attend another meeting the king was dead.

Shortly before Henry died, Denny suggested that he should have a priest at his deathbed. The king agreed to see Cranmer, after first taking a 'little sleep', but by the time he had awoken and Cranmer had arrived Henry was unable to speak. Cranmer asked the dying king to make some sign that he put his trust in God and Henry squeezed his hand. At 2 a.m. on Friday 28 January 1547 Henry VIII left the people of England under the rule of a 9-year-old boy. Throughout the realm there was great sorrow at the king's passing. For one man, however, the news would be greeted with relief and hope. The Duke of Norfolk was in his cell at the Tower waiting to learn the day of his execution. Although he did not know it at the time, Henry VIII's death would save his life.

For Hertford, fate was about to offer an unimaginable opportunity. Edward VI's reign would offer a unique chance to wield power. Due to his good fortune, skill and judgement during the past years, Hertford now found himself in an unprecedented position. He just needed to seize this chance.

7

Creating the Protectorate

The story of Edward VI's reign is not primarily about the young king but rather about the men who governed England in his name. In particular it is the story of the two who were pre-eminent among those governors – Hertford and Lisle. Henry VIII had never intended either man to hold precedence and his failure to recognise the inherent weakness in the terms of his will left the government of the country at the mercy of ambitious men. The transfer of power from one monarch to another was always a time of uncertainty but never more so than when the new king was a child. Any appearance of weakness left the new regime open to challenge and the most vulnerable time would be in the days immediately after the old king's death. Hertford was very aware of this.

Even as the king lay dying Hertford was planning for the future. Away from the privy chambers he and Paget were secretly formulating their plans to take control. A letter written by Paget two years later reminded Hertford of their discussions:

> Remember what you promised me in the gallery at Westminster before the breath was out of the body of the king that dead is. Remember what you promised immediately after, devising with me concerning the place which you now occupy … and that was to follow mine advice in all your proceedings more than any other man's.[1]

Edward's reign would offer unprecedented opportunities for ambitious men to exert authority and pursue their own designs. Hertford intended to make sure he held the greatest power.

Hertford already knew the terms of the will and who Henry VIII had chosen to govern the country for his son. During a term of minority rule it was usual to appoint a regent or Lord Protector, often a brother of the dying king.[2] Henry, however, had no close relatives and, anyway, such appointments had not always been successful in England. Richard III's usurpation of the throne from his nephew, Edward V, was well known.

Henry instead selected sixteen men to act as both executors of his will and as a regency council until Edward reached the age of 18. The council was to include all the prominent officers of state – the Archbishop of Canterbury, Cranmer; Lord Chancellor Wriothesley; Hertford (listed as Lord Great Chamberlain); Lord Great Master St John; Lord Privy Seal Russell and Lord Admiral Lisle. Another cleric, Bishop Tunstall of Durham, was included together with men who either brought special skills or in whom the king had placed great trust – Sir Anthony Browne, Master of Horse; the chief judge Sir Edward Montagu; Justice Bromley; Sir Edward North, Chancellor of the Augmentations; secretary William Paget; Sir Anthony Denny and Sir William Herbert, chief gentlemen of the privy chamber; Sir Edward Wotton, treasurer of Calais, and his brother Dr Nicholas Wotton, an experienced diplomat. Henry also named a further twelve assistant executors, among whom were Thomas Seymour and the Earls of Arundel and Essex, who were to assist the council when required.[3] Thus the king had included his three brothers-in-law among his son's advisers.

Of most importance to Hertford was the exclusion of both Gardiner and Norfolk from the list of executors. Even before Norfolk had confessed, the king had turned against him and decided he was unfit to govern for his son. During the revision of the will Sir Anthony Browne had queried the omission of Gardiner's name from the list of executors but Henry had replied that he had left him out for good reason. If he was one of the executors, the king continued, 'he would cumber you all, and you should never rule him, he is of so troublesome a nature … I myself could use him, and rule him to all manner of purposes … but so shall you never do'.[4] Henry had been strong enough to control the factions at court but he knew that his son would be at their mercy. Only by establishing a council of like-minded men could he hope to leave Edward a stable government that would not be split by discontent and political disagreement.

With the exclusion of Gardiner and Norfolk, Henry had ensured that the majority of Edward's most influential advisers favoured further religious reform. He knew these men would maintain the Church in England as he had left it and might even move forward towards Protestantism. He could be confident they would not turn back the clock. Henry VIII still believed in much of the Catholic doctrine when he died, but not in the supremacy of the pope. He feared that Gardiner and Norfolk would attempt to return England to the control of the papacy, thereby ending the royal supremacy that he had worked so hard to create. Although the two men had been left out of the council, Henry needed to ensure that they could not be appointed after his death. To prevent this he imposed an extraordinary condition in his will that permanently excluded the two men, or anyone else, from joining the privy council during Edward VI's minority.

A regency council without the leadership of a regent was an innovative but untested idea. In a bid to ensure it would be a success, and to impose some control over the actions of the councillors, Henry laid down certain restrictions on the new council. Its members were granted full authority to govern in all matters as they thought best until Edward reached the age of 18. The sixteen men were all to be of equal power and authority and none of them would be able to do anything alone without the written consent of the majority of the rest. In other words, no single man or small faction could assume overall control of the council – or so Henry VIII intended. Importantly, there was no provision in the will for councillors to be replaced or removed. Throughout his son's minority the composition of the council was to be fixed. If a councillor died before Edward reached the age of 18 then his position would remain vacant. This meant that even if Gardiner should return to court, he would be permanently excluded from the privy council and from any part in the minority government. Similarly, if Norfolk had been declared not guilty and released, this clause would have also excluded him from office.

Henry VIII's choice of executors illustrates the extent to which 'new' men had established themselves at court. Historically the monarch's advisers had been predominantly clerics and noblemen, but among Henry's executors the Earl of Arundel was the only scion of an ancient family. All the other noblemen – Hertford, Lisle, Wriothesley, St John, Russell and Essex – had risen from the gentry and only lately received their titles for their kinship or service to the king.

Henry had not given Hertford any singular position of precedence over these councillors but once the king was dead Hertford moved quickly to assert his pre-eminence and take control. He and Paget had known the contents of the will for four weeks, and it had given them plenty of time to decide their course of action. Early in the morning of 28 January the two men met to finalise their plans for the future; although they had already discussed their intentions it was only when they were sure that the king's end had come that they could commit themselves to a definite plan. Taking action any earlier would have risked the possibility that Henry might recover, as he had done before, or that the political situation at court might change or their plans be uncovered. They had recently witnessed, in the case of the Earl of Surrey, where pretensions to power could lead. The two men agreed that the news of Henry VIII's death should be kept secret until the new king had been brought to London. Meanwhile this allowed time for Paget to garner support for what was to come next – Hertford's assumption of power with Paget as his principal adviser. Their plan was audacious and contrary to Henry VIII's will: Hertford was to become Lord Protector of England.

Hertford, now the uncle of the King of England, left Westminster soon after his meeting with Paget. He rode quickly to the town of Hertford where Edward was lodged, and then accompanied the boy to join his sister, Elizabeth, at Enfield before telling the two children the news. That next night he did not sleep much. Shortly after 1 a.m. a letter arrived from Paget. Hertford immediately penned a reply, advising that the will should not be opened until he had returned to court and that it was unnecessary to make public its full contents. He may have been trying to hide the fact that the will made no mention of a Lord Protector. Only a few people were to know of the king's death immediately and Hertford intended that before the news became commonplace the two men would meet and agree on certain matters to avoid any future disagreements between them. Hertford had, though, forgotten that the will was locked away and in a postscript he added that he had enclosed the key for the will, which had presumably been stored in a chest. It seems that in his haste to reach Edward he had taken the key with him.[5]

Hertford soon started gathering support for his bid to take control. Sir Anthony Browne had accompanied him on the journey to Enfield and while they walked in the garden together their discussion turned to the future government. Browne believed that Hertford should be Lord Protector as it was 'both the surest kind of government and most fit for that Commonwealth'.[6] Browne was a religious conservative and a supporter of Gardiner, but he was quick to accept the idea of Hertford as Protector despite their religious differences. In London Paget had been similarly busy and by Sunday evening the other executors were already deferring to Hertford, seeking his opinion on when a general pardon should be granted. Hertford responded in a suitably authoritative tone and advised them to notify Anne of Cleves of the king's death before the official announcement was made.[7]

On Monday 31 January Hertford accompanied the new king on his journey into the city. For the next three weeks Edward and many of his councillors were to be lodged in the Tower until the coronation. It must have been a disconcerting experience. The Tower of London was rarely used as a royal residence but served primarily as a jail and a storage facility for ordnance and gunpowder. Apart from the period prior to a coronation, the only occasion when courtiers might expect to live in the Tower was if they were incarcerated there as prisoners. Hertford was unaware that in the future he would twice enter that mighty fortress as a prisoner and would spend the last days of his life imprisoned within its grey walls.

At 3 p.m. Hertford and Edward arrived at the Tower. As they rode through London, where the news of Henry's death had been announced that morning, they were greeted by a great celebratory firing of guns from the Tower and the ships along the river. For three days the news had been kept secret while the daily routine of court life had continued as if Henry was still alive. Even the usual fanfare of trumpets had announced the arrival of each royal meal in the privy chambers. The members of Parliament had been unaware of what had happened, and that they had consequently met illegally on the day following Henry's death, until Wriothesley announced the news to them on 31 January. This secrecy was not unusual. For example, when Henry VII had died late on 21 April 1509 his death had been unknown outside the privy chamber until the evening of 23 April and was not announced to the people until the following day. The delay gave Hertford and the other councillors time to prepare for a smooth transition of power. However, on this occasion it was not to the new monarch that power was to pass.

The men Henry VIII had nominated to be his son's privy and assistant councillors were essentially the same men who had comprised his own privy council but the role they were to play for Edward VI would be very different. Under Henry they had advised and enforced his policies; under Edward they were to govern England. For over eight years they were to decide policy and would not be answerable to the young king for their actions. This was a novel situation and one which allowed Hertford and the councillors to interpret their roles as they saw fit.

Henry VIII had presented the executors with a formidable undertaking. Never before had minority rule been by a privy council of sixteen executors nominated by the previous sovereign. The concept of a council assuming full responsibility for all aspects of government was totally alien to these men who were conditioned to having a governor in control. Their own experience of government involved the king making decisions, usually in concert with councillors who then implemented the orders. The ultimate decision had rested with the monarch and even when Thomas Wolsey and Thomas Cromwell were Henry VIII's chief ministers, the king was the final arbiter in decisions. The executors' only knowledge of what should happen during a time of minority rule came from history where government of the kingdom had rested with a regent or Lord Protector advised by a council. None of them had experience of being ruled by a child king and they were stepping into the unknown. They decided to do what they thought was the best solution to overcome the possible problems they might encounter during the reign – and that meant creating a *modus operandi* with which they were familiar.

Later that Monday evening Hertford joined twelve other executors for the first meeting of the new privy council, a meeting that was to set the course of the new reign. The absent members were Justice Bromley and the two Wotton brothers, who were serving overseas. However, none of these three was to be a big player in the council. Those councillors whose support Hertford needed were all present.

The thirteen men heard Henry's will read and agreed to maintain 'every part and article of the same to the uttermost of our powers'. However, their very next decision overturned the intent of the will. Over-ruling objections by Wriothesley, they decided unanimously that for sending important letters and for 'sundry other great and urgent things' it was necessary for good government and for the honour of the king that 'some special man ... should be preferred in name and place before others ... who for his virtue, wisdom and experience' would be best placed to oversee matters. They were in agreement that Hertford should be this man because of his kinship to the king and his experience as a military leader, a diplomat and a politician. Hertford was to have 'the first and chief place among us' with the titles of Protector of the Realm and Governor of the King.[8]

The appointment was against the terms of the will but the executors believed they had the power to appoint Hertford 'by virtue of the authority given to us by the said will' to do whatever they thought best to uphold the king's honour. They did, though, impose the special condition that Hertford should take no action without the advice and consent of the other executors. He was to be their representative and leader but was not granted absolute authority. They mistakenly believed that although they were creating him first among equals they were not empowering him to act independently. As they would later find, this restriction would be insufficient to bind Hertford to their will. It may be that, even as the executors imposed this condition, Hertford had already decided to sideline them.

The councillors' intention was to create a chairman or president of the board but their decision had created the very situation that Henry VIII had tried to avoid – the vesting of over-riding power in one man. Or rather in two men. Hertford had already agreed that he would follow Paget's advice before that of any other councillor. As long as Hertford acted upon Paget's advice, Paget would be a power behind the throne and continue to maintain the influence he had wielded during the final years of the previous reign. Which of the two men was the prime mover behind this plan is impossible to ascertain but Paget's later assertiveness in reminding Hertford of his promise to follow his advice must raise the possibility that Paget had instigated the initial proposal.

The following day, Tuesday 1 February, after hearing the will read for a second time, the executors took their oaths of allegiance to the king and swore to uphold the principles of the will. It was necessary to tell the king their decision regarding Hertford and at 3 p.m. they joined noblemen and bishops who had gathered in the presence chamber. As Edward stood before them, Hertford led the way as each man knelt to kiss the king's hand in an act of homage with the words 'God save your Grace'. It fell to the Lord Chancellor to put their plan to the king. Dwarfed by the great chair of state upon which he sat, Edward listened to the proposal before confirming that his uncle should be Protector of the Realm and Governor of his person. It was an announcement that was met with approbation by all the assistant executors, the lords and bishops who gave their unanimous consent to the appointment. As Hertford told the listening audience that he would put his trust in God to help him do right, he could congratulate himself on achieving what he and Paget had planned.[9]

The councillors retired to start work, writing letters to the emperor, the King of France and the regent of Flanders telling them of Edward's accession and the appointment of Hertford. Although written in the name of the king, the letters were signed only by Hertford. It was an early indication of how Hertford would assume control. As England mourned, in France the news of Henry VIII's death was greeted with elation. When word reached the French court, Madame d'Etampes went running through the palace to the queen's bedchamber early in the morning, crying out as she reached the door, 'News, news! We have lost our chief enemy'.[10]

There was much for Hertford and the council to do, not just running the country but also planning the funeral of the dead king and the coronation of the new one. Next day the thirteen executors set about preparing for these two events. On this occasion they were joined by Thomas Seymour, who attended again on Sunday 6 February when he witnessed Hertford bestowing a knighthood upon the new king. Even allowing for the sparseness of privy council attendance records, with just one further recorded attendance and an occasional signature on council warrants, Thomas appears to have attended council meetings infrequently.[11]

Thomas may have been present at these early meetings as an assistant executor, although his appointment as Lord Admiral a few days later would, under normal circumstances, have warranted him being admitted as a full privy councillor. However, the terms of Henry VIII's will precluded such an eventuality. Nevertheless, it appears that Hertford may have appointed his brother to the privy council as a compromise.[12] One contemporary writer believed this was the point at which the enmity began between the two brothers. In an attempt, he wrote, both to reduce Hertford's new authority and to drive a wedge between the two Seymours, Lisle may have encouraged Thomas to seek appointment as Governor of the King leaving his brother to be only Lord Protector. Thomas supposedly asked Lisle to propose the idea to the council on his behalf but Lisle distanced himself from the enterprise, leaving Thomas to do that for himself. Hertford was annoyed by his brother's request and Lisle, playing the two men against each other, told him that he believed Thomas would always envy his position and try to overthrow him.[13] Whatever the truth of this account, Thomas continued to seek greater power and authority. His resentment at being denied the governorship of the king festered and the friendly relationship the two brothers had shared during the previous reign quickly soured. In reality the idea of both men sharing responsibility for governing king and country had precedent but for some unknown reason Hertford made an early decision to exclude his brother from such a prominent position.

At some point during these early days of the reign, Paget made a long deposition to the council outlining what he believed to be the dead king's wishes regarding new honours for the councillors. It was a matter he had discussed with Henry during his final days and Hertford may have had some influence on these decisions when, on one occasion, he and Paget had spent two or three hours alone with the king.[14] Paget had been the king's closest confidant and knew Henry's intentions better than anyone. He explained that Henry had intended to advance certain men to higher titles to increase the number of noblemen since they were 'much decayed' by attainders and the failure of some men to produce heirs. The king had initially proposed raising Hertford to a dukedom, Essex to be a marquis, Lisle, St John, Russell and Wriothesley to earldoms and ten other men, including Thomas Seymour, to be barons. However, after Paget had spoken with the intended recipients about the proposals, the king changed the details of some of the awards. Hertford was to be created Duke of either Somerset, Exeter or Hertford and his son would be created Earl of Wiltshire if his father became duke of Hertford. Essex was to become Marquis of Essex while Lisle would be elevated to Earl of Coventry, Wriothesley to Earl of Winchester and Thomas Seymour, Rich and four other knights were to be created barons.

Paget also confirmed Henry VIII's intention that Hertford should become Lord Treasurer and Earl Marshal, filling the positions left vacant after Norfolk's downfall. These appointments allowed further promotions as offices were passed on. Hertford's position as Lord Great Chamberlain was to be filled by Lisle, Thomas was to step into his shoes as Lord Admiral and Sir Philip Hoby would take the post of Master of the Ordnance. Although it was a great jump in the court hierarchy for Thomas, he was still in his brother's shadow and increasingly came to resent this inequality between them. For Hertford, his promotion was further acknowledgement of his pre-eminence.

Hertford decided to be styled as Duke of Somerset, a choice of ducal title that perhaps indicated his aspiration for status. The title 'Duke of Somerset' was a senior one, traditionally associated with Henry VIII's Beaufort ancestors, and more recently held by his son, Henry Fitzroy. It may also have been that Hertford claimed a connection to the county through his title of Viscount Beauchamp of Hache in Somerset. However, his determination to hold this dukedom was at the expense of his son, who could only hold the courtesy title of Earl of Hertford rather than the hereditary title of Earl of Wiltshire with an associated seat in Parliament.[15] Essex, Lisle and Wriothesley all chose not to accept their proposed titles but instead took respectively the titles of Northampton, Warwick and Southampton.

The late king had also intended the recipients to receive grants of land. However, after speaking to the men about the size of their awards, Paget had encouraged Henry to increase his initial proposals. Hertford was awarded land with an annual value of £800 instead of an initial award of 1,000 marks (£666 13s 4d); his brother received land worth £500 instead of £300 (a substantial addition to his annual income of £458 6s 8d) and several other councillors received various sums up to £300.[16] With no written record of the king's wishes, Paget did have the opportunity to further increase the awards to profit Hertford and his supporters but for two reasons such deception seems unlikely. The recipients had been informed of their good fortune while Henry was still alive and Paget's statement was corroborated by Denny and Herbert, who had also spoken with the king about these matters. The privy council accepted Paget's account without question.

Although the will contained a clause instructing the executors to distribute any grants and awards which Henry had promised but not executed during his lifetime, there was concern about the legality of this distribution of honours and, especially, of land. After Edward's coronation one of the executors' first actions would be to instruct lawyers to examine the will and determine whether they had the right to give away Edward's land to satisfy his father's wishes. The judges confirmed the distribution to be legal but imposed certain provisos on how the grants were to be recorded.[17]

However, when the land was distributed it was often worth more than the value of the award. Thomas Seymour's lands were probably worth at least a further £200 above the £500 he was due. Hertford also did well from his land allocation, choosing which lands he liked by being, in his son's words, 'his own carver'.[18] When the grants were confirmed in July he received an extensive collection of manors, lands and forests including the castles of Marlborough and Christchurch and the sites of the dissolved monasteries at Glastonbury and Syon. With a 'clear yearly value of £800' these properties may have been worth substantially more. Shortly afterwards Hertford exchanged a selection of his lands and manors with the king and in return received innumerable parcels of land and properties closer to his estates in Somerset, Dorset and Oxfordshire.[19] Later in 1547, when Edward decided to reward Hertford with £500 for his victory against the Scots, Hertford chose to receive more land in Somerset, further increasing his land-holding in the south-west.[20] Many of the parcels of land he received were small and it was much easier to manage them and collect rents if they were close together.

Thomas Seymour later tried to dissociate himself from the rapaciousness of both his brother and the other councillors, saying that he would 'not be in some of their coats for five marks when he [the king] heard of these matters'. He also let it be known that he would return Sudeley Castle to Edward upon his coming of age when, Thomas believed, the king would claim back all the lands that had been given away.[21] He made his point very firmly at the end of 1547 when Parliament passed an act confirming all the land and property grants made by letters patent during that year, which effectively legalised the land-grab that the councillors had carried out. Thomas voted against the act.[22] Only the Marquis of Dorset, one of his supporters, joined him in this display of truculence.

Before Edward could be crowned his father had to be buried. Henry's body lay in state at Westminster until Monday 14 February when, at 7 a.m., a great procession set off towards Windsor Castle. It was a magnificent spectacle, a fitting tribute to a man whose own magnificence had dominated England and its court for nearly thirty-eight years. For two days hundreds of people accompanied the dead king on the 24-mile journey, stopping overnight at Syon where the coffin was placed in the monastery church while the mourners retired to lodgings. In a bid to ease the passage of men, horses and carriages, orders had been sent out days earlier that all overhanging branches along the route should be removed and all broken bridges repaired.

At the head of the cortege, two porters carrying black staves preceded 250 'poor men'. Dressed in long black mourning gowns, each man carried a torch that was lit whenever they passed through a town or village. Behind them, hundreds of mourners were arranged in order of precedence with those of highest rank closest to the coffin which lay upon a carriage at the centre of the procession. Around the coffin banners displaying Henry's ancestry were held aloft and sixty pages carried more torches.

The townsfolk and villagers came out to see the cortege pass, no doubt marvelling at the robed effigy of the king that lay upon a cloth of gold spread over the coffin. The robe was of velvet decorated with gold and precious stones and around the neck was placed a Garter collar. In the effigy's right hand was a golden sceptre, in the left an orb; upon the head was a crown of inestimable value. Denny and Herbert, who had served as their master's closest servants, sat within the carriage at the head and foot of the coffin. Neither Hertford nor his brother were allocated specific roles during the proceedings and they travelled among the other noblemen.

At Windsor Castle the coffin was placed in St George's Chapel in readiness for the burial the following day. The mourners rose early on Wednesday to hear a mass for the king's soul, a service that had been held daily since his death, before taking breakfast and returning to the chapel for the funeral where Hertford watched as Henry was laid to rest beside his late wife, Hertford's sister Jane Seymour. The service finished and, following a meal at the castle, the lords separated and hurried back to London. Hertford and the privy councillors needed to prepare for the coronation.[23]

In the days before the coronation Hertford took his oath as Lord Treasurer and was appointed Earl Marshal. The latter position brought little financial reward – just £20 – but the prestige was enormous and came with its own symbol of office, a golden baton, ringed with black at each end and engraved with the seal of the king's arms on the upper end and Hertford's on the lower.[24]

It had been decided that all the men who were to be advanced to higher titles should receive them before the coronation. With little time to spare, on the day after the funeral Hertford and the other recipients gathered in the council chamber at the Tower. In a stately procession Hertford was led into the presence chamber accompanied on either side by Dorset and Henry Brandon, second Duke of Suffolk. Ahead of them processed Garter Knight and four noblemen carrying the accoutrements of the honour. Garter held the letters patent, Derby bore Hertford's cloak, Shrewsbury the rod of gold, Oxford the cap of estate with the coronet, and Arundel carried the sword. As Hertford knelt before the king, Paget read out the letters patent and it is recorded that as he did so Edward put the cloak upon Hertford, girded him with his sword, placed the cap and coronet upon his head and gave him the rod of gold. Considering Edward's small stature, he undoubtedly needed help in carrying out these offices. After the newly created Duke of Somerset had received his letters patent he moved to stand beside the king to assist in the creation of the other noblemen.[25]

Hertford was also created Baron Seymour 'so that the name of Seymour may not be forgotten'. It seems there was concern, perhaps from the king, that his family name could be lost among the plethora of other titles awarded to his uncle. This new honour was added to Somerset's impressive list of titles: Lord Protector of the Realm, Duke of Somerset, Earl of Hertford, Viscount Beauchamp, Lord Seymour, Governor and Protector of the King, Lieutenant-General of his Majesty's land and sea armies, Lord Treasurer and Earl Marshal of England, Governor of Jersey and Guernsey, Knight of the Garter.[26]

The other elevations followed: Essex to Marquis of Northampton and Lisle and Wriothesley as Earls of Warwick and Southampton. For Thomas it was also a day of high achievement. He and Rich, Willoughby and Sheffield were created barons, Thomas taking the title of Baron Seymour of Sudeley which was accompanied by the grant of Sudeley Castle and a substantial number of manors and other property. He was also made a Knight of the Garter and received his appointment as Lord Admiral.[27] Henry Seymour and Somerset's son, Edward, also benefitted from their relationship to the king. Before the coronation, Henry was promoted to Knight of the Bath and Edward was made a knight.

Attention now turned to the coronation as the people prepared to celebrate the beginning of a new era. It was only three weeks since Henry VIII had died but preparations for the coronation had been carried out quickly. There may have been an urgency to see Edward VI crowned. When the 12-year-old Edward V had become king in 1483 his coronation had been delayed, which had given Richard III time and opportunity to seize the crown. No-one wanted to risk a repeat of such an eventuality.

It was thirty-eight years since the last coronation and for many people this would be the first such event they had experienced. There was great euphoria. In 1509 the people had taken a handsome 18-year-old prince to their hearts and had then watched as Henry VIII gradually evolved into an unpredictable, bloated and sometimes dangerous old man. Now there were high hopes for the 9-year-old Edward – a young boy, pure and untainted. For the next few years, though, Edward would have little influence in the government of England.

Throughout London there was great preparation in readiness for the coronation. Streets were graveled and railings erected to keep a way clear for the procession and to stop horses stepping into the watching crowd. Banners, streamers and tapestries, some of cloth of gold, were hung from buildings along the route. In Westminster Abbey a stage was built to enable the congregation to see Edward. A proclamation was issued inviting people who believed they had a right to perform some official duty, either during the ceremony or at the following celebrations, to register their claims. Many of these duties were traditionally held by particular families or accompanied certain court appointments. The Earl of Shrewsbury, for instance, claimed the right to support the king's hand while he held the sceptre; Nicholas Leghe believed he had the right to make a bowl of pottage to be served to the king.[28]

Whatever their reason for applying, all the claimants sought the opportunity to be part of the greatest event in England since Henry VIII's coronation. It was to be an occasion of splendid pageantry and ceremony. It would also provide an opportunity for Somerset to demonstrate that nothing had changed. England's new king might be just a boy but the monarchy remained strong. Edward would be crowned and imbued with the same regal authority as his father during a ceremony which had remained essentially the same and been used by English kings for nearly six hundred years. It was an event full of symbolism in which the dependence of subjects and king upon each other would be re-affirmed when they acknowledged Edward as their new monarch and he promised to protect the state and the Church. The sacred element of the service, the anointing, would consecrate the king and finally the investiture with the presentation of the symbols of office and the crowning would confirm him as sovereign.

As Earl Marshal, Somerset (as he will now be known) had the responsibility for organising the coronation but the executors agreed that on the day of the event he should act as Lord High Steward with the honour of carrying St Edward's crown.[29] The king was to be crowned with three crowns. St Edward's crown and the Imperial crown were heavy and intended for an adult. Because Edward would be unable to wear these for any length of time during the ceremony, Somerset selected some gold and jewels in the royal collection to be fashioned into a crown especially for the occasion.[30]

On the afternoon of Saturday 19 February a great procession wound its way from the Tower through the city to Westminster Palace. This was the opportunity for the citizens to see their new king and for him to see them. There was an air of excitement and celebration. The streets were thronged with people, some of whom were perhaps more interested in the wine running from the fountains than in the pageantry. It was a magnificent sight. At the heart of the procession rode Edward, dressed in a gown of silver cloth embroidered with gold and with a doublet and cap of white velvet. Even his horse looked splendid, covered in a cloth of crimson satin embroidered with pearls and gold. Somerset had a prominent position, riding in a place of honour close to his nephew. Ahead of them Dorset, Warwick and Arundel carried the three swords of state and, stretching into the distance before them, the nobility and officers of the royal household rode on horseback, preceded by esquires and knights, gentlemen, chaplains and servants, all arranged according to their rank. Behind the king followed hundreds more men – members of the privy chamber, household servants, yeomen and soldiers.

The journey took four hours and along the route the participants were regaled by choirs, pageants and tableaux all praising the new king. Somerset was no doubt proud of the tableau symbolising Edward with his parents where Jane, represented by a phoenix (the emblem she had chosen as queen) and Henry VIII, a crowned lion, were depicted with Edward as their lion cub offspring being crowned by angels. Amid all the pomp and ceremony, the entertainment which most appealed to Edward was the sight of a man sliding downwards, his arms outstretched, on a long rope stretching from the top of a steeple to the ground.[31]

Early the following morning Edward travelled by boat the short distance to Whitehall. There he was dressed in his crimson velvet coronation robes before walking in a long procession to the abbey as Northampton and Warwick held his train. Southampton, St John and Russell each carried a sword, Somerset held St Edward's crown and Suffolk and Dorset the orb and sceptre.[32] Changes were made to the proceedings to shorten the event due to concern that the 'tedious length' of the traditional coronation service 'should weary and be hurtsome peradventure to the King's Majesty being yet of tender age'. In the abbey Edward was carried in a chair to the four corners of the stage to be presented to the people who, upon being asked for their assent to the coronation, all replied loudly 'Yea, yea, yea, King Edward, King Edward, King Edward'. He was led to the altar where he made an offering of gold coins and swore the oath to preserve the laws and freedom of England and to protect the Church.

Instead of giving a sermon Cranmer addressed a speech to Edward in which he set out the young king's duties and the future direction of religion in England. Even before Edward was crowned, Cranmer – with Somerset's approval, one assumes – had decided on further reform of the Church. Edward's authority, he said, did not come from the pope but directly from God. It would be the new king's responsibility to ensure not only that God was worshipped, and the tyranny of the Catholic Church stopped, but also that idolatry should cease and images be removed from churches.

The next part of the ceremony was the anointing. After Warwick had removed Edward's outer clothing and opened his shirt, Cranmer used holy oil to anoint the boy upon his hands, breast, back, arms and head before Edward was clothed in his ceremonial gown, sandals and spurs. These last, though, were immediately removed for fear that he might trip over them. Finally, as the young king sat in his chair before the altar, Cranmer and Somerset placed the three crowns upon his head in turn – St Edward's crown, followed by the Imperial crown and finally the one made especially for the occasion and which Edward continued to wear for the rest of the ceremony.

Somerset was the first to pay homage to the new king. Kneeling before Edward with his hands raised together he vowed to:

Become your liege man of life and limb and of earthly worship, and faith and truth I shall bear unto you against all manner of folks, as I am bound by my allegiance and by the laws and statutes of this realm, so help us God and Allhallows.

He kissed the king upon the left cheek and all the noblemen and bishops followed suit. The service ended with mass, before the procession re-formed to walk to Westminster Hall for the feast where Somerset and Cranmer sat with the king at the top table.[33]

With Henry's funeral and Edward's coronation completed Somerset and the executors had fulfilled the immediate demands of the will and were able to concentrate on their role as privy councillors and turn their attention wholly to the government of the country. For the next few days council business was routine. Warrants were issued for payment of money, import licences granted and arrangements made for negotiations to continue with France about the ongoing dispute over Boulogne and to discuss a defensive league.

During all this executive activity there was, however, concern among the councillors as to whether their authority and that of Somerset as Lord Protector was legal. Although England had a living king, the form of government to be exercised during the minority had been laid down by the previous monarch. Henry VIII had granted 'full power and authority' to the councillors to do whatever they thought 'meet, necessary or convenient for the benefit, honour or surety' of Edward and England. This authority, though, was given only to the men named in the will, or to those of them who were still alive, and there was no provision for new councillors to be added during the minority. Henry had also instructed that when Edward came of age he could not 'charge, molest, trouble or disquiet' the councillors for any of their actions, a condition intended to allow them to govern without fear of later reprisals.[34] The councillors, though, were worried that Henry VIII's intentions might not be legal in his son's reign.

Somerset had his own, different, concerns. The decision for him to be Lord Protector should have made no difference to his authority among the other councillors. He was to be *primus inter pares* – first among equals. But he had other ideas. He wanted complete control of the council. To achieve this he needed greater authority to exercise his new office. Although the king had, by word of mouth, endorsed the executors' decision that he should be Lord Protector, Somerset had no legal authority for his appointment and he was keen to ensure his position could not be challenged. It might be months before Parliament would be called and his position ratified by that august body. However, letters patent confirming his position could be granted by the king and authorised under the great seal by the Lord Chancellor almost immediately.

Thomas Wriothesley, Lord Chancellor and newly created Earl of Southampton, had studied law at Cambridge University before beginning his career at court in 1524 through the patronage of Thomas Cromwell. He proved his worth as an administrator and in 1540 had been appointed privy councillor and joint principal secretary to Henry VIII. Four years later he had been rewarded with the prominent position of Lord Chancellor in which post he was noted for handing out harsh punishments to Catholics and Protestants alike.

Southampton was concerned at Somerset's assumption of power and was later described as having been 'sore against' his being created Lord Protector, telling the Imperial ambassador van der Delft that he would never agree to any 'innovations' in the matter of government beyond what was stipulated in Henry's will.[35] He may only have accepted Somerset's appointment because he believed the Protector's authority would be limited by the condition that he could act only with council agreement. Somerset knew that Southampton would not support the action he was about to take to increase his power. He needed a Lord Chancellor who would do as he was bid. Then, very conveniently for Somerset, Southampton's own actions provided a reason to depose him as Lord Chancellor, leaving the way open for Somerset to appoint a more compliant replacement.

In a move to reduce his duties in the law courts and give himself more time to attend to privy council duties, Southampton had issued a commission on 18 February authorising certain cases to be determined in the court of chancery rather than in the common law courts. Several common lawyers had brought this to the attention of the privy council, complaining that this subverted the natural course of the law. Somerset had lost no time and the decision to act against Southampton was taken on 28 February. He and the other councillors claimed that, because they had not authorised the commission, Southampton had acted illegally. Somerset also complained that Southampton had used 'unfitting words' towards him.

The Lord Chancellor was called before the council a week later to answer the charge of acting without authority and, after waiting in an adjoining closet while they deliberated, Southampton was deprived of his office and ordered to return to his house at Ely Place and remain there under house arrest. That evening, after supper, Thomas Seymour, Sir Anthony Browne and Sir Edward North visited him to collect the great seal. There was no sound reason for his deprivation except that he would be an obstacle to Somerset's plans. Southampton had not needed permission from the council for his actions. His authority to issue commissions had previously been granted to him by Henry VIII and re-granted by Edward VI on 31 January when he had gone through the formality of surrendering the great seal to Edward and then receiving it back from him.[36]

Once again Somerset had demonstrated his ability to seize an opportunity and turn it to his advantage. Southampton would never have agreed to extend Somerset's authority and that was why he had to be removed from office. His action in issuing the commission gave Somerset the means to do this.

Similarly, when the terms of Henry VIII's will had presented the opportunity for Somerset to become Lord Protector, he seized the chance. He was undoubtedly among the courtiers who took the opportunity to remove Gardiner and Norfolk from court before Christmas. Gardiner's disagreement with Henry had provided a way of securing his exclusion and Surrey's indiscreet use of the royal arms had provided a means to establish charges against Norfolk. None of these events had originated from deliberate schemes to remove the three men or to create the Protectorate. But they had all provided an opportunity for Somerset to advance his plans and he was quick to turn them to his favour. What is unknown is the extent to which Paget influenced his decision to capitalise on these opportunities.

With Southampton's removal Somerset had taken the first step towards establishing himself more firmly in control. The following day the king gave the great seal into the custody of Lord St John, 'some special man of great trust' and one upon whom Somerset could rely for support.[37] The following Sunday, 13 March, Somerset took the action that Southampton would probably have resisted when he and the councillors presented the king with a commission that gave legality to their government. It granted them the power and authority they needed to deal with any matter, foreign or domestic, and confirmed in writing the verbal agreement that Edward had given to his uncle's appointment as Lord Protector. The commission also granted them immunity from any future charges against their actions. The king signed the commission, giving it his royal assent, and it was then delivered to St John to be passed under the great seal as letters patent.

This document, however, contained other clauses that went much further than either Henry VIII's will or Edward's verbal agreement. Under the new letters patent the structure of the council was changed. Instead of a privy council aided by assistant councillors all the men were listed as councillors with the exception of Southampton, who was now excluded from office and court, and Somerset, who stood apart as Protector of the Realm and Governor of the King. The new terms granted extensive extra power to Somerset. The greatest change, and the one which most increased Somerset's authority, was his freedom to appoint whomsoever he chose to be a privy councillor and to consult with 'such and so many of our privy council or of our councillors as he shall think meet to call unto him from time to time'. Somerset could, if he wished, pack the council with his supporters and seek advice only from those he chose, giving himself unrivalled control. This was expressly against the terms of Henry's will.

One further detail in the letters patent maintained that all decisions taken by the councillors since the death of Henry VIII should stand and could not be challenged. Specifically the men would not incur any loss of lands or property, ensuring that the lands granted to support their new titles could not be taken away from them. Edward was legalising the transfer of crown lands that his councillors had instigated as part of the unfulfilled gifts clause in his father's will. Somerset appears to have been worried about the security of the document and, unusually, he insisted that it was entrusted to his care for safe-keeping, rather than being lodged with other official papers, and that the contents were recorded *verbatim* in the council register.[38]

There is no evidence of any objections so it must be assumed that all the councillors supported the content of the letters patent. However, when the commission was presented to the king only seven councillors were in attendance – Somerset, St John, Russell, Northampton, Sir Thomas Cheyne, Paget and Browne. For now, though, Somerset felt secure. His assumption of power had been quick and complete. Indeed, the transition of power from Henry VIII to Edward Seymour and the privy council had been extraordinarily smooth. Paget would later sum up the extent of Somerset's authority when he reminded the Protector that 'saving for the name of a king and that you must do all things in the name of another, your grace is during the king's majesty's young age of imperfection to do his own thing as it were a king and have his majesty's absolute power'.[39] Somerset was king in all but name.

Somerset's authority had achieved near regal status, something borne out by a prayer he composed in which he asked God to aid him in his role as Lord Protector.[40] Although there is a recognition of conciliar government when he asks God to 'pour his knowledge' upon all those who shall counsel him, much of the prayer suggests individual sovereign rule:

> Thou Lord, by thy providence hast made me to rule …
> Govern me, Lord, as I shall govern; rule me, as I shall rule …
> Give me power, Lord, to suppress whom thou wilt have obey.

But perhaps more striking is his reference to 'a shepherd for thy people', a phrase more usually associated with the religious leadership of Christ or of a king:

> I am by appointment thy minister for thy King,
> a shepherd for thy people, a sword-bearer for thy justice.

Eventually Somerset would realise that the final words of his prayer, concerning the actions of those who would counsel him, had fallen on deaf ears:

> And forgive them, that in their offence
> I suffer not the reward of their evil.

Somerset and Religion

Somerset's time in power was dominated by three issues: religious reform, war against Scotland and civil unrest. His policies on these matters defined the early years of Edward's reign. Given the uncertainty and vulnerability engendered by having a child king, it is surprising that Somerset chose to embark upon a matter as contentious as religious reform and to incur the expense and trauma of fighting a long and protracted war in Scotland. Neither event was inevitable but he was determined to pursue both courses and they would become contributory factors in causing the civil unrest. As early as February 1547 Gardiner recommended to Somerset that, until the king came of age, it would be best to maintain calm in the country and not force through change. If anything should go amiss, he warned, it would be blamed on Somerset, either for causing the problem or for not having the foresight to prevent it.[1]

In some respects Somerset did not see the Protectorate as an opportunity for radical change but rather as a continuation of Henrician policy. Changes to worship in both services and ceremonies, dissolution of chantries, the policy against Scotland and France, enforcing enclosure statutes, attempts to control vagrancy and even the reform of education all had their origins in the previous reign. It was a point used by Somerset to justify his policies. However, his approach to implementing these ideas was often different from that of his former master. Some policies he took much further forward than Henry had ever intended, others he handled in a more extreme manner. He may have adopted the previous king's proposals but he appears not to have absorbed his style and skill of government. It was to be a failure that would cost Somerset dearly.

It would have been perfectly reasonable for Somerset to adopt a more cautious approach to ensure peace and stability within both the country and the privy council. Without the strong control of a mature king, stable government was dependent upon a united council. To avoid the divisive effect of rival factions among the councillors, Somerset needed to ensure that they all shared the same convictions. His position as Protector was secure only as long as they supported his policies. When he chose to follow a course that deviated from their expectations, he would find himself increasingly isolated.

With his new authority to choose his own councillors, Somerset quickly set to work to revise the council membership and create a privy council that suited his purposes. By the end of April he had selected a total of eighteen men, fifteen of whom had served on Henry VIII's final council. It was a conventional choice which reflected his trust in the late king's judgement. All the men, with the exception of Northampton, were officers of state or of the household. All had been listed as executors or assistant executors in Henry's will. Throughout his time as Lord Protector, there would be little innovation in Somerset's choice of privy councillors. Of a total of twenty-six men appointed over the next three years, only three were not named in the will.

Despite the terms of the new letters patent, which enabled him to appoint whomsoever he wished, Somerset made no attempt to pack the council with men who might be especially loyal to him. In the spring of 1547 Somerset's position appeared unassailable and he expected to rule England for nearly nine years until Edward VI took control. He did not foresee any need to enhance his support. All the councillors had supported his appointment. The very nature of his position demanded the same loyalty from all men that they would give to the king. Somerset had the strongest personal claim to be Lord Protector and his appointment by letters patent had been approved by all the privy councillors. He could only be removed by the king. However, as time would tell, his expectation of secure tenure was to be sorely ill-judged.

There was one good reason for Somerset to select the men he did – they were mostly supporters of the new religious beliefs that would become known as Protestantism. Only five of the initial eighteen councillors were Catholic. This was an imbalance he maintained throughout the Protectorate and one which quickly assumed importance as he began to implement his religious policy.

When Somerset came to power England was on the cusp of change. Though it was still a Catholic country, Henry VIII had created the opportunity for Protestantism to take root. By the time of Edward's accession it was ready to be nurtured and encouraged to flourish. In his choice of tutors for his son and in the religious persuasion of many of the new councillors, Henry had knowingly left England under the leadership of men who favoured religious reform. What he could not control was how far they would deviate from the religious ideology that he considered acceptable.

Religion was a central part of early sixteenth-century life, defining the pattern of the year as the Church moved through its calendar of festivals and saints' days. It determined all the major rites of passage through life – baptism, confirmation, marriage and death. Few people, though, really understood their religion. With services in Latin and instruction from priests, some of whom had limited education, the finer points of Catholicism were a mystery. But instilled in all was the fear of what lay beyond. For many people life was hard and religion offered the prospect of an eternal life of peace and comfort. While some men and women gave more attention to religion than others, none could ignore its existence.

Henry VIII had created a religion that satisfied his beliefs and his needs. Though still nominally a Catholic, he denied papal authority in England. He had taken steps towards reformation but then, towards the end of his reign, had pulled back and reversed some earlier reforms. Henry's religious journey had not been prompted by a desire to introduce new religious beliefs but by his perceived need to replace a wife and his wish to remove the excesses of the Catholic Church. In order to achieve this he had found it expedient to appoint himself Supreme Head of the Church in England with control over not only church administration but also its liturgy. With this unfettered authority he released the two convocations (assemblies to oversee Church matters) from many of their responsibilities, relying instead on Parliament to authorise Church matters both spiritual and administrative.

Cranmer had become Archbishop of Canterbury in 1533 and for the remainder of the reign had encouraged Henry along the path towards Protestantism. Action had been taken against religious 'superstitions'. For example, images which had been venerated with candles or by pilgrimages were removed. The number of holy days had been reduced and each parish was ordered to provide a Bible in English instead of Latin for the people to read for themselves. The Ten Articles of 1536, which were statements of religious belief, were a compromise intended to satisfy both conservatives and evangelicals. By not referring directly to transubstantiation, they were more acceptable to people who refuted the concept of consecrated bread and wine changing into flesh and blood.

However, in 1539 with the authorisation of the Six Articles, Henry had stepped back from the tentative advances he had made towards Protestantism. He reaffirmed his belief in transubstantiation and communion in one kind, clerical celibacy, private masses and the necessity for auricular confession. In 1543 the reading of the Bible became restricted to the upper echelons of society and it was asserted that masses for the dead should not be for specific souls but for all the departed together. Then, in early 1546, the king suddenly moved forward again. He ordered the abandonment of the Catholic practices of bell-ringing at Halloween, the covering of images during Lent and the ceremony of creeping to the cross on Good Friday. Yet, almost immediately, he changed his mind and halted the proposals, possibly after being warned by Gardiner that the changes could jeopardise treaty negotiations with the Emperor Charles.

By the time of Somerset's ascendancy, England still worshipped according to the Catholic rites but there were many Englishmen, including Somerset, who were ready for change. Protestants believed that the 'superstitions' of the Catholic Church – purgatory, images, candles, processions, Latin services – were unnecessary and that the way to God was through reading the Bible and understanding their faith. Somerset was ready to lead England towards these new beliefs. As he told Gardiner, his greatest desire was that when Edward came of age England would be 'rather more flourishing in men, possessions, wealth, learning, wisdom and God's religion and doctrine, if it were possible, and God's will, than we found it'.[2]

Somerset left no evidence of any particular interest in theology but he was considered by his contemporaries to hold strong Protestant sympathies and to be a 'great enemy' of the pope.[3] His leanings towards the evangelical cause had been evident early on. He supported the royal supremacy over the Church and in 1539 had taken great pleasure in the news that Henry VIII was to marry a Protestant princess, Anne of Cleves. Six years later he was firmly in the reformers' camp. When Paget wrote to Somerset in 1545, asking for his secret opinion on a radical proposal to 'borrow' some of the gold and silver plate from the churches to raise funds, Somerset had been enthusiastic about the idea. Such items in churches, he replied, were unnecessary because 'God's service, which consisteth not in jewels, plate or ornaments of gold or silver, cannot thereby be anything diminished, and those things better employed for the weal and defence of the realm'.[4]

He was a devout man, 'well disposed to pious doctrine'. The speech that he would make at his execution indicated a man of firm faith who, at the end of his life, truly believed that he had taken the best course in the matter of religion. Somerset held a strong belief in the power of God. Among the last words he wrote, on the night before his death, was a quote from the Psalms: 'Fear of the lord is the beginning of wisdom'.[5]

His few writings that have survived suggest he may have been closer to the Calvin doctrine of predestination and the concept that men were saved unconditionally by God's grace regardless of what they chose to do, rather than to the Lutheran understanding that God's grace is given to those who have found faith through the word of scripture. Evidence of this is suggested in the wording of the preamble to a statute from Edward's first Parliament in 1547 where Somerset authorised a reference to 'the good and Godly elect'. Similarly, when appealing to God for assistance in his office of Protector, he composed a prayer that specifically noted: 'I am the work of thy hands: thy goodness cannot reject me … I am recorded in the book of life … Thy inestimable love will not cancel then my name.'[6]

This Calvinistic outlook may explain his apparent lack of compunction in ordering the destruction of a cloister at St Paul's Cathedral in 1549 to provide building materials for his new house. Around the walls of the cloister was painted the *Danse Macabre*. These images of people from all ranks of life being encouraged to dance towards their death were a powerful reminder of the need to avoid sin and prepare for death. It was a decidedly Catholic image and for a man who believed in predestination it was unnecessary.[7]

Somerset's contact with Calvin began in 1548, by which time he already shared the reformer's views. In July Calvin dedicated his *Commentary on the Epistles to Timothy* to him, praising Somerset for his 'distinguished piety'.[8] This was followed shortly afterwards by a long letter, the first of several, advising Somerset how to advance reform of the English Church. However, this does not explain how Somerset first came into contact with Calvin's ideas. Although he had close contact with some of England's leading reformers, with whom he could discuss Calvin's views, this appears to have been after his appointment as Lord Protector. Of these John Hooper, who was recommended to him by Calvin in 1549, and Thomas Becon, who served as Somerset's chaplain, were both part of his household for a time.

It appears, then, that Somerset must have already been well disposed towards Calvinism during Henry VIII's reign and his interest may have been nurtured by contact with Katherine Parr. The queen was intensely interested in religion and set her hand to several religious works. In November 1547 her book, *The Lamentations of a Sinner*, was published. Although the work was decidedly Lutheran, some passages were more akin to Calvinism. Katherine was certainly acquainted with Calvin's works. In 1546, Princess Elizabeth had translated the first chapter of Calvin's *Institutes of the Christian Religion* and presented it to her stepmother as a New Year gift. Anne Seymour was part of the circle of close confidantes who shared Katherine's theological interests and no doubt discussed Calvin's ideas with the queen. She became a great supporter of religious reform, inviting English reformers to visit her at home, and was highly regarded by the exiles with whom she and her daughters maintained a friendly familiarity through their letters. As thanks for his dedication to her husband, Anne sent Calvin a ring that he rather disparagingly described as 'not of great value, not being worth more than four crown pieces'.[9] During the latter years of Henry VIII's reign Somerset was well acquainted with Katherine and the ladies of her court, including the Duchess of Suffolk, who sponsored *The Lamentations of a Sinner*. It is highly probable that Somerset's Calvinist beliefs were encouraged by his wife, who in turn was greatly influenced by the queen. This certainly gives credence to the later assertions that Anne was a major influence on her husband's programme of religious reform.

However, despite his leanings towards Calvinism, Somerset was certainly not an ardent reformer. He was not intent on expunging Catholicism from England and imposing a new religion upon the people in the shortest possible time. Many of his early proposals were for reform of the existing Church rather than the creation of a new one. Although he shared many of Cranmer's reformist religious views it was probably the archbishop who was the driving force behind change. Some of the early reforms were ideas that Cranmer re-introduced after having failed to instigate them under Henry VIII. Somerset was aware that the task they set themselves would not be easy and that they would not satisfy everybody. However, he wanted to maintain unity. His intention was to steer a middle course between those people who feared 'every reformation to be an assault upon all religion and good order' and those who would rashly rush in and change everything.[10] Somerset was cautious, choosing to take reform forward by gentle stages in the belief that if handled gently the people would follow his lead. He was in no hurry. He had plenty of time to complete his task before Edward came of age.

Unlike Charles V and Francis I, Somerset had no desire to enforce his country's religion elsewhere. When the Act of Six Articles was repealed later in 1547, the final clause of the new statute was included at Somerset's behest and stated that the government did not condemn the religion of other countries. Although this may have been included to placate the emperor, who was becoming increasingly concerned at the direction of Somerset's religious policies, it was also something in which Somerset firmly believed. His opinion was quite progressive. In 1549 he wrote to Cardinal Reginald Pole that 'friendship between nations should not be hindered by differences in ceremonies, since we all believe in one God and Christ'.[11]

Somerset's attitude to religion was not dissimilar to that of Elizabeth I – allowing tolerance in the expectation that people would choose to follow the new religion of their own accord. However, as they both eventually realised, pressure had to be exerted to ensure conformity. Unfortunately, Somerset's dislike of coercion was an issue that put him at odds with the majority of the privy council. There was no apparent opposition to the idea of religious reform from the councillors. With Gardiner, Norfolk and Southampton excluded, the remaining Catholics lacked a spokesman. It would not be Somerset's religious reforms that would be questioned in the future; rather, it would be his decision to allow people tolerance and greater freedom to express their thoughts in religion and other matters. This tolerance was also disliked by some of the reformers who believed that Somerset should be more authoritarian. The German Protestant

John ab Ulmis, writing in 1551, believed that 'he was of a more gentle and pliant nature in religious matters, than was befitting a nobleman of so much authority'.[12]

With Edward VI favouring Protestant ideas, Somerset and Cranmer were able to forge ahead knowing they had the support of the young (though powerless) king. Initially the two men sought to remove those aspects of Catholicism they considered were inconsistent with their vision of religion in England. They wanted to remove the 'superstitions' of Catholic worship, for example, and for all men to have access to the Bible in English so that they might read the word of God for themselves. However, the introduction of some religious reform early in the reign may have been determined as much by external forces as by government intent.

With Edward's accession many people throughout England believed the time for religious change had come and the reformers had high hopes that Somerset would support them. In expectation that the government would act quickly, and being impatient for change, some men took matters into their own hands. Somerset was no doubt encouraged by early reports of the enthusiastic although unauthorised actions of some reformers but he initially took a cautious approach. In February 1547, for instance, it was brought to his attention that the wardens and curate of St Martin Pomary Church in London had removed the crucifix on the roodscreen and various images of saints, replacing them with texts of scripture and the king's arms. Although they escaped a prison sentence by pleading that the crucifix was rotten and the roof falling down, the men were ordered to replace the crucifix.[13] However, it would not be long before the council ordered the removal of crucifixes from roodscreens throughout the country.

In his address at Edward's coronation, Cranmer had spoken out against religious imagery and may even have been encouraging acts of iconoclasm. Bishop Gardiner was strongly opposed to this, maintaining that people were not misled by images but instead found them useful as a means of instruction. After similar destruction at Portsmouth in May, and concerned that the wholesale destruction of images might be encouraged, Gardiner tried to discuss the matter with Somerset. The Protector, however, refused to take his concerns seriously saying that he was over-reacting. In reality, Somerset objected strongly to the idolatry given to statues and images by kissing, kneeling and lighting candles before them while little veneration was given to the Bible. It would be better, he believed, to abolish all images for a time rather than have the people at odds over them.[14]

The removal of imagery continued. Statues in some churches were destroyed, stained glass removed and religious paintings covered in lime-wash. At the beginning of March 1547 van der Delft reported that some people, including many of the councillors, were openly against Catholicism and that preachers derided the old religion in their sermons to the young king.[15] The reformers were moving ahead of government policy but Somerset and the council did little to prevent this behaviour. The conservatives retaliated by spreading seditious rumours of changes to church ceremonies and worship. In May Somerset was forced to take action against rumour-mongers by threatening jail for the miscreants.[16]

On 31 July 1547 Somerset and Cranmer took their first steps towards establishing a Protestant Church when they issued a set of injunctions, or commands, for religious reform.[17] These were only small steps, reforming the existing Church rather than creating a new one, but they signalled the direction the government was to take. The injunctions ordered every church to have a copy of a new book of *Homilies* and *Erasmus' Paraphrases upon the Gospels*. The *Homilies* were a collection of twelve sermons – a means by which to 'plant true religion' – that non-preaching clergy were to read in church as instruction for the congregation. Cranmer was the major contributor to the book, which was Protestant in tone, denouncing Catholic superstitions and espousing justification by faith and through reliance on the Bible. *Erasmus' Paraphrases* was a new translation of most of the New Testament accompanied by his commentary on the contents. Cranmer and Somerset hoped that through these books people would come to a better understanding of both the reformers' beliefs and of their interpretation of the Bible.

The injunctions also ordered that each church be provided with a large Bible in English for anyone to read. The Lord's Prayer, the Creed and the Ten Commandments were to be recited in English so that people might learn them by heart. Four times each year the clergy were to preach a sermon denouncing the 'Bishop of Rome' (the pope). Fundamental changes were to be made in church ceremony with Catholic traditions such as kneeling before and the kissing of images being denounced. These 'abused' images were to be removed and rosary beads, superstitious relics and shrines were to be banned. Henceforth, candles would be used only upon the altar. The money that had previously been spent upon candles, pilgrimages and pardons was to be collected and given to the poor as alms. This was only moderate reform as it left the doctrine of the Church untouched but it did change the ceremony of worship with which people were familiar. The removal of images, for example, was to have a major impact on the visual appearance of the churches. The use of English, though removing some of the mysticism of the service, did give people an opportunity to understand their religion more easily. However, this was not to be the end of the reforms. Notice was given that all services should be held according to these injunctions until further orders came from the king.

For people who were strongly attached to the Catholic religion, the injunctions were a major blow. Gardiner was the chief opponent of religious reform, claiming that no significant changes should be made to the country's religion during the king's minority. He objected to the injunctions, saying that they were contrary to the Six Articles which had been authorised by Parliament and to the *Homilies* because they taught justification by faith alone. Somerset had great respect for the bishop and believed that with his qualities of 'wit, learning and persuasion' he could have encouraged widespread support for the reforms.[18] He and Cranmer had been keen to accommodate Gardiner and win his agreement to their proposals. The bishop, however, refused their invitation to join in the preparation of the injunctions and *Homilies*, preferring instead to write numerous letters to Somerset, expounding on his views and offering advice.

Somerset and Gardiner had been friends for some years and had served together in Brussels. Gardiner often remarked that he felt able to offer advice because of the familiarity they had previously shared and the 'special acquaintance' he had with Somerset and his family. Initially his advice had an almost fatherly quality. On 21 May 1547 he commended Somerset for the 'gentleness and humanity' he had shown since his elevation to power. Reminding him of the responsibility he held, Gardiner warned Somerset that he should act with care because God had placed him in a position where, under the king, governance was 'chiefly yours and, as it were, yours alone'.[19] However, as time went on, relations between the two men became increasingly difficult as the Protector failed to persuade Gardiner to his way of thinking and Gardiner realised that the Protector now took little heed of his words.

In order to enforce his reforms, Somerset needed the co-operation of the bishops. As a means of achieving this he took steps to reinforce both royal and government authority over them. New commissions were issued, re-confirming their ecclesiastical authority and thus establishing that government authority over the Church was not reduced during a royal minority. This was followed by a parliamentary act late in 1547 authorising that in future bishops would be appointed by the king, not by election within the Church. As the ability of the English Church to follow its own path was being eroded, most of the bishops were quick to fall into line and embrace the reforms. However, Gardiner and Edmund Bonner, Bishop of London, would prove to be thorns in the side of the privy council.

The injunctions had enabled Somerset and the council to legalise selective destruction of images and in early September van der Delft reported their removal from churches all over London. Many men needed little encouragement to rid their churches of idolatry. However, in some places the removal and destruction led to disputes about what constituted abuse of an image. On 18 September, the privy council issued an order to the Lord Mayor that all images to which no offerings or prayers had been made should be left in place as adornment of the churches. If they had been removed without permission they were to be restored. This led to further disagreements between conservatives and reformers over the status of images. The privy councillors were beset by trouble. Seemingly unable to take control of the situation, on 26 September they decided that to restore images might inflame the situation and that, therefore, no further action should be taken on the matter until Somerset returned to London.[20] Throughout the previous weeks Somerset had been in Scotland fighting the Scots. Rudderless, without a leader, the privy council seemed unable, or unwilling, to make and enforce a decision on this matter without Somerset's guiding hand.

The councillors were, though, firm in their approach to recalcitrant bishops. During Somerset's absence Gardiner had addressed his protest letters against the injunctions and the *Homilies* to the council. On 25 September the councillors sent him to the Fleet prison for refusing to use the *Homilies* in his diocese of Winchester. Bonner also objected to them and despite later retracting his comments he, too, spent time in the Fleet.

On his return from Scotland in October, Somerset was quick to take control, coming down on the side of the reformers. As he travelled south, he settled a dispute at St Neot's, in Cambridgeshire, where a group of parishioners had removed images from the church and then refused to replace them when ordered to do so by the local gentry. His response was to favour the parishioners.[21] Once he was back in London the decision was made to order the removal of all the remaining images in the city churches. The previous May Somerset had told Gardiner there was no need to destroy all images, only those that were abused, unless it was necessary to prevent trouble over disputed images.[22] On this occasion the implementation of his policy was determined by the reformers. Although Somerset had initiated reform, for now he had intended moderate reform, not the wholesale removal of images.

Action by the reformers against Catholic worship in churches continued to escalate. In December, although no authority had been given to remove crucifixes from churches, Somerset told van der Delft that many had been removed from altars to prevent people making offerings to them. Two workmen were crushed late one night as they pulled down the rood-loft in St Paul's in London. At Canterbury Cathedral the clergy sold the crucifix and were planning to sell other items to pay for repairs until ordered to stop by the privy council. There were reports of disorder and insolence against some clergymen, of apprentices 'tossing' them over and taking their caps. In Hertford, John Newport was committed to the Fleet after slandering the curate by calling him 'whoremonger and other misnames' as he preached.[23] Even men in authority appear to have been moving ahead of government policy. Although Somerset told van der Delft in December that mass was still celebrated in the king's chambers, the ambassador believed it was no longer held in the Protector's own house or in those of Thomas Seymour and Warwick.[24] There had been noticeable changes in England's religion during the year but Somerset had only just begun. He would need parliamentary authority to carry through his next reforms.

9

Victory at Pinkie Cleugh

Somerset had returned to Scotland during the summer of 1547 to renew hostilities across the border. When Edward VI came to the throne, England was technically at peace with Scotland, France and Spain. That is to say, there was no declared war between any of the parties. However, it was a fragile peace engendered primarily by the treaties between the various monarchs, and Somerset's ambition upset the balance. England's relationship with Scotland was unfinished, personal business for him. His earlier campaigns had failed to bring about the union of England and Scotland which would have paved the way for his nephew to become king of both countries. He intended to unite the two countries through the marriage of Edward and Mary and, if necessary, he was prepared to use military force to achieve this.

Henry VIII's plan to achieve this union through a peaceful solution had foundered when the Scottish lords threw out the marriage treaty in 1543 and his 'rough wooing' over the next three years had further alienated the Scots. English rule of Scotland was necessary to ensure the security of England. Scottish raids over the border were a constant irritation. Of more concern, however, was the 'auld alliance' between the Scots and French, which provided mutual support in time of war and presented the prospect of the French using Scotland as a back door into England. Scotland, rather than England's traditional enemy, France, was to be the focus of Somerset's military aggression. He was aware, though, that war against the Scots would be easier if he could maintain peaceful relations with France. It was a situation which was doomed from the start and Somerset soon found himself facing both countries in concert.

Peace between England and France had been reached in 1545 when Henry VIII and Francis I signed the Treaty of Camp and resolved the future of Boulogne after

Henry agreed not to invade Scotland without provocation. England was to be allowed to hold Boulogne for eight years and then return it to France in exchange for 2 million gold crowns. But the French continued to resent this new English foothold in their country and were constantly testing the defences at Boulogne and the other English forts at Calais, Guisnes, Newhaven and Blackness. Somerset's visits to France had shown him how vulnerable these strongholds were. Within days of his appointment as Lord Protector he began to take measures to raise more soldiers and to improve the defences in France and along the south coast.

There was the additional concern that, with a boy king, England might be perceived as being more vulnerable to attack. At the beginning of March, in an attempt to placate France and tie the two countries closer together, Somerset and the privy council proposed a joint meeting of commissioners. The French, too, were keen to avoid war because Francis I was dying. The two sides set to work quickly and by the middle of the month the commissioners had reached agreement on a new treaty between the two kings and settled the disputes regarding the boundaries and fortifications at Boulogne. The treaty was sent to Paris for ratification by the king but it was too late – Francis died on 31 March. This was a disaster for Somerset. Francis had been keen to avoid war but his successor, Henri II, was defiant and refused to endorse the treaty, instead demanding the immediate return of Boulogne to the French.

Worse still for Somerset, Henri was in league with the Catholic Mary of Guise. Mother of the young Scottish queen and herself the Dowager Queen of Scotland, Mary held a powerful position on the Scottish regency council. She and Henri favoured the marriage of Mary, Queen of Scots to the Dauphin, which would bring Scotland under French control. It would also destroy Somerset's plans for Scottish union with England. Any English attack on Scotland now would increase the likelihood of conflict with the French king. Tensions rose as Henri's accession heightened the fear of an attack on Boulogne. English construction of a jetty to protect shipping at Boulogne was viewed by the French as a defensive work and they countered by building a new fort overlooking the lower town. Somerset, though, held a trump card. Henri II would not attack until he knew which side the emperor would support.

Emperor Charles V was caught in the middle, unwittingly cast in the role of peacekeeper. By earlier defensive treaties, he was pledged to aid England if France attacked Calais. Although this agreement did not include Boulogne, Henri dared not attack the fort in case Charles tried to intervene there too. However, Charles was reluctant to help England for fear of antagonising the French king and provoking him to attack the duchy of Milan, which he had recently inherited and which Henri wanted. Charles had another reason for wishing to avoid being embroiled in war against France. He was already heavily involved in bringing the German Protestant states back into line. However, his victory over the Schmalkaldic League, a defensive alliance of Lutheran princes, in April soon freed him from this burden.

Somerset did not need direct aid from Charles against the Scots; he just needed to be sure the emperor would not join Henri against him. He was trying to play off one ally against another while maintaining good relations with both. Frustratingly, he was hampered by an agreement between England and Spain whereby neither country could agree any treaty with a common enemy without their mutual consent beforehand. During the treaty negotiations with France in early 1547 Somerset and Paget frequently reassured van der Delft that any pact they made with the French would not conflict with their treaty with the emperor and they would make no agreement with the Scots without Charles's consent. But there was a certain amount of duplicitousness on both sides. Somerset could not be seen openly to aid the German Protestants against the emperor but secretly sent them money. Charles later refused to allow Somerset to hire German mercenaries for fear of upsetting the French, but then let him raise 2,000 men in secret.[1]

With Henri II on the French throne it became even more important for England to have control of Scotland. Henry VIII's repeated invasions had shown the futility of a policy of using force to coerce the Scots into obedience. Many Scotsmen were alienated from the English by the trauma inflicted upon them and after each invasion the people had recovered from the devastation their country had suffered. Somerset knew the invasions had pushed the Scots into closer alliance with the French and he planned to approach the problem in a different way. Violence had been ineffective, so he was prepared to try persuasion. He believed that a network of English garrisons across the country could maintain continuous control of a large area of Scotland.

The idea of using garrisons was not new. Somerset had recommended their use during the previous reign but Henry VIII had given only half-hearted support to the scheme, preferring instead to concentrate on his campaign against France. In 1544 Somerset had been especially keen to fortify Leith to provide a permanent entry point into Scotland and a base from which to intercept military aid from France. Garrisons would keep the surrounding areas in subjection, provide bases for further expansion across Scotland and serve a defensive purpose against assaults by both the Scots and French.[2]

Garrisons would be difficult to maintain without local support; however, Somerset was confident that the promise of protection for 'assured' Scots would encourage more people to join the English cause. These assured Scots were the men he hoped would help him win over and control Scotland; men who had sworn an oath of allegiance to the English king and promised to promote the marriage between Edward and Mary. They were primarily Protestants opposed to the strong Catholic pro-French party that ruled in Scotland, and were often tempted by the promise of pensions from England. Somerset believed they would welcome union with a country that favoured the new religion. Nearly 200 noblemen and gentlemen were already committed to the English cause including Patrick Lord Gray, who offered his castle of Broughty Crag and promised to deliver and hold St Johnston for the English, and the Earl of Glencairn, who promised to raise 2,000 men to fight.[3] If Somerset's scheme was to be successful, it was vital for him to win over more of the Scottish Protestants. Early in February 1547, the privy council ordered the continuation of pension payments, instigated by Henry VIII, to ensure the continued loyalty of certain Scotsmen who were holding the castle of St Andrews for the English.

Before Somerset could put his garrison plan into action he needed to establish a foothold in Scotland, which could only be achieved by another invasion. The regular incursions by Scotsmen across the border into England could be used as a reason for retaliation, but by the terms of the Treaty of Camp Somerset needed to show good cause for his actions. In March the council asked Thomas Wharton, Warden of the Western Marches, for a letter detailing recent raids into England. However, aware that the figures might be insufficient for their needs, they also instructed him to send a separate report exaggerating the number of Scotsmen involved and the number of villages attacked. England was in a high state of alert as Somerset ordered watch to be kept along the coast for Scottish and French ships, and called for a survey of the number of weapons, including bows, arrows, pikes and hand guns, that were available throughout the country.[4]

By the beginning of July 1547, Scotland and England were preparing for war. Somerset received regular reports from Wharton and Lord Eure in the eastern border area, from assured Scots and from spies in Scotland; he still hoped there might be a way to avoid confrontation. On 8 July he sent Bishop Tunstall and Sir Robert Bowes to meet Scottish commissioners at the border in an attempt to persuade the Scots to ratify the marriage treaty and terms for peace. The Scots refused to attend the meeting and England was left praying for peace and future union of the two countries.

French troops soon landed in Scotland and on 31 July they scored the first victory of the engagement when they took St Andrews Castle from the assured Scots who were holding it. The captured gentlemen were put into prison but the remainder, including the Protestant preacher, John Knox, were sent to serve in the French galleys. After six months of uncertainty all the expectation of war was about to be fulfilled. Somerset intended to lead the invasion force himself and on 11 August he was confirmed as Lieutenant and Captain-General for war both on land and at sea.[5]

Somerset's decision to invade was not taken lightly. The challenges of both finance and logistics were enormous: one official document suggests that over 6,000 men travelled north overland while another 6,000 were transported by sea. An eyewitness estimate of 18,000 may also have included all the troops already on the borders.[6] Estimates of the quantity of goods needed for an army of 18,000 men on a thirty-day campaign demonstrate the magnitude of the venture. Food and drink were provided by the king and then charged to the soldiers at a sum calculated so that the king accrued a small profit. Each man received 2lb of meat, 1lb of bread, and drink but such apparently generous daily rations were only available as long as supplies lasted. If the campaign overran or sufficient provisions did not reach the army, the men might go hungry. The quantities victuallers were controlling were gargantuan – among other commodities was sufficient flour to bake 144,000lb of biscuit (cakes of hard, dry bread) and 22,000 gallons of wine for the journey from Berwick to the Firth of Forth. Flour for a further 360,000lb of biscuit, 120,000 gallons of beer and 28,000 gallons of sweet wine were to be sent to the Firth to victual the troops for twenty days in the field. Vast quantities of corn and hay were needed for the horses and the oxen that pulled the 900 carts, wagons and guns, including fifteen large pieces of ordnance. It is no surprise that the army could only remain in Scotland if supplied by sea, and supply vessels formed part of the eighty-strong fleet of warships, galleys and merchant ships.[7]

During his preparations for the invasion Somerset visited Sheen, where he composed an accompanying letter for a proclamation that was to be sent to the Scots. His power as King's Lieutenant gave him authority to treat with foreign powers, and this was a rare proclamation issued in Somerset's name alone without the endorsement of either the king or the council. Entitled 'To Scotland concerning the projected marriage' the proclamation set out the peaceful intention of the English invasion. Somerset came, he said, 'as a friend only to chastise rebels, and bring about the marriage: to unite both realms, under the name of Britons, to preserve the laws of Scotland, and abolish the jurisdiction of the Bishop of Rome'. Copies of the proclamation were to be nailed to the castle gate at Stirling and to church doors in Edinburgh, Glasgow and Dumfries and distributed among sympathetic Scottish noblemen.[8] Although the proclamation professed friendship, the Scots were not to be persuaded.

One of Somerset's final actions before travelling to Scotland was to ensure that the English defences were ready to withstand any invasion attempt by the French during his absence. With the main army in the north, the risk of a French attack in the south was high and on 21 August he appointed his brother Thomas to have military control of all the southern counties and the English lands in France. It is notable that van der Delft believed Thomas' influence and authority were sufficient for him to be nominated to preside over the council.[9] Thomas, though, with little experience for such a role, had hoped for another position. He was particularly annoyed that he was not given governorship of the king during Somerset's absence. That position was awarded to Sir Richard Page, chamberlain of Edward's household since the previous reign, whom Thomas complained was a drunkard.[10] Page had become Somerset's stepfather-in-law when he married the duchess's mother, Elizabeth Stanhope, after she was widowed. Nepotism was accepted to be a moral duty and an accepted route to preferment, and even distant relatives sought shelter under the umbrella of patronage offered by an influential member of their family. However, Somerset failed to satisfy Thomas's expectations. His decision not to give his brother control of either the privy council or the king may have been because of a growing antagonism between the two men, something which would come to the fore after Somerset returned from Scotland.

Somerset left London and quickly rode the 250 miles to Newcastle where, on the afternoon of 27 August, he was welcomed by the mayor as a saluting volley of gunfire rang out.[11] The following day the troops were given an early warning that indiscipline would not be tolerated in Somerset's army. As he was receiving forty Scottish gentlemen and hearing their pledges of loyalty to the king, the gallows were set up in the marketplace to hang a soldier who had been caught brawling. Somerset resumed his journey, covering another 60 miles to Alnwick in two days, and soon joined Warwick and the main army at Berwick from where Admiral Clinton and the fleet set sail to the Firth of Forth. As a precautionary measure, Somerset spent the next three days leading a raiding party across the border to survey the route north. The road ahead was clear and on 4 September, with banners flying, Somerset rode at the head of the army as it began its journey northwards.

For five days he led the long procession of footsoldiers, horsemen and carriages loaded with victuals, munitions and large guns. They covered less than 10 miles each day but as they moved they took control of the country through which they travelled. Dunglas Castle surrendered and the settlements of Thornton and Innerwick were soon taken and destroyed. Scottish opposition had been light so far – Warwick had successfully won a skirmish near Haddington – but on 8 September, as the force approached Prestonpans on the Firth of Forth just east of Edinburgh, 600 Scottish horsemen appeared upon the hillside. The riders dispersed after Somerset ordered two field guns to fire at them. However, the following day groups of Scotsmen harried the English army while it remained in camp, and Somerset sent out a large cavalry force which was engaged by Scottish horsemen. It was a huge mistake by the

Scots. James Hamilton, Earl of Arran and Governor of Scotland, who commanded the Scottish army, sent most of his cavalry, amounting to fewer than 2,000 men, into the attack. After an engagement which lasted three hours, hundreds of the Scotsmen were dead and their cavalry severely weakened. It was a sad reminder to the Scots that on this same date thirty-four years earlier they had suffered the loss of 10,000 men at the hands of the English in the Battle of Flodden. As they counted their losses that night they were not to know that the following day they would suffer another great slaughter of their countrymen.

Somerset set up camp about two miles from the Scots, overlooking an area known as Pinkie Cleugh, with his battalions ranged along the slopes of two hills facing towards the enemy to the west. The Scots had chosen a strong position for their camp, protected by the Firth to the north and a marsh to the south and with Edinburgh to their backs. To the east, and between them and the English, was the River Esk, the only bridge across the river heavily protected by Scottish guns. Somerset and his officers rode to the hilltops to survey the battlefield and the Scots camp. It was quickly apparent to Somerset that command of the hills, especially of Inveresk hill close to the bridge, gave good vantage points for artillery fire across the Scots position.

On the return journey to camp they were overtaken by a Scots herald with a proposal from Arran that if the English would leave Scotland he would offer good terms for peace. It was too late. Somerset was ready for battle. He refused the offer and the accompanying challenge from the Earl of Huntly for the matter to be settled in a fight either between himself and Huntly or between twenty or thirty men from each side. As Governor of the King, Somerset explained, he could not accept such a challenge and he also forbade Warwick accepting on his behalf.

Early on the morning of Saturday 10 September, Somerset moved his army into position. Although outnumbered by Arran's army of over 20,000 men, Somerset had the superior force. Most of the Scots were untrained, armed only with pikes and were supported by a depleted cavalry and poor ordnance. With over 4,000 horsemen, a large contingent of professional mercenaries supported by the gentlemen pensioners and a large number of guns, Somerset commanded substantially more power.

As with many battles, why this one developed as it did is not always clear but it is possible that the Scots misunderstood Somerset's intentions, causing them to leave their strong position. Somerset intended to take the small hill of Inveresk close to the Scottish camp. As the English moved westwards, advancing on the Scots position, their left flank swung northwards closer to the hill. To the Scots it may have appeared that Somerset was moving his troops towards the coast, perhaps with the intention of abandoning the battle and withdrawing to Clinton's ships which lay in the Firth just north of the battlefield. Fearful of losing this opportunity to engage with the English, the Scots abandoned their position. As they poured across the Esk towards their foe, Somerset's military expertise came to the fore. Making a quick reassessment of the situation, he stopped the English advance and ordered the troops to re-form in battle order facing the approaching enemy. Meanwhile, cannons were pulled to the top of the hills behind the English line. As the Scots, already under bombardment from Clinton's ships, marched towards their enemy they moved further within range of the cannon. With his army in position, Somerset rode to the guns on the hill, a good vantage point from which to survey the battle and despatch orders.

The Scots stopped their advance and stood shoulder to shoulder. Armed with pikes, they formed a nearly impenetrable barrier. The first English cavalry charges suffered heavy losses against the pikes but the bombardment from land and sea slowly began to break apart the solid mass of Scottish footsoldiers. It was a terrifying experience for all the participants, vividly recorded by William Patten who accompanied the English army as a judge: 'Herewith waxed it very hot, on both sides, with pitiful cries, horrible roar, and terrible thundering of guns besides, the day darkened above head, with smoke of shot.' Bullets, shot and arrows were flying from every direction and every man feared injury as much as death. The English were sure that as prisoners of the enemy they would suffer cruelly without any hope of mercy.

An attempt by the English troops to move forward was hampered by the furrowed unevenness of the ground and the marshland to the south. At one point a company of Scots managed to press forward and kill twenty-six Englishmen, mostly gentlemen. Lord Grey, captain of the horsemen, and Edward Seymour, Somerset's son by his first marriage who was captain of Somerset's personal band, were lucky to escape; Grey was struck in the face and Seymour's horse was hacked by swords. Somerset ordered his troops to re-form and then sent forward the harquebusiers who approached as close as they dared before firing their guns.[12] The archers followed, sending a rain of arrows down upon the Scots before the ordnance was fired, preparing the way for an English cavalry charge upon the enemy. As the dust from the horses settled the Scotsmen, seeing thousands of footsoldiers marching towards them, turned and ran. With a cry of 'They fly! They fly!' the English were after them. For 5 miles horsemen chased after the terrified Scots, showing them little pity and sparing few. The area was strewn with bodies and the accoutrements of war – pikes, guns, swords, even clothes discarded by fleeing, terrified men. At 5 p.m. Somerset recalled the cavalry standard and ordered the trumpets to blow retreat. William Patten estimated that as many as 13,000 Scots had been killed. Other chroniclers set the figure at 10,000.

English dead were probably fewer than 600.[13] The battle of Pinkie Cleugh was a massive rout that damaged relations between England and Scotland even more and pushed the Scots further into the arms of France. It was, though, to be the last battle fought between English and Scottish armies.

The following day, after the English dead had been buried and the discarded Scottish ordnance collected, Somerset marched the army towards Leith. They met no resistance and that night he joined the troops in the camp outside the town rather than using lodgings within. For the next week the English remained at Leith. Edinburgh was only a few miles away but Somerset made no move to take the capital. He had learned in 1544 that the castle was practically impregnable. Any assault on it required great planning and although an 'exploit' against the castle was planned for the following winter, it came to nothing. Anyway, there was no immediate need for Somerset to follow up his victory with any further show of military power. The Scots no longer had an army to oppose him and many Scotsmen were coming to Leith, offering their loyalty and asking for English protection.

With the defeat of the Scottish army, Somerset was free to fulfil his plan to establish garrisons in Scotland and he quickly identified the first sites. One afternoon he was rowed a few miles up the Firth to inspect the isle of Inchcolm. Half a mile across and with an abandoned abbey, it made a perfect location from which to control shipping travelling upstream. Clinton took a small flotilla further up the river to take the castle at Blackness, west of Edinburgh, before setting sail for Broughty Castle, close to Dundee on the Firth of Tay. The residents of the castle knew there was no Scottish army to come to their aid. Resistance was relatively minimal and, as Patrick Lord Gray had agreed, the castle was soon handed over to the English.

On Sunday 18 September, before leaving Leith, Somerset knighted thirty of his commanders including Andrew Dudley, Warwick's brother, and ordered that the town and the ships in the harbour were to be set alight. He also ordered the hanging of 'English William', a robber from Lincolnshire who had run away to Scotland and was caught spying for the Scots. Spying was a dangerous occupation. That same month a Scot spying for England had been caught and hanged in Edinburgh.[14]

The army met no opposition as it returned south towards the border. Hume Castle was surrendered by Lady Home, wife of George, Lord Home who had led the disastrous assault by the Scottish cavalry. There was no resistance at Lauder or at Kelso where, although they found the town empty, many Scots came in to swear allegiance. Somerset was keen that the town of Roxburgh should be fortified before he left and for four days the troops set to work improving the defences. It was noted that even Somerset was seen wielding a spade as he helped the men build earthworks of stone and soil which were then covered in turf. By 28 September Roxburgh was tenable.

Before leaving the army and returning to London, Somerset knighted a further forty-eight men for their exploits during the battle, including his son, Edward, and two of his servants, John Thynne and Miles Partridge. The expedition had gone to plan and he had been away from the city for just over six weeks, as he had predicted to Paget and van der Delft.[15] This was to be Somerset's last military exploit and, like all his previous campaigns, it had been a success. Although councillors and noblemen would later make many accusations against him, no one questioned his ability in the field. Even allowing for the superiority of the English troops over the Scots, victory had only been assured by Somerset's skill as a general and his ability to react to the changing military situation. As time would tell, though, his skill in dealing with changing political situations was not so well honed.

Somerset was welcomed back to London by the Lord Mayor and aldermen at Finsbury Field on 8 October. His victory in Scotland was hailed as a triumph, further strengthening his hold on power and his dominance as 'king in all but name'. Nevertheless, despite his achievement, he declined the city's offer of a triumphal entry. Patten remembered that, shortly before venturing into Scotland, Somerset had a dream in which he returned victorious to court after defeating the Scots and was greeted by the king and courtiers. Yet all the while he knew that he had achieved nothing because Scotland would soon recover and the great cost and effort would have been in vain.[16] Somerset did, however, accept a substantial reward for his victory although he declined the initial package of land worth £500, asking instead for the palace and certain lands of the bishopric of Bath and Wells, to the annoyance of the bishop. The palace was a more useful commodity than the many small parcels of land spread across several counties which the king insisted on granting his uncle in addition to the bishop's property.[17]

On this occasion Somerset had good cause to believe he had finally subdued the Scots and that they would agree terms for peace and for the marriage. However, he still faced opposition from Catholic Scotsmen who supported French intervention. In a bid to encourage them to agree to the marriage union, Somerset sent a herald to Arran and Mary of Guise. His message was that God had shown his support for Somerset by giving him victory and any refusal by the Scots to co-operate would be met by further force. Somerset had reckoned without the French, though, who persuaded Arran and Guise against any agreement.[18] England's Protector had not yet finished with Scotland and English troops would soon return to the country in force

It was not long after Somerset left Scotland that flaws became apparent in his plan. His belief that with garrisons he would be 'able to win not a battle alone, but a country' was eventually to be dashed.[19] At Broughty Crag, Sir Andrew Dudley had been left in command with 100 men, victuals for six weeks and three ships to provide protection. However, as Somerset arrived back in London, Dudley wrote the first of a series of letters complaining about conditions in the garrison. He was in a desperate situation: the house they lived in was more like a lodge than a fort, there was no wood or coal, no glass for windows, no locks or bolts for doors. The soldiers were lazy and sick, there was a lack of gunners and with enemy soldiers not far away there was a constant threat of siege and attack. At the end of the month, after Dundee had surrendered following a bombardment from the ships, Dudley had to ask the townspeople to return any shot they could find because the English had insufficient. Only weeks later much of it was re-used when Dudley repulsed an attack by 3,000 Scotsmen. This was not what Somerset wanted to hear and as winter came upon them and the rains started, conditions deteriorated at other garrisons. Roxburgh had neither brewhouse, bakehouse or kitchen, nor mills for wheat or malt for beer. The supply of drink was one of the most difficult logistics problems faced by any army. At Norham, where over 500 horses were unfit, the men wanted their pay. Somerset's response to this was that it was usual for them to wait three to four months for their money. Men were sick, both in the garrisons and on board the ships which patrolled the coast, and at Berwick the commander, Lord William Grey, asked for a good physician and surgeon for the soldiers.[20]

By the end of the winter, garrisons had been established at Eyemouth, Ayton and Coldingham along the coast, at Norham on the border, Castlemilk near Dumfries and at Lauder and Yester Castle, but the largest was to be at Haddington. The fort provided a well-positioned base for an attack on Edinburgh and gave control of the area between the city and the coast to the east. Most of the forts held no more than a few hundred men but Somerset proposed putting 2,500 men into this garrison in the belief that by 'keeping Haddington, you win Scotland'.[21] But Haddington, like many other forts, was to suffer from the scourge of being difficult to victual. Ideally the garrisons would have been supplied with food from the local area and indeed, for a time, some Scotsmen did bring in goods to sell to the troops. But as winter passed, and Somerset ordered destructive raids across the countryside to try to bring the Scots to heel, there was little food to be had off the land for either men or horses. The Haddington garrison needed vast quantities of victuals and was reliant on supplies arriving by ship. Unfortunately, it was some distance from the coast. Munitions and food continued to arrive by sea but then needed to be transported over land, an almost impossible feat across the moors of Scotland in winter. A fort on the coast at Aberlady or Dunbar might have resolved the problem but was never established.

Somerset's garrison plan was beset by problems – lack of money, the difficulty of victualling and the large body of Scottish opposition he still faced. If the invasion had served to convince the Scots of the benefits of union, control of the country might have been maintained by a few garrisons. However, without the support of the majority of Scots, Somerset needed more forts. Grey and Dudley encouraged him to establish new garrisons at St Andrews, St Johnston, Dundee and Dunbar but for this he would need thousands more troops and, as always, money was in short supply. In February 1548 – only five months after Pinkie – Paget begged Somerset not to establish any new fortifications that year because they could not fund them.[22] For the next eighteen months it would be a familiar theme of their relationship.

With an insufficient number of garrisons, Somerset turned to other, more subtle, means of establishing control by winning the support of individual Scotsmen. Many of the assured Scots who took the oath of loyalty to Edward VI were ordinary people but Somerset especially wanted the support of the nobility, the men who had influence. However, they wanted favours in return for their support and often gave their loyalty to the highest bidder, or even professed allegiance to both sides. Pensions were not always sufficient. The Earl of Bothwell, for instance, made the ambitious and unacceptable proposal that as reward for his support he should marry either the widowed Duchess of Suffolk or one of the Princesses Mary or Elizabeth. Some men were tempted away by the offer of rich rewards from the French. The earls of Argyll, Angus and Huntly were all rewarded with pensions and membership of the French order of St Michel.

Somerset thought he had the measure of George Gordon, Earl of Huntly, but was easily deceived by him. Huntly had been captured at Pinkie and, along with other influential prisoners, taken to London. The intention was that, after having professed loyalty to England, they would be allowed to return to Scotland to support the English cause and pursue negotiations for the royal marriage. Huntly consented to these conditions for his release and also agreed to leave his wife and three sons in England, which Somerset believed would ensure his loyalty.[23] It was a vain hope. Huntly's family soon escaped and joined him across the border and he quickly returned to the pro-French party.

Somerset also turned his attention to spreading his religious reforms in Scotland. If the two countries were to be fully united, Somerset believed they must have a shared faith – a Protestant faith. With the governing pro-Catholic faction still holding out against England, he needed to win over the many Scots who were already followers of the new religion. After the people of Dundee had surrendered, Dudley asked for a preacher to be sent to them with Bibles, Testaments and other English books 'which would do more good than fire and sword'.[24] No doubt it was a request that Somerset was pleased to fulfil but it was one which, like the other schemes, had only limited success.

Somerset had returned home but Scotland would continue to demand his attention throughout the remainder of his Protectorate. There would never be long-term peace between England and Scotland until the two countries were united. It was an intractable problem and one that would become even more so after the French joined the war in 1548.

10

Somerset and Thomas Seymour

Following his victory at Pinkie, Somerset had made a hasty return to London. He had always intended to leave Scotland after six weeks, probably to prepare for the opening of Parliament in November. Rumours that his brother was plotting against him may have been another reason that he did not remain in the north. If Somerset and Thomas had shared common ideals and a strong friendship they could have been a powerful force together; both men had faults but 'the defects of each being taken away, their virtues united would have made one excellent man'.[1] Indeed, as uncles of the young king, and with command of both the army and the fleet, some may have felt they had the potential to be too powerful. However, as Somerset's authority grew, the gulf between the two men widened.

While Somerset handled the governance of the realm, Thomas attended to his own secret business, a matter that would infuriate Somerset when he learned of it. With unseemly haste, less than a month after the death of Henry VIII, Thomas proposed to the dead king's daughter, Elizabeth. In sixteenth-century society, marriage was a well-practised means of rising in social class. The earlier prospect of marrying Norfolk's daughter would have allied Thomas with the most powerful noble family in England; that plan had failed but the new Lord Admiral now saw a way of advancing even higher. Marriage to a member of the royal family would be even more prestigious.

On 27 February, after receiving 'the most eloquent letter in the world' from Thomas, Elizabeth replied to him politely declining 'the happiness of becoming your wife'. Neither her age nor her inclination, she explained, allowed her to think of marriage. Indeed, she was astonished that anyone should even speak to her of marriage so soon after her father's death, for which she must have at least two years' mourning.[2] It had been an extraordinary proposition, not only on account of its untimeliness but also because Thomas apparently thought the privy councillors would sanction such an audacious proposal. Elizabeth was most unlikely to marry without their agreement because by the terms of her father's will she would forfeit her right to the crown and lose the dowry of £10,000 which would be granted if she married a foreign prince.

Thomas was undeterred and instead turned his attention to Henry VIII's widow, Katherine Parr. It is surprising that he had not addressed himself to her before trying for Elizabeth's favour, since he and Katherine had nearly married four years earlier when she had instead decided to wed the king. Katherine had been aged 30 at the time and already twice widowed. Her first husband, Edward Borough, had died within four years of their wedding and in 1534 she had married John Neville, Lord Latimer. After Latimer's death in March 1543 Henry quickly made known his feelings for Katherine but by then the king was 52 and in poor health. Grossly overweight and suffering from an ulcerous leg, which would later necessitate the use of a sedan chair to move him around the palace, Henry was no longer the golden prince of his early years.

Katherine had hoped that when Latimer died she might marry Thomas Seymour, the man with whom she had fallen in love. After marriages to a young man and a middle-aged widower, she was entranced by Thomas, one of the most exciting men at court. He would have been a good catch: dashing, athletic, good-looking, charming and ambitious. He was a very physical man, highly skilled at jousting. At the May Day jousts in 1540 he and five other knights had taken on forty-six defenders but his energy was not always directed so constructively. Later that year he and Edward Rogers, a fellow courtier, were both bound over for £1,000 to keep the peace against each other.[3] 'Fierce in courage, courtly in fashion, in personage stately, in voice magnificent', he typified the ideal courtier. A later portrait shows him with short cropped dark hair and a full beard and moustache. He is wearing expensive black clothing with a fashionable black feather in his cap beside a badge proclaiming his admittance to the Order of the Garter. But looks were not everything. He was arrogant and headstrong and, being 'somewhat empty of matter', he ultimately brought about his own downfall by his 'vanity and folly'.[4]

Marriage to Thomas would have offered Katherine the prospect of life with an exciting and virile young man rather than with an ageing and increasingly sickly and demanding king. However, Katherine was a devout Christian and eventually she decided it was her duty to both God and her king to take Henry as her husband. It was a difficult decision and in a letter written in 1547 she explained her feelings to Thomas.

I would not have you to think that this mine honest good will towards you to proceed of any sudden motion or passion; for as truly as God is God, my mind was fully bent the other time I was at liberty, to marry you before any man I know. Howbeit God withstood my will therein most vehemently for a time, and through His grace and goodness made that possible which seemeth to me most impossible; that was, made me to renounce utterly mine own will, and to follow his most willingly.[5]

All was not lost, though, and the couple now had another opportunity to marry. Undoubtedly, this man 'Of person rare, strong limbs, and manly shape / By nature framed to sea or land' was likely to excite Katherine more than the old bloated king. Katherine, however, like Elizabeth, expected to mourn her late husband for two years before re-marrying. Thomas was not prepared to wait and tried to persuade her to change the two years into two months. By May 1547 their relationship was developing; Thomas visited her house at Chelsea in secret, arriving across the fields from the river very early in the morning and leaving by 7 a.m. They may even have already considered themselves to be married. On 17 May Thomas ended a letter with words from the marriage vow: 'from him whom ye have bound to honour love and in all lawful things obey'. Katherine wrote of herself as 'her that is and shall be your humble true and loving wife'. [6] A marriage was considered to be legal from the time a couple had exchanged vows, not necessarily in front of a priest, and Thomas and Katherine may have already done this.

The couple had a problem. They knew there would be outrage that Katherine had married with such unseemly haste after Henry's death. As a king's widow, she should not remarry without approval from the privy council and such a marriage should certainly not have occurred for at least a year after the king's death. This was to allow not only for a period of mourning but also for sufficient time to pass to ensure Katherine was not carrying Henry VIII's child. Thomas set to work to win support for the idea of their marriage before they announced that it had already taken place. He did not expect his brother to be pleased at the news and Katherine suggested that Thomas should first gain the support of the young king.

In the event, the route he chose to follow was devious. Keeping their established relationship secret, he told King Edward of his desire to marry Katherine and asked the young boy to use his influence and write to Katherine favouring Thomas as a suitor. Involving Edward in the matter would make it more difficult for Somerset to object. The ploy was successful and the king wrote to Katherine encouraging her to marry his uncle. Aware of the couple's concern about Somerset's response, Edward naively promised that they should not 'need to fear any grief to come, or to suspect lack of aid in need'. He was confident that Somerset would not trouble them if they had the king's support. 'I will so provide for you both, that hereafter, if any grief befall, I shall be a sufficient succour', he wrote.[7]

A similar attempt at the beginning of June to gain help from Princess Mary was a dismal failure. Mary refused to be a 'meddler'. If Katherine were minded to accept Thomas, she wrote to him, her letters would be of little use and if she was still in mourning and did not wish to marry her letters would again be of little use.[8]

Although there is no record of when the marriage was solemnised, rumours of it were circulating by 16 June and on 10 July the Imperial ambassador reported it as a fact.[9] The king was delighted that Katherine had, supposedly, followed his suggestion to marry Thomas. His two sisters were appalled, Elizabeth suffering great 'affliction' upon hearing the news that her father had been 'so shamefully dishonoured by the Queen'. Demonstrating their disdain for the relationship, they agreed to make no comment and Elizabeth, who was concerned about the protocol of returning visits to Katherine, who had been kind to her, delayed visiting the new bride lest 'I should be charged with approving what I ought to censure'. The king's diary entry that Somerset was 'much offended' by the marriage failed to illustrate the extent of Somerset's anger as he made no effort to hide his annoyance with his brother and new sister-in-law.[10]

It has been accepted historically that there was great animosity between Somerset's wife and Katherine, primarily because Anne Seymour resented the dowager queen's precedence over her, and that this discord led to the estrangement between the brothers. The first reports of Anne's relationship with her sister-in-law were made in the 1550s by Catholic writers who had cause to despise Anne because of her staunch support for religious reform, and their disparaging comments have been repeated ever since.[11] There is, however, no evidence that any dislike between the two women originated over an issue of precedence. It is unlikely that Anne should have become resentful of Katherine's precedence following Henry's death and her own husband's elevation. As dowager queen, Katherine held precedence over Anne despite the latter being the wife of the senior peer in England. Similarly, Anne of Cleves, demoted from queen to 'king's sister', held precedence over Anne. Katherine and Anne Seymour had been friends since Katherine became queen and Anne had served as a lady-in-waiting. Katherine often visited Anne and had attended the christening of one of her daughters in August 1544.[12]

However, there may have been an issue over the precedence that Thomas claimed. His marriage to Katherine as dowager queen had changed his status. As he intimated at the end of 1548, he believed that marriage to a royal personage would raise him above other noblemen. If there was a dispute over precedence, was it because he claimed the right to be placed at his wife's side, ahead of Anne? In 1548, after the birth of his daughter, Thomas was overheard remarking that when she came of age the girl, as a queen's daughter, would take pride of place over the duchess.[13] It seems likely that any disagreement concerning precedence was between Anne and Thomas, not Katherine.

Somerset's anger at his brother's marriage was probably the initial cause of discord between both the two brothers and the two sisters-in-law. The family disgrace caused by Thomas's precipitate marriage to Katherine was an acute embarrassment for Somerset and his wife. After Katherine's death in 1548, one of Thomas's servants, Wightman, told him that:

> If ever any grudge were borne towards him [Thomas] by my Lady of Somerset, it was as most men guess for the queen's cause, who now being taken away by death, it will undoubtedly follow that she will bear him as good heart as ever she did in her life.[14]

With Katherine dead, Thomas could have no claim to precedence and the disgrace of the marriage was expunged.

There were other issues that contributed to the rift between the two couples. Significantly, in the correspondence between Thomas and Katherine their animosity was directed at Somerset, not Anne. The relationship between Somerset and Katherine was decidedly strained, especially after the two fell out over her manor of Fausterne Park which was leased to Sir Henry Long. Somerset bought the lease from Long and then refused to allow Katherine to pasture her cattle in the park. After one especially tense meeting Katherine became very heated and agitated at how to respond to Somerset, later asking Thomas how she should treat him for he 'hath this afternoon a little made me warm. It was fortunate we were so much distant, for I suppose else I should have bitten him. What cause have they to fear having such a wife?'[15]

Shortly before Katherine died, a further dispute arose between Somerset and Thomas concerning her jewellery. Somerset claimed that certain jewels which Henry VIII had given to Katherine were crown property and had only been lent to Katherine for the duration of her time as queen. Thomas disputed this, maintaining that the jewels were gifts from the king to his wife and that Katherine should be allowed to keep them. After her death, he continued to claim that the jewels then belonged to him, much to the annoyance of Somerset who may have intended that, if the jewels were in his custody, his wife could wear them. In an attempt to prove his case, Thomas wrote to various gentlemen and to Princess

Mary asking if any of them knew the words Henry VIII had used when giving the jewels to Katherine, whether they were a gift or a loan.[16] The issue was never resolved and it served as yet another irritation between Somerset and his brother. The tension between the two men soon became apparent to other courtiers. The French ambassador believed that Thomas and Katherine left a large gathering at Greenwich in February 1548 because Somerset and his wife were present.[17]

It could be argued that Somerset had reason to be angered by his brother's behaviour – the family disgrace of a hasty marriage and the attempt to enhance his status through the union. He may also have resented any challenge to his own pre-eminence. Underlying Thomas's animosity towards his brother was his own desire for more authority. At the end of 1547 Somerset would be granted a special seat of precedence in Parliament because, among other reasons, he was the king's uncle. It was an honour that Thomas believed he should have shared. As Lord Admiral, he ranked high among the other courtiers but he still sought recognition that would set him apart from other men. Somerset's special seat in Parliament, his use of the royal 'we' in letters and the ceremony of a mace being carried before him in procession all presented him as a regal persona and were intended to elevate him above his contemporaries. Even at an event as inconsequential as a baptism, Somerset claimed the place of precedence. When he, with the king and Princess Mary, stood as godparents to van der Delft's son in 1547, it was decided that Somerset should act as proxy for the king while Warwick would represent Somerset. Lady Russell would stand in for Mary (who was in mourning for her father) thus elevating Somerset above the other proxies.[18]

Somerset may have been further annoyed by the regal manner in which Thomas maintained his wife, living in a household to rival that of Somerset. As a dowager queen Katherine was entitled to live in great state, as befitted a Queen of England, with her own privy chamber staff of gentlewomen and maids, surrounded by 120 gentlemen and yeomen.[19] However, this had the effect of creating a court, at the heart of which was Thomas:

Her house was deemed a second court, of right,
Because there flocked still nobility.
He spared no cost his lady to delight,
Or to maintain her princely royalty.[20]

The prestige of this household was enhanced by the presence among Katherine's ladies of Princess Elizabeth and Lady Jane Grey. In a bid to win the friendship and support of Henry Grey, Marquis of Dorset, Thomas had proposed that Grey's eldest daughter, Jane, should live under his roof and that he would endeavour to further a plan for her to marry the young king. A granddaughter of Henry VIII's sister, Mary, Jane was well educated, pious and meek. She appears to have been happy with the arrangement and was fond of Thomas, describing him as 'a loving and kind father' towards her.[21]

However, the relationship between Thomas and Elizabeth was rather different. It appears that Elizabeth quickly overcame her apprehension at visiting Katherine and moved into the dowager queen's household soon after news of the marriage became public. Elizabeth was 14 years of age, a woman by the standards of the time and very attractive. She was, no doubt, attracted to this tall, good-looking man who excelled at manly pursuits, including that of courting women, but his familiarity with her overstepped the bounds of propriety. Early in the morning Thomas would sometimes enter her bedroom and, if she had already risen, he would strike her familiarly upon 'the back or buttocks'. If she was still in bed he would open the curtains and make as though he would join her. On one morning he tried to kiss her in bed and on another he came into her chamber 'bare-legged' in his night-shirt. Katherine Ashley, Elizabeth's governess, told Katherine about her husband's boldness but the new bride thought little of it and may even have joined him in tickling their charge while she sat in her bed. There was even talk that Katherine had held Elizabeth while Thomas cut her gown into a hundred pieces.[22] Nothing untoward came about as a result of his ribald behaviour. However, eventually, when Somerset and the council would no longer tolerate his cavalier attitude in other matters, the remembrance of these antics and Thomas's overfamiliarity with the princess would cast a poor reflection upon his reputation.

It was no secret among the privy councillors that Thomas was ambitious. By the end of 1547 he was talking openly to several of them about enhancing his status at court. Many men would have been content to reach the pinnacle of achievement that he held but some courtiers still took precedence over him and Thomas believed he should be second in importance only to his brother. He began to give vent to his frustration in a bid to win support among his friends. He had a scheme and while Somerset was in Scotland Thomas had been free to act openly against his brother. News of this may have reached Somerset.

Thomas knew that as Edward grew, authority and power would rest with the men who had most influence over the king. Thomas still wanted to be Governor of the King. It would allow him access to Edward and give him the pre-eminence he craved. He appealed to historical precedent to demonstrate that it was unreasonable for Somerset to govern both king and country. During Henry VI's minority, Thomas claimed, responsibility for the realm and for the king had been divided between the child's uncles. Humphrey, Duke of Gloucester, was Protector of the Realm, John, Duke of Bedford, controlled English lands in France and Thomas, Duke of Exeter, was Governor of the King. Thomas believed he was entitled to hold the latter position and thought to pursue the idea through Parliament. However, his efforts to win support for the scheme among his friends were fruitless. He eventually discarded his plan after Paget reminded him that he had given his written assent to Somerset's appointment as Governor of the King.[23]

Thomas sought another way to gain unrestricted admittance to the king. If he was to hold any influence over Edward he needed access to his nephew but this was strictly controlled by the chief gentlemen of the privy chamber. Richard Page and later Somerset's brother-in-law, Michael Stanhope, supervised the king closely. Such an appointment would suit Thomas's purposes and, with this in mind, he bribed one of the king's attendants, John Fowler, to act as a go-between, passing letters and praising Thomas's virtues to Edward. In particular, Fowler was to encourage the king's support for Thomas to be appointed chief gentleman of the privy chamber, effectively the king's keeper.

At some point during these machinations, Thomas decided to seek wider support. Aware that Somerset might not endorse his bid for greater recognition, Thomas planned to submit a bill to the forthcoming Parliament 'to have the king better ordered and not kept close'. His later confession suggested that the bill was to seek support for him to be chief gentleman, although such an appointment would not have needed parliamentary assent. That would be required only if he sought approval to be Governor of the King.[24]

Thinking the bill would gain more support if endorsed by the king, he wrote a letter for Edward to copy in his own hand and sign. It was a simple letter: 'My Lords. I pray you favour my Lord Admiral mine uncle's suit, which he will make unto you.' Somerset, though, had ordered that the king should sign nothing unless already authorised by him. Edward's tutor, John Cheke, refused to let the king write the letter. It was a decision supported by the young king who agreed that his uncle Thomas 'should have no such bill signed nor written' by him.[25]

Nothing came of Thomas's attempt to wrest influence from his brother but it may have been a factor in Somerset's decision to seek parliamentary approval of his own position. The letters patent, issued in March and appointing him to be Protector and Governor, although authorised by the king, had been signed by only seven executors beside himself and lacked legal authority. Somerset intended to use Parliament to ensure that his position could not be challenged.

On 4 November 1547 the king, accompanied by the bishops and nobility dressed in their parliamentary robes, rode from Westminster Palace to hear mass at the abbey church. For the first time before a Parliament, the *Gloria*, Creed, *Sanctus*, *Benedictus* and *Agnus Dei* were sung in English. Returning to the palace, Edward VI opened his first Parliament. Sitting on his chair of state at the head of the Parliament chamber, the 10-year-old boy faced all the influential men of the kingdom. Seated on benches along the right-hand side of the chamber were the bishops, and on the left were the secular lords. The commons faced him from below the bar. It was an occasion of special significance for Somerset as the king acknowledged his pre-eminence by appointing him to a special seat of honour in Parliament. There he would 'sit alone, and be placed at all times, as well in our presence, as in our absence, upon the midst of the bench or stool standing next on the right hand side of our siege royal, in our parliament chamber'.[26] When the king was not present Somerset would hold pride of place at the head of the chamber. It was yet another reminder to Thomas Seymour of how high his brother had risen and of his own lack of recognition as the king's uncle.

The formal confirmation of Somerset's position came on 24 December, the final day of Parliament, with the ratification of new letters patent re-appointing him as Lord Protector and Governor of the King. The terms were similar to the original letters patent, granting Somerset the same authority as before to rule in the name of the king. They declared him to be the 'chiefest and highest of our privy council' with the power to appoint and consult whomsoever he wished on the council. They also confirmed his appointment as Lieutenant and Captain-General with authority to declare war, make peace and summon an armed force.

There was, however, one important change. He was no longer to hold the position until Edward reached the age of 18 but only during the king's 'pleasure'. While this opened up the possibility of Somerset continuing to govern after the king reached his majority, it is unlikely that he asked for this amendment since it also presented the opportunity for him to be removed from the Protectorate early. The amendment may have been proposed by his brother in an attempt to weaken him. Thomas had told the Earl of Rutland that he thought the king should begin to rule earlier than planned with Somerset acting as chief councillor. Such a plan would, of course, be simpler to instigate if Somerset could be removed with ease from his position as Lord Protector. Thomas also spoke to Sir William Sharington about a patent concerning Somerset, saying that the king had thanked him secretly 'in his ear' for the patent. Sharington believed that, because of the difficulties between the two men, Thomas was working against his brother.[27] The patent referred to was probably the same that allowed for the Protectorate to be curtailed early.

Although Warwick had not yet conceived any intention to replace Somerset, this amendment to his security of tenure as Protector would certainly make his future removal easier. Of immediate importance to Somerset was that the letters patent was endorsed by the signatures of the king and sixty-two lords, including his brother, bishops, councillors and justices. Somerset's appointment as Lord Protector had been confirmed with the consent of the king, Parliament and nearly all the men in high authority.[28] Notwithstanding that the Protectorate might be foreshortened by the king's wishes, his position appeared to be unassailable. Time would, however, prove otherwise.

11

Advancing the Edwardian Reformation

Somerset was in a powerful position. After a resounding victory in Scotland and with this new recognition of his authority it was an opportune time for him to seek parliamentary approval for his policies. Thus far the limited changes he had made to the religious practice of the country had been only by proclamation. His next step required the full weight of parliamentary authority and would show the future direction of his intentions. He was, though, concerned about how his proposals would be received. Soon after the opening of Parliament, van der Delft challenged him about the need for further religious innovation and the harm it might do to Somerset's reputation. Acknowledging the risk, he replied: 'I know very well that whatever is done ill will be laid on my shoulders, and consequently I shall strive my utmost in all things to do what is best for God's service.'[1]

For seven weeks, at the end of 1547, Somerset watched as legislation was scrutinised, amended and finally approved. He made no obvious attempt to control the actions or decisions of Parliament and he allowed freedom of debate and voting. Although a few government bills were defeated, members of the privy council who voted against them suffered no censure. It served the government well to have councillors in both parliamentary chambers where they performed the dual role of councillors and members of Parliament. When the lower house requested that 'the King's Privy Council in this House may make request to the Lords', the expectation was that the request would be passed between the councillors.[2]

Somerset did, though, have influence over the selection of members of the lower house who were elected to represent boroughs of which he held the patronage.

At least twelve men who represented Wiltshire in 1547, for example, had direct links with him. These included his son John; his secretary Thynne; Thomas Smith; his servants Ralph Pickerell and John Young; and his chaplain William Turner. Similar numbers were also elected through the patronage of both Thomas Seymour and Katherine Parr, and it may be that the opposition in Parliament to Thomas's attainder for treason in 1549 came from this large number of dependants in the lower house.[3]

The most far-reaching statute of Somerset's first Parliament – and the one that would have the greatest consequences for the Protectorate – repealed most of the treason legislation passed during the previous reign. Some offences were to remain: plotting the king's death, denial of the royal supremacy in writing, counterfeiting, and forging the king's signature were among these. Denial of the king's supremacy of the Church by the spoken word, however, would not be treasonable until the third offence. In a bid to improve the working of the law, the act also decreed that in future two witnesses, rather than one, would be needed for a charge of treason to be made.[4]

Somerset also used the act to extend religious freedom. Some earlier acts for the punishment of heretics were repealed. The prohibition on the printing, sale and reading of the Bible and certain other works in English was lifted, opening the floodgates to a great wave of Protestant books and propaganda. Then Somerset took a large step away from Catholicism and towards Protestantism by repealing the Act of Six Articles. Henceforth, denial of transubstantiation, whereby consecrated bread and wine were converted into the body and blood of Christ, would not be a crime. The Eucharist could be considered to be a memorial rather than a re-enactment of Christ's sacrifice. This was re-enforced by a further act permitting the sacrament to be offered in two kinds, as both bread and wine. Somerset and his fellow reformers could practise their religion as they chose without fear of retribution.

At a stroke, Somerset had removed the stranglehold of power that Henry VIII had created to control the actions and thoughts of his subjects. His reasoning was that while Henry's reign had necessitated 'straight and sore laws', life under Edward could be different. The preamble to the statute explained that 'as in tempest or winter one course and garment is convenient, in calm or warm weather a more liberal rase or lighter garment both may and ought to be followed and used'. It was a bold move that would allow people freedom to express their thoughts on religion and other matters without fear of punishment. However, Somerset's belief in the inherent obedience of people and his expectation that they would not abuse such indulgence and royal clemency displayed a naïve understanding of human behaviour. Relaxing the controls on the populace made it more difficult to control them and would lead to trouble in the future.

These two acts underwent much change during their passage through Parliament. Somerset must have been encouraged, though, that the convocation of clergy, which was sitting at the same time as Parliament, approved the administration of the sacrament in two kinds. Convocation also agreed to the idea of clerical marriage, although Parliament did not enact this idea until a later session. The support of many of the bishops and clergy would make his task so much easier in the future.

The new freedom offered by the act was welcomed by the people and did much to raise Somerset's popularity. Paget, who was best placed to know the Protector's thoughts, believed that Somerset's desire to have the good opinion of the people was one factor that determined his policy of leniency. The common folk responded to his concern for them and in 1549 they would say of him that 'there was never man that had the hearts of the poor as your grace'.[5] In 1556 Bishop John Ponet referred to him as 'the good duke of Somerset', a term that was taken up by John Foxe a few years later.[6] Ponet was a supporter of Somerset but it is possible that this epithet was first used by the common folk as a popular response to the greater freedoms granted during this Parliament and to later attempts to improve their living conditions in the countryside.

Not everyone was satisfied with the final draft of the repeal act. Thomas Seymour took great exception to the degree of freedom of speech it permitted. He believed that people would now be free to repeat scurrilous talk against his wife by claiming that she had not been lawfully married to Henry VIII. Thomas's request to include a clause that would prevent this was denied. He was furious and went about threatening to make this the 'blackest Parliament that ever was in England', claiming that he would live better without the Protector than the Protector would without him.[7] In his bid to change the bill, Thomas may have once again tried to enlist the king's support by asking him to write a letter to Parliament. Edward recalled that when he asked what the letter was for, Thomas replied 'it was none ill. It is for the queen's matters'. Edward, though, refused to write favouring the request, saying that 'if it were good the lords would allow it, if it were ill I will not write in it' and then asked Thomas to leave him alone.[8] The Lord Admiral may not have been as high in his nephew's favour as he might wish.

Among the other statutes passed during that first Parliament was one to abolish chantries. These were endowments to maintain priests to pray for the souls of specific people after their death and were often funded by income from land or property. Somerset believed that these endowed prayers encouraged a misguided belief in purgatory and were unnecessary. The statute, which followed an earlier act of Henry VIII, granted the existing endowments to the king so that this wealth could be put to better use for education and the maintenance of the poor. In effect, however, the measure became a means of replenishing the royal coffers, which were severely depleted after the Protector's foray into Scotland. By the following April, when commissioners were instructed to sell the chantry lands, the money was unequivocally intended for military purposes.[9] Somerset's intention to use the money for schools and education was probably sincere and his failure to do so was largely occasioned by the heavy demands upon government money for other expenses.

One unforeseen aspect of the abolition of chantries was the recognition that charitable giving was a social responsibility. Money that testators had previously allocated to establish chantries was now often assigned directly to fund schools, almshouses and even hospitals. This new form of charity accorded well with Somerset's belief in the need to help the poor and oppressed. Although little changed during his tenure, there was a noticeable increase in such funding during the second half of the reign.

While many of the statutes present Somerset as a benevolent governor, one shows a harsher side to his character. Despite the strong moral responsibility he felt for people unable to help themselves, he had no tolerance for those who intentionally lived on the edge of society. Previous legislation to help people in need had often been poorly enforced. This new act took steps to ensure that people who were sick, maimed or elderly should be housed and cared for in their own villages and towns using funds from a weekly collection at church. In contrast, people deemed able but unwilling to work were to be physically branded with a letter 'V', set to work as slaves for two years and punished by beating, chaining and being fed with only bread, water and waste meat.[10] The government believed that vagrancy and idleness often led to robbery and hoped this act would prevent such crime. However, this was a draconian response. Just two years later, when Somerset was no longer in power, the act was repealed on the grounds that it had not been effectively enforced, probably on account of its harshness.

One final statute was intended to give protection to Somerset and his co-councillors from any future charges of malpractice during their term of government.[11] When the king reached the age of 24 he would have authority to repeal any Act of Parliament made during his minority. This left the possibility that Somerset and the others could be accused of unlawful activity should Edward, or anyone else, object to something they had done. The new statute ordained that an existing act could only be annulled from the time of its repeal, not retrospectively, giving Somerset the freedom to pass whatever laws he thought fit without fear of later retribution. Regarding the laws for religious reform, Somerset could be hopeful that by the time Edward came of age the country would have adjusted to the new religion and there would be no call for a return to the old.

Somerset's hope that the reforms instigated both before and during Parliament would be peacefully assimilated into the Church's pattern of worship was not entirely satisfied. Throughout England the response to reform varied. Some parish churches were reluctant to change and waited for the government to enforce the new orders. Others instigated the changes immediately, even moving ahead of the government to follow their own ideas. Many churches stopped elevating the host at mass and abandoned the use of Latin. Some clergy spoke out from the pulpit against the concept of transubstantiation, others maintained their belief in it. Disagreements continued over identifying and removing idolatrous images. Somerset's liberality was leading to abuse as people took it upon themselves to decide how they would worship. Eventually he was forced to take action against men who were fomenting trouble, even though he may have agreed with some of their ideas. Parliament ended on Christmas Eve and three days later Somerset issued a proclamation banning any discussion of the interpretation of the Eucharist. It was an attempt to prevent dissenters speaking out against the changes and was to be the first in a series of proclamations intended to contain the excesses of the reformers.

Proclamations were issued in the name of the king and privy council and were used to enforce existing laws. They also enabled Somerset and the council to regulate people's behaviour without recourse to parliamentary statutes, often for a limited time and to deal with an immediate crisis. Their use was wide-ranging, covering major issues such as the defence of England and the penalties for rioting, together with more routine matters including short-term controls of food prices, export of goods, changes to coinage and controls on movement during times of plague. Ironically, considering his desire to lessen the burden of authority on people, Somerset made greater use of proclamations than either Henry VIII or the Duke of Northumberland (during the second part of Edward VI's reign). He issued about twenty-nine per annum compared with ten by Northumberland and fewer than six by Henry. However, the greater number of proclamations reflected the turbulent conditions of the time, and many dealt with disorder that resulted from his own policies.

It is apparent that by February 1548, just twelve months after Somerset came to power, Paget was already concerned about his master's style of government, including his use of proclamations for matters he considered were properly the responsibility of Parliament. He was worried that their use enabled Somerset to enforce far-reaching policy, especially with regard to religion, which had been agreed by only a few men rather than after wider consultation. On 2 February he advised Somerset to appoint a number of 'learned men' to consider which laws should be retained, which should be repealed and the form of services to be observed in the churches. He further proposed the 'staying of all things unto the parliament time' when decisions should be taken 'with advice and consent of the body of the realm and the learned men'.[12] Paget wanted Somerset to use statutes rather than proclamations to instigate further changes to religion. Parliament had just authorised Somerset and the privy councillors to pass whatever laws they thought fit without fear of later retribution, but this immunity did not apply to orders issued by proclamation. Somerset, though, was following his own course.

By 24 April 1548 a further three proclamations had been issued.[13] One enforced the statute ordering that communion should be given as both bread and water. Another banned 'private innovations in ceremonies', permitting only church services authorised by the king and Parliament, and relaxed the necessity to use ashes on Ash Wednesday and palms on Palm Sunday. Somerset knew, though, that many reformers felt he was moving too slowly and a common feature of these proclamations was the repeated acknowledgement that further reform would follow.

The third proclamation prohibited unlicensed preaching. Some preachers were reported to be inciting subjects to disobedience and talking of new fees of half a crown to be paid at marriages, baptisms and funerals. To stop the spread of false rumours, Somerset and the council needed to control what was preached from the pulpit. In future, they agreed, only clergy licensed by the king, Somerset or Cranmer would be allowed to preach. All other clerics would be restricted to reading Cranmer's *Homilies* to their congregations. The order was unsuccessful, though, and in September Somerset issued a further proclamation prohibiting all clergy from preaching sermons and allowing only the *Homilies* to be read from the pulpit. A straitjacket was being applied to restrict freedom of speech. This was not what Somerset had intended when he relaxed the restraints on the people.

The proclamation against unlicensed preaching in April had also ordered that there should be no public orations on bigamy and divorce. Some priests were preaching that it was now acceptable for a man to have two wives, putting one aside and marrying the second, with the inference that the sanctity of marriage was only assured under the old religion. This clause was probably inserted because of the marital indiscretion of William Parr, Marquis of Northampton, who was known to be a supporter of the religious reforms. It had become public knowledge that he had wed Elizabeth Brooke while still married to his first wife.

It was an issue that could challenge the morality of the new religion and would create a rift between him and Somerset.

After Northampton's first wife, Anne Bourchier, had eloped and given birth to her lover's child, Northampton had obtained a legal separation. In 1543 a bill had been passed in Parliament to bastardise her children, thus preventing them inheriting either property or title from him. This was not an uncommon occurrence and was something he shared with Somerset who had also used Parliament to disinherit the eldest son of his first marriage. However, by 1547 Parr had fallen in love with Elizabeth Brooke. Since he had been granted only a separation from Anne, not a divorce, in April he had appealed to the privy council to decide whether he might re-marry while Anne was still alive. It was a protracted inquiry and eventually Northampton became impatient and married Elizabeth in secret. When Somerset discovered the truth in January 1548, he and the council were horrified at the precedent this might set to other people. If the council was seen to be taking no action, especially when the person involved was someone of high repute, others might follow suit and 'breed manifold disorders and inconveniences within the realm'.

On 28 January Northampton was ordered to present himself at Somerset House to explain his conduct. He might have expected sympathy from the Protector who had suffered similarly from the behaviour of his first wife, but Somerset had waited for Katherine Fyloll to die before remarrying, and any sympathy he felt was outweighed by concern regarding the morality of the issue and the need to maintain public order. Northampton and Elizabeth were ordered to separate; the council eventually found in favour of their union but the legality of their marriage would prove to be a thorny issue for years to come. Of more significance, the treatment he received from Somerset no doubt contributed to Northampton's later decision to turn against the Protector.[14]

In February 1548 the privy council ordered the removal of all images from churches across the country, extending the ban already in place in London.[15] This was a step too far for some parishioners. They had so far suffered the assault on their religion – the imposition of wine with bread at communion, the use of English in services and the cessation of some ceremonies – but for some people images of saints were necessary as the focus of their prayers.

That spring Somerset was faced with his first rebellion. On 6 April an outbreak of violence in Cornwall resulted in the murder of William Body at Helston. An unpopular local official and supporter of the new religion, Body was confronted by a hostile crowd while he checked that religious images had been removed. Cornwall was a staunchly Catholic part of England and the local people wanted the laws and tenets of religion to remain as they had been at the end of

Henry VIII's reign until Edward reached the age of 24. The crowd increased to about 3,000 and, when the local justices of the peace were unable to restrain the rebels, soldiers from local garrisons were brought in. Arrests were made but Somerset issued a general pardon to all the rioters except for twenty-eight, ten of whom were executed primarily for the murder rather than the rioting.[16] The rising was put down quickly and firmly and the executions were a warning. Somerset had reason to be pleased with the result but it may have lured him into a false sense of security regarding how easy it was to suppress a rebellion. The following year he would find matters to be very different.

The number of clergy who opposed Somerset was relatively small, but one of the main protagonists was Bishop Gardiner. As soon as Somerset had returned to London from Scotland in 1547 the bishop had resumed writing letters to him. The Protector, though, was either too busy to respond or, perhaps, was becoming annoyed with Gardiner's interference and continual haranguing against the Paraphrases, Homilies and injunctions. Gardiner wrote six times in October and November before he received a reply. Somerset took exception to some criticism from him and his annoyance was apparent in his response to the bishop. Gardiner replied that he had not meant to upset Somerset but that the latter had misinterpreted his words and had taken 'my fly as it were a bee, which I thought should have stung no man'.[17] While languishing in the Fleet prison, Gardiner had been a notable absentee from Parliament, despite his pleading to be released so that he could attend. Somerset was understandably reluctant to have this powerful and persuasive orator in the upper chamber where he could oppose the government legislation.

Gardiner was released from the Fleet in January 1548, after Parliament had adjourned, and allowed to return to his diocese at Winchester despite failing to agree to support the new reforms. However, after local disturbances he was soon ordered back to London. Somerset was doing his best to rehabilitate the bishop but Gardiner would not be coerced and as the Protector persevered, the Earl of Warwick believed his chances of success were slim. Referring to Gardiner, he wrote: 'I fear his accustomed wiliness and the persuasions of his friends will again let the fox deceive the lion.'[18]

Somerset was swimming against the tide of opinion with regard to Gardiner. His secretary, William Cecil, confided to the bishop that some men thought the Protector 'favoured him overmuch' and that if he had followed their advice he would have already sent Gardiner to the Tower. Somerset, though, believed he was making progress and on 29 June 1548 he permitted Gardiner to speak at the new 'preaching place' – an open air pulpit in the privy garden at Whitehall – on articles dictated by the council. Somerset warned him that he could be deprived of his bishopric if he ignored their instructions but it was to no avail. Once he had taken the platform, with Somerset and the king seated at a window in the gallery and the council and a large audience in the garden, the bishop ignored the council's instructions and proceeded to uphold the doctrine of transubstantiation and failed to acknowledge the privy council's authority over religious matters.[19] Somerset finally lost patience with Gardiner and the following day ordered him to the Tower. He remained there for five years until the accession of Mary and England's return to the Catholic Church.

If Gardiner had opposed Henry VIII in the way he opposed Somerset he would most certainly have been imprisoned more quickly, deprived and possibly even executed. Somerset was more tolerant than Henry and, perhaps because of their earlier friendship, continued to believe that he could bring Gardiner round to his way of thinking. He did not deprive him of his bishopric – that decision was taken by Warwick after Somerset's fall. In comparison with the persecution during the reigns of Henry, Mary and Elizabeth, the treatment of religious dissidents and heretics was notably lenient during Edward's reign. Somerset displayed great tolerance and while he was in power no Catholics appear to have suffered unduly for their religious beliefs. No bishops were deprived and only Gardiner and Bonner suffered extended imprisonment. No-one was executed although Joan Bocher, an Anabaptist condemned for heresy, languished in prison as long as Somerset was ascendant only to become one of the two heretics executed under Northumberland.

Many of Somerset's most powerful supporters in religion came from the literate educated class. The new freedom to print and sell books in English led to a wave of religious publications, the majority supporting reform and denigrating Catholicism, which encouraged much discussion of the new ideas. Somerset and Cranmer needed educated men to promulgate these ideas further. They welcomed reformers from Europe into England, not only Englishmen, such as John Hooper, who had fled the Henrician regime but also Europeans who were under threat of persecution on the Continent. The presence of some of Europe's leading reformers gave enormous impetus to the burgeoning movement for change.

Somerset had close contact with several of these men, providing ample opportunity for him to discuss and develop his own religious beliefs and ideas for reform. Three men in particular lived in Somerset's household for a time and must have been highly influential. John Hooper, who described Somerset as his patron, spent a short time with him. Thomas Becon and William Turner both served as chaplains to Somerset and the latter also offered his skills as a physician and herbalist.[20] From these men Somerset heard the ideas of reformers such as Zwingli, Bullinger and Calvin and, although they may not have been in complete agreement on all aspects of theology, they all rejected the concept of transubstantiation.

If they had not shared these men's beliefs, Somerset and his wife would never have taken them into their household where they would have daily contact with their children. Anne Seymour's sympathy for religious reform had been apparent when she served Katherine Parr and had been suspected of knowing Anne Askew. After Somerset became Protector, her enthusiasm for change became even more apparent as she openly encouraged the reformers. She even chastised Thomas Smith, one of her husband's servants, for being 'neutral' in religion. Indeed, van der Delft believed she was a powerful influence on Somerset and held her responsible for encouraging him to pursue his religious reforms.[21]

Somerset and his wife ensured that their children were exposed to religious debate both through casual contact with the reformers and through their education. The couple were praised by Thomas Becon for training their children in 'good literature', by which he was referring to religious works.[22] Somerset attached great importance to education, describing the universities as the 'storehouses or great nurseries of letters and piety' from which teaching should spread throughout England. In 1549 he attempted to reform university teaching in a bid to improve the breadth and quality of education at Oxford and Cambridge. The universities had been founded essentially to train clerics but Somerset wanted greater emphasis given to training civil lawyers who could practise in the London law courts and assist in government. His intention was to create one college teaching civil law with a further college to be dedicated to teaching medicine. It was an innovative idea and one that he maintained had been intended by Henry VIII.[23] However, with the advent of rebellion that year there was insufficient time for this scheme to succeed during his tenure as Protector. Both this idea and his plan to use chantry money for schools would prove to be a failure.

Somerset's progressive attitude towards his daughters' education and the quality and extent of their tuition was certainly unusual. During their early years his children, including the girls, were well tutored. Edward and Henry spent time with their cousin, the king, being instructed by Cox and Cheke, while the three eldest girls were educated at home. The daughters were taught first by John Crane and then by Nicholas Denisot, who was resident as their French master and probably also served the duke as a French secretary.[24] From 1550, Thomas Norton, who later translated John Calvin's 'Institutes of the Christian Religion', served in Somerset's household as a tutor and secretary. The novelty of this treatment of young Tudor women was captured by Calvin in his letter to Somerset's daughter, Anne, in 1549 when he refers to her 'liberal education (which is very unusual in a lady of such birth and station)'.[25]

Anne and her sisters Margaret and Jane won literary fame in England and on the Continent for an elegy they wrote in tribute to the recently deceased Marguerite of Navarre. Marguerite had written works on religious meditation and it is probable that Denisot, who had spent two years at the court of Marguerite, introduced the girls to her work. Their elegy, *Hecatodistichon*, of 104 couplets in Latin, was published in England and translated into French for circulation on the Continent.[26] At a time when there were few published works by women, this was even more remarkable considering the young age of the girls – Anne was 14, Margaret 10 and Jane just 9. Despite the fact that they may have received help from their tutor this work demonstrated the extent of their education and their skill received many plaudits. A year earlier Jane had been corresponding with Martin Bucer and Paul Fagius, two German Protestants in Strasbourg, thanking them for their praise and for the books they had sent. While she was still aged 8, Thomas Becon dedicated his *The governaunce of vertue* to her. Nicholas Grimald, who wrote songs celebrating the sisters' qualities, particularly praised Jane for her linguistic skills at such an early age – Latin, French, English, Italian and an understanding of Spanish.[27] It should be noted, of course, that while these men may have admired Jane's achievements, their praise for her would be known to her father, whose patronage they sought.

Although not a scholar himself, Somerset was well educated and wrote the preface to two religious tracts. The first, for Coverdale's translation of a German work, *A Spiritual and Most Precious Pearl*, was written in 1550 after Somerset found great comfort from reading the book during his imprisonment in the Tower. The same year he also wrote the preface to *An epistle both of godly consolacion and also of advertisement*. This was a letter written to Somerset by Calvin that was translated from French into English before being published.[28] It has been suggested that he may have also written a short poem – 'The pore estate to be holden for best' – in which the first letter of each line together with the last letter of the final line spell out the name Edwarde Somerset. However, it is possible that this was written as a eulogy to him. The words 'Desired pomp is vain, and seldom doth it last; / Who climbs to reign with kings, may rue his fateful sore' suggest that it was written after Somerset's execution and was exhorting the reader to eschew ambition and be content with humble estate.[29]

Somerset and his wife were the recipients of numerous book dedications, many from the reformers. Somerset received dedications in twenty-four books and manuscripts, a similar number to that made to the king during the same period, and the duchess received seven.[30] Although the books Somerset received covered a variety of topics and included a history chronicle, a medical treatise and two herbals, many were on religious themes and often praised him for his service to the Protestant cause. In 1549 Thomas Cooper applauded his 'Christian and virtuous governance' in advancing the reformed faith and hoped that through his benign and merciful government he might bring about an end to diversity of religious opinion in England.[31]

The reformers saw Somerset as the way forward and may have hoped that through their fulsome praise they might recruit him further to their cause. However, since Somerset received no dedications under Henry VIII and the majority were made during his time as Lord Protector this suggests that they favoured him primarily for his authority rather than his faith. On the other hand, dedications could also be a means to gain patronage. Somerset could influence appointments in both his own and the royal household and in the universities and the Church. For example, Hooper dedicated 'A declaracion of Christe' in 1547 while in exile in Zurich and was then taken into service by Somerset when he returned to England two years later.[32]

These intellectual reformers were not alone in travelling to England. Many other groups fled from persecution on the Continent after the Emperor Charles suppressed the Schmalkaldic League. Some of the refugees set up home in London and in towns along the east coast. Those settling in the city were allowed to hold their services in disused churches. Despite the privy council's later insistence that all the people should use the new prayer book, the refugees were allowed to use their own form of worship and liturgy. Somerset was very sympathetic to the plight of Protestants fleeing from Europe. His relationship with one group, in particular, demonstrates a social conscience and vision that set him apart from many of his contemporaries and led to him becoming an early proponent of modern philanthropy.

Somerset became aware of a congregation of Flemish weavers who had fled to England with their superintendent Valerand Poulain. The group wanted to stay together and Somerset offered them the opportunity to establish a community at the old Glastonbury abbey, a dissolved monastery that had been granted to him by Edward VI. In the belief that 'no greater benefit can be conferred on any people than the introduction of crafts, of which none is more useful than weaving', Somerset agreed the terms of their residency with Poulain. It was to be a formal charter under his own seal and with the agreement of the king and Parliament. Initially Somerset was to provide houses and sufficient land to maintain cattle for at least fourteen families. He planned to lend money for wool, tools, madder, woad and alum for dyeing and for essential living costs. The first cloths to be made were to be used to pay off part of their debt to Somerset. Once the weavers were established he was to have an option to buy their cloth at market rates and their remaining debt would be paid back in instalments.

Although the scheme could have been an opportunity for Somerset to make a financial gain, the terms of the agreement suggest he chose not to.[33]

Somerset lent the weavers £484 14s 8d to establish their business and ordered houses to be built and meadows assigned, but his servants were not very diligent in overseeing the project. By the end of 1551 the number of refugees had grown more quickly than expected. Thirty-four families with widows and spinsters had arrived and more were expected. The Glastonbury community quickly outstripped its facilities and was short of money. Somerset was by this time unable to participate in the project so the king and privy council, believing the enterprise to be worthwhile, stepped in to provide funding and the use of a park for cattle. After a slow start the community showed every promise of being successful but after the accession of Mary Tudor the members returned to Europe. It had been a generous plan and had shown that Somerset possessed foresight and a charitable instinct that was rare at the time.[34]

12

Uncertain Times

Throughout 1548 the difficulties in Scotland would demand an increasing amount of Somerset's attention. At the beginning of February he sent another declaration to the Scots: he did not intend to conquer or win the country by force, he explained, but through friendship and by making 'of one Isle one realm'. If the Scots would agree to the marriage of Edward and Mary their heirs would inherit both England and Scotland, removing any likelihood of future wars between the two countries. The united realms would use the 'indifferent' old name of Britain and Scotland would be allowed to keep her own laws, customs and free trade. 'Having the sea for wall, the mutual love for garrison, and God for defence', the two countries united could withstand all assaults, Somerset declared.[1] The rhetoric may have sounded convincing but, like the earlier proclamation, it did little good.

It was the arrival of the French in Scotland later in the year that rang the death knell for Somerset's plan. When he had proposed the invasion and establishment of garrisons it was with the hope that, once he had overwhelmed the Scots army, the only opposition would be from small pockets of resistance that would eventually be subdued. The garrisons were then to maintain peace locally and provide protection for an increasing number of assured Scots. However, the presence of the French would quickly defeat this purpose as the strongholds were increasingly forced to take on a defensive role, preventing them carrying out the function Somerset had intended. Ironically, it was the establishment of the garrisons which forced Henri II to send an army to Scotland. Without the permanent presence of English troops, the Scots would not have needed the support of a large French force.

Somerset had taken steps the previous year to discourage French involvement in the conflict. In August 1547 he had met secretly with the French ambassador, Odet de Selve, and raised the possibility of returning Boulogne to France before the treaty date in exchange for a sizeable payment. Besides releasing the king from the great expense and trouble of maintaining the fort, the forfeiture of Boulogne would bring in a large sum of money that Somerset desperately needed for the war in Scotland. Furthermore, he hoped that the promise of such a prize might discourage the French from joining the Scots. He was acutely aware of the objections the privy councillors would raise against the scheme and of their probable anger towards him for even considering returning such a hard-won prize. During his absence in Scotland he had left Paget to continue the negotiations, suggesting that it would be better if the French could be persuaded to make a proposal so the council would think the first advances had been made by them, not by Somerset.[2]

The foreign ambassadors had quickly become accustomed to dealing with Paget. It was apparent that he and Somerset worked closely together and that Paget exerted enormous influence. He had given up the position of principal secretary the previous June to take on the less onerous post of comptroller of the household (which could be treated as a sinecure), enabling him to spend more time assisting Somerset. The post of secretary had lost much of its appeal since the death of Henry VIII. As secretary to a governing king and the vital link between the monarch and the privy council, Paget had been in an enormously influential position, but with a child king there was little interaction between monarch and secretary. Now it served the purposes of both Paget and Somerset for him to be free to assist the Protector.

By the time Somerset had returned from Scotland the matter of Boulogne had moved no further forward. With the realisation that there was no imminent likelihood of a marriage between Edward and Mary, Somerset changed his approach. In November 1547, as he talked with Selve at Westminster, he had proposed returning Boulogne in exchange for other French forts and the promise of French support for the marriage. Henri II, unsurprisingly, had refused the idea and countered with an equally unacceptable offer. After several weeks of further proposals and counter-proposals that culminated in Somerset's suggestion that Boulogne could be exchanged on the terms of the original treaty if France would support the Scots marriage, the idea faltered as fifty French soldiers landed in Scotland to survey the country.[3] Negotiations between Somerset and Selve continued but without success.

Amid rumours that 6,000 Frenchmen were ready to sail to Scotland, the English garrison commanders worked through the winter to improve their fortifications, despite the local problems and what they perceived to be a lack of support and understanding from Somerset and the council. When Andrew Dudley was chastised in January for asking for the same quantity of munitions as was needed for Calais, he replied that Broughty 'is another Calais' and should have sufficient stores for itself, for the ships and for the surrounding country.[4]

In April 1548 Sir John Luttrell, who joined Dudley at Broughty after he was forced to abandon Inchcolm, wrote a scathing attack on Somerset, his officers and ministers. Among a catalogue of complaints that was becoming familiar to Somerset, Luttrell bemoaned the lack of victuals, powder, shot and fit men, especially stonemasons. What was the point, he railed, of raising and turfing bulwarks when, because of lack of masons, they fell down again. Somerset, he continued, knew that Broughty was in the front line of danger and yet never sent men to relieve his soldiers. Believing that the Protector had little regard for him and considered his demands to be unfounded and unimportant, Luttrell warned that if his concerns continued to go unheeded it would lead to disaster for the garrison. He asked to be released from his command and suggested to Somerset that if he would replace him with someone he trusted, Luttrell would be happy to 'trail the pike' again.[5] Sadly, we do not have Somerset's response but he did not replace Luttrell and was soon chastising him for undermining the authority of his deputy. The following year Luttrell came in for more criticism when Somerset accused him of not managing his supplies properly. The constant interference in Luttrell's management suggests that, in some respects, he was ineffective yet in 1549 Somerset would again refuse his request to be released from his post.[6]

Somerset's readiness to criticise his officers may have been one reason why some were reluctant to make decisions without first seeking his advice. Somerset expected to be kept closely informed of what was happening in Scotland and there was a constant stream of letters from the garrison commanders. However, often they concerned matters which could have been referred to the local commander, Lord Grey, rather than to Somerset. It appears that Grey, too, frequently sought the Protector's counsel and Somerset urged him to deal with urgent business himself before referring matters to London. He also took the opportunity to point out to Grey that during his own campaigns in Scotland he had not constantly sought direction from the council.[7]

While the commanders no doubt valued Somerset's advice, they had good cause to be fearful of his displeasure. He could be a difficult man to please; he set himself exacting standards and expected much of his officers. During 1548 he became increasingly dissatisfied with progress towards his goal and with the way some of his commanders were managing the situation. In a bid to bring round the Scots he frequently ordered destructive raids. After one such raid in January 1548, for example, Somerset chastised Grey, accusing him of achieving less than he himself had done in Scotland yet spending more money in the process. Grey was annoyed and in his defence sent back a list of the towns and men that had declared allegiance to him, explaining that he was attempting to control a large area and that a lot of money was being spent to keep the local Scots as friends. Grey hoped that once Somerset had a more favourable opinion of him, he would be recalled 'from the perils of the weary business of this country'. Like Luttrell, Grey was fed up with Scotland. With the bareness of the country, the lack of lodgings, shortage of food and the rain and cold, war in Scotland was 'more painful than elsewhere'.[8]

Nevertheless, Grey remained where he was and Somerset continued to criticise him. In June 1548 it was for not spending sufficient time raiding the Scots, although Grey explained he had done the best he could while still maintaining work on the fortifications at Haddington. Only two days later Somerset was complaining that the horses were being under-used. The complaints were, no doubt, becoming tiresome to Grey as he was forced to defend himself once again. The horses, he explained, were constantly used for convoys between Berwick and Haddington, moving victuals and night scouting, and with only poor-quality fodder many of them were dead.[9]

However, the following month Somerset was so critical that Paget felt compelled to call the Protector to order. Grey had sent a large force to harry a besieging army at Haddington. Among the commanders was Sir Thomas Palmer, who had been warned to 'adventure nothing', but, ignoring these instructions, he and Sir Robert Bowes were captured and about sixty of their men killed.[10] Somerset was furious and vented his wrath on both Palmer and Grey. He would not countenance what he perceived as failure in others. Paget, though, accused Somerset of provoking Palmer to act in a reckless manner by having written letters accusing him of 'stillness, slackness and sleeping'. Knowing Palmer's desire to please Somerset, Paget believed that he had taken the Protector's words to heart. As Protector of the Realm, Paget reminded him, men treated Somerset's words as if they were those of a king and acted upon them accordingly. Paget took it upon himself to suggest that the Protector should write some 'words of comfort' to Grey who was in despair at the debacle. Somerset could be an unsympathetic master and it is ironic that, earlier in 1548, he had taken Grey to task for his style of writing, suggesting that he should use a 'more doulse and gentle manner'.[11]

Surprisingly, Somerset's criticism of Grey does not appear to have damaged their relationship and he would later be very liberal in his generosity to Grey. Service to the king had left Grey in a beggarly position. In August 1548 he would complain about being expected to pay a subsidy towards the cost of the war and argue that men who served in the war should be quit of such payments. He was already in debt, he claimed, having spent a large sum during the campaign and was worried that he would have no money to leave to his wife and children. He petitioned Somerset for a manor and land to provide income to allow him to rebuild his finances. Somerset took all this to heart and in 1551 it was noted that Grey was living in part of one of the Protector's houses, with twenty or thirty gentlemen to attend him, all at Somerset's expense.[12] Somerset's compassion for people in poor circumstances extended to members of his own class, and his help for Grey earned him a loyal supporter who would later speak out in his defence. However, his quickness to criticise men earned him enemies and some of these, including Palmer, would remember their dealings with him when the Protector needed help in the future.

As summer had approached, the situation in Scotland improved only marginally. Efforts had been made during the winter to improve fortifications and, with better weather, communications were easier but there was still a shortage of men. Thomas Wyndham, who controlled the northern fleet, complained of sick men, lack of victuals and leaking ships. Meanwhile Grey, increasingly dismayed at the burden of command, asked for some 'lusty' young gentlemen to be sent who could spare him from continual 'drawing in the plough'.[13] But matters were about to get even worse. There was an old saying that the French king would rather lose half of the French realm than that Scotland should be English.[14] On 16 June 1548 several thousand Frenchmen landed at Leith, about 17 miles from Haddington, with the intention of taking the garrison. It served as a base from which the English could threaten Edinburgh and only two weeks earlier a raiding party from there had burnt crops close to the town. However, Haddington was the jewel in the crown of the English garrisons and Somerset would not relinquish it lightly.

By 2 July Haddington was besieged and government of Scotland was reported to be under French control.[15] It was apparent to Henri II that with a sustained effort by Somerset, Scotland might eventually fall to the English. If Henri was going to ensure that Mary married the Dauphin, and Scotland became a dominion of France, he needed to expel the English who would only be able to remain in Scotland while they held the garrisons. Estimates of the number of French and Scots besiegers vary but it is likely to have been well over 10,000.

Somerset's response was to send the Earl of Shrewsbury to Scotland with a similarly massive force. However, before he could do that, the worst happened. At the beginning of August the 5-year-old Queen of Scots sailed for France as the future bride of the Dauphin and Henri soon claimed that the marriage agreement between his son and Mary meant that he was now the rightful King of Scotland.[16] This was not what the Scots had intended.

With Mary gone from the country, and far from his control, Somerset had lost the primary reason for the invasion and the continued presence of the English in Scotland. This was not the time to turn back, however, and by 23 August Shrewsbury was camped just 5 miles from Haddington with an army of nearly

15,000. The French were not prepared to face such a large force and within six days they withdrew. Once the garrison had been relieved and provisioned with stores and men Shrewsbury moved his force to Berwick, but the enemy soon returned. The garrison was well prepared and in October the English troops successfully withstood a massive assault. It was heartening news for Somerset and was followed by reports that the French and Scots had fallen to fighting each other within the town of Edinburgh. English hopes rose that soon the Scots would grow to hate the French and would revolt against them.

Shrewsbury's expedition had achieved its aim but the cost had been enormous. The garrisons were intended to be an alternative to sending large and expensive armies into the north but the arrival of the French had shown otherwise. Unless he could soon force the country into submission, Somerset would not be able to maintain the garrisons. Funds were short and, although control of Scotland was of more importance to him than full coffers, he could not spend money that was not there.

With the advent of winter, Somerset feared the prospect of being forced to abandon any garrisons. This would jeopardise his plan and, as Paget reminded him, spending time, money and men on holding a place and then losing it to the enemy would also besmirch the honour of both the king and Somerset.[17] When Sir James Wilford at Haddington lamented the desperate state of his men and the loss of thirty horsemen bringing in supplies Somerset ordered him to 'keep well at home' and not to risk the garrison. He must 'keep fast the key in hand' for the forts were the key to opening the door to future enterprises against the Scots. Somerset gave similar advice to Luttrell. Lacking men and horses, Luttrell was losing control of the area around Broughty and Somerset advised him to 'lie there as you were dead'.[18] The garrisons must be held at all costs. But it was to no avail and slowly they were lost or abandoned – Inchcolm, Blackness, Dumfries, Yester, Jedburgh, Hume and the town of Dundee. Somerset's policy towards Scotland was falling apart, and his hope of winning the country through the support of assured Scots faded. As England's position weakened, and the garrisons were unable to offer protection, many assured men returned to the Scottish cause.

As the remaining garrisons in Scotland prepared for winter, Somerset turned his attention towards France. Although the two countries had been engaged in warlike activity in both Scotland and France they were technically at peace. On 3 October 1548 Somerset met with the privy council to consider issuing a declaration of war against the French but the council decided otherwise.[19] Somerset could not afford to engage in a major offensive in France while a large number of troops were already committed to Scotland. Nevertheless, England remained in an unsteady state of apprehension as tensions rose following increased French aggression against English-held territory in France. The previous December, when negotiations for the return of Boulogne had foundered, the French had launched a raid near the town, killing a number of Englishmen. On that occasion, in the interests of maintaining some form of cordiality, Somerset had refrained from making any response. However, during the summer French provocation had escalated and firing broke out between Boulogne and a new French fort on the opposite side of the river. Amid rumours of an invasion, warning beacons were erected in England and plans prepared to assemble a force should it become necessary. Efforts were made to improve defences and in October, for the second time that year, Somerset spent several days inspecting fortifications at Portsmouth and other ports along the south coast.[20]

Negotiations over Boulogne continued between Somerset and Selve but to no avail. Somerset also sought to resolve the issue of Scotland with the ambassador. If he could not achieve union through marriage he hoped there might be a way through law. At the end of 1548 he showed Selve documents which he hoped would prove Scotland's historic feudal allegiance to England. The ambassador declined to either read or comment on the content, replying only that the French king was seeking to establish a similar claim.[21] It was stalemate as neither side would give way.

During his first year in power Somerset's priorities had been Scotland and religion. It was not until the summer of 1548 that he took the first steps towards instigating any major programme of social reform when he turned his attention to enclosures, an issue that troubled many people. In May he opened access to Hampton Court park, which had been enclosed for Henry VIII to make it easier for him to hunt as increasing infirmity had made riding difficult. While the park was closed people had been denied access to the common land for grazing and, as the tenants moved away, their houses had fallen into disrepair. More importantly, Somerset and the council were concerned that, with fewer tenants, revenue from the estate had fallen. The following month, on 1 June, he appointed commissioners to examine the wider effects of enclosures upon the populace, particularly the problems caused by loss of grazing land, the lack of property and the dearth of both food and soldiers.[22]

Historically, landowners had assumed responsibility for their tenants and in return the tenants provided agricultural labour and military service. However, by the mid-sixteenth century this feudal system was declining and the relationship between the lower orders and their landlords was weakening. As the number of ancient noble families declined, land passed into the hands of the new aristocracy and the growing class of gentlemen. Land ceased to be just a source of manpower. It became a valuable commodity and a source of income as some men sought to breed great numbers of sheep to satisfy the demand for wool and cloth for England's growing export trade with Europe. It was more profitable to run large flocks, so landlords often combined several smallholdings, maintaining just one farmhouse and allowing the others to decay, thus depriving their tenants of both land and homes. Large areas, including common land that tenants traditionally had a right to use, were enclosed by hedges and fences, denying people access to pasture for their cattle and pigs. Confronted with the choice of losing their livelihood or paying increased rents, many families were forced to leave the countryside and move to the towns. Contemporaries complained of decayed villages as England was brought into 'a marvellous desolation'. Where there had once been 100 men to serve the king, there were now only half as many, and where there had been forty or fifty ploughs, there were now fewer than ten.[23]

The conversion of large areas of arable land to sheep pasture also presented the risk of a shortage of grain and beef. This threat to food production was exacerbated by a rapidly growing population. In the ten years from 1541 to 1551 the population of England rose from 2.774 to 3.011 million people, a jump of over 8 per cent in just ten years. Food production was not keeping pace with this growth, particularly in years of bad harvests. For the poor, the scarcity of food was aggravated by inflation. Prices of agricultural products during the 1550s were nearly double those of two decades earlier. There was often insufficient employment for the growing workforce in London and other large towns and wages did not keep pace with inflation.[24] Inflation had risen partly as a result of the currency debasement that had taken place during the previous reign; Henry VIII had reduced the gold and silver content of coins to raise money to fund his wars against France and Scotland. However, this had the effect of pushing up prices because people felt that, with a lower precious metal content, the value of the coins was less.

The issue of enclosures was not new but the decline of the rural population held an increasing significance. The ability to maintain an army in Scotland was of paramount importance to Somerset. With the threat of war against France, the prospect of a continuing reduction in the number of fit men to serve as soldiers was deeply worrying and may have been one reason for him taking action when he did. It was increasingly difficult to summon large numbers of suitable men from the country and this seriously weakened the king's ability to defend England. The realm needed 'force of men', not 'flocks of sheep and droves of beasts'. Men who were unable to afford food had difficulty purchasing a bow and lacked the strength to be effective archers. As one commentator remarked, 'shepherds be but ill archers'. The Bishop of Rochester, John Scory, described starving and weak Englishmen and likened them to the peasants of France rather than to the ancient yeomanry of England.[25]

There was one other impotant reason for the commission. The maintenance of law and order was paramount and much government policy was directed towards this end. Displaced and hungry people presented a potential threat to the peace and quiet of the realm. By ensuring the populace was adequately provided for, the council hoped to prevent any outbreak of disorder.

The commission established in 1548 was not intended to redress complaints immediately, only to gather information about instances where land had been enclosed and arable land converted into pasture. It is likely that Somerset intended the matter to be considered during the next Parliament before he set about enforcing existing statutes against the practice. Attempts had been made by Henry VIII to address the issue of enclosure but ineffectual enforcement had allowed the practice to continue.

One leading supporter of the commission was John Hales, a prominent campaigner for social and economic reform. He was one of a group of outspoken men who believed in the Christian principle of charity and sought to improve society for the common good of all. Generally known as 'Commonwealth' men, many of them were prominent Protestants who were influenced by the ideal of compassion for the poor that was a central theme of the Gospels. They accepted the existence of poverty but believed that those in authority had a responsibility to maintain poor folk in a condition where they could provide for themselves and their families. They believed that removing enclosures and making grain farming more profitable than sheep grazing would increase the food supply and provide work. To what extent Somerset's own ideals were influenced by these reformers is impossible to say, although he had close contact with several of them, including Bishop Latimer, Hooper, Becon and Turner. Thomas Smith, a political theorist closely allied to Somerset, suggested that Anne Seymour favoured the reformers so it may be that she encouraged her husband to adopt their ideas.[26] However, it is likely that Somerset, too, had been influenced by the New Testament emphasis on compassion and, because his policies accorded so well with their beliefs, it is probable that he needed little encouragement.

Hales's suggestion that Somerset sought to create a society 'without one having too much, and a great many nothing at all' was not an ideal shared by all the privy councillors. Despite initially having much conciliar support for the enclosure commission, Somerset was later to find himself isolated from the councillors, many of whom were landowners and opposed to the Commonwealth men's ideas. It had been intended to establish commissions throughout the country, but only one, in the Midlands, operated that year. When riots broke out in response to the government failure to make immediate improvements, Warwick, in particular, was quick to condemn the commissioners as the cause of the trouble.[27] The limited operation of the commission was undoutedly the reason that no large-scale measures were taken against enclosures in the next Parliament.

Somerset did, however, introduce a bill to improve the rights of some of his own tenants. This bill was granted out of his 'charitable mind and accustomed goodness' and gave greater security of tenure to some of his tenants who, lacking a strong claim to their land, could easily be evicted.[28] The terms of the bill were probably not a great encumbrance to him. However, by binding his heirs to these new conditions, Somerset did choose to put his tenants' interests before those of himself and his family. It set an example to other landlords, although few chose to follow his lead.

Somerset himself had been involved in the agricultural practices he denounced. At his death he was recorded as owning 2,000 sheep and he did enclose his own land.[29] However, he took his responsibilities as a landlord seriously. Tenants whose properties were affected by his plans for a new park in Wiltshire were rehoused and retained their access to common land. In 1548 he began enclosing the park with a circumference of nearly 3 miles as part of the preparations for building a new mansion near his house at Wulfhall. Where the enclosure encroached upon a pond used by the tenants of Wilton, a pathway was left, enabling them to move their livestock to a new pond that was to be dug on a new area of common land. Arrangements were put in hand to find another house for one tenant, Bushell, whose property was to be enclosed within the new park; other tenants whose lands had been taken were provided with alternative fields on which to plant the following year's barley crop.[30]

More than many other landlords, Somerset accepted his responsibility towards his tenants and went to great lengths to practice the charity that he espoused to others. Although much of his public social programme for reform would prove to be a failure, the private initiatives he took, such as the tenancy bill and his involvement in the Glastonbury community, proved to be successful.

13

King in all but Name

By the end of 1548 Somerset had been granted or had assumed many of the prerogatives of kingship. Like a king, he selected his own advisers and consulted them only when he chose to do so. He had the power to declare war, to raise a military force and to make peace, all issues that were usually reserved for royal consideration. Through the use of symbolism he assumed the persona of royalty. His special seat in Parliament, beside the king's throne at the head of the chamber, set him apart from his peers. Early in Edward's reign van der Delft had reported that two gilt maces were carried before Somerset when he went in procession.[1] Even his new coat of arms played a part, proclaiming an unfounded connection to the kings of England by incorporating the royal arms as used by his sister, Queen Jane. Depicting three golden 'lions of England' between six blue fleurs de lys quartered with the Seymour arms of two joined wings, Somerset's standard was a powerful way of proclaiming his precedence. However, nowhere was his assumption of regality more evident than in his dealings with the privy council.

By the mid-sixteenth century, the privy council was the mechanism of government. Councillors were responsible for every aspect of life in England, ensuring the peace and security of the country and maintaining the social welfare of the people. Routine day-to-day business was handled by them and covered a wide range of issues from maintaining food supplies, regulating manufacturing and minting new coins to individual matters such as issuing passports. Important decisions were taken by the king, with or without the advice of the councillors who then carried out his instructions. In the absence of a monarch competent to make such decisions – for instance, during a period of minority rule or when the king was ill – the government of the country would normally be placed in the hands of a regent or Lord Protector who acted as the king's representative. He assumed the absolute power of the monarch and the council deferred to him.

The Protectorate established by Edward VI's council was different. Although Somerset was to have primacy, it was intended that he should act only with the advice and consent of all the councillors. He was to be their spokesman and figurehead. Unfettered by any monarchical interference, the councillors expected to have unlimited power to make decisions with Somerset on all matters. He and they together were to make decisions and govern England.

Somerset, though, chose to interpret his role differently. In June 1547 he had explained to van der Delft that, although he thought it better to communicate matters to the council, 'he could act by himself if he pleased, according to his own discretion'.[2] In the event, as time passed he did increasingly make decisions without taking account of the councillors' views. His failure to consult them fully limited their influence upon some government policy. It was a situation that was of the councillors' own making. The letters patent they had granted to Somerset gave him enormous control over the operation of the privy council. The freedom to accept their counsel, as and when he chose, effectively negated the earlier condition that he should govern only with their advice. They had undermined their own position. In December 1548 Paget wrote to Somerset pleading with him to listen to the councillors' opinions. It was an appeal he would make repeatedly the following year. However, as the months passed, Somerset ignored even Paget's counsel as he forgot the promise he had made, which was to heed his advice at all times.[3]

This is not to say that the Protectorate was a time of autocratic rule, although Somerset was the dominant figure and led the direction of policy. In principle, he and his colleagues agreed on much of the policy they followed – their desire for union with Scotland, the necessity of dealing with internal dissension and religious and agrarian reforms, for instance. Their disagreement often stemmed from the implementation of that policy and Somerset's practice of making decisions outside the council.[4]

Undoubtedly on some issues his policies were out of step with the views of his peers. On matters that he knew would face conciliar opposition, he may have found it more expedient to avoid initial confrontation and follow his own course. In 1549, for example, he would issue a bill against enclosures without council support. During the summer of 1547 he had been especially intent on keeping his meetings with the French ambassador secret while he tentatively pursued the idea of returning Boulogne to the French, a matter that was likely to enrage several of the councillors. Somerset actively sought to exclude councillors from his meetings with the ambassadors. Early in the reign van der Delft and Selve would speak with the Protector and the council together. As time passed, however, he increasingly dealt with them alone, encouraging them to seek audience with him rather than with the councillors. In August 1549 Selve would meet with Somerset alone to deliver the French declaration of war.[5]

Somerset's style of government was a reflection of the way he commanded the army, where strong leadership and discipline were what counted, not management and persuasion. As an army commander he took complete control and responsibility for making decisions and issuing orders, only accepting advice when he chose. He failed to appreciate that he needed to use a different approach with the privy councillors who considered him to be their equal, not their commander. As his authoritarian stance weakened the councillors' influence, they became resentful at their inability to participate fully.

Somerset's ability to govern independently was enhanced by his habit of conducting council business at his London house, Somerset Place. Much of the routine business was handled at Westminster by a small group of councillors that included St John, Rich, Paget and Petre, who were all reliable administrators. However, Somerset increasingly met with councillors and despatched whatever business he chose at his home, bypassing the conventional procedure whereby the principal secretaries handled all correspondence for the council. Secretary Petre later admitted that he had given council papers to Somerset and his servants, some of which had since been lost. At Somerset Place incoming documents were opened and drafts for new letters were prepared for the Protector by Paget (who was no longer a principal secretary) and Somerset's servants, John Thynne and William Cecil, aided by council clerks.[6] It was an effective way for Somerset to keep control but, without the oversight of the secretaries, records of business were sparse, with few decisions of any importance being recorded and no reliable lists of council meeting attendance being kept.

Many letters regarding business that would routinely have been handled by the council were instead addressed personally to Somerset rather than to the councillors, and it must be assumed this was at his insistence. During 1548 much of the correspondence from the commanders in Scotland was sent directly to Somerset, who responded to their questions in place of the councillors. In September 1548, while he was away from the court for a few days, the council had opened several letters addressed to the Protector from the commanders on the Scottish borders and taken action on several matters. However, they appear to have felt that this practice was so unusual that it warranted an explanation. In their letter to Grey they acknowledged that they had opened correspondence during Somerset's absence 'as it was his grace's pleasure we should'.[7] There was concern among the councillors that Somerset issued many letters under his signature alone without their counter-signatures. After the Protectorate, when he was no longer in power, they would ensure that all letters issued by the council carried at least six signatures.[8]

Because of their proximity to Somerset, his principal servants held an important position as the link between their master and the court. As quasi-monarch, people sought Somerset's attention as they had previously done with Henry VIII and his home quickly became an extension of the court. While Edward VI was afforded all the respect due to his position, he was a child living in an adult world. His court did not have the prestige of his father's and for much of the time he was isolated from what happened around him. Somerset was the real power and source of patronage. Visitors and petitioners did not hasten to the king's chambers but to those of his uncle. Requests for patronage would usually have been passed through the privy chamber to the king but only five weeks after Edward's accession van der Delft noted that people were advised to present all petitions to Somerset. Since few men had easy access to the Lord Protector, petitions were passed via his servants. Even privy councillors relied upon this method to submit their requests and there were numerous occasions when Warwick sought Paget or Cecil's help in securing Somerset's favour in a suit. In matters of council business, too, Warwick routinely addressed questions to Cecil in the expectation that he would report back with the Protector's response.[9]

The Protector's wife also served as an effective channel to gain patronage. She was particularly well-placed to present petitions to her husband on behalf of other people and to influence his decisions, and men and women went to great lengths to keep her favour. For example, in the spring of 1549 Paget, horrified that he might be opposing the duchess, withdrew from pressing a suit for a parcel of land in the mistaken belief that the other supplicant was Anne, a situation, he wrote, that 'went to my heart like a dagger'.[10]

In the future, however, one of the criticisms levelled against Somerset was the extent of Anne's perceived influence over him, particularly with regard to his policies. Historically, the duchess has been portrayed as ambitious, arrogant, domineering and a malign influence on her husband. Undeniably loyal to Somerset, Anne was conscious of the pre-eminence his position as Protector bestowed upon them both. She had a strong personality and it is easy to understand how her criticism, for instance, of courtiers whom she considered were failing to maintain the standards expected of them, could be interpreted as arrogance. She was very critical of the respective wives of John Cheke and Thomas Smith, complaining in particular that Smith's wife dressed below her status and that he failed to 'keep house' in London because of the expense.[11] A tract against Somerset, probably written in 1551, attacked Anne as 'that imperious and insolent woman his wife, whose ambitious and mischievous persuasions led him and directed him even also in the weighty affairs and government of the realm'.[12] It would be easy to believe that such unfavourable views of Anne were held by Somerset's enemies but it seems that even his closest supporter may have had reservations about her involvement. In August 1549, during a meeting with van der Delft, Paget conceded that Somerset had 'a bad wife' to which van der Delft rejoined that he was unworthy to govern if he allowed himself to be ruled by his wife. Some people would later hold her partly responsible for the rebellions of 1549 in the belief that she had influenced Somerset's policy on enclosures. Undoubtedly, as van der Delft asserted, Anne had a hand in influencing his religious and social views but there is no evidence that she was instrumental in formulating policy.[13] That was Somerset's preserve.

One aspect of Somerset's government that particularly irked the councillors was his supposed involvement in the Court of Requests. This court at Westminster provided access to justice, especially for the poor seeking redress against powerful men, often in disputes over ownership of land and property. Councillors claimed that Somerset held a private Court of Requests in his own house, managed by his servants.[14] Although there is no evidence that this happened, two of his servants, Thomas Smith and Cecil, were appointed masters of the court and it is easy to see how such misunderstandings could arise, especially if Somerset signed request documents while he was at Somerset Place. However, he did exert some influence over the court at Westminster by writing letters in favour of suitors, an activity that Paget criticised. A letter in March 1548 left no doubt of the verdict Somerset expected. The complainant, he wrote, should receive all 'that in conscience he ought to have'. It is difficult to know how often he interfered, and it may have been only after an appeal had been made directly to him, but it was sufficiently frequent for Paget to be concerned. There is, though, no evidence that Somerset ever tried to pervert the course of justice, only to see justice done.[15]

Somerset felt strongly that all men should be treated equally by the law. As he told his brother: 'We are ready to receive poor men's complaints, that findeth or thinketh themselves injured or grieved, it is our duty and our office so to do.' All men in authority received requests for help but people believed that because of his 'affability and clemency' he would be most sympathetic to their plight.[16] It was perfectly acceptable for someone in high office to have sympathy with people who needed help. However, some men believed Somerset's concern for the common people went beyond that usually expected of a member of his social class. His concern, though, was to ensure that people who appealed for help were properly treated. It was the role of a king to see that justice was dispensed – in the absence of a monarch competent to do this, Somerset took the role upon himself. Of course, it may have been this assumption of quasi-regal power to which the councillors really objected.[17]

Throughout the Protectorate, Somerset governed in an increasingly regal manner, as was apparent in his handling of documents. Important papers would usually be authenticated by the monarch using either his signature, a stamped imprint of his signature that could be inked over, or a signet ring that left a wax impression. Understandably, Somerset would not allow Edward to sign any document unless he had previously authorised and signed it himself – a precautionary measure against anyone trying to take advantage of the king, which Thomas Seymour did attempt to do. However, Somerset would later be accused of having used the king's stamp of his own accord to authorise letters. He would also be charged with having issued orders concerning 'weighty affairs' on his own authority, under his own signature and seal without the accompanying signatures of any councillors. Since Edward was not in a position to challenge his uncle's decisions, Somerset's power was so great that he could, if he chose, govern as a king. It was an impression reinforced by his use of the royal terms of 'we' and 'our' in his letters.[18] Writing after Somerset's death, the Protestant Francis Bourgoyne told John Calvin that Somerset had been 'all but king, or rather esteemed by everyone as the king of the king'.[19]

Somerset, though, had no intention of overturning the natural order and assuming the exalted position of king. When it later became known that his brother, Thomas, sought to raise his status by marrying one of the king's sisters, Somerset was quick to remind him of his position, saying that 'neither of them was born to be king, nor to marry king's daughters'.[20] They should be satisfied, he said, with the honour and benefit they had received because their sister had married a king. Edward VI had no need to fear being usurped by his uncle.

Somerset may have had no designs on the crown but he certainly lived in a regal manner. Not only was he the most powerful man at court, he was also by far the wealthiest. In July 1547 he had awarded himself an annuity of 8,000 marks (£5,333) to cover the costs associated with his appointment as Lord Protector and Governor. This came in addition to the money he already received from other sources. The majority of his income came from lands he had inherited, acquired through his two marriages and bought or received as gifts and rewards from the king. By the end of Henry VIII's reign he had amassed land with an annual value of £4,500 and another £3,000-worth was added during Edward's reign. This, together with his annuity, gave an annual income approaching £13,000, to which was added the fees from various appointments. It is difficult to give a comparison but one estimate for the average income of peers in 1559 is £2,380.[21] By the standards of his time Somerset was very wealthy.

The new Protector was, however, adept at spending his money on a lifestyle commensurate with his position. Thynne recalled that 'he had neither money or treasure for his revenues and moneys were always spent or they were due to be paid'. In June 1545 Somerset had claimed that his financial state was so bad and his debt so large that he would either have to reduce the size of his household and live quietly for a while or sell some land. Since land was his primary source of income this course would be his last resort.[22]

During Henry VIII's reign Somerset had certainly been stretching his resources to the limit, borrowing large sums of money, probably to complete land acquisitions, and he appears to have been rather dilatory in paying his debts. Drapers' accounts in 1539 included over £80 for outstanding bills and a goldsmith, Nicholas Trapps, offered him credit after one charge was larger than Somerset had expected. Some bills suggest he was extravagant. In June 1545 he paid Peter van der Wall nearly £1,000 for several deliveries of gilt bowls and decorated cups, and two years later made similar purchases for a further £854. However, in a time when there were no banks these purchases did serve as investments. Between April 1545 and September 1548, for part of which time he was not receiving his annuity, his expenses averaged nearly £8,000 per annum. Household costs were around £2,500 each year, £618 was spent on clothes, nearly £800 was accounted for by the duchess and large sums were spent on wages, horses and building works. At the height of his ascendancy, Somerset kept 167 domestic servants in addition to a large number of people to work on his estates and a further 200 gentlemen retainers entitled to wear his livery badge. In the space of three years many of his expenses increased by over 50 per cent, except for his spending on building houses, which trebled.[23]

Somerset acquired a reputation for extravagance and nowhere was this more gloriously displayed than in his grandiose buildings. With such a large annual income he was well placed to finance a large building project but his ambitious plan to fund three such concurrent projects stretched his resources to the limit. Even his steward, John Thynne, who supervised much of the building work, believed that Somerset should cease building rather than put himself into debt.[24]

Somerset planned to build three new houses, one in London, one outside the city at Syon and the third near his home in Wiltshire. Image was an important aspect of Tudor society and these three properties were an important part of the Protector's projection of himself. Somerset Place, in particular, was intended to be the setting for his own court. One reason for establishing himself as a man of property was to emulate the image associated with men of authority who traditionally came from ancient aristocratic families. Somerset was a parvenu with no noble lineage and none of the visual signs of a long ancestry. No doubt he remembered the aspersions Norfolk and his son had cast upon the Seymours' gentry background. To establish his family as a prominent noble house he needed to be able to rival the great magnates such as the Dukes of Norfolk who held substantial inherited estates and property.

It was expected that Somerset should live in a manner appropriate to the dignity of Lord Protector but Chester Place, his existing London house, was too cramped. As was commonplace, he had quickly renamed the property after himself as a means of identifying the house and its owner, firstly as Beauchamp Place and then Somerset Place immediately following his elevation. The house was in an ideal position, on the banks of the Thames with easy access to Westminster, Whitehall and the city both by boat and on land along the Strand. However, enclosed by other properties, the site was too small for Somerset's aspirations and he set about carving out a piece of London on which to build a glorious palace. In a bid to acquire land he was ruthless in his acquisition of property and soon demolished several of the surrounding buildings – a chancery inn called Strand Inn, the inns or London lodgings of the bishops of Chester and Worcester, together with all the adjoining tenements, and the church of St Mary le Strand – to create a large house with gardens covering about 6 acres and a river frontage of around 600ft.[25]

He was equally ruthless in acquiring building materials. The steeple and most of the church of St John of Jerusalem near Smithfield was 'undermined and overthrown with gunpowder' to provide stone. Rubble was collected from the partially demolished St Paul's cloister and charnel house, the bones of the dead who had been laid to rest there being dumped unceremoniously on Finsbury field.[26] The destruction of these buildings and the desecration of human remains undoubtedly brought criticism and condemnation upon him.

Somerset Place was one of the first houses in England to incorporate the new Renaissance style that was spreading from the Continent. Although not showing the finesse of later buildings, it demonstrated the emergence of the blossoming interest in the classical style of Greece and Rome. It was an innovative design, possibly by an Italian architect, John of Padua, which demonstrated that its owner was progressive and educated. Somerset was knowledgeable about architecture and construction, albeit with regard to military fortifications, and no doubt took a close interest in the design. Thynne, who was closely involved with supervising work at two of his master's houses, also took a keen interest and later built his own grand Renaissance residence at Longleat in Wiltshire. Somerset Place was a substantial palace, two storeys high and built around two courtyards with gardens stretching down to the water's edge, and had all the usual chambers expected in such a building – great hall, presence chamber, privy chamber, withdrawing chamber, bedchamber and a long gallery.[27]

Somerset, though, was never to see or enjoy the finished palace. Letters written by him from Somerset Place show that he was living at the property while it was being built, perhaps in the original part of the building. However, a 'number of tall and comely gentlemen and yeomen' he kept as attendants had to be lodged elsewhere for lack of accommodation during the building works.[28] Somerset was executed before the palace was completed in 1553. The building passed into the hands of the crown, and the Somerset House which stands on the site today was built for George III in the late eighteenth century.

The granting of Syon Abbey to Somerset in 1547 presented an opportunity for him to create a substantial Renaissance-style mansion away from the city but close enough for quick access to the court. As with his palatial London property, Somerset had little opportunity to enjoy Syon without the chaos of building works. Because his attendance upon the king was his priority, Somerset spent only limited time at his country houses. As the king moved between his palaces of Windsor, Greenwich and Hampton Court, Somerset stayed with the court, using the queen's chambers that were prepared for him. While the court was in London, however, he was able to spend much time at Somerset Place with the duchess by his side.[29] For Anne, life at court was very different under Edward VI. As a lady-in-waiting to Henry VIII's queens she had spent much time in the queen's chambers but now there was little reason for her to be in residence except when ceremonial events or festivities took place at court.

Somerset's third proposal was for a grand new country estate at Bedwyn Brail about 3 miles east of Wulfhall.[30] The park included 109 acres of woodland and 476 acres of meadow. It was a vast scheme and for one year enormous effort was made. Two hundred and eighty workmen were involved in the project. Great quantities of stone were quarried, including 300 tons of chalk. During 1549 sufficient clay was dug for 'twenty hundred thousand' (2 million) bricks, some of which were for a water conduit. This was an impressive and progressive example of sixteenth-century engineering that diverted local streams into a covered brick-lined channel 1600ft long to transport water to the property. The scheme was a grand enterprise, intended to impress, but it came at a cost and Bryan Tesh, the clerk of the works who oversaw the building project, was very concerned at the enormous expense. As a cost-cutting measure he suggested that, rather than using quarried stone for the lowest course of the building at grass level, they should use flints that could be gathered from the estate free of charge. Like the privy councillors and the military commanders in Scotland, Tesh found Somerset difficult to work with and was reluctant to make decisions himself for fear of annoying him. Somerset took a close interest in the whole project, among other things examining samples of stone sent to him in London and selecting the gorse plants for a new warren. However, when matters in London demanded his attention and he failed to reply to Tesh's many questions, such as whether a new well should be round or square, work on the house was delayed. The clerk's frustration would not last long, however. It appears that the building never progressed further than the foundations after Somerset's downfall and there is no longer any evidence of work on the site other than the remains of the conduit.

Somerset was not alone in this visual display of wealth and many noblemen built large houses. Thomas Seymour, for example, substantially rebuilt a large property on the Strand, next door to his brother, and Lord St John built a great mansion in London and a magnificent house at Basing in Hampshire that was later described as 'the greatest of any subject's house in England, yea larger than most of the King's palaces'.[31]

What set Somerset apart from his contemporaries was not his building aspirations but the symbolism he employed in portraying his image. His seat in Parliament, his coat of arms, the use of the terms 'we' and 'our' in letters and the two gilt maces all marked Somerset with a veneer of royalty. Yet in the future it would be his building projects that would draw the greatest criticism. Somerset's schemes were considered to be excessive, and he would later be accused of extravagance and of seeking glory through building such sumptuous and costly houses. One estimate put the amount spent on Somerset Place and Syon House at £15,000.[32] Yet, why should he not have grand houses? As Paget reminded him, 'you supply the place of a king ... you are now not the Earl of Hertford, nor the Duke of Somerset'. Edward Seymour was king in all but name and could 'do his own thing as it were a king and have his majesty's absolute power'.[33] Somerset was the most important man in England, after Edward VI, and he expected to live in a manner appropriate to his position.

14

A Brother's Treason

By the end of 1548, it was not only Somerset's autocratic government which gave the privy councillors cause for concern; they had also become alarmed by his brother's behaviour, as Thomas's schemes became increasingly wild. Following his appointment as Lord Admiral, Thomas Seymour appears never again to have served at sea. In 1547, while Somerset and the army were in Scotland, Clinton was despatched to command the ships while Thomas remained in the south of England to repulse any invasion attempt by the French. It is unclear why he failed to lead the fleet the following year, but he would later be accused of making excuses or just refusing to take part.[1] In a society where great accolades were showered on military prowess, it was unusual for a man who had proved his martial skills both on land and at sea to choose not to participate, although he did continue to send orders to the fleet from the comfort of his home. Some men considered him lazy in his 'slothfulness to serve'. When asked why he declined to put himself forward, he answered that 'it was good abiding at home to make merry with one's friends in the country'.[2]

One of Thomas's responsibilities as admiral was to counter piracy around the English coast but he quickly turned the office to his own advantage. Soon after his appointment he had been ordered to intercept a pirate called Thompson who had established a base for several ships on the Scilly Isles. The pirates were to be pardoned if they surrendered voluntarily. Instead, it seems that Thomas came to an agreement with them, leaving them unmolested and offering them protection in the Admiralty courts in exchange for part of their plunder. His conduct was known to the councillors, yet they appear to have taken no action despite complaints against him. In April 1548 goods seized by English pirates from Spanish vessels were found in his house but when van der Delft complained of this Paget's only response was that Seymour had been 'a great rascal'.[3]

Somerset, too, failed to take any decisive action. When merchants complained that they received no justice against the pirates because of Thomas's overbearing control of the courts and his use of corrupt judges, Somerset imprisoned one of the judges. His only punishment of Thomas was to chastise him in the tone of an elder brother remonstrating with a younger sibling who needed guidance. Nevertheless, in a letter appealing to him to redress earlier faulty judgements and ensure that in future justice was dispensed in a more upright manner, there is a hint that Somerset had become weary of the complaints against his brother.[4]

There was one reason why Thomas may have been reluctant to serve with the fleet in 1548 – Katherine was pregnant. On 9 June he wrote to his wife that he hoped recent French hostilities would not prevent him spending time with her at Sudeley Castle where Katherine was to lie in while she waited for the birth. Concerned for her well-being, he offered the advice to 'keep the little knave so lean and gaunt with your good diet and walking that he may be so small that he may creep out of a mouse hole'. His delight at the news that Katherine could feel the 'little man' moving was heightened further by the idea that one day his son would revenge the wrongs done to them by Somerset.[5]

But Thomas was to be disappointed in his hope for a son. His 'pretty' daughter, Mary, was born on 30 August. His disappointment was shared by his brother, who believed 'it would have been, both to us, and, as we suppose also to you a more joy and comfort if it had been this the first a son'. A son and heir was of primary importance to perpetuate the family name and, despite the friendly terms in which the letter was written, it may have served to increase Thomas's envy of his brother. Only a few weeks earlier Somerset had become father to another son, also named Edward, who was to be the king's godson.[6] Sadly, any hope of future sons for Thomas was dashed when Katherine died only six days later, most probably after developing puerperal fever, and was buried at Sudeley. She was only 36 and after four marriages died giving birth to her first child. Thomas was overcome at his wife's death – 'so amazed, that I had small regard either to myself or my doings' – but soon recovered and within two weeks was planning how to maintain the large household the couple had kept together.[7]

After Katherine's death her cousin, Sir Nicholas Throckmorton, hoped that Thomas would change his attitude towards his brother. Encouraging him to be more humble towards Somerset, Throckmorton offered the advice that if he were 'either wise or politic he would become a new manner of man both in heart and service'. He condemned Thomas for both his laziness and his 'greediness to get' and recommended that he should 'alter his manners, for the

1. Edward Seymour, Duke of Somerset, Lord Protector of England.

2. Jane Seymour. Although Jane was queen for less than eighteen months, she gave Henry VIII the greatest gift of all: a son and heir.

3. Henry Howard, Earl of Surrey. This image of a casually dressed man belies the truth; Surrey was an arrogant, haughty man whose excessive pride led to his downfall.

Edward Prince of Wales

4. Prince Edward, the child who changed Edward Seymour's fortune. Edward was the first heir to the throne to receive an education to fit him for the role of king.

5. William Paget. Ambitious for power, Paget held great influence first as secretary to Henry VIII and later as adviser to Somerset.

THE PROCESSION OF KING EDWARD VI.
FROM THE TOWER OF LONDON TO WESTMINSTER, FEB. XIX, MDXLVII, PREVIOUS TO HIS CORONATION.
ENGRAVED FROM A COEVAL PAINTING AT COWDRAY IN SUSSEX, THE SEAT OF LORD VISCOUNT MONTAGUE.

6. The coronation procession of Edward VI. Along the procession route the houses are hung with banners, and people crowd at the windows and on the rooftops to watch the king pass by.

7. William Parr was neither particularly ambitious nor politically astute, but his alliance with John Dudley brought him both land and a position as Lord Great Chamberlain. However, his later support for Lady Jane Grey led to a charge of treason in Mary's reign.

8. John Dudley. A Machiavellian character, Dudley was a ruthless opponent of the Lord Protector. He led the *coup d'état* that deposed Somerset, and finally brought him down by fabricating evidence against him.

9. Thomas Cranmer, Archbishop of Canterbury. Cranmer's success in advancing the Edwardian Reformation was only possible because of the support he received from the Duke of Somerset and, later, the Duke of Northumberland.

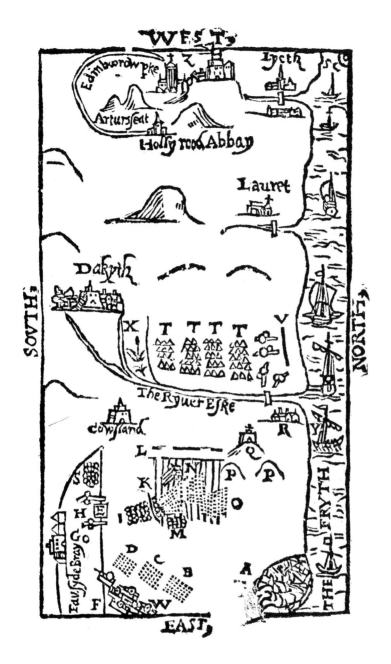

10. The Battle of Pinkie Cleugh. The troops are positioned ready for the battle.

Key: B, C, D: English troops.
G: Duke of Somerset watching from the hilltop.
H: English guns.
M, N, O: Scottish army.
T: Scottish tents.
Y: English galley with other English ships in the Firth of Forth.
Z: Edinburgh Castle.

11. Thomas Seymour. A man of action whose ambition led to his downfall and execution – yet his expectation to be Governor of the King did have precedent in earlier minority reigns. This portrait was painted by Nicholas Denisot, who taught French to Somerset's daughters.

KATHARINE PARRE

12. Katherine Parr had been widowed twice before her marriage to Henry VIII. She wed Thomas Seymour early in Edward VI's reign but died a year later following the birth of her only child.

13. Edward VI in Parliament. The young king sits upon his chair of state. On the left-hand side sit the bishops and on the right are the lords; two clerks rest upon the woolsack as they record the proceedings.

14. King Edward VI. On the threshold of becoming king, Edward is portrayed in the familiar pose adopted by his father. Although he was still only 9 years old his direct look, his stance and his wide-shouldered gown were intended to project an image of strength and authority.

A defcription of Maifter Latimer, preaching before Kyng Edward the fyxt, in the preachyng place at Weftminfter.

K. Edward.

M. Latimer.

15. Bishop Latimer preaching. Latimer stands in the covered pulpit erected in the privy garden of Whitehall Palace; Somerset and Edward VI are listening at the window on the left-hand side.

The Lady Mary after Queen.

16. Princess Mary. Throughout Edward's reign Mary steadfastly refused to accept the new prayer book and she quickly re-introduced Catholicism to England upon her accession.

17. Princess Elizabeth. Painted shortly before Edward VI's accession, this shows Elizabeth aged 13, a few months before she refused Thomas Seymour's proposal of marriage. As queen she would later carry forward the establishment of the Anglican Church begun by the Duke of Somerset.

18. Sir William Sharington used his position as treasurer of the Bristol mint to defraud the king of nearly £4,000. He also agreed that he could mint £10,000 in coins for Thomas Seymour to fund his own personal army.

William Sharinton

19. King Edward VI and the pope. An allegory of the Reformation: Henry VIII indicates his successor, Edward VI, at whose feet the pope is crushed by an English Bible. Somerset stands beside Edward as Archbishop Cranmer and John Dudley sit upon the bench.

20. The Tower of London. Somerset lived in the Tower on three occasions: before Edward VI's coronation and twice as a prisoner. However, he never entered the fortress through Traitors' Gate, which can be seen in front of the Tower.

21. Richard Rich. As Lord Chancellor, Rich was able to promote Somerset's policies. Known for having given evidence against both Sir Thomas More and Thomas Cromwell, in 1549 he also turned against the Lord Protector.

22. Sir Philip Hoby. An administrator who served as resident ambassador to Emperor Charles V; his brief return to England in 1549 enabled him to act as negotiator between Somerset and the privy council during the *coup d'état*.

Phillip Hobbie Knight

23. 'Ceirtein pointes of waighty matters'. Originally intended as a reminder for the privy council to decide the punishment for Somerset's accomplices, the insertion of a few words changed this to an order for the council to decide on Somerset's execution.

Ceirtein pointes of waighty matters to be immediatly concluded on by my counsell. 18. Januarij. 1551°.

1 The conclusion for the payment of our dettis in February next comming.

2 The matter for the stiliard to be so considerid that it may be to our profit, and wealth of our subiectis.

3 The matter for the duke of Somersetes confederates to be considered as aparteineth to our suretey, and quietnes of our realme, that by there punishement and his execution according to the lawes, example may be shewed to others.

4 The resolution for the bishops that be nominatid.

24. Somerset's final devotions. Inscribed inside an almanac, these may have been the last words he wrote. Poignantly, the final words read: 'frome the toware the day before my deth 1551. E. Somerset'.

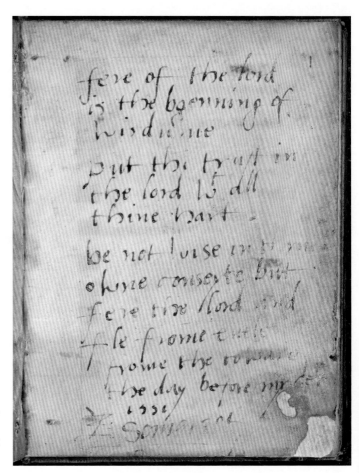

25. The Duke of Somerset's execution. Somerset met his death bravely; in his execution speech he claimed that his reform of the Church was the achievement of which he was most proud.

The D. of Somerset L. Protector Beheaded

world beginneth to talk very unfavourably of him'.[8] In a world where success often depended on supporters, men were wary of greed and ambition. Thomas risked antagonising his friends and leaving himself isolated.

Still smarting from his failure to gain any authority over the young king, Thomas continued scheming to wheedle his way further into his nephew's affections and increase his influence over the boy. Aware of Edward's lack of money to reward men for their services, Thomas used Fowler as a go-between, sending coins whenever the king asked. On one occasion Edward needed money to give to Bishop Latimer as a reward for preaching. Thomas sent £20 for the bishop with a further £20 for the king to distribute among his servants. Another gift of money for Edward was accompanied by £20 to solicit the support of John Cheke.[9] Both Thomas and Fowler knew Somerset would be annoyed at their scheming and Fowler, referring obliquely to the king as 'my friend', begged the admiral to destroy his letter so that it 'shall tell no more tales after your reading'.[10]

Such attention from his younger uncle was probably a novelty to the king. Edward had been brought up by attendants and his governess, Lady Margaret Bryan, but he had lacked the close familial attention and affection of his parents. Somerset failed to treat his nephew with tenderness. He was stern and lacking in affection towards him and this made it easier for Thomas to work against his brother. Having failed to increase his own power, he resolved to reduce Somerset's. Henry VIII had intended his son to take control when he reached his 18th birthday but Thomas encouraged Edward to assume power earlier, which would effectively reduce Somerset to being chief councillor. It was a plan that would be easier to execute since the issue of the letters patent by Parliament. These had given the king authority to remove Somerset from his post as Protector at any time. However, the king would not be party to such a ploy. When Thomas tried to persuade Edward to speak up for himself and not be 'too bashful' in matters, the young boy replied that he was 'well enough'. Thomas suggested that within two years Edward might start to take a part in government for 'your uncle is old and I trust will not live long'. Edward responded abruptly: 'It were better for him to die before'.[11] It was a damning verdict on their relationship. There was little love between the king and the governor of his royal person.

Somerset had no control over his brother as his intrigues became even wilder. By late November 1548, as members gathered for the second session of Parliament, many of Thomas's friends were aware of his scheming and especially of his intentions towards Princess Elizabeth. Elizabeth had been removed from Katherine's household a few weeks before the dowager queen's death, possibly after Katherine one day came upon the young princess in her husband's arms.[12] Whatever the reason, soon after Katherine died rumours started that Thomas was intent on marrying one of the king's sisters. Riding to Parliament one morning, Thomas fell into conversation with Lord Russell and their talk touched upon gossip that the Lord Admiral intended to marry either Princess Mary or Princess Elizabeth. Russell warned him against this but Thomas denied the rumour. However, two or three days later, as they again rode to Parliament, Thomas questioned Russell why he should not marry one of the princesses. On another occasion he asked what Russell would think if Thomas were to rise above him. This was too much and Russell reported the conversations to Lord Rich.[13]

Thomas's servants were aware of his talk and tried to dissuade him from such a course. Yet he already knew his scheming would probably fail. He admitted to Thomas Parry, Elizabeth's cofferer, that the marriage was unlikely to happen because his brother would never agree to it. Parry recollected that Thomas had become angry and stammered, saying 'I am kept back or under, or such like words'.[14] Like his brother, Thomas Seymour could be very single-minded and failed to recognise when he should give up a scheme.

Without doubt, there was good cause for the rumours. Thomas's earlier proposal to Elizabeth, his behaviour with her under his own roof, his interest in the size of her marriage dowry and his talk with Russell all gave credence to the story. Both Elizabeth and Thomas vehemently denied the accusation of any impropriety between them and Elizabeth became furious at the suggestion that she was expecting his child. While she may have been flattered by his flirtation she retained her view of him as a 'disinterested person', knowing that the council would be unlikely to consent to a marriage between them.[15] Somerset was increasingly concerned at his brother's behaviour, advising him against this folly. By the end of the year he even resorted to threatening to clap him in the Tower if he visited Elizabeth.[16]

Thomas talked in a similarly careless manner with other lords. Dorset, Northampton, Clinton, Rutland and Southampton would all later remember conversations with him as they rode to and from Parliament or when they visited him at Seymour Place.[17] He spoke openly against Somerset, voicing his annoyance with his brother for denying him greater authority and talking of his plan for the king to assume control before the appointed time. Most worrying, and somewhat sinister, was his boasting to Dorset and Rutland about how many friends he could call upon and his encouragement for them to increase their own power base by building up a large retinue of trustworthy gentlemen and yeomen. He even advised Dorset to cultivate their friendship by taking gifts of wine and venison and dining with them. Worried at the breach between the brothers and concerned at what Thomas might be planning, his friends could only try to discourage him from any attempt to wrest power from Somerset.

Council members had known for many months of Thomas's ambitious ideas but since nothing had come of his plans no action had been taken. However, early in the Parliament, as rumours of his intention to marry Elizabeth became more widespread, the extent of his scheming became apparent during an investigation into Sir William Sharington, the vice-treasurer of the mint at Bristol. At the beginning of January 1549 an inquiry was made into possible fraud by Sharington after it was suspected 'that more money hath been made than doth appear by the indentures and books of account'.[18] Sharington was found guilty of debasing currency by lessening the quantity of bullion he used in coins and of keeping the surplus. During the investigation it also became apparent that he had been working with Thomas who was in debt to him for nearly £3,000. Sharington admitted that they had discussed whether he would be able to make £10,000 in coins for Thomas, the amount they had calculated would be sufficient to support an army of 10,000 for a month.[19] This news, taken together with Thomas's boasting about how many men he could raise, gave the councillors good reason to believe that he was planning to raise an army against Somerset.

On 11 January Somerset called his brother to appear before him. Thomas, aware that questions were being asked about him, was suspicious of the purpose of the meeting and asked if it could be postponed until the following day and held in the presence of the council. He believed that his brother 'should do me wrong' and wanted witnesses for their discussion.[20] Late at night on 16 January matters took a turn for the worse for Thomas when Henry Manners, Earl of Rutland, gave evidence against him to Somerset. Matters looked bleak and, aware that he might be imprisoned, Thomas sent a message that he would question Rutland and answer any charges before the council as long as he was at liberty but that he would answer nothing if he was imprisoned.[21]

The following day Somerset and the council decided they had sufficient evidence against Thomas to commit him to the Tower. There were many accusations against him: firstly, of wanting to take control of the king and inducing him to write letters to Parliament in support of his bid for authority. Thomas had threatened to make the 'blackest parliament' and bribed the men of the privy chamber. There had been talk of his plan to arrange the king's marriage to Jane Grey and of his own attempt to marry Elizabeth.[22] None of this was new but the other 'diverse' points against him which had recently come to light were just too serious to be overlooked. The councillors could not ignore his association with Sharington and the possibility that he had been conspiring to raise a large force.

Most startlingly, there was talk that he had planned to 'dispose' of the king. Thomas had complained to Fowler that the young king was so poorly protected, that a man might 'steal' him away. After Thomas's arrest there was a rumour, which appears to have been more commonplace around the courts of Europe than in England, that Thomas had attempted to enter the king's bedchamber late at night, with the intention of abducting him. It was reported that he had startled the royal pet dog, which he had shot and killed.[23] Courtly gossip soon exaggerated this to an attempt to murder the king.

Thomas was arrested on 17 January and taken to the Tower. The day after his incarceration the Lord Admiral's signet was taken from his secretary and men were sent to make inventories of all the goods in his houses and at the foundries he kept in Sussex. His man, Harrington, was sent to the Tower, followed the next day by Sharington and Fowler and then by two of Elizabeth's servants, Sir Thomas Parry and Mistress Ashley. All the prisoners and many of Thomas's associates, including several privy councillors, were examined in an attempt to build a case against him. It may have been a coincidence but on 23 January the council issued a proclamation prohibiting the carrying of weapons or wearing of armour within 3 miles of the court. Although the document referred to soldiers recently returned from the Scottish borders the council may have been taking precautions in case Thomas really had raised a private army.

On 25 January, Russell, Southampton (readmitted to the council) and Petre interrogated Thomas. He admitted that he had encouraged the king to take the reins of government early, when Somerset should stand aside to be just the chief councillor, but he would admit to no other charges. For over three weeks Thomas languished in the Tower. It would have been an unpleasant experience as the cold and wet of a London winter seeped into his chambers. A small log fire was little comfort against bare, damp walls and he was cut off from life in the outside world. Like many prisoners before him, he found he had few true friends as men were quick to dissociate themselves from a prisoner in the Tower for fear of sharing his fate. Thomas, however, was confident of his own innocence and that no great harm would come to him. With the bravado of a pirate, he boasted to his servant, Harrington, 'I am sure I can have no hurt, if they do me right. They can not kill me, except they do me wrong: and if they do, I shall die but once.'[24]

As the days passed Thomas became anxious, wondering why there was no message from the council. At last, on 18 February, a delegation of noblemen visited him before dinner and, after being questioned, Thomas felt in 'better cheer' believing that the answers he had given would satisfy them.[25] But it was not to be. By 22 February Somerset and the council had gathered sufficient evidence to charge him with high treason. The following day Rich, with most of the councillors, rode to the Tower to speak to Thomas. Somerset did not accompany them. In a chamber at the side of the king's gallery, Rich read out thirty-three charges against Thomas and gave him an opportunity to either deny them or to offer excuses for his behaviour. The council appear to have believed that quantity might achieve what quality could not. Many concerned Thomas's marital advances and his intentions regarding control of the king; several regarded his conspiracies with pirates, while others related to his attempts to garner support amongst the nobility, raise 10,000 supporters and provision a castle on the Welsh borders to sustain such a force.[26]

To what extent Thomas was guilty of all of the charges is questionable. He had married Katherine and made approaches to Elizabeth. He had given money to the king and tried to gain some control over his nephew. He had consorted with pirates. But some of the crimes of which he was accused were just the talk of a man who had big ideas that he failed to put into action, a man who felt belittled by his brother and was constantly striving to achieve the precedence he believed was his right.

Thomas refused to comment on the charges unless faced by his accusers or in a trial. On the next day, 24 February, Somerset listened as the councillors reported the details of their meeting with his brother and they decided to seek the king's consent to proceed further in the matter. After dinner the men made their way to the king's chambers where, after Rich had read out the charges, each councillor gave his view. Somerset was the last to speak, declaring that he would not think himself worthy to live if he had committed such offences against the king. Thomas's behaviour, he said, was a great sorrow to him and he had done all he could to stop matters reaching this point. His first duty, he acknowledged, was to the king and crown rather than to his own brother and he agreed not to oppose the councillors' decisions. Somerset was washing his hands of his brother and, on this occasion, following the will of the council. The king gave the councillors permission to continue and it was agreed that Thomas would be charged with treason and tried by attainder.[27] This was a parliamentary procedure where the evidence would be heard by the lords in Parliament but Thomas would be unable to present a defence. The judges who had decided in what manner Thomas should be charged had considered whether he should be tried in court but Sir Edward Montagu, the chief judge, was worried that, if he was found guilty and executed, the king might later lay the blame for his death on the judges. It would be better, he decided, for all the lords in Parliament to carry responsibility for Thomas's death.[28]

In a final attempt to resolve the matter before it went to Parliament, Thomas was given a last opportunity to defend himself. Rich, Warwick, Shrewsbury and Southampton, together with four representatives of the lower parliamentary house, went straight to the Tower where, after much persuasion, Thomas gave answers to the first three charges. He admitted that he would have liked to have the king in his custody and had told Fowler how Edward could be brought secretly to his house but he insisted that he never meant to harm his nephew. He also admitted giving money to the king and to Fowler and that he had planned for Edward to write a letter to Parliament supporting his bid to have the 'governance' of him. He would admit to nothing else and, after he refused to answer any more questions unless it was before a jury, the councillors returned to report the meeting to Somerset.[29]

The decision to proceed had been taken and the council lost no time. The following day Somerset sat in his chair of state in Parliament as the bill of attainder against his brother was read out, the evidence heard and the bill passed. The following day he heard it read and passed a second time but at the third reading, on 27 February, he asked 'for natural pity's sake' to be absent.[30] Although he is recorded as being present it is probable that he left the chamber after attending to the other business to avoid witnessing the vote which would send Thomas to the block. On that day the name of Lord Seymour of Sudeley was removed from the list of lords eligible to be called to Parliament.

The lords immediately sent the bill down to the lower house with the offer that the noblemen who had given evidence against Thomas would declare it likewise to the commons. There was much debate in the lower house, with many men arguing that it was wrong to find a man guilty without allowing him to make his own defence. As already mentioned, the strong support for Thomas among the commons may have been due to the large number of members who owed their places to his patronage. Eventually they asked for Thomas to appear before them, a request which the king, on the advice of his councillors, declined. On 4 March, after four days of discussion and with the lower house being 'marvellous full' with nearly 400 people, the attainder for treason against him was passed with only ten or twelve dissenting voices. The following day the bill for the attainder was passed by the Lords.[31]

On Sunday 10 March Somerset met the privy councillors at Westminster to consider how the case should proceed. Late that morning, after dinner, they presented themselves before the king to explain the seriousness of the charges against Thomas and to convince Edward to agree to his uncle's execution. His treason had been so dangerous to both the king and the country, they agreed, that he must be punished. However, since 'the case was so heavy and lamentable' to the Lord Protector, they proposed that they should proceed 'without further troubling or molesting' either Somerset or the king.[32] Perhaps, too, there was some fear among the councillors that as the dread moment of Thomas's execution neared Somerset might lose heart and try to save his brother, or that the king might choose to spare his uncle. The following Sunday Somerset did not attend the council meeting when Rich and the other councillors agreed that Thomas should be executed three days later. The council record authorising the execution is signed by fourteen councillors and foremost among the names is that of Somerset. However, his signature has been written in a different ink to the other signatures and was probably added after the event, possibly because the severity of the decision warranted the approval of the most powerful councillor.[33]

On the morning of Wednesday 20 March, Thomas Seymour, aged 40 and one of the most ambitious men at court, walked out of the Tower up to Tower Hill, his dreams in tatters. Yet, even until the end, he may still have been scheming. Bishop Latimer asserted that, during his last days in the Tower, Thomas had taken an aglet from a point of his hose and made ink in 'some crafty way' and penned two tiny letters to the Princesses Mary and Elizabeth. These suggested that Somerset wanted to deprive them of their place in the succession and encouraged them to conspire against him. The letters were sewn between the soles of one of his velvet shoes where they could be retrieved by his servant after his death. The story may have been a fabrication since it is possible that Latimer had been instructed to preach against Thomas. If that was the case, his condemnation of the admiral as 'a man the farthest from the fear of God that ever I knew' was also probably intended to blacken his reputation even further.[34]

With two strokes of the axe Thomas's head was severed from his body. His separated head and body were carried back into the Tower where they were buried. There seems to have been little sadness at his death. His nephew, the king, who featured so largely in his downfall, recorded simply that 'the Lord Sudeley, Admiral of England, was condemned to death and died the March ensuing'.[35] Princess Elizabeth, upon hearing of his death, remarked 'this day died a man with much wit, and very little judgement', but some years later she did accept the gift of a portrait of him.[36] Perhaps the person who showed most regret was Somerset. When she became queen, Elizabeth recalled him saying that if Thomas had been allowed to speak to him he would never have died. Somerset may have believed his position was insecure while his brother was alive, but the suggestion that his wife had told him that 'if your brother does not die he will be your death' was probably intended to discredit Anne.[37]

It might have been better for Somerset if he had spoken with his brother and so prevented the execution. Fratricide was seen by many as an unnatural act, and his part in the affair damaged Somerset's reputation. He may not have participated in the final vote in Parliament but he, too, held responsibility for his brother's death. He wielded more power than any other man in England and could have stopped the proceedings or at least ensured that Thomas was not charged with treason. He examined the evidence, agreed with the councillors to proceed against Thomas and attended the privy council meetings where the charges had been agreed. He sat in Parliament while the charges were read. Perhaps on this occasion he was reluctant to stand alone against the decision of all the lords; there was undoubtedly an overwhelming agreement in Parliament that Thomas was guilty and deserved to be executed.

Thomas Seymour was condemned to die yet an alternative punishment might have been imprisonment in the Tower. Although several of the charges against him were for acts of treason, he had not carried them out. Only his plan to marry Katherine had been put into action. He never intended to harm the king and he lacked sufficient support to be a real threat to his brother. All he wanted was greater authority in recognition of his relationship to the king – and by historical precedent, it was a reasonable expectation. His behaviour was, though, inappropriate for a man in his position and it dishonoured the king.

He was refused the opportunity to defend himself in open trial, yet all the privy councillors, the Lords and most of the Commons voted for his execution. Did they really believe him guilty of the crimes or was this an indication of his unpopularity or the fear that he might commit treason in the future? One commentator believed 'his climbing high disdained by his peers was thought the cause he liv'd not out his years ... Thus guiltless he, through malice, went to pot'.[38]

The one person who might have lamented his passing in years to come, and who might have avenged the wrongs which aggrieved Thomas, was his daughter Mary. After her father's death the child, now an orphan, lived for a short time at Syon House under the protection of Somerset before being removed to the care of the Duchess of Suffolk. Somerset, though, was slow to arrange for the payment of a pension for the girl's upkeep, and for the transfer of nursery items from Syon, which left the duchess short of money to pay the child's servants.[39] During the Parliament which began in the November following Thomas's death Mary was granted restitution in blood, restoring her legal rights which had been forfeited by her father's attainder, and removing any taint from her name. But that is the last we hear of her and it appears that she died before reaching adulthood.

15

From Triumph to Dissent

Parliament had been adjourned on 14 March, six days before Thomas Seymour's execution, after a momentous session in which agreement had been reached on the form of the first English prayer book. By late summer 1548 Somerset and Cranmer had been preparing to codify England's religion. Their reforms so far had been piecemeal, creating a hotchpotch of the old religion with the new ideas. They were determined to instil uniformity through one doctrinal interpretation of faith and one authorised service. This would also remove the anomalies that existed throughout England where, over the centuries, variations in worship had developed. The differing beliefs among the reformers had further widened the spectrum of religious ideas in England. Somerset was aware of the need for religious unity within the country – in 1549 he would blame the riots in Cornwall on 'all these divergencies in religion' – but Catholicism was deeply ingrained in English culture and would not be easy to erase.[1]

Although the new prayer book was primarily Cranmer's work, there can be no doubt that Somerset agreed with its contents. It was to need the skills of both men to create this book – the ideas and theological knowledge of Cranmer and the authority of Somerset. Although the Protector claimed that he and the council were continuing the work that Henry VIII had begun, Somerset allowed Cranmer the freedom of expression which he had never enjoyed under Henry. Undoubtedly Cranmer was the driving force behind the creation of this book and it was due to him that the work received such extensive consultation. During the autumn, in a bid to ease the path of their proposals through Parliament, Cranmer had consulted the bishops about the new prayer book. Although there were aspects of the service about which they had concerns, all the bishops, except George Day, Bishop of Chichester, agreed to the proposals in the expectation that contentious issues might be resolved in Parliament. Unlike earlier religious policy that had been enforced through proclamation, often after only council consideration, the prayer book was to receive widespread debate and would carry the full weight of parliamentary authority.

Parliament had reopened on 24 November and at 10 a.m. on Saturday 15 December the lords and bishops began to discuss the Act for Uniformity of Service that would define the beliefs to be enshrined in the prayer book. It was the most important piece of legislation enacted during Somerset's Protectorate and the one that would have the most enduring effect. The session was well attended – eighteen of the twenty-six bishops were present and thirty-two of the forty-five peers. Somerset acted as moderator and opened the debate by proposing that the lords and bishops should first discuss 'whether bread be in the sacrament after the consecration or not'.[2] Although it was an open discussion, the participants were primarily the bishops. Somerset oversaw the proceedings, ensuring that they adhered to the agreed topics and that the arguments were based upon scripture and 'ancient' writers rather than upon the works of recent reformers such as Erasmus.

Tunstall led the dispute on the Catholic side but when he attempted to move the discussion to other aspects of the mass Somerset promptly reminded him that they had agreed only to discuss the consecration at that point. Thomas Smith attended the proceedings as secretary but his interjections that the idea of Christ's body being in the bread was loathsome and that 'it is more horrible to eat flesh than to break it' can only have served to annoy the Catholic bishops. On Monday Somerset opened the debate by reprimanding Bishop Thirlby for his ill-conceived comments on the Saturday when the bishop had claimed that he had never agreed to the proposed doctrine. Somerset reminded the gathering that the details they were discussing had not been agreed by the bishops but only put forward for consideration and Bishop Day had been alone in voting against the proposals. The earlier consultation, he continued, had been intended to establish limited unity before the matter was presented to Parliament and he expected the bishops to accept a majority vote in the same way as the privy councillors did. The debate became increasingly heated as Thirlby made further objections. He argued that he could not support the proposal to abolish the adoration and elevation of the bread and claimed that the word 'oblation' had been removed from the service after the bishops had agreed the book's content. This was too much for Somerset, who responded angrily, objecting to Thirlby's 'vehement sayings' and accusing him of being wilful and obstinate yet not presenting any proof to sustain his argument. Quoting from scripture Somerset referred to Christ's commandment that whenever they should eat bread and drink wine it was as a memorial of his sacrifice. His views on the significance of the mass were clear as he asked the gathering: 'Who can take this otherwise but there is bread still?'

After four days of dispute the discussion closed on Wednesday and the Act for Uniformity was passed to the Commons for their deliberation. On 15 January 1549 the Lords voted to accept the act and the Commons followed suit a few days later. Three noblemen – Derby, Dacre and Windsor – together with eight of the twenty bishops present voted against the bill.[3] Somerset and Cranmer did not have complete support but it was a resounding victory. Later in the year, Somerset no doubt took pleasure in pointing out to Cardinal Pole that the content of the new prayer book had been reached by the agreement of the most learned men in England and with the consent of both houses of Parliament.[4] Of all the religious reforms Somerset supported, this received the most widespread consultation. It is notable that when the council would later bring various charges against him, none concerned the changes of religion. It was one of the few areas of major policy where he enjoyed the long-term support of the councillors.

England now had a single prayer book, *The Book of the Common Prayer and Administration of the Sacrament*. It contained a clearly defined doctrine and patterns of worship that included the complete order of the services for all occasions including Holy Communion, morning prayer, evening prayer and occasional services such as marriage, baptism and funeral. For the first time uniformity was to be introduced in all churches throughout England. The book was nevertheless a compromise, intended to be acceptable to both reformers and Catholics. While much of the content was familiar – the order of the Eucharist remained unchanged – the use of English and the lack of a sense of adoration had removed much of the former mysticism. However, the consecration remained, and, although the concept of sacrifice was absent from the text, the words could be interpreted, as indeed they were by Gardiner, to imply transubstantiation.

It remained to be seen whether everyone would accept the new prayer book. Somerset had no wish to force men to participate in a service they abhorred and it was decreed that, at the time of communion, those who wished to partake should remain within the choir while others could leave before the bread and wine were placed upon the altar. Ministers, though, were given no such freedom. Those who failed to use the book were threatened with deprivation and imprisonment. In an attempt to prevent opposition and encourage conformity, the act included stringent penalties against people who decried the prayer book through plays and songs or who tried to prevent clerics using the book.

Somerset and Cranmer had achieved much of what they wanted, a simpler service with no superstition presented in a language that people could understand. It was a remarkable and long-lasting achievement. With this prayer book and their earlier reforms, the two men had laid the foundations of the Protestant Church in England. *The Book of Common Prayer* was a precursor to that of 1662 which has been used throughout England for over 300 years and still underpins the order of service used in Anglican churches throughout the world today.

The first prayer book may have been prepared by Cranmer but it was due to Somerset that it became enshrined in law. This momentous piece of legislation was not enacted by the Church or by a powerful monarch but by the bishops and men of Parliament in the name of a child king. It came into being not with the religious authority of Church convocations but on the legal authority of Parliament. Somerset had gone even further than Henry VIII by using Parliament to change religious doctrine in an act that was his most outstanding achievement.

Yet had he been pushed further along the path of reform than he had intended? Somerset did intimate to van der Delft that this was the case but that it had been necessary in order to stop the extreme religious sects that were springing up. He may have allowed himself to be coerced into greater reform by Cranmer as the best means of creating a unified religion and achieving religious stability in the country but this prayer book was as far as his moderate beliefs would allow him to go. There were some men who certainly believed that Somerset had achieved as much as he wanted. Both Francis Burgoyne and John Knox would later suggest that he had become lukewarm with regard to religion and Knox commented that Somerset had become 'so cold in hearing God's word' that he preferred to visit the masons at work on his buildings rather than listen to a sermon.[5]

The country had taken a major step along the road towards a Protestant Church of England but distributing the new prayer book would not alone be sufficient. People needed to be encouraged to use and understand it. The country needed more preachers and numerous and generous stipends were granted to encourage theology students. Somerset was fearful that people would be alienated by too much change introduced too quickly so vestments continued to be worn by the clergy. Candles, commemoration for the dead and chrism oil were also retained but this was to be only for a short time until people had become accustomed to the changes.

When the new prayer book came into use in June 1549 the privy council was forced to deal with Bishop Edmund Bonner and Princess Mary, two of the most prominent opponents of the religious reforms. After his release from the Fleet, Bonner had obeyed the edicts on religion even, probably reluctantly, ordering the use of the new prayer book within his diocese of London. As the summer months passed the councillors became concerned that some people in the city continued to use the Catholic services. They ordered Bonner to preach a sermon denouncing this and touching upon other issues dictated by them. However, when he took the stand at Paul's Cross he did as Gardiner had done and ignored the council's instructions. Instead he preached about transubstantiation, refused to confirm that Edward's power as king was undiminished during his minority and failed to denounce the rebellion against religious reform that was then taking place in the west of the country. The council was furious and after a series of hearings Bonner was committed to the Marshalsea and, like Gardiner, spent the remainder of Edward's reign imprisoned. Unlike Gardiner's downfall, Bonner's was sudden and it may be that Gardiner's behaviour was tolerated for so long because Somerset favoured him on account of their long friendship. A few weeks after his imprisonment Bonner spoke out vehemently against Somerset, accusing him of being one of 'my deadly enemies' who had in 'sundry ways studied and laboured my ruin and destruction'.[6]

Mary was decidedly more difficult to deal with. Somerset had always had a good relationship with her and she was a friend to his wife, referring to her as 'my good Nann'.[7] He was, though, acutely aware that Mary was Edward's sister and heir to the throne. Although Edward was young and healthy there was always the possibility that one day Mary might be queen, so it would not do to alienate her. Since her brother's accession, Somerset had permitted Mary to worship as she thought fit but with the embodiment of the new doctrine into law she expected to be pressurised to conform. Mary was determined not to give way, claiming that she would not change her religion until Edward came of age and could decide for himself. It was a stance that her cousin, the Emperor Charles, supported.

In May, Somerset told van der Delft that he would not inquire into how Mary chose to worship, thus allowing her the same freedom she already enjoyed. This situation might have continued unchallenged if the emperor had not pressed Somerset for a written assurance, claiming that a verbal promise did not ensure her future safety from reprisals. Somerset refused to give one. He believed that if Mary was seen to have official permission to follow a different religion to the king, it could lead to dissent within the kingdom. Although he was prepared to be tolerant, his first loyalty was to Edward and there was a warning in his words that he would continue to favour her in 'everything that is not prejudicial to the king'.[8] It was clear that if Mary's religious practice should have any consequences for Edward, Somerset might turn against her.

Somerset's continued tolerance of Mary and his unwillingness to restrain her or many other Catholics prompted the reformer John ab Ulmis to comment 'that he was of a more gentle and pliant nature in religious matters, than was befitting a nobleman possessed of so much authority'.[9] In some men's opinions, Somerset did not always exhibit the strength expected of a leader and this was one of his greatest failings as Lord Protector. His lack of ruthlessness and his mildness of character were considered to be inappropriate in a man ruling with the power of a king. However, in the case of Mary, Somerset's tolerance was partially dictated by the need to remain on friendly terms with the emperor.[10]

The prayer book came into official use on 9 June and three days later Rich and Petre visited Mary, ostensibly to discuss the possibility of a marriage with Don Luis of Portugal. However, before they left they also reminded her that the new law ordered everyone to conform in religion. Despite Somerset's concession to Mary, which had been made only the previous month, it appears that the councillors were losing patience. As England began to use the new prayer book, Mary clung resolutely to the mass. The following month the council began to put pressure on her servants to persuade her to conform to the king's laws and celebrate the new communion service.[11] The difficulty had arisen because whereas before the reforms Mary had heard mass twice a day, now it was three times and with greater ceremony. In July Somerset explained to van der Delft that although he must enforce the king's laws he had not forbidden Mary to hear mass privately in her own chamber. He was doing his best to be tolerant and leave her in peace – if she did not wish to conform, he insisted, she might do as she pleased but do so 'quietly and without scandal'.[12] One of his primary concerns must have been that Mary could become a focus for religious discontent, particularly for the Catholics in the West Country who were naming the new prayer book as one reason for inciting rebellion.

In early September, St John and Paget reiterated Somerset's promise to van der Delft that, since they all wished to avoid discord and as Mary was heir to the throne, she could continue to hear mass as she was accustomed. However, the emperor again asked for this undertaking in writing, claiming that councillors had previously broken their promises and if St John and Paget were absent the others might not feel bound to abide by it. Having hoped that his earlier response to Mary would satisfy the emperor, Somerset was greatly annoyed by Charles' reply and accused him of making 'a reflection upon his honour' by suggesting that he would break such a promise.[13]

However, Somerset's promise would soon become irrelevant. His lenient approach to Mary was just one of many issues that put him out of step with the other councillors and in particular with Warwick. Within a few weeks Somerset would no longer be in power and Mary's case would wait until Warwick could deal with her more firmly. For a time the subject of Mary paled into insignificance against the other difficulties Somerset faced during 1549.

The parliamentary authorisation of the prayer book probably marked the peak of Somerset's primacy. By the time Parliament had adjourned on 14 March, Somerset had begun to lose his firm control of government. Overwhelmed by a plethora of important matters – Scotland, France, religion, lack of money, attempts to improve the lot of the common man and the problem of his brother – the business of government slowed. Parliament had continued to sit but latterly no great matters were considered and on many days the little business that was done could have been left for a later time. Paget believed Somerset should have ended the session before Christmas. Members of both houses were becoming impatient at the length of time they were spending tied to London and on 12 March he had implored Somerset to adjourn Parliament.[14]

Somerset was no longer coping with governing the country. He failed to make decisions or to implement those he had made. He took hasty decisions and was then forced to change them. Paget became increasingly anxious, writing six letters to Somerset between Christmas Day 1548 and 12 March 1549 and a further five by the end of August, each offering advice and encouraging him to look at the future consequences of his decisions.[15] On 25 January he had tried to ease his master's predicament by identifying the matters that needed resolution in the hope this would encourage Somerset to move forward. It was a tactic he would adopt on several occasions. His letters and memoranda became increasingly forthright but the Protector was slow to act on the advice. The councillors became increasingly frustrated at the inaction and at Somerset's reluctance to delegate despite Paget's appeals for him to accept their assistance.

What may have eventually prompted the adjournment was the passage through Parliament of a finance bill to raise revenue for the crown. Paget had been imploring Somerset to address this issue since Christmas and in March the bill received assent. Money was a primary concern for both the privy council and the people but it was one that Somerset did little to address. Throughout the Protectorate the government was short of funds, a situation that was exacerbated by Somerset's military ambitions. The royal finances had been in a poor state when Edward came to the throne, severely depleted by the outlay of over £2 million on his father's costly military ventures during the latter years of his reign. Somerset's commitment to continue the war in Scotland needed further vast sums of money. During the first five years of Edward's reign a total of £1,356,687 was spent on defence and war in Scotland and France.[16]

As Lord Treasurer, Somerset controlled the exchequer and formulated policy with the councillors to ensure funds were available to finance their programmes. The collection and distribution of money was then authorised through the finance courts on the orders of the privy council. However, beyond raising funds for his wars, Somerset did little to re-establish a sound financial base. It was a failure that severely weakened his credibility with the councillors and was one which they would work hard to rectify when he was no longer in power.

Historically, the king was expected to live off his own income, especially income from crown lands, which had increased greatly as a result of the Dissolution of the Monasteries. However, Edward's annual income had been reduced by the disposal of land as rewards to the executors soon after his accession and by the later sale of land. Somerset was forced to seek an alternative source of funding. In times of exceptional expense, such as war, it was usual for the king to demand taxes from his subjects – never a popular move – and this had been one of the reasons for calling the Parliament in 1548. Somerset needed money to finance his military ambitions.

The revenue bill ordered a tax of 1s in the pound on people with money or goods valued at over £10 and introduced a sheep tax, an idea proposed by the 'Commonwealth' man John Hales. Owners were to pay between 2d and 3d per head for sheep kept on enclosed land, less for sheep kept on common land, and there was to be a tax of 8d in the pound on the value of woollen and other cloth.[17] It was primarily aimed at men who owned large flocks – people with fewer than twenty sheep paid a lower tax – and was yet another policy which increased the alienation between Somerset and the landowners. However, even before the bill had been passed, Paget warned Somerset that the income would be insufficient.[18] In 1549 it brought in only £54,000, a fraction of what was needed. His alternative suggestion for a subsidy based on both the value of movable goods and the income of all men would have brought in more money more quickly but was ignored by Somerset.

On 24 January, in an attempt to re-establish confidence in the currency, the government announced the issue of new coins. The coinage had been greatly debased during the previous reign and there had been much counterfeiting. New gold coins – sovereigns, half-sovereigns, crowns and half-crowns – were ready to be issued, together with silver shillings and half-shillings.[19] However, although the coins were of increased fineness, with a higher content of gold and silver, they weighed less, thus diminishing the quantity of precious metal in each coin. The teston had become so small that this 'pretty little shilling' could easily be mistaken for the much less valuable groat.[20] Unfortunately, although these changes to the coins brought in income for the government, they had the undesirable effect of encouraging inflation and counterfeiting. Somerset did, though, avoid resorting to devaluing the coinage as Warwick would later do in a move that reduced the value of shillings and groats by half.

Despite the government's lack of money, Somerset was already intent on his next great military exploits and in April was making plans for a further campaign in Scotland and another against France. At the beginning of June, Paget would be despatched to Brussels for unsuccessful negotiations with the emperor for a joint invasion of France and the inclusion of Boulogne in their existing treaty of mutual support. Paget was increasingly alarmed by the lack of money to pay for Somerset's existing military commitments and in February, March and April he wrote despairingly that they owed more than they could pay and could not maintain the cost of the wars.[21] The Spanish ambassador accused Somerset of not being 'lavish but rather tends to parsimony' with regard to government money but in reality Somerset had no choice because there was no money.[22] Whether Paget's pleas eventually had any effect on the Protector is difficult to establish. As unrest spread throughout England during the summer, Somerset would be unable to spare money or men for his foreign commitments. However, Paget's repeated comments do suggest that he believed his advice was being ignored.

Paget was Somerset's most loyal supporter and understood him better than any other man but he was also one of his harshest critics and not afraid to criticise him both to his face and by letter. His letters were always couched in very respectful even self-deprecating tones but their frequency demonstrates his growing concern. Even when he was at court with Somerset, Paget wrote to the Protector, probably in the expectation that letters would serve as a long-term remembrance better than a conversation. On 2 January 1549, in lieu of a New Year gift, he had presented Somerset with a 'Scedule' of advice 'wherein as in a glass if your grace will daily look, and by it make you ready, you shall so well apparel yourself as each man shall delight to behold you'.[23] The 'Scedule' was a list of points for good government, intended as a reminder to Somerset. In reality it was probably a litany of his failures in government and included the advice to follow the counsel of 'wise' men, to execute his decisions quickly, to punish offenders and to accept no bribes and use no corrupt councillors.

Somerset was becoming increasingly authoritarian. On Christmas Day, only a few days before writing the 'Scedule', Paget had written a letter that was particularly hard-hitting but which summed up well the councillors' views. As he laid all the criticism squarely at Somerset's door, Paget demonstrated that the Protector was the driving force behind many decisions.[24] Somerset's mistakes, Paget maintained, were in trying to please everybody and in his reluctance to use punishment. He had moved from one extreme to another, from the constraints of the previous reign, where men were afraid to speak their thoughts, to this new liberty where men could say what they pleased. Policies were changed to accommodate the views of people who increasingly despised the noblemen and gentlemen for their apparent lack of authority. Somerset failed to listen to councillors' comments and views and was too quick to believe what he wanted to hear. His policies had left the country with no money and had put England 'in discord with all the rest of the world besides dissension at home now at liberty to burst out'. Not only was Somerset alienating his peers, he was damaging and endangering the realm. It was a critical but true condemnation of his government.

Less than six weeks later Paget was moved to voice his concerns yet again. On 2 February he called upon Somerset to 'lift up, lift up the eyes of your heart' and consider how matters stood. There were signs of discord at home, England was at war with Scotland, close to war with France and had no money to maintain Somerset's military ambitions. He urged Somerset to send men of authority throughout the country to collect the forthcoming tax and to execute the laws, especially those for religion, and so put an end to the dissension among the people.[25] Paget, fearful that poor enforcement of the laws and lack of respect for the nobility could lead to unrest, believed that a display of authority would restore obedience and deference to those in authority. If his advice had been followed all the troubles of the approaching summer might have been avoided.

Somerset's management of affairs had increasingly put him at odds with the men who should have shared the burden of government with him and they were worried. When they had granted Somerset quasi-monarchical powers, they had intended that he should govern on their behalf and only execute those powers with their agreement. Somerset might believe that he alone was answerable to the king but, if he failed, the men who had appointed him would also be answerable for his actions.

There was growing annoyance at Somerset's increasingly abrasive manner with all those about him as 'of late your grace is grown into great choleric fashions, when soever you are contraried in that which you have conceived in your head'. On 8 May he was especially harsh dealing with Sir Richard Lee, a military engineer and architect with whom he had worked closely for many years in France and Scotland. After a severe dressing-down by the Protector, Lee had retreated to Paget's chamber in tears. Paget was concerned for the future of the Protectorate. Somerset had recently ignored councillors' advice to send more troops to Boulogne and became so angry when contradicted that they were afraid to voice their opinion for fear of his response. He even spoke sharply to Paget who admitted that, although in private Somerset heard him speak 'very gently and graciously', in council 'your grace nipps me so sharply'. Paget begged him to listen to the councillors, pointing out that while a king who refused to take advice imperilled his realm, a mighty subject such as Somerset endangered himself as well as the country. Even more than a king, the Protector had a duty to take advice.[26]

It is striking that for a man who governed in such an authoritarian manner, Somerset continued to accept severe criticism from Paget. Yet despite the fact that he was the one man whose opinion Somerset could trust, and knowing that Paget gave sound counsel, he was slow to follow his advice. Paget had a personal interest in the Protector's survival. He must have realised that if Somerset lost his position, Paget would lose the opportunity to wield such great influence at court. He was right to be concerned. Trouble was already brewing: not from the council, but among the people.

The first riots had begun in April 1549 as men became frustrated by government inaction over enclosures. Although the commission of the previous year had held no authority to remedy matters, Somerset hoped it would encourage landlords to reform themselves. It had not and on 11 April he had issued a proclamation enforcing the Henrician statutes against enclosures. Landlords, he claimed, had continued to enclose, forcing tenants from their land and houses, thereby decreasing the number of people who could be called up for the defence of the realm. In the hope that a gentle approach would bring people to heel and avoid the need to resort to punishment, Somerset offered a pardon to landowners who would open up their enclosures. All those who would not conform, however, were to be punished with no exceptions. This was a challenge to many landowners whose main concern was to protect their own interests. In the future the privy councillors would charge him with issuing this proclamation without their full support.[27]

Somerset wanted to govern well, however, his desire to improve the well-being of the poor had put their needs above the desires of his peers. He was an idealist who believed social injustice could be overcome and the plight of the common man improved. His efforts to help those with whom he had close contact – in the Court of Requests, securing land tenure for his own tenants and his support for the community at Glastonbury – showed clearly his humanity and charity. As Paget acknowledged, Somerset's intention was 'good and godly' and had earned him popularity with the people.[28] The Protector's sympathy for the poor was not unusual. Men of his class shared a conventional concern for the condition of the poor that was related to the need to maintain peace in the country. But his sympathy for the lower orders stretched beyond the natural concern of his peers. He was prepared to support the cause of the common folk at the expense of his own class. This brought him into direct conflict with the landowners, among whom were many councillors. These were the men whose support he would soon need.

Ironically, it was his efforts to remove social injustice that would ultimately lead to discontent throughout the country and in the privy council. Only days after the proclamation was issued, unrest broke out in several counties. The following month this developed into something more serious when 200 rioters pulled down hedges and fences at Frome in Somerset, claiming that their actions were allowed by the April proclamation. The disturbance in Somerset was soon followed by commotion in other counties as riots sprang up in Wiltshire, Gloucestershire, Hampshire, Sussex, Surrey and Essex.[29] This was only the beginning. Much worse was to follow as England teetered on the brink of civil war.

Somerset had not understood the ordinary people of England. He had never intended to release them from the constraints of the law, but he believed that by lifting the oppressive control of the previous reign to give them more freedom, they would respond by behaving well. He believed that by promising them social reform and raising their expectations they would wait patiently for their lives to improve. He was to be proved wrong on both counts. Once the people knew their grievances had been acknowledged by the country's governors, they wanted immediate improvement. As Henry VIII had known, only force would keep the lowest orders in their place once they were roused.

16

Rebellion

For much of the sixteenth century England was a relatively peaceful country but at times, when significant numbers of the populace became dissatisfied with their condition, the resulting dissension could lead to a breakdown in law and order. In each county the law was enforced by the gentry, in their role as justices of the peace, using the sheriffs and local men to apprehend offenders. The extremities of the realm had always been difficult to govern and kings had depended upon loyal and powerful landowners to maintain control, men such as the Percy family in the north, the Courtenays in Devon and Cornwall, the Dukes of Norfolk in the east and the Earls of Shrewsbury along the Welsh borders. However, the removal of the powerful nobles in the east and west had left a power vacuum. Norfolk was languishing in the Tower and Henry Courtenay, Marquis of Exeter, had been executed for treason in 1538.

In 1540 Henry VIII had tried to establish the Lord Privy Seal, John Russell, in the west with lands and the title of Lord President of Devon, Cornwall, Dorset and Somerset. In the event, because of his influential position on the privy council, Russell spent little time on his estates and had only limited contact with the local people. A similar dislocation arose between some gentlemen and their tenants after much property from the dissolved monasteries was distributed to absentee landlords. In times of trouble kings relied upon these gentlemen to use their tenants to restore order. Russell would later blame the rise of the 1549 rebellion in the West Country upon 'the lack of such aid and assistance as the gentlemen of the county should have given'.[1]

During the spring of that year, riots started in different counties as men complained about rent and food prices and pulled down fences and hedges to open up enclosed common land. Where local landowners and justices took swift action the disturbances were soon quelled. In Wiltshire, for instance, after men destroyed the fences of Sir William Herbert's new house and park the justices prevented further riots. Lord Rich suppressed trouble in Essex, Lord St John and the Earl of Southampton in Hampshire. The Earl of Arundel in Sussex invited people to present their complaints directly to him at Arundel Castle. In Surrey, he also reduced the town of Guildford to a 'quavering quiet' but complained that there were insufficient justices because the county was 'weak of worthy men'.[2] A plan by men from Sussex to join rebels in Hampshire was stopped by the local authorities but in Cornwall and Devon, where the government was slow to back up the ineffective local control, the rebellions soon spiralled out of control as different groups of rioters joined together.[3] Justices and gentlemen who were not already in their counties were ordered to return home but, as Somerset was soon to discover, local manpower was only sufficient to quell relatively small risings.

As summer approached Somerset faced the prospect of losing control as the riots spread, flaring up in one area as they were suppressed in another. The situation demanded firm action and on 23 May he issued a proclamation ordering sheriffs and justices to use any force necessary against people pulling down hedges and fences. While the rebels were absent from their homes, the officials were even authorised to 'spoil and rifle their houses and goods to their utter ruin and destruction, and the terrible example of others'.[4]

However, Somerset accepted that the rioters had good cause for their actions and he also announced that measures would be taken against unlawful enclosures in due course. For many country folk, though, this response was too slow. The previous year they had sensed that improvement might be forthcoming and now they were impatient. Reform would take time as reluctant landowners were forced to co-operate and Somerset miscalculated by believing that a mere promise would be sufficient to calm the people. Riots continued around the country and noblemen were despatched to maintain order. On 11 June, for instance, Somerset sent an urgent letter to the Marquis of Dorset and Francis Hastings, Earl of Huntingdon, who were both in Leicestershire, ordering them to be ready with the local gentlemen to repress any trouble from 'lewd men' and 'seditious priests' who tried to destroy enclosures.[5]

Three days later, as the privy council struggled to bring the country under control, Somerset tried a different approach and offered a pardon for all rebels who would stop rioting. There was, though, a sting in the tail. In future men who continued to offend would suffer loss of their land and goods and even the death penalty. It was a policy that Somerset had seen Henry VIII use with success against the rebels in the Pilgrimage of Grace in 1536. He also absolved the rioters of any blame for their actions, attributing their earlier behaviour to misunderstanding the April proclamation which had ordered landowners to reform.[6]

Somerset was sympathetic towards the rioters. Some of their complaints were 'fair and just', he believed, and he laid much of the blame for the troubles on the 'covetousness of gentlemen' who seized common land, leaving their tenants with no grazing land.[7] He was naïve, though, in believing that a policy of tolerance was the best way to achieve calm. His later insistence on making repeated offers of pardon to the rebels would irreparably damage his reputation and leave him open to the charge of favouring their cause. His reluctance to take an aggressive stance from the very beginning showed a disturbing lack of forcefulness and left him ill prepared for the trouble that was about to break out in the west of the country.

On 9 June 1549, Whitsunday, the priest at Sampford Courtenay in Devon recited the service in the new *Book of Common Prayer* which came into official use that day. The villagers refused to hear it again and the following day they prevented the priest using the book and forced him to revert to the traditional celebration of mass. Riots broke out when the justices and gentry tried to stop this and one of the gentlemen was murdered. Feelings were running high on both sides as the number of rioters grew and unrest spread to other villages, through Crediton and Clyst St Mary and across north Devon.

Meanwhile, in Cornwall, riots had broken out at Bodmin where men, already incensed by the destruction of religious imagery the previous year, rebelled against the new liturgy. Under the leadership of Humphrey Arundell, a local gentleman, they drew up a list of complaints and set out along the road towards London to present it to the government. However, at Crediton they met the Devon rebels with whom they joined forces. As the rebellion gathered momentum, Somerset sent Sir Peter Carew and his uncle, Sir Gawen, to offer a pardon to the people if they would stop rioting. However, both men were staunch supporters of the new faith and not the best choice of intermediaries to deal with a rising which seemed to have its roots in religion and the attack on Catholic beliefs.[8]

Across England the rioters' complaints were primarily about agrarian and social issues but in the west they were more concerned with the religious reforms. Due to the distance of Cornwall and Devon from London, the local inhabitants were less influenced by events in London and the area had remained staunchly Catholic. They considered the new communion service to be like a 'Christmas game' and wanted to return to the old Catholic services as they had been at the end of Henry VIII's reign with images and ceremonies, the Six Articles, the sacrament in just one kind and all services in Latin since some Cornishmen understood no English (the west of Cornwall was culturally distinctive and many people spoke only Cornish). However, this request did draw surprise from London that men who spoke no English would prefer to hear Latin that they also did not understand.[9] Undoubtedly the lists of grievances sent to the government particularly reflected the views of the rebel leaders who wrote them down. Unlike the Pilgrimage of Grace in 1536, the rebellions of 1549 had little support from gentlemen. In the west the leaders were primarily yeomen and minor gentry, such as Arundell, and members of the clergy. Although their initial demands had included complaints about the sheep tax and the dearth of food, the focus of their concerns shifted to reflect the views of the priests who concentrated on religious issues.

On 22 June the Carews met an armed crowd near Crediton, but the meeting was a disaster after one of their party set fire to a barn, causing the rebels to panic. A second attempt to talk with the rioters also failed and Sir Peter Carew left for London to ask Somerset for more support. The Protector had little patience with failure and, in his accustomed brusque manner, he rewarded Carew's efforts by chastising him for the burning of the barn. Somerset had, however, already despatched the Lord Privy Seal, Russell, in the wake of the Carews with instructions to try to remedy the rebels' grievances through 'gentle persuasion'. Only if that failed was he to raise local men to augment the small force that accompanied him and subdue the troublemakers.[10]

Russell, who was approaching the age of 65, was a poor choice to oppose the rebels. Although he had been one of Henry VIII's commanders at Boulogne in 1544 he had never held sole command and he appears to have been overly cautious. In 1536 he had been accused of 'slackness' for his hesitant response during the Pilgrimage of Grace, a matter which he blamed on a lack of men. Somerset appointed him because of the authority his lands and local office should have given him. Throughout the campaign, though, Russell lacked confidence, once again complaining that he had insufficient support. With no large cohort of soldiers he was left to recruit forces in the west, an unsuccessful enterprise since men were reluctant to join him to fight against countrymen whose grievances they shared.

Hindered by the slowness of communication, it may not have been until Carew's arrival in London that Somerset fully appreciated the seriousness of the situation. Messages took at least two days to travel between London and the western counties and it took substantially longer for an armed force to make the same journey. The local situation could change drastically before the authorities in London could react. Matters were moving faster than Somerset and the council were aware, and Russell arrived in the area just as 2,000 rebels besieged the city of Exeter on 2 July.

A plethora of proclamations that month demonstrate the council's increasing anxiety. On 11 July protesters in Cornwall and Devon were ordered to submit to Russell or forfeit all their property and be treated as traitors. The following day this strong rhetoric was followed by a proclamation throughout England which appeared to contradict the earlier order, pardoning all rebels who repented of their behaviour and then, on 16 July, they were ordered to cease all unlawful behaviour or be subject to martial law.[11] Somerset probably lacked the full support of all the councillors for the further offer of pardon. As news of the proclamations filtered out to the countryside, the apparent uncertainty of the council must have fuelled the rioters' resolve to continue.

It was over a month since the first offer of pardon had been made and it seems extraordinary that Somerset continued to use this same policy. However, for a government with limited money and troops, reasserting control through offers of pardon and reform was the cheapest and most appropriate solution. Some areas had been calmed and this may have encouraged him to believe the policy was working. Writing to Russell and Paget early in July, Somerset and the councillors reported that 'stirs' in some areas had been quieted and they expected other riots to be similarly suppressed in two or three days.[12] He was too optimistic and events would soon prove him to be wrong. In the west the proclamations were completely ineffective. For over three weeks, as Exeter held out against the rebel siege, Russell sat with his army near Honiton, afraid to move and pleading for more men. Somerset and the privy council were unable to send further soldiers because of the increasing need for troops elsewhere in the country.

Paget was growing agitated at Somerset's handling of the rebellions. On 7 July he had put quill to parchment yet again and written another long letter to the Protector, damning his actions and bewailing the fact that if Somerset had listened to his advice matters would not be as they were. Society, Paget wrote, was maintained by means of religion and laws where the Church provided moral guidance and the government enforced order. But England now had neither, and the net that held society together was broken. Somerset had relaxed the laws, giving people too much liberty, and he had forbidden the old religion before people were ready for the new. He had the 'absolute power' of a king but failed to act as one and keep the people obedient. The whole council, Paget wrote, objected to the Protector's decisions. He believed Somerset should have used force against the first rebels as an example to others and then granted a pardon. By offering a pardon first, men had become emboldened. The only way forward was to use force, he advised. By hanging some of the rebels and sending others to serve in the north or in Boulogne he would not lose the love of good people but he would be feared by evil men.[13] Paget's advice was sound and Somerset ignored it at his peril.

On 8 July the councillors had finally taken action against enclosures. Commissioners had been ordered to investigate the loss of land and houses but this time they also had limited powers to enforce the existing statutes against enclosures and reinstate common land and rights of way. It may have appeared to be a reasonable response but if Somerset hoped it would remedy the situation, he was wrong. It would have taken weeks before the commissioners could resolve matters across the whole country. Not unexpectedly the work of the commission was in vain and months later the privy council would claim that it had further enflamed the insurrections.[14] People's hopes had been raised yet again and trouble soon followed when a quick remedy was not forthcoming.

The decision-making was undoubtedly being steered by Somerset, who had become increasingly alienated from the councillors. As he ignored their opinions and dominated their meetings they dared not speak out against him. He caused resentment when he ordered the councillors and commissioners to reform their own estates as an example to other landowners. Warwick placed the blame squarely on Somerset's shoulders when he was forced to stand by and allow men to plough and sow oats in the best pasture at one of his parks.[15] Somerset no longer had the full support of the councillors, who believed that this was not the right time for the enclosure commission. With England at war with Scotland and poor relations with France, they believed that matters such as this should have been left until the country once again enjoyed 'fair and quiet weather'.[16]

As trouble spread through the counties, in London the councillors were isolated from the immediate effects of the rioting. The city remained relatively calm, probably due to the presence of a number of troops. Rebels from the counties were brought in to be hanged as a further deterrent. At the beginning of July watches were ordered around the city and two weeks later martial law was declared. To prevent rebel groups marching into London, artillery was moved from the Tower to the city gates where new portcullises were fitted. In June the inhabitants of Staines had been ordered to destroy their bridge over the Thames, severing a major route into the city from the west. The townspeople were horrified, complaining that to do so would be to the 'utter undoing of the town', and a compromise was reached when the townsfolk offered to send scouts out along the road to keep watch. Preparations were made for the protection of the king. Weapons were placed at Windsor Castle, which was furnished ready to receive Edward, and 4,000 horsemen and 2,000 footsoldiers were assembled for his protection.[17] On 23 July Somerset accompanied the king in procession through the city to dispel a rumour that Edward was dead but before the month was out he would move him to the safety of Windsor.[18]

Early in July serious riots broke out around Oxfordshire, where the rebel leaders included several priests whose grievances concerned religion. Although Somerset had sympathy with agrarian complaints he had no intention of reversing any of his religious reforms. He warned Russell to keep news of this religious dissension secret for fear that word of religious fervour spreading to other areas might encourage the western rebels.[19] In an attempt to resolve the trouble without using force he sent a conciliatory letter to the rebels questioning their continued disobedience even after receiving an offer of pardon. He then gave them the benefit of the doubt by offering to send a second pardon in case the first had not arrived. The rebels were not to be persuaded, however, and Somerset finally acknowledged the need to use troops. Lord Grey, who was on his way with 400 horsemen to support Russell in Devon, was diverted to control the Oxfordshire rioters, which he did successfully, leaving several rebels to be hanged and their heads displayed as a warning to others.[20]

The privy councillors were fearful lest the rebellions around Oxfordshire should provide a bridgehead for rebels from the west to join a new rising in East Anglia. On 7 July a few men had pulled down the hedges of John Flowerdew, an unpopular lawyer-landlord at Wymondham near Norwich.[21] The crowd grew quickly as they moved around opening up enclosures, especially after one of their victims, Robert Kett, a local landowner, offered to take down his own hedges and act as their leader. On 9 July, after several hundred men had set up camp near Norwich, the city authorities sent a messenger to London to warn the council of the rising. Three days later the growing crowd had moved on to higher and more easily defendable ground at Mousehold Heath, east of the city. As their number quickly rose, reportedly to 16,000, Kett set about organising the men into a disciplined army by forming them into smaller bands and arranged with Thomas Codd, the mayor of Norwich, for a sufficient supply of food. Meanwhile, further camps were established at Downham Market in Norfolk and at Ipswich and Bury St Edmunds in Suffolk.

The rebellion in East Anglia grew so quickly and the camps were so large and widespread that the local gentlemen were powerless to do anything about it. By 17 July Somerset had ordered the Marquis of Northampton to take a small force to Norwich. He was another poor choice for military commander. Northampton had held no major military position and had only limited success serving on the Scottish borders but, as Paget remarked, there was a 'great scarcity of chieftains to conduct the wars' and other more experienced commanders were already employed elsewhere.[22]

As Northampton prepared to journey to Norfolk, Somerset and the council pursued peace in East Anglia through conciliatory letters, negotiation and promises of pardon, a policy that had proved effective in some parts of the country. In Suffolk, where Sir Anthony Wingfield, the head of an established Suffolk family and vice-chamberlain to the king, could exert substantial authority, this ploy was successful and the rising was quickly suppressed. It had less success in

Norfolk, however, and Somerset's offer to control prices of food, rents and wool and to consider further complaints in Parliament failed to placate the rioters.[23] On 21 July, Kett and the rebels at Mousehold rejected an offer of pardon. The gates of Norwich were closed against them and the city prepared for battle but its defences were inadequate and two days later the rebels took the city. One commentator believed this was partly due to the city archers losing heart when rebel boys ran into the midst of the hail of arrows and turned their backsides towards the archers who were shooting from the walls.[24]

Northampton reached Norwich on 30 July with Lord Wentworth, Lord Sheffield, Anthony Denny, Ralph Sadler and their men. Because of Northampton's inexperience and his lack of troops, Somerset had advised him not to engage in battle with the rebels but to cut their supply lines and negotiate with them. However, Northampton quickly demonstrated his incompetence by ignoring the orders. Kett had left the city poorly guarded and after quickly overwhelming the rebel defenders, Northampton set his own guards. However, that night under cover of bombardment, Kett attacked and hundreds of his men broke into the town. By the end of the following day Sheffield had been killed, the city was again under rebel control and Northampton, defeated, was retreating towards London. If he had obeyed Somerset's orders he might have been successful but he had underestimated the strength of the opposition. The rebels were prepared to fight it out, better 'to die like men, than after so great misery in youth to die more miserably in age'.[25] By the end of August many of them would be dead.

The Norfolk rebels joined other groups in sending lists of their grievances to London but the demands were so diverse that even Somerset seemed perplexed. As he related to Sir Philip Hoby in August, it could be difficult to discern what they wanted: 'Some cry, Pluck down enclosures; some for their commons; others pretend religion; a number would rule and direct things, as gentlemen have done.' In East Anglia, especially, the rebels had 'conceived a wonderful hate against gentlemen, and take them all as their enemies', forcing many of them out of their homes and taking others prisoner.[26] This area was well attuned to the new religion – daily Protestant services were held in the Mousehold camp – and the main thrusts of their grievances were social and economic. The breadth of their concerns is clearly demonstrated by the origins of their leaders who included numerous farmers, four clerics and artisans from Norwich who, although they had little issue regarding land usage, were affected by food shortages, high prices and rents.[27]

About half of the Norfolk rebels' twenty-nine articles of complaint were concerned with restricting the rights of landlords and increasing those of the common folk. In particular they objected to the men in authority locally, especially self-interested landlords whom the clergyman, Robert Crowley, likened to 'cormorants, greedy gulls; yea, men that would eat up men, women and children', who were failing to manage the land for the benefit of their tenants.[28] Their complaints demonstrated the widening gulf between the different expectations of peasants and of the gentry and nobility. The common folk in Norfolk wanted a resumption of what they considered the traditional, more responsible, relationship between their landlords and themselves.

Despite his abhorrence of the violence and his contempt for the troublemakers whom he considered to be the 'vilest and worst sort of men', Somerset was sympathetic to many of the rebels' demands, believing them to be 'for the most part founded upon great and just causes'.[29] But he would not deal with troublemakers and repeatedly reminded the rebels that the Bible taught obedience to the king. Only after they had assumed the position of supplicant would he consider their grievances and then he would go to great lengths to appease them. After the men of Suffolk had quietened, Somerset and the council not only agreed to most of their demands but also offered to recall Parliament one month early for speedy redress of their complaints. Similarly, he agreed to replace some of the enclosure commissioners at Thetford with others named by the local people and to return the local manor to the king with the land available for farming.[30] This manor had been leased to Somerset in 1548 and his decision to relinquish the estate shows his determination to do anything reasonable to secure peace.

Somerset's conciliatory attitude was alien to the councillors and it is clear to see why they would later accuse him of favouring the protesters' cause. Government was the responsibility of the upper echelons of society but his repeated offers of pardon and his efforts to satisfy the rebels complaints left him open to the damaging charge that policy was being dictated by the rioters. Yet, although it may have appeared that Somerset was allowing the people a voice in government, on one issue he remained firm. He was prepared to consider grievances concerning agrarian and social complaints but not the demands of the men in the West Country who wanted a return to the old religion. That was a challenge to the authority of the king and his government.

Despite Somerset's attempts to bring about peace without bloodshed, he did not hesitate to use force once other options had failed. When he realised the Oxfordshire rebels would not accept a pardon, his reaction in sending Grey had been quick and effective. However, in the extreme east and west his response was hampered by several factors. The inadequacy of the local authority allowed the risings to grow rapidly. Somerset had been given a warning of this weakness the previous year when the gentry were unable to suppress the rising in Cornwall without using troops, but he had failed to make any attempt to address the issue. He was often unaware of the seriousness of the local situation and in the time it took for news to reach him the rebel numbers had increased even more. His initial response, conditioned by the expectation of resolving the issues by negotiation, had been quick but ineffective. The forces he sent to both the eastern and western counties were too small and lacked robust leadership. He was seriously hampered by a lack of experienced men to command the soldiers and he suffered from a paucity of troops, particularly in the early stages of the rebellions, and in the time it took to assemble and move a force.

By the end of July, as government authority in parts of England disintegrated, Somerset and the council faced a dire situation. Some areas of the country were out of control. Exeter was under siege, Norwich in the hands of rebels and in many counties that had been quietened, rebellion could very easily be reignited. These were the most widespread rebellions in England during the sixteenth century. Somerset was facing the threat that every government feared – civil war and the need to use substantial force against its citizens. His over-riding concern, though, was to avoid violence because what he most desired was 'to spare as much as may be the effusion of blood, and namely, that of our own nation'.[31]

Somerset was a soldier, a man who could be brutal on the battlefield and who had turned his guns upon his own mutineering men. Yet even then he had exhausted all other avenues first, offering the soldiers an opportunity to return to their units peacefully. In Scotland he gave the Scots the opportunity to agree to his terms before he made the decision to invade. Now he was following the same principle with the people of England, using gentleness with the offer of pardon. Somerset was an optimist, confident that he knew what was best for his countrymen and that they would concur with this. But his overconfidence was misplaced. His stubbornness and reluctance to alter his course prevented him from adapting to a changing situation. He had never accepted the need to withdraw from the conflict in Scotland and he was slow to recognise the futility of his approach towards the rebels. His mistake was to prevaricate so long before admitting defeat and using greater force.

As Northampton responded to the Norfolk rising, in Devon Russell had remained near Honiton, afraid to engage the rebels without the aid of further troops. While he pleaded for more help, Somerset and the councillors became increasingly annoyed at his inactivity and he began to take offence at their continual stream of advice, thinking that they were casting aspersions upon his ability to command. Efforts to send men westwards had been hampered by the changing situation throughout the country. Orders were being constantly amended. A promise on 10 July to send Russell 400 horsemen under the command of Grey was rescinded two days later when Grey was sent to control the trouble in Oxfordshire. With its proximity to London, suppressing riots in this county had to take priority. Somerset had abandoned his plan to send Warwick with an invasion force into Scotland that summer which left him free to join Russell. However, on 22 July the western commander was informed that Warwick would no longer be joining him because he was needed in Norfolk. The councillors were instead sending Herbert with an army. However, the additional proposal to send over 1,000 German mercenaries to Russell was also quickly changed because they were 'odious to our people'.[32] The use of foreign soldiers against Englishmen upon English soil was viewed as an abhorrence.

Somerset and the council wrote a scathing letter to Russell on 28 July, again criticising his lack of action and pressing him to attack the rebels. But by then Russell was on the move.[33] Marching his men towards Exeter, he overcame strong opposition at Fenny Bridges then, fortified by Lord Grey's arrival on 3 August, he won significant victories at Clyst St Mary and the following day at Clyst Heath. The rebel forces were routed and together the two commanders continued towards Exeter and freed the city on 6 August.

It had been a long protracted situation, largely due to Russell's reluctance to engage the rebels. However, there was no time for elation in London. East Anglia was in turmoil and on 8 August, just two days after the relief of Exeter, the French ambassador had met Somerset at Whitehall to give him his king's 'defiance'. Henri II had declared war on England as a prelude to attacking Boulogne. As Somerset sought to bring order to the country this declaration of war was an especially unwelcome intervention. With all available troops dealing with the insurrections, Somerset had insufficient force to counter either a major French offensive against Boulogne or an invasion attempt. That night letters were sent to the mayor of London to set a watch around the city and to apprehend all Frenchmen who were not recognised as permanent residents and might be spies.[34]

It had become imperative to have peace in England. Somerset could not wage war against France while he struggled to control internal rebellion. Russell, who had failed to capitalise on his success at Exeter, was ordered to capture the remaining rebels and then reduce the number of his troops to allow them to return home to prepare for a feared invasion by the French. On 16 August he left Exeter with what he had craved – Grey and Herbert by his side and an army of about 8,000 men. Two days later, after a well-planned military assault, they routed the rebel force at Sampford Courtenay, capturing and killing many while the rest fled. By the end of the month those who escaped had either come to Russell to beg pardon or been hunted down by the royal forces. Devon and Cornwall were once again quiet.

Russell, however, continued to incur Somerset's displeasure due to his reluctance to execute one of the rebels. The Protector was adamant that those who had incited the rebellion should be executed as traitors – including Paget's brother, who had been one of the leaders. Russell hesitated, probably in the expectation that although Somerset had consented to his own brother's death, he would 'wink' at this and show mercy for his friend's sake. But Somerset had no intention of changing his mind and was annoyed at Russell's failure to follow his order. After refusing any mercy to Thomas Seymour he could never spare Robert Paget, he explained, since 'it should much import us if we should spare any other man's brother'. For a month Russell delayed the execution, until, on 18 September, Somerset wrote angrily, claiming that the delay impugned his honour and ordering Russell to carry out the sentence.[35] As the Lord Protector would realise only weeks later, his authoritarian stance against Russell throughout the troubles had not endeared him to the Lord Privy Seal. Russell would not forget the haranguing from Somerset when the latter needed his help.

Once Exeter had been relieved, Somerset could devote more attention to the problems in Norfolk. Concerned that the rebels at Norwich had found greater courage and confidence after their victory against Northampton, Somerset had decided to take to the field himself. By 6 August he had assumed command of the army. However, as was becoming commonplace, within days the plan had been very suddenly changed. On 10 August a proclamation had been issued calling upon gentlemen in the eastern counties to attend upon Somerset, who would be marching towards them with all speed. Yet later that same day a commission was issued to Warwick ordering him to command the troops in Norfolk.[36] It was just two days since the French had declared war. The possibility of an imminent attack on England was an even greater threat to the country than the rebellion in Norfolk. Such a potentially dangerous situation demanded Somerset's presence in London. Coincidentally, this also avoided the possibility of him being personally involved in the wholesale massacre of his own people.

As Warwick amassed his army, events in Norfolk were moving towards a bloody climax. On 23 August, accompanied by Northampton and Lords Willoughby, Powis and Bray, Warwick set up camp 3 miles from Norwich with 12,000 men. He had asked that Northampton might retain his commission and be given a second chance to prove himself, because he believed that no-one should be discarded for making one mistake, which anyone might have done.[37] That day the king's herald rode out to the camp on Mousehold Heath to offer the royal pardon. However, when one of the herald's guards shot and killed a boy who made an obscene gesture the crowd became angry and prevented Kett from meeting Warwick.[38] The opportunity for peace was lost. The following day and night the royal army drove the rebels out of Norwich. Warwick tightened his control over their supply routes, forcing Kett to move his men from Mousehold to a less easily defended site. On 27 August, after the rebels had rejected a second pardon, Warwick attacked. It was a resounding victory; about 3,000 rebels were left dead together with several hundred of the king's army. It is possible that in all over 10,000 people died as a result of the 1549 rebellions.[39] Even after striving so hard, Somerset had failed to avoid bloodshed.

As peace returned to the country, Somerset and the councillors took pre-emptive action to prevent further outbreaks of trouble. Somerset was determined that the rebel leaders should be hanged as an example to others. Judgement against Kett and his brother, William, was harsh. Kett was reportedly tied in chains and, with a rope about his neck, was lifted alive from the ground up to the gibbet built on the top of Norwich Castle. His brother was hanged from the tower of Wymondham Church.[40]

England was calm but the threat from France continued. By the end of August the French, by the judicious use of bribery, had taken control of Ambleteuse and Blackness and were laying siege to Boulogne. The rebellions had seriously affected the privy council's ability to counter French aggression. However, it appears that Somerset was trying to keep this hidden, even from many of the councillors. On 7 September a message was sent to the emperor admitting that they were unable to send men and supplies to Boulogne and begging him to keep this secret since it was known to only a few councillors. A draft for an unsent letter illustrated the seriousness of the situation as the council asked the emperor for the loan of 2,000 horses and 4,000 men with sufficient money to pay them for two months.[41]

The rebellions had shown that there was a fracture in society between the people and the nobility and gentry. As the old system of feudal allegiance slowly crumbled the mutual respect, reliance and support that had existed between the common folk and those in authority had also declined. But there was also a fracture between Somerset and his peers. The ruling class had little sympathy for the common people when they upset the natural stability of society by resorting to rebellion. This is why Somerset's attitude set him apart. His compassion for the poor, and his reluctance to use force against troublemakers whose demands he believed were just, was seen by many as a sign of weakness, even as a sign that he wished for the 'decay of gentlemen'.[42] Yet while he might sympathise with men's complaints, Somerset's intention was to right wrongs – not to change society. He wanted to help but he would not stand for unrest and the rebellions put him into an unenviable position. The landowners expected him to take strong action to protect their interests. What he succeeded in doing was losing the support of both common folk and governors, the one by not providing what they wanted and the other by opposing their interests.

Somerset failed because he was a poor political leader who was reluctant to exercise strict authority to keep the king's subjects under control. He lacked the skill to deal with the privy councillors effectively and he failed to understand fully the ordinary people and their reaction to events. His experience of wielding power was based upon his command of an army, where men followed his lead without question, and he expected the people of England and the councillors to follow in a similar fashion. They did not and his reluctance to use severe force against his own countrymen allowed the rebellion to get out of hand. This was his real failure – to lose control of the people and endanger the country. He had failed to carry out the primary role of a ruler, to maintain peace and order within the realm. He might eventually have brought the rebellion to an end, but he should have prevented it in the first place.

17

Coup d'État

As the country recovered from the rebellions, the final footnote for Somerset's military ambition came with the abandonment of Haddington. It had been evident for a long time that the policy to garrison Scotland was failing, but Somerset persisted. The war had drained the coffers and was no longer seen as an honourable enterprise. Realising that England could never win, Paget had sent Somerset an appraisal of the merits or otherwise of the fighting men of Scotland and England. The Scots, he wrote, had the determination to avoid the English yoke, sufficient money and military help from France. They had captains and men willing to serve. The English were short of money, lacked good commanders, were lazy, disobedient and unwilling to fight. After eight years of war, Paget observed, the English were 'exhausted and worn to the bones'. At the end of August he had advised Somerset to abandon Haddington and give all his attention to the restoration of peace at home. What good is it to conquer foreign realms and yet lose control of England to the people, he would later ask.[1]

With the threat of increased hostilities from France, and unable to spare extra support for Haddington, Somerset reluctantly agreed with Paget's assessment. The garrison, under constant assault and short of supplies, could hold out no longer. In mid-September a large force was sent to bring the men and guns out of the fort and Somerset's *pièce de résistance* was razed to the ground and abandoned. The other garrisons remained under pressure from Scots and French forces until they were all either taken by the enemy or were surrendered in 1550 as part of the negotiations over Boulogne. For now the dream of a united Britain was over. It would not be until 1603 that England and Scotland would share a monarch, and a further hundred years before the two countries became one kingdom under the title of Great Britain.

Somerset had known that once he withdrew there would be no way back into Scotland. With Queen Mary of Scots removed to France, he would never convince the council or the country that there was any reason once again to invest time, men and money in an enterprise that would place them against the combined might of France and Scotland. At one stage, there had been a chance that his dream could become a reality. Twenty-five of the thirty-nine garrisons he proposed were built near the Scottish border and along the east coast.[2] Yet the French had arrived before Somerset had been able to move further into Scotland to establish forts in the north and west. He had failed because as long as the Scots had French support they could not be forced into submission and the garrisons could not survive independently of sustained support from England. Moreover, the hope that the Protestant lords could bring about the marriage needed more time; but when Mary went to France the opportunity was lost. Time was a luxury which was also about to run out for Somerset.

At the end of the summer Somerset's policies were in tatters and now England was formally at war with France. Some of his policies, such as those concerning enclosure, taxes and education, needed more time or had been insufficiently powerful to achieve their purpose. His plan for Scotland had failed. His policies to relax the treason laws and control vagrancy had been too extreme and would eventually be repealed. Only his religious reforms were showing evidence of success. In general his ideas were not necessarily unworkable, and the privy councillors had been content to give him their support as long as his policies worked. However, they were his policies and when they failed the councillors could lay the blame at his door. They no longer trusted his judgement and were fearful of where his future designs might lead. By 23 September 1549, van der Delft predicted that Somerset could not survive much longer as Lord Protector.[3]

As Warwick returned to London, victorious after his defeat of the rebels, England settled back into an uneasy calm, unaware of the new rebellion that was fomenting. This time, though, it would not be played out across the country but within the privy council. Warwick had finally lost patience with Somerset's arrogance and with the flawed policies that had brought England close to civil war – and he was not alone. Somerset had alienated many people both through these policies and in his demeanour. With his authoritarian and abrasive manner, men had cause to be wary of him. He had isolated himself both politically in council and socially through his regal lifestyle. His failure to cultivate friends and appoint personal supporters in the privy council left him dangerously exposed and vulnerable to attack. He failed to appreciate that his position was not an inalienable right but one that was dependent upon the support of king, council and nobility. The privy councillors had lost confidence in his ability to govern responsibly. They had tolerated his policies and manner of operation for long enough and they were prepared now to exert their combined authority against him. Even Paget had become disenchanted with his master's government, telling van der Delft in September that some other means of governing must be found.[4]

Many of the privy councillors held personal grudges against Somerset. Southampton had never forgiven him for stripping him of the office of Lord Chancellor, and in September 1549 he delayed returning to court after an illness because of the ill will between him and Somerset.[5] Northampton had been let down by Somerset over the issue of his divorce. By taking much of the policy-making away from the privy council, Somerset had reduced the authority which St John should have held as Lord President. Somerset's disagreements with his brother, Thomas, and the latter's execution ended Dorset's hopes for his daughter to marry the king. Herbert had been one of the first landowners to suffer when his enclosures were pulled down during the rebellions.

The rift between Russell and Somerset had widened during the rebellions, with the latter's increasingly abrasive letters, but there had been earlier disagreements between the two men. One, in particular, shows how fragile the relationships between these powerful men could be. In 1544 differences over a land lease and the control of one of the king's wards had resulted in Somerset allegedly making a threat against Russell. Russell – angered – claimed that he had always been his friend, speaking out on his behalf, and he demanded a letter of explanation from Somerset. Somerset responded that he had never made the threat – it may have been a rumour started by men trying to make trouble between the two – and he wanted to resolve their differences 'for I entend to disguise with no man and had rather have an open enemy than a feigned friend'.[6] In the ambitious world of the Tudor court, it was best to know who your enemies were.

Most serious was Somerset's growing rift with Warwick, one that worsened during 1549 and was well known throughout court circles by the middle of September.[7] Warwick's objections to Somerset's policies during the rebellions were compounded by the ploughing up of his own parks, and he had become especially incensed by Somerset's failure to grant patronage to his nominees. The previous year his request to the Protector to appoint John Gosnold as a justice was refused and, although Warwick believed that his enemies were influencing Somerset against him, it drove a wedge between the two men.[8] However, Warwick took even greater offence on his return from defeating the rebels. He had asked Somerset for two offices for his son, Ambrose, in recognition of his service in Norfolk. Again he was refused and, to compound matters, Somerset awarded the offices to one of his secretaries, Thomas Fisher, a man whom Warwick counted as his enemy. Realising that he might never gain any favours from Somerset,

Warwick began to gather support against the Protector. When Fisher travelled north to the Scottish borders he noted that many people were speaking out against his master and in favour of Warwick. He promptly wrote to Somerset, warning that great trouble would follow if Warwick was not won over, and suggesting that he should be well rewarded for his exploits in East Anglia.[9] Once again, Somerset failed to heed the warning.

Establishing precisely the chain of events that led to the *coup d'état* against Somerset is problematic. Undoubtedly the councillors wanted to change the manner of his government. Some may have even talked of his removal, although this would have been a last resort. Who would replace him? Somerset's position as Lord Protector rested partly upon his relationship to the king (a connection which no-one else could claim), upon the support of the councillors and on the letters patent. Somerset held his office at the king's pleasure. If Warwick intended to overthrow Somerset, he needed to be sure that Edward would support him. The young king may not have been on especially good terms with his uncle but Somerset was his only relative and the person most likely to have Edward's best interests at heart. It is unlikely he would remove his uncle without a strong motive.

Somerset's opponents in the council wanted change. They wanted him to be less authoritarian, and, at the beginning of October, in what may have been a final attempt to resolve their differences, they decided yet again to try to persuade him to a more conciliar mode of operation. It is possible that at this point Warwick and his supporters did not plan to stage a coup against him. However, that became the inevitable consequence of the Lord Protector's confrontational stance. If Somerset had met with the councillors and agreed to their terms, the ensuing coup might have been avoided. It was his extreme response to the news that they might be gathering a force against him that made it imperative to remove him.

Over the years Warwick has acquired a reputation for duplicity. Some commentators believe he made an agreement with Southampton and Arundel, offering to halt the reformation of the Church and reinstate Catholicism in exchange for their support to bring down Somerset, while in reality he intended to further the reformation.[10] However, this seems unlikely. It would have been a very risky plan to form a government with powerful men such as Southampton and Arundel with the intention of later opposing them. If Southampton and Arundel had been persuaded there would be a Catholic revival, they were quickly disabused of this idea. At the height of the coup the two men were present when the council informed the Lord Mayor and aldermen that there was no intention to alter the newly established religion. A few weeks later, and again in December, proclamations would be issued, denying rumours that the country would return to the old religion.[11] Perhaps more importantly, the king was showing distinctly reformist views and was expected to assume his royal authority in six years' time. If Warwick had any long-term intention of maintaining influence it would be unwise to oppose Edward's beliefs. Suffice it to say that Warwick made an alliance with the men who had most cause to wish for Somerset's demise, men such as Southampton, Arundel and St John, who were all Catholics.

Towards the end of September the king left Westminster and travelled to Hampton Court Palace. For a time both Somerset and Warwick left court, Somerset to enjoy hunting near Odiham in Hampshire and Warwick to visit Greenwich.[12] Away from the Protector it was easier for Warwick to plot. In fact, he may have already been busy. At the end of August, Princess Mary had reported to van der Delft that Warwick, Arundel, Southampton and St John were working against Somerset and planning to charge him with *lèse-majesté* (offence against the crown). There was a rumour that they intended to sound her out to see if she would lend her support to this. Mary had appealed to the emperor for advice on how she should respond if the matter was raised with her. But plot and counter-plot were rife and everyone was suspicious. Charles V did not trust Somerset and warned Mary that it might be a trap to involve her in a plot against the government in response to her objections to the changes in religion. But it all came to nothing. The four men never did contact Mary directly and, in response to rumours that they wanted to make her regent, they later wrote to her that they never 'by word or writing, hath opened any such matter to your Grace, as your honour knoweth'.[13] It would have been very risky for Warwick if people knew he was considering such a course of action. However, the four men named by Mary were the leading protagonists against Somerset a few weeks later and were almost certainly already discussing how to deal with him.

On 1 October Somerset left his wife in Hampshire and rode to join the king at Hampton Court Palace. For the next three days life went on as usual. Somerset was aware that he did not command the full loyalty of all the councillors, and he had become very suspicious of any who were seen talking together secretly. Only St John, Paget and the two secretaries, Petre and Smith, together with Thynne and Cecil, were with Somerset at the palace. In London the number of councillors meeting together was growing and rumours that they and their servants were openly carrying weapons as they passed through the city galvanised Somerset into action.[14] By Saturday 5 October, St John had returned to London. Somerset, convinced there was a conspiracy against him, issued a proclamation ordering all the king's 'loving subjects' to hasten to Hampton Court to defend the king and his uncle against 'a most dangerous conspiracy'. This was followed by a series of letters summoning help from men he believed to be his supporters. Assured of family loyalty, he called upon his brother, Sir Henry Seymour, to bring as many men as he could. He secretly instructed the Earl of Oxford to be ready with his men.[15] Somerset also summoned Russell and Herbert, who had reached Hampshire on their journey from Devon to London. Although Herbert had probably already dismissed many of his men to their homes in Wiltshire, Russell still commanded a large force. Somerset's request that Herbert might travel to him post haste may have been intended to increase the number of privy councillors around him.[16]

In an attempt to resume control, Somerset ordered all the councillors in London to be at Hampton Court on Sunday 6 October.[17] With Herbert beside him and the expectation of Russell's arrival, he might soon have had sufficient council support to overcome the threat from his opponents. That evening carriages came from London carrying the councillors' 'stuff' in readiness for their arrival next day. The duchess, who had earlier been summoned by her husband, arrived from Hampshire after sunset. But Somerset was wary and posted guards around the palace that night.

By the following morning matters had become more serious. News arrived from London at 4 a.m. on Sunday that 2,000 horsemen were gathering on the streets of the city, preparing to ride to Hampton Court. Apparently, when they heard that Somerset and his supporters had risen from their beds and were armed and ready for an assault they remained where they were. The facts may have been exaggerated but the news galvanised Somerset into action as he prepared for an attack on the palace. Hampton Court had not been built as a fortified structure and was not designed to withstand an assault. For the only time in its history, the palace prepared for battle. The stones paving the courtyards were dug up and carried to the roof above the west gate, ready to be hurled down on to attackers. Heavy logs were piled up at the back gate so that assailants could only enter at the west gate and armed servants, including kitchen boys, were placed around the courtyards. Throughout the morning people flocked to the palace from the local towns in answer to the summons of the previous day, including Cranmer, who brought with him sixty men. By noon, 4,000 of the king's subjects had arrived carrying weapons and armour for his defence. Due to the insufficiency of food and drink at the palace, Somerset was forced to appoint captains to select the most suitable and send the rest away.

With the king at his side, Somerset gathered everyone around him in Base Court and addressed the people in a rousing speech. Warwick, he explained, intended to remove him from power and make Mary regent. He reminded the audience of Richard III's usurpation of the throne and even suggested that perhaps it was really the king that Warwick sought to replace, not him. Edward, he continued, was 'as the apple of my eye' and his death would be Somerset's downfall and ruin. With his declaration that he would be one of the first to die defending the king, a loud cheer went up from the crowd. Edward joined in with the spirit of the moment, affirming his support for his uncle and calling upon the people to join him 'for he himself was clothed, and ready to arm'.[18]

Tensions rose as each side responded to rumours and prepared to oppose a perceived threat which had not initially existed. In London the councillors were booted and ready to ride to Hampton Court to talk with Somerset when news arrived that he was raising an army. Abandoning their plan, they were soon busy outlining their grievances to the Lord Mayor and aldermen and issuing orders that no men or arms should be sent to him. Around the city, guards were set at all the gates to prevent Somerset sending in a force.

Opposition to the Protector was growing. On Sunday, ten councillors met at Ely Place where Warwick lived – St John, Warwick, Arundel, Southampton, Petre, Sir Edward North, Sir Edward Wotton, Sir Richard Southwell, Sir Edmund Peckham and Dr Wotton.[19] In a move possibly intended to exonerate themselves from future charges of disloyalty to the king, the councillors in London kept a careful record of the situation as it appeared to them, citing the reasons for their actions. They blamed the recent rebellions upon the 'ill government' of Somerset, who had failed to listen to their advice and had chosen instead to 'follow his own fantasies', which had led to the loss of both Haddington and the French forts. Their earlier intention, they said, had been only to have 'friendly communication' with Somerset about reforming his manner of government, but they were now afraid to come to court for fear he would destroy them. The situation had very quickly deteriorated into a stand-off.

During the day Somerset sent Edward Wolf, a member of the privy chamber, to London to secure the Tower for the king. With its store of weapons he did not want the fortress to fall into the hands of the London councillors, but he was too late. St John reached the Tower before Wolf, and the lieutenant, following instructions from the council, placed it under his control. Petre was also sent to London with a letter from the king accusing the councillors of failing in their loyalty to him. Their response the following day was in suitably grovelling tones as they tried to convince the king of their fidelity.[20]

It must have been heartening for Somerset when support arrived in the figure of Sir Philip Hoby, a skilled diplomat and negotiator who had returned home briefly from his post as resident ambassador to the emperor. Hoby, who had served under Somerset in Scotland in 1545 and had been one of his strong supporters, was described by Warwick as 'entirely devoted to the Protector, as his creature'.[21] However, he had the advantage of being trusted by both sides in this dispute and would play a major role in the negotiations that were to follow.

Nevertheless, Somerset became increasingly worried and his appeals for help became urgent and more desperate. He despatched his son, Lord Edward Seymour, with a further letter to Russell to emphasise the gravity of the situation. In expectation of Herbert's imminent arrival, Somerset addressed his letter only to Russell calling upon him to bring 'such force and power' as he could to defend the king.[22] The situation had changed and he no longer wanted just the support of a few councillors; he needed an army to withstand a possible attack. However, he ordered Russell to bring his force not to Hampton Court but to the king at Windsor Castle. Somerset planned to move to the fortress, built to withstand assault and more easily defended than the palace.

At 5 p.m. on Sunday Somerset sent his wife to Beddington Manor in Surrey, a royal manor of which her brother, Michael Stanhope, was keeper. With the threat of armed confrontation he wanted to ensure Anne's safety but as she left the palace, weeping, she had to endure the taunts of courtiers and peasants who believed her influence on her husband had led to much of the trouble. Two hours later Somerset accompanied King Edward as he rode out of the palace surrounded by his courtiers, servants and guard.[23] Creeping away under cover of darkness without the ceremony of an impressive procession was not what Edward was used to. The young king, who was only six days away from his 12th birthday, did not enjoy the long ride to Windsor.

The party reached the castle around midnight. Three hours later a carriage arrived from Hampton Court with some of the king's belongings but Windsor was to prove a dismal place after the comforts of Hampton. Edward's palaces were sparsely furnished and when he moved from one to another supplies of food were organised in advance and items such as beds, tapestries and kitchen goods were moved so that when the king arrived all was in readiness and his move between houses was seamless. This occasion could not have been more different. No preparations had been made. One can imagine that the walls were still bare – there had been no time to hang tapestries – and the fires were still cold. They found little provision of food, only four large casks of wine and a little beer. The following day, however, on being informed that Somerset had taken the king to Windsor, the council arranged for all manner of provisions to be delivered to the castle, together with a letter assuring Edward of their loyalty and good intentions.[24]

To Somerset's surprise Petre had not returned from London and the councillors admitted that they had 'caused' him to remain since most of the council were there together – and he was, after all, the council secretary. As he read the list of signatures on their letter Somerset became aware of the strength of opposition against him. The arrival in London of Rich, Sir Thomas Cheyne, Sir John Gage, Sir Edward Montagu, Sir Ralph Sadler and Sir John Baker brought the number of councillors to sixteen. Even with the backing of Russell and Herbert – who had so far failed to respond to his calls for help – and with only Cranmer, Paget and Smith beside him, Somerset was facing overwhelming odds. As he realised that he might soon be facing defeat and the possibility of reprisals, he sought to salvage what he could from the situation. Writing to the councillors that day, Somerset conceded that if they offered reasonable conditions, and the king was not harmed, he would agree to their terms. Above all else he would not jeopardise Edward's safety and he added that he would fight to the death if they should attempt anything against the king.[25]

Letters between Windsor and London were passing in opposite directions on the road. On Monday the council in London wrote to the three councillors who remained at Windsor reciting their main grievance against Somerset, that he would never listen to their advice, and explaining that because he had assembled so many men they had been forced to follow suit. They offered a solution – that he should leave the king, disperse his forces and 'be ordered according to justice and reason'.[26] This final vague statement gave no hint of what they planned to do with Somerset. The letter ended with a threat. If Cranmer, Paget and Smith refused a peaceful agreement, caring more for 'one man's ill doings' than for the execution of the king's laws, any disturbances that followed would be of their doing. In a bid to stop more people rallying to Somerset's side, the London councillors also issued a strongly worded proclamation calling him 'a great traitor' whose 'malicious and evil government' was the cause of all the recent sedition. He was 'ambitious and sought his own glory' which was proved, they said, by his building the 'most sumptuous and costly houses' at a time when the king was at war – surely an allusion to the unfounded idea that he had used royal funds to finance his ambitious projects.[27]

After his flight to Windsor, Somerset was aware that if he should be found guilty of some extreme charge his property and belongings would be forfeit to the crown. If matters turned out badly for the Lord Protector, the court vultures would soon be circling in hope of rich pickings from goods confiscated by the king and distributed as largesse among his favourites. So, in a well-managed plan, over the next few days his servants spirited goods out of Syon and Sheen and removed them to their own houses. Coffers and other items were conveyed to the homes of Somerset's brother-in-law, Michael Stanhope, his household chamberlain Richard Whalley, and his clerk, Ravys. Even the duchess helped, taking four square caskets by boat to Whalley's house at Wimbledon. In Richmond, Somerset's porter, footman, yeoman of the scullery and carter all moved coffers, bedding and other objects to their houses by day and night. 'Certain stuff' was transferred to Kew by boat at night. No onlookers were allowed to see what was moved. 'Scouts' were set on the roads to stop people coming out to watch. Despite being aware that three of Somerset's servants, including his physician, William Turner, and Miles Partridge, dwelt at Kew the councillors would later be unable to identify exactly where the goods had been stored. The duke's surgeon, Huddy, removed two geldings from Sheen and broke a door to get into Syon to remove three beds and a coffer to Turner's house. Bedding, carpets, hangings and other items were moved by Somerset's surveyor of the works to his own house at Isleworth. The bailiff at Syon even sold as much wood as he could, in order to realise money.[28]

On Tuesday 8 October, Lord Edward Seymour returned to Windsor and Somerset at last received a response from Russell and Herbert, but it was not what he had hoped for. The two men were not prepared to aid him. Although Somerset had maintained that the London councillors were conspiring against the king, Russell and Herbert were now aware that their grudge was not against Edward but on account of 'private causes' between the councillors and Somerset. Knowing that the majority of the council had already turned against Somerset, the two commanders' decision must have been influenced by their own instinct for survival. They were unlikely to support a lost cause. Their great fear, they wrote, was that the noblemen might turn upon each other and that 'the quarrel once begun will never have end till the realm be descended to that woeful calamity that all our posterity shall lament the chance'. So they intended to use the force at their disposal to maintain peace between the two sides and they urged Somerset to 'conform yourself' to avoid greater trouble.[29]

It was only three days since Somerset had first summoned help but the response from Russell and Herbert ended all his hopes. Somerset realised he could no longer continue as Lord Protector and that day he wrote to the councillors admitting defeat. He had never intended to harm them, he explained, and had only prepared to defend himself and the king after hearing that they had armed themselves. In the hope of reaching a favourable settlement, he agreed to accept any reasonable terms to ensure the safety of the king and the peace of the realm.[30]

His letter was accompanied by another, from the king, with a plea and also a warning to the London councillors to treat his uncle gently. However much they considered Somerset to be wilful, Edward wrote, he and his council at Windsor had 'found him so tractable' and he hoped that his uncle would continue to serve him 'by your good advices'. Acknowledging that Somerset had faults, Edward warned them against harming him, pointing out sharply that:

Each man hath his faults; he, his, and you yours; and if we shall hereafter as rigorously weigh yours, as we hear that you intend with cruelty to purge his, which of you all shall be able to stand before us?

Somerset, Edward continued, had not used himself 'so discreetly' in his government as he might have done. However, the king did not believe this warranted extreme punishment and he forgave him because 'he is our uncle, whom you know we love'.[31] It would be a brave councillor who would be cruel to Somerset after this exhortation.

Despite the threatening letter from the London councillors and the realisation that the Protectorate was coming to an end, Cranmer, Paget and Smith had not deserted Somerset, although Smith wrote to Petre that he was in a 'most miserable case', unable to leave the king or 'him who was my master, of whom I have had all'. Accepting that Somerset must resign, the three men set about securing reasonable terms to protect his life and property. When Hoby left the castle to take the letters from the king and Somerset to London he also carried a letter from the three councillors in which they pointed out that it was unreasonable for Somerset to surrender without knowing what conditions the councillors would impose. 'Life is sweet, my Lords, and they say you seek his blood and his death.' They implored the councillors to allow him to live peacefully and to treat him with 'kindness and humanity; remembering that he hath never been cruel to any of you'.[32] Somerset may never have been cruel to any of the lords but he had certainly upset several of them. The final letter in Hoby's package was from Somerset to Warwick lamenting why, after such a long friendship, Warwick should have such enmity for him and, perhaps rather pathetically at this point, asking him to remain his friend.[33]

In London, still unaware that Somerset had capitulated, the lords were busy working to blacken his reputation further. At 4 p.m. trumpets were blown around London to signal the reading of a proclamation detailing Somerset's 'evil government, false and detestable proceedings'. It called upon the people to aid the council in releasing the king from the 'hands of so great a traitor'.[34] Meanwhile, various bills were being circulated favouring Somerset. Deriding the councillors and praising the Protector for his support for the common folk, the bills were intended to be inflammatory. One, for example, accused the councillors of seeking to prevent Somerset calling Parliament to redress the recent complaints by the rebels. Unsigned and couched in terms that suggested they had been written by one of Somerset's supporters, they may have originated in Windsor Castle. The bills were proving effective. Russell and Herbert had reached Andover just in time to prevent a force of over 5,000 men marching to Windsor to join the Protector.[35]

The Duchess of Somerset had been kept informed by Stanhope of what was happening to her husband. On Tuesday she wrote begging Paget to do what he could to resolve the differences between the two sides. Anne was distraught, unable to understand why the lords had turned against Somerset, for she knew he was innocent of all the charges against him. 'What hath my lord done to any of these noble men or others that they should thus rage and seek the extremity to him?', she asked Paget. Anne was convinced the trouble had been caused by 'wicked' men but was equally sure that God would defend her husband from his enemies 'as he hath always done hitherto'.[36]

On Wednesday 9 October the London councillors penned their replies to the letters which Hoby had delivered the previous evening. They were rather cautious in their response, as if they were not entirely convinced by Somerset's acknowledgement of defeat, and later that day they issued a further proclamation accusing Somerset of continuing his 'wilful doings'.[37] Hoby set out for Windsor with the replies but during the journey he turned back, claiming that he had lost the letters to the king. Not wishing to trust anyone else, he returned to London to find them or to obtain another copy and sent his servant on to Windsor to tell them that all was well. However, this may have been a ruse to gain more time until the councillors were sure which side Russell and Herbert had chosen to support, a factor that would make a crucial difference. Hoby may well have chosen to favour the London councillors' case. It would appear that he too had been upset by the Protector when Somerset gave appointments vacated at the death of Anthony Denny to one of his own men rather than to Hoby.[38]

The following day, after the welcome news had reached London that Russell and Herbert supported the councillors, Hoby made the journey to Windsor. Fearful that the guard might attempt to protect Somerset, Hoby first secured the castle, announcing that all was well, and gave orders for the soldiers to depart. That done, the gates were shut with the instruction that only the king's servants would be allowed in and permitted to carry weapons within the court.

Inside the castle Somerset and the king waited. The letters Hoby carried were to be read before the whole court so that everyone understood the situation. In a solemn procession Somerset followed the king into the presence chamber where he stood as Hoby read the letters. In them the councillors implored Cranmer, Paget and Smith to join with them and impressed upon the king their hope for clemency since they had done only what they believed to be best for him. They had no desire, Hoby read, to take away Somerset's lands or goods and intended no hurt against him. They would continue to honour him as the king's uncle and only wished to 'give good order for the Protectorship, which hath not been so well ordered as they think it should have been'. At the news that Somerset was not to be harmed, men wept with joy. Paget fell to the ground clasping him about the knees and weeping as he praised the generosity and leniency of the councillors.[39]

Somerset had lost, but he had survived and his relief must have been overwhelming. He had expected to be treated harshly and had asked only that he should be allowed to live quietly but it appeared his life could continue as before. He was to be deprived only of his position as Lord Protector. However, the lords had drawn up a list of twenty-nine accusations condemning his conduct towards them and his actions as Protector. The councillors had no intention of leaving Somerset at liberty in the immediate future and Hoby quickly assigned twelve guards to accompany him back to his chamber. Smith, Stanhope, Thynne, Wolf and Cecil were similarly confined.

On Friday morning, when Wingfield arrived at the castle with 500 horsemen, Somerset was under guard and it was the king who greeted him 'with a merry countenance and a loud voice' and asked about the London councillors and when he would see them. Despite suffering with a cold brought on partly by riding through the night and partly by the cold air of the castle, Edward appeared to be none the worse for his ordeal. 'In good health and merry' he was, nevertheless, ready to leave Windsor. 'Methinks I am in prison; here be no galleries nor no gardens to walk in', he complained. Because Somerset's chamber was next to the king's he was moved to the Beauchamp Tower, well away from his nephew. Somerset's two sons, Edward and Henry, who had accompanied the king as his companions, were sent home to join their siblings. The previous day Whalley had been sent to Bedington to comfort the duchess.[40] The duke's fall from power also meant her fall from grace.

On Saturday 12 October, just one week after the first sign of trouble, Warwick and the other councillors arrived at Windsor. Presenting themselves before the king, they explained their actions and waited for his approbation of what they had done. Somerset no longer had his nephew's full confidence and Edward was quick to give his support to the councillors. The following day their first action was to issue letters patent in which the king revoked the earlier letters patent appointing Somerset to be Lord Protector and Governor of the King.[41] In one quick move Somerset was removed from a position which had earlier seemed unassailable.

Two days later, after being interviewed by the councillors, Somerset was accompanied on the long journey to the Tower by the Earls of Sussex and Huntingdon and a large guard contingent. As the cavalcade rode along Cheapside, the deposed Protector proudly declared to the watching people that he was 'no traitor, but as faithful a servant of the king as any man'.[42] Somerset's downfall also signalled the fall of his adherents. Stanhope, Thynne, Wolf and Smith (who was deprived of his office as secretary of state) were all moved to the Tower where they were kept confined apart. In all, ten of Somerset's supporters and servants were imprisoned including his secretary Fisher, clerk of the works Richard Paldye and John Hales. Their servants were also unable to leave, remaining continuously with their masters 'to avoid secret practices and intelligence'.[43] Somerset could still be dangerous to the councillors and they could not risk any attempt to release him. They now faced a difficult decision. If they executed him the king might later revenge his uncle's death but if they did not, Somerset might one day destroy them.

Somerset's overthrow was undoubtedly his own fault. His independent style of rule and his actions during the previous few days had left the councillors with no alternative. However, the king and the executors of the will, who had granted Somerset such unfettered authority, should bear some responsibility for the situation they faced. They had failed to consider that such power could be abused, even unintentionally. Somerset never meant any harm to the king, the country or its people but his instinct for what was needed was not always right. If he had been allowed to continue unchecked there was no way of knowing where he might have taken the country. Perhaps England was saved from further strife by this coup.

The Protectorate was finished and would not be re-established. There had been nothing wrong in the idea of having a Lord Protector; it was Somerset's manner of exercising the office that had been wrong. If he and the privy councillors had shared the same understanding and the same vision he might have remained as Lord Protector until Edward came of age. But he had interpreted his role in a different way to the councillors and had been too confident in his own capabilities. Ultimately he fell from power because he became isolated. At the end, only Cranmer, Paget and Smith stood by him. He had alienated many men and failed to recognise the strength of opposition to both himself and his policies. Somerset had lost sight of his place in government and assumed that all men would give him the same unquestioned loyalty they gave to the king. In reality, he needed to court their friendship and support. Although he was the king's representative, the Protector of his realm, underneath he was a courtier like any other. The king held authority by divine right but Somerset had held it only with the consent of the king and the support of the other notable men of the day.

18

Restoration

As Somerset languished in the Tower, Warwick took control of the privy council. He had no intention of establishing himself as Lord Protector but, without the authority which the position endowed, he needed to be sure of the councillors' support. The best way to accomplish this was to fill the privy council with his allies. Henry VIII had intended the composition of the council to remain unchanged but Parliament had granted Somerset authority to remove and appoint members as he chose, and Warwick intended to assume this authority. He also intended to win the trust and support of the 12-year-old king. By establishing a good relationship with him and introducing him to the art of government, Warwick would be in a strong position when Edward assumed power. In the meantime, he needed to have influence over him and the best way to achieve that was through control of the privy chamber.

The day after Somerset was taken to the Tower, the council agreed that the king should have new men among his attendants. Six were to be noblemen – Warwick, Northampton, Arundel, St John, Russell and Lord Thomas Wentworth – at least two of whom were always to be in attendance, together with four principal gentlemen – Sir Andrew Dudley, Sir Thomas Wroth, Sir Thomas Darcy and Sir Edward Rogers (whom Warwick quickly replaced with Sir John Gates). The office of Governor of the King was effectively shared between the six noblemen. Although they were appointed ostensibly for the 'good government' and 'honourable education' of Edward, these ten men gave Warwick control of the privy chamber.[1] They controlled access to the king and could use their influence on Warwick's behalf.

Immediately after the coup many men, both Catholics and reformers, believed that with Somerset out of power the country might return to the old religion. The Catholics' hopes were soon dashed. Apart from Arundel and St John, the king's new attendants all held reformist views, as did more than half the privy councillors. In November Warwick announced that further reformation would take place and on Christmas Day 1549 a proclamation ended rumours of any return to the old Latin service. Instead, it upheld the use of the new prayer book and ordered the bishops to collect and destroy all books of Catholic worship.[2]

Realising that their hopes were in jeopardy, the Catholics had been thrown into disarray during November when Southampton was very ill and close to death. A few councillors were well disposed towards Catholicism, but only Southampton was sufficiently powerful to be an effective opponent to the reformers, whose numbers had increased during November when Warwick made his first two council appointments – Thomas Goodrich, Bishop of Ely, and the Marquis of Dorset.

Southampton was ambitious and influential but much of his authority had derived from his office of Lord Chancellor. He had insufficient support to oppose either Somerset or Warwick and take overall control of the council for himself. He could, nevertheless, exert enormous power working alongside Warwick and for a few weeks van der Delft certainly believed that the two men were governing in partnership. Warwick has acquired a reputation for being a Machiavellian character, partly due to the supposition that he had planned to use Southampton and Arundel to remove Somerset and then to cast them aside while he continued religious reform. However, it seems that Southampton may have been the real conspirator.[3]

In December, Southampton's health improved and he joined Arundel and St John in examining Somerset concerning 'treasons in his government'. Southampton was intent on his ruin, 'very busy to follow him to death' in revenge for past grudges. Questioning went on for several days. An authoritative contemporary report stated that Somerset did not deny the allegations against him but maintained that everything he had done was with 'the advice and consent' of Warwick. Although not entirely true, this assertion gave Southampton the solution to another problem – how to deal with Warwick. Somerset had, unwittingly, shown him a way forward but it was one that would unexpectedly secure Somerset's life.

Aware that Warwick would be an obstacle to a complete Catholic resurgence, Southampton now saw a way to be rid of him. By accusing Warwick of being an accomplice to Somerset, he could remove both men in one stroke for 'they were both worthy to die'. When their examination of Somerset was completed, Southampton explained his plan to Arundel and St John. Arundel was enthusiastic, agreeing that on the day of Somerset's execution they would arrest Warwick. St John said little but that night went secretly to visit Warwick at his home to tell him of Southampton's plan and warn him that if he pursued Somerset's death he was sealing his own fate too.

One day soon afterwards, when the councillors were gathered at Warwick's house, Southampton made his move. Confident that he had Warwick's support against Somerset, he declared the deposed Protector to be guilty of treason and deserving to die. Warwick knew the moment had come and that his own condemnation would follow, but he was prepared. Laying his hand upon the sword by his side, he faced Southampton with 'a warlike visage' and accused him with the words 'my lord, you seek his blood and he that seeketh his blood would have mine also'. Stunned into silence by this completely unexpected response, Southampton was defeated and Somerset was saved.

By mid-December Warwick was seeking a way of securing Somerset's release. He was even on good terms with the Duchess of Somerset, who often visited his house.[4] On 23 December Somerset signed a document acknowledging his 'offences, faults and crimes' and submitted himself to the mercy of the king and council with a plea for pity on himself, his wife and children. This document contained twenty-nine charges. Nine of them accused him of abusing his authority as Lord Protector by ignoring councillors' advice, acting without their consent, rebuking them and concluding business alone with ambassadors. Ten concerned his actions during the rebellions and included the charges that he had favoured the rebels and had blamed the landowners' greed as one cause of the disturbances. The enclosure commission of the previous summer and the proclamation he issued ordering landowners to open up enclosures, both 'against the wills of all the council', were cited as being contributory causes of the rebellion. Eight of the charges concerned his treatment of the king and councillors during the previous October and two were related to his failure to strengthen Boulogne, Newhaven and Blackness. Yet, surprisingly, no mention was now made of Somerset's Scottish policy and the recent loss of Haddington. There were also no charges against him in connection with his religious reforms.[5]

It was questionable whether any of these charges could take Somerset to the block but they were sufficiently serious to remove him from office. There does appear to have been an emphasis on quantity rather than quality, and many of the extreme charges made against him at the time of his arrest had been dropped. He was no longer accused of malicious and evil government, for instance, or described as a great traitor who was ambitious and sought his own glory. However, to regain his freedom Somerset had no choice but to admit to all the charges whether or not he believed himself guilty. Upon this admission of guilt Warwick felt able to relax the conditions of Somerset's imprisonment and on Christmas

Day the duchess was allowed to visit her husband.[6] The warders of the Tower made great efforts to ensure Somerset's comfort. He was so impressed by their diligence that after his release he secured the privilege for them to wear the same livery as the Yeomen of the Guard and they became known as Yeomen Warders.[7]

Warwick, though, was worried. He could no longer trust Southampton and rumours, at the time of the coup, that Mary might become regent, although unfounded, increased his concern about the Catholics. It was a time of plot and counter-plot. The only way to ensure his own safety was to remove Southampton from the privy council. By 14 January 1550 orders had been issued for Southampton and Arundel to leave court and be placed under house arrest. Southampton left hurriedly at night, before the order arrived, and never returned. He was seriously ill and died the following July. Arundel was removed from his position as Lord Chamberlain and confined on the rather feeble charge of 'certain crimes of suspicion against him, as plucking down of bolts and locks at Westminster' and giving away the king's belongings. Bolts and locks for doors in the royal chambers of the palaces were of high quality, decorated and valuable. It was not unusual for them to be purloined and the penalty if caught could be imprisonment. In this instance the charge does seem bizarre. Whether guilty or not Arundel's fine of £12,000 was extreme, a rather vindictive response from Warwick, and before it had been paid much of the fine was remitted.[8]

Somerset remained in the Tower until Warwick felt sufficiently secure. On 16 January two more reformers – Sir Thomas Darcy and Walter Devereux, Viscount Hereford – were appointed to the council and during the next few weeks Warwick extended his control by placing his own men in the chief positions at court. It was something that Somerset had singularly failed to do. These rewards and promotions were thanks for past aid and inducements for future support; Warwick intended to use them to keep power in the hands of just a few men, his adherents in the privy chamber. Only five days after Southampton's removal St John was well rewarded for his timely warning to Warwick when he and Russell were advanced to the earldoms of Wiltshire and Bedford respectively. The following month St John was appointed Lord Treasurer while Russell remained as Lord Privy Seal. Northampton was appointed Lord Great Chamberlain, Lord Wentworth became chamberlain and Darcy vice-chamberlain of the household. Shortly afterwards Warwick took overall control when he assumed the office of Lord Great Master with the associated post of president of the privy council, two appointments which increased his authority over both the court and the council.

Before his arrest Somerset had summoned Parliament to meet on 4 November. It had been his intention to pass legislation addressing some of the rebels' complaints. However, this was an issue which the other lords had no intention of considering and hopes of reform were dashed. Warwick was unsure how the two houses would respond to Somerset's arrest but he needed Parliament to repeal some of the Lord Protector's legislation. Fearful of further outbreaks of violence, he believed that only a return to the harsher regime of Henry VIII would guarantee a peaceful country. One new bill in particular, which overturned Somerset's attempts to lessen the authoritarian control over the people, would have ramifications for the deposed Protector two years later. This act against unlawful assemblies was intended to prevent any reoccurrence of the rebellions but it was also a return to the more stringent controls and punishments of the previous reign. It introduced tougher penalties to prevent crowds gathering. Inciting an unlawful assembly, for example, became a felony and carried the death penalty. In particular, it became treason for twelve or more people to meet with the intention of imprisoning or killing a member of the privy council and then failing to disperse when ordered to do so. Notably, this act contained no requirement for there to be two witnesses before a charge could be brought.[9]

This was government by fearful men. The bill had a difficult passage through Parliament, presumably on account of its severity; there were many men who preferred the lighter touch of Somerset's laws. Warwick did, though, make a concession towards less severe punishments by repealing Somerset's act against beggars and vagabonds. The harshness of this act, that had condemned some people to a life akin to slavery, had been almost unworkable. In future, refusal to work would be punished by whipping, time in the stocks and labouring for a living but not by the brutality of Somerset's act.[10]

Warwick also curtailed the freedom of speech which Somerset had encouraged. Worried that the publication of 'fantastical prophecy' against the king and councillors might encourage disorderly behaviour, he imposed restrictions upon what people could print or say in public. Other new measures favoured landowners over the common folk. Somerset's tax on sheep and wool was lifted, although a wealth tax was imposed to replace the lost revenue. A further act gave landowners more power to enclose their land. Somerset was powerless as he saw his attempts to allow people more freedom being swept away. He must have been greatly heartened, however, by legislation which reinforced the recent proclamation that the new prayer book was to remain and all Catholic books and remaining religious images were to be destroyed.[11]

Somerset's most important social and public order legislation must be considered to have been a failure, since Parliament quickly saw fit to repeal so much of it. Some of his ideas were visionary but they were either unworkable or inappropriate for the time. The people did not know how to use their newly granted freedom. As Paget had written, society was maintained by religion and laws. Without the control of law England became ungovernable. It was also a very hierarchical society: everyone knew their place and those in authority were not prepared to give up their rights to those they considered inferior. Somerset's contemporaries did not share his generosity of spirit towards the lower classes.

By mid-January there were rumours that Somerset would soon be released and he was allowed frequent visits from his wife and friends.[12] A deputation from Parliament had visited him at the beginning of the month to establish whether his confession to the twenty-nine charges had been given freely and not under duress. Once satisfied of this, Parliament ratified his confession and on 14 January he was formally deposed as Lord Protector and the fine for his release was set. It appears that the initial sum was quite substantial. On 2 February, the day after Parliament adjourned, Somerset wrote a grovelling letter to the council pleading for pardon and asking them to reduce the fine since he was unable to pay such a large amount. However, fearful of a more stringent punishment he was grateful that his penalty was only a fine. His plea may well have been successful, for the king later recorded that Somerset had been made to forfeit nearly £2,000-worth of land, a sizeable but not impossible fine for a man of his wealth, together with all his valuable movable goods and his appointments.[13] At his imprisonment, all his goods, buildings and land had become the property of the king but during the year much of this would be granted back to him.

The council ordered an investigation to establish what property belonging to the king was in the duke's possession. From this inventory, together with others made earlier in the year, it appears that Somerset and his wife had been rather free in taking items for their own use. Lists of goods that had been removed from the king's 'secret' houses at Westminster Palace and elsewhere indicate a couple who enjoyed the good things of life and who, perhaps in the belief that Somerset had supreme authority, had no qualms about helping themselves. In August 1547 crimson velvet had been taken from the silk house to cover a wagon for Somerset's use, but the bill was still unpaid. The following summer silk and satin intended for the Earl of Ormond were delivered instead to the duke's chamber at Sheen. Michael Stanhope had helped the duchess to carry coifs, cloths, counterpanes and pillows, wrapped in a sheet, to her chamber. On another occasion he helped her to remove a wooden coffer, a desk, a looking glass and an alabaster hourglass.

Items that might ordinarily have found their way into the king's houses were also delivered to Somerset. The best plate, altar cloths and hangings from St Stephen's Church in Westminster went to the duke, the rest to Vane and Thynne. Jewels and other items that had belonged to Somerset's brother and to Norfolk, and tapestries, down beds, woollen quilts, silk canopies and table linen (worth over £300) removed after Sharington's arrest, also went to the couple. There was evidence of duplicitousness. A diamond and a white ruby, worth at least £100, were taken by Fulmerston for Anne Somerset, who later told Lady Sharington that they were of no value. Somerset's acquisitiveness stretched outside his household chambers. He had sold lead, stone and 'stuff' from several properties, the profits of which should have gone to the king. There was even the suggestion he had kept 1,000 marks given by the city of London to the king at his coronation.[14]

On 6 February Somerset was escorted by the lieutenant of the Tower and taken by barge to the wharf at Vintry, upstream from London Bridge. From there they travelled by horse to the house of Mr York, one of the London sheriffs, where Warwick was recovering from a long illness. Van der Delft noted that Warwick had also taken up residence at York's house in October, when he had been scheming against Somerset, and believed it was done to ensure he had the support of the city officials for his intrigues. Somerset was escorted to Warwick and the privy council where, in an act of subservience that had become unfamiliar to him, he doffed his cap and remained with his head uncovered.[15]

Somerset was to be freed. The terms of his release were explained and then, accompanied by Wentworth and Herbert, he left the council and took his barge to Somerset House to visit his wife before making his way out of the city.[16] He was free of the Tower but did not have complete freedom. He had been ordered to live under house arrest at either Syon or Sheen and was not permitted to travel more than 4 miles from the property. Additionally, if either the king or any privy councillor should pass nearby he was not to approach them. Warwick and the council would not allow him any opportunity to inveigle his way back into favour. As a further incentive for good behaviour, he was reputedly placed under a bond of £10,000.[17]

The king's pardon followed a few days later and for six weeks Somerset enjoyed the comforts of confinement in his own house rather than the Tower until, at the end of March, his bond was lifted and he was allowed to return to court.[18] Warwick was confident of his position and felt sufficiently secure to release Somerset. The following month van der Delft described Warwick as 'absolute master here' because nothing was done without his consent. Illness frequently kept him away from court but he retained control of government. Councillors visited him at home, documents were sent for his perusal and amendment and Warwick sent instructions and advice to the councillors by letter.[19]

It is quite remarkable that the transition of power from Somerset to Warwick had been completed so smoothly. The Lord Protector had been toppled and yet England remained stable and government continued to function. Without a powerful monarch to control the activities of ambitious councillors, there was every opportunity for war between factions within the privy council. Yet the council was unified and the councillors appear to have demonstrated a remarkable sense of purpose and resolve to maintain calm. The majority of the councillors had united and turned against Somerset. At the end he had stood alone, a single man against the rest.

Somerset, nevertheless, still commanded respect from the councillors and he was soon back at court. On 8 April 1550, before dining with them, he was allowed into the king's presence for the first time since they had been together at Windsor Castle in October and soon after that he was restored to the privy council and readmitted as a gentleman of the privy chamber. When he took his place at the council table on 24 April it was no longer as Lord Protector and Lord Treasurer; he was recorded only as 'The Duke of Somerset', with no official appointment. He was, though, given precedence over all the other officers including Archbishop Cranmer, the Lord Chancellor and the Lord Treasurer, whose offices generally placed them above other men of higher rank.[20] His rehabilitation was completed at the beginning of June with the return of many of his movable goods (household items including his gold and silver plate, jewels and money) and his land and property, although the king kept some as payment for Somerset's fine. He was re-granted numerous manors and houses including Somerset Place, Syon and Glastonbury and woods, parks and land in Wiltshire, Somerset, Hampshire, Dorset, Devon, Gloucestershire, Berkshire, Oxfordshire, Buckinghamshire, Middlesex and Lincolnshire.[21]

Both Somerset and Warwick knew it would be difficult for the former Protector to adapt to a more subservient position in the privy council. Both men were ambitious and sought power and each was fearful of the other. Somerset feared that Warwick might try again to bring him down – the expulsion of Southampton proved that Warwick could remove anyone who stood in his way. Warwick, meanwhile, feared the support that Somerset still held throughout the country and at court; lacking the title of Lord Protector and kinship to the king, he could not expect to exercise as much authority as Somerset had done. Warwick had good reason to be cautious about Somerset's return to court. By the end of April men already sought Somerset's company in the expectation that he would return to power as president of the privy council or Governor of the King. The diplomat Sir John Mason told van der Delft on 12 April that he believed Somerset would 'come back into authority as before, and this will happen because there is no one else to take his place'. At the beginning of May, van der Delft was still referring to Somerset as Protector.[22]

Warwick made great efforts to ensure he maintained control of the privy council. He had learned from Somerset's mistake and attempted to minimise the risk of being overthrown by surrounding himself with his adherents. With the removal of some councillors and the periodic appointments of a further twenty men, the council sometimes numbered over thirty members. In reality, however, only a few of them regularly attended council meetings. Many of them either held no official appointment or occupied positions that usually did not warrant membership of the privy council. Warwick, though, hoped that he could rely upon the loyalty of all these men if required and it is notable that half of them were noblemen who could each raise an armed force.

His appointment as president of the privy council was a supervisory role that gave Warwick limited authority over the council's decisions. He was empowered to call and preside at meetings, to set agenda and to speak towards the end of debates with the advantage that his comments were fresh in the councillors' minds as they made their decisions. He did much to improve the machinery of government by using the privy council in a more democratic manner than Somerset had done. Meetings of councillors were held more frequently and records were kept of attendance and business. Yet Warwick's grip on the council was so strong that no one dared oppose him, and his pursuit of power left the practice of government not so very different from what it had been under Somerset.

It is likely that Warwick was confident he could control the privy council but knew he could not control Parliament. If Somerset had sufficient support in the lower house there might be a move to reinstate him as Lord Protector. After the parliamentary session had finished on 1 February 1550 Warwick chose not to use the legislative assembly again during Somerset's lifetime and Daniel Barbaro, the Venetian ambassador, believed that many matters that should have been referred to Parliament were instead settled by the council. Despite the opposition of Lord Chancellor Rich, Warwick ensured that Parliament was repeatedly prorogued throughout 1550 and 1551.[23]

Warwick was also consolidating his position with the king. If he was to maintain any authority after Edward took control he needed to establish a good relationship with him. Edward had so far played a minor role in government – only his signature was important – but he had now reached an age where he was ready to be introduced to the business of governing the realm. He was the first king to receive an intensive education to fit him for his future role. Cox and Cheke gave him sound instruction in Greek and Latin and trained him to think and write clearly. An intelligent child, he took a natural interest in government and, encouraged by Warwick, he began attending occasional meetings of the privy council. He examined council documents, added his own comments and then wrote his own papers, agenda and memoranda of matters to be considered by the council and even Parliament. Initially these inputs were probably drafted from ideas propounded by Warwick and his tutors but as time passed they increasingly became his own work and show a particular attention to detail.

His papers covered a wide range of topics, often displaying an especial interest in financial matters. In one lengthy document, where he used the device of comparing society to the body and showing how each part of the body contributed to the well-being of the whole, he wrote of the evils of enclosure, of men owning vast flocks of sheep and of the criminality of unemployed people, echoing some of Somerset's social concerns.[24] However, his belief that dissension in society was exacerbated by the 'slack execution of the laws' suggests that he did not share his uncle's reluctance to use punishment. Edward was also encouraged to take a keen interest in religion. He listened intently to sermons, making a copy of them for later study. Early on he came to appreciate the importance of his position as head of the Church, noting proudly in his diary that the oath he took ratifying a treaty with the French proclaimed him to be 'Supreme Head of the Church of England and Ireland'.[25]

Somerset and Warwick were to have an uneasy time in government as the deposed Protector watched the reversal of some of his policies. The two men shared the traditional concern for peace and stability but their views and approach to handling these issues were different. While Somerset wanted to relieve the oppression of the people, Warwick believed that this path led to rebellion. On religion Somerset supported moderate Protestantism; Warwick was more evangelical. Somerset was intent on maintaining Henry VIII's foreign policy; Warwick's attention was turned inwards to maintain peace in England. While he was tough and repressive at home, abroad he was weak and withdrew from confrontation to leave him free to concentrate on events at home.

After the past three years of war in Scotland and fighting against France, England needed peace. The cost of maintaining an English presence in Scotland, Calais and Boulogne had been enormous and nothing was left in the coffers. Somerset had considered returning Boulogne to the French but his reasons for doing so were driven by concern for his policy towards Scotland. He was prepared to use the town as a bargaining tool to win French support for the Anglo-Scottish marriage. His failure to reach an agreement with Henri II and the French declaration of war left England facing military conflict on two fronts. Warwick did not want any war and Somerset could only watch his foreign policy being dismantled as Warwick gave up the conquests which Somerset and Henry VIII had made.

Warwick worked quickly and by 24 March 1550, before Somerset had been readmitted to the council, a peace treaty had been negotiated with the French. Boulogne was to be returned to France in exchange for 400,000 ecus

(French crowns). England gained little from the agreement, though: the English were to give up the town four years earlier than agreed in the previous treaty, for half the original sum, and there was no agreement that the French would support Mary's marriage to Edward. Plans were made for the the exchange. On 6 April the sons of nine peers, including Somerset's son, the Earl of Hertford, sailed to France as honorary hostages. They would return to England once Boulogne was in French hands. Similarly, French hostages travelled to England to be returned home after the money had been paid.[26]

However, since the terms of the treaty also forced England to cease any attempt to control Scotland, it left her northern neighbour under French influence and destroyed any chance of the Scottish marriage. Warwick agreed to stop fighting in Scotland and to cease border raids. Boulogne was handed over on 25 April but even before that date the English commanders in Scotland had started to surrender their forts to the Scots. Nothing remained of Somerset's victories in Scotland. The enormous cost in men and resources had all been for nothing.

Henry VIII's victory at Boulogne had been a mark of honour and a reminder of the English claim to the throne of France. It had served as a symbol of power and was an irritation to Henri II. However, although it did not serve any great military purpose, its loss weakened English ability to support Calais. Freed from the constraints of fighting against Boulogne and in Scotland, France could in future concentrate all its forces against this remaining English enclave. Of course, Henri II knew that if he attacked Calais the Emperor Charles was still bound by treaty to aid the English.

The relationship between England and the emperor was, however, a little tense. Charles V was becoming increasingly concerned at the growing entente between England and France, firstly with regard to the agreement for Boulogne and then later, in 1551, when a marriage treaty would be agreed between Edward VI and Princess Elizabeth of France. Trading relations between England and Charles's subjects in the Netherlands were fraught as merchants on both sides complained of bad treatment and piracy from the other side. Meanwhile, the new Imperial ambassador, Jean Scheyfve, objected to recent taxes imposed on merchandise by the English. More serious was the discord generated through disagreements over religion, particularly by Warwick's treatment of Princess Mary.

Somerset and Warwick were of the same religious persuasion but differed in the extent to which they embraced the new ideas. Somerset had moved only a short distance along the path of doctrinal reform and was tolerant of people who were slow to agree with his beliefs, hoping that with persuasion they would eventually follow. Warwick, whom the reformer John Hooper considered to be the 'fearless instrument of the word of God', ultimately went further in religious reform than Somerset.[27] In the *Second Book of Common Prayer* that was issued in 1552, the 'real presence' of Christ in the sacrament, which could be implied by the words of the first prayer book, was denied and it was plainly stated that the Lord's Supper was a commemoration or remembrance of Christ's sacrifice. Warwick also lacked the patience which Somerset had shown towards hard-line conservatives although it is possible that, after two years of having to cajole Gardiner and Mary to reform, Somerset, too, might have become less tolerant.

Somerset had worked hard to reach a compromise with Mary that did not impugn the king's honour as head of the Church. Mary was apprehensive, though, about whether Warwick would allow her to continue to worship as she chose. Demands by the emperor for Somerset's promise to Mary to be stated in writing, and the collapse of two schemes to spirit her out of England, further worsened the situation. The king was annoyed by her adherence to the old faith, an annoyance that can only have increased after she processed through London in March 1551 with her attendants all carrying rosary beads. Remonstrations from the king and council regarding her religious practices were met by the threat of a declaration of war from the emperor.[28] Matters intensified when the council imprisoned some of Mary's household officers after repeatedly ordering her to stop celebrating mass in her household. However, the crisis was eclipsed by the French declaration of war on the emperor in September 1551. For a time the matter of Mary's religion held less significance for Charles and the council reached a compromise with her whereby, for the time being, she was allowed to hear mass in her private chambers although there was to be no mass for her household.

Somerset played a prominent role in the council throughout the months of dispute over Mary's religious practice, often attending meetings with the Imperial ambassador, Scheyfve. Within three weeks of returning to the council, in 1550, Somerset had already been exerting his influence. The reformer John ab Ulmis believed that he had persuaded the council to appoint John Hooper, a noted Protestant preacher who had lived in Somerset's house, to be Bishop of Gloucester, against the opposition of many of the bishops. It is probable that in June Somerset was one of the proponents of the idea for Gardiner to be given an opportunity to regain his freedom if he would agree to support the religious reforms. The same day, also at Somerset's intercession, a prisoner named John Rybaulde was granted his release from the Tower.[29]

Somerset's efforts on behalf of Gardiner were to no avail. Although his old friend eventually agreed to use the prayer book and acknowledge the king as head of the Church, he refused to admit that his earlier beliefs had been wrong. Warwick, Somerset and the council tried hard to accommodate his objections and in July they gave him a further three months in which to agree to their demands.

Yet he still refused and the following year he was finally deprived of the See of Winchester.[30] During his time in power, Somerset had shown great patience towards the Catholic bishops but he, too, might eventually have felt obliged to follow the same course as Warwick. Up to the end of the Protectorate, only Bonner had been deprived and his deprivation was not confirmed until after Somerset's downfall. Warwick removed three more bishops – Nicholas Heath of Worcester, George Day of Chichester and Cuthbert Tunstall of Durham – although Tunstall's removal was probably brought about by the personal animosity of Warwick.

Perhaps the most noticeable – and extreme – difference in the religious views of Somerset and Warwick was the burning of two Protestant heretics who held unorthodox views. During Somerset's tenure no-one was sent to the stake. When Joan Bocher had been condemned as a heretic in April 1549 he refused to let the sentence be carried out. She was, instead, left in the Tower in the hope that she would recant. However, on 27 April April 1550, on a day when Somerset was absent from the council, a writ was issued for her to be burnt and the sentence was carried out five days later. The following year George van Parris, a Dutch surgeon living in London, followed her to the stake.[31]

Somerset's attempts to exert influence after his return to the council were not welcomed by Warwick. In late June 1550, Warwick expressed his concerns to Richard Whalley, Somerset's steward and a relation of his by marriage. Warwick was especially concerned at Somerset's bid to gain freedom for Gardiner and for Sir John and Thomas Arundell, who were also in the Tower. 'The whole Council', Warwick told Whalley:

> Doth much dislike his late attempts … Thinks he to rule and direct the whole
> Council as he will, considering how his late governance is yet misliked? neither
> is he in that credit and best opinion with the King's Majesty, as he believeth, and
> is by some fondly persuaded.

Whalley wrote details of the conversation to Cecil in the hope that he would encourage Somerset to change his ways. It had little effect.

Warwick's particular concern at this time may have been because the Arundells were related to the Earl of Arundel, with whom Somerset had recently spoken. Arundel had been released from house arrest at the beginning of March and Warwick was aware of the enmity the earl held for him since being cast aside in January. He may have been fearful that the men were plotting some conspiracy against him.[32]

Warwick had good cause to be worried. He had been absent from the court and council almost continuously since the beginning of March, suffering from a chronic illness that plagued him throughout his ascendancy. It is uncertain what the condition was but on one occasion his doctor had prescribed that he should take a bath and Warwick was perturbed that council business might interfere with this necessary treatment.[33] As he languished at home, reports that Somerset was re-establishing himself among his contemporaries made Warwick fearful that his adversary might regain the ascendancy in the council. Yet, despite ambassador Scheyfve's belief that Somerset was 'reinstated in honour and pre-eminence', when Warwick returned to court in July he was still very much in control of events.[34]

During his absence the court had celebrated the visit of French ambassadors to ratify the treaty for the return of Boulogne. For five days at the end of May, banquets and entertainments including bear- and bull-baiting and hunting were held for the guests. On the final evening Somerset hosted 'a fair supper' before the participants took to boats on the Thames to watch as a bear was hunted through the water. They were also entertained by what was, perhaps, a Tudor version of fireworks as 'wildfire' was shot out of boats.[35]

Warwick had been too ill to join Somerset at Sheen for the marriage of his son, John Viscount Lisle, to Somerset's daughter, Anne, on 3 June. Anne was only 14 but it was quite usual for children of influential families to be married at an early age to ensure the future of hereditary estates and to seal alliances. Both men must have hoped that this outward show of friendship and the union of their families would bring some concord between them. The celebrations were a magnificent affair, attended by the king who gave Anne a ring worth £40. After the banquet the guests were entertained with dancing, jousting and a tournament that they watched from two 'chambers' made of tree boughs before the festivities finished with supper.[36]

Somerset had ambitious ideas to forge similar alliances through his other children. He planned to match Jane with the king and Edward with Lady Jane Grey – a scheme which had caused further discord with Thomas Seymour, who had wanted Lady Jane to marry the king. Somerset also had it in mind for Margaret to marry Lord Strange, the son of the Earl of Derby, and for Henry to marry Catherine, daughter and heiress of the Earl of Oxford. In 1548, when Somerset and Oxford had agreed on a marriage between their two families, Henry was just 8 and Catherine 10. It was settled that, if for any reason Henry failed to marry Catherine, one of his brothers might take his place and the dowry would remain intact, thus maintaining the alliance. Somerset drove a hard bargain. As well as agreeing the financial settlement of the dowry he also demanded a bond of £6,000 to ensure the earl did not change his mind.[37] No doubt the clause enabling one of Henry's brothers to take his place was to allow for the possibility of the boy's early death before the wedding, but it was to be Somerset's death that prevented the marriage. Before the nuptials could be fulfilled Somerset had fallen from power. His children were no longer such a good prospect and his plans all came to nothing.

Somerset became fully involved in the government of the country, both in council and in maintaining peace throughout the realm. After the rebellions of the previous year councillors were especially fearful of dissension. Holidays were a popular time for people to cause trouble since it did not interfere with working days. At the end of April a group of men were arrested on suspicion of planning an insurrection on May Day. In May the council received reports of disturbances planned for Whitsun Monday in Sussex and Kent, and another conspiracy was stopped when a group of men were arrested in Essex. In an attempt to prevent further trouble, the number of nightwatchmen in London was increased during June. The council issued proclamations ordering that vagabonds must leave London and offering rewards for information about sedition and rebellion. However, any hope that these orders and the recent act against unlawful assemblies would be effective was soon dashed as trouble spread through south-east England. In July and August Somerset spent time away from court quelling unrest at Reading and in the surrounding counties of Oxfordshire, Sussex, Wiltshire and Hampshire.[38] Yet, although London remained unsettled until the end of September, there was no return to the major disturbances of 1549.

Despite their marriage alliance, Warwick was still wary of Somerset. A rumour in August 1550 that the deposed Protector had declared himself king demonstrated a widely held view that he might return to power. The rumour-monger was put in the pillory and had both ears cut off so that he could hear no further rumours.[39] In mid-October, after his mother died, Somerset received a clear message about the decline of his status. Margery Seymour had not frequented court but, as grandmother of the king and perhaps in acknowledgement of his own status, Somerset asked if she might be accorded a state funeral with all the trappings of mourning. The council response was the reformist view that the wearing of mourning clothes had no benefit for the dead. Private grief should be kept at home and not cast a cloud around the king. However, the following March, at an elaborate state funeral for the Lord Chamberlain, Thomas Wentworth, the mourners all wore black.[40] It was a warning to Somerset that his position at court was not as exalted as he might think.

At the beginning of November, Somerset may have considered making a bid to take control. For a few days the young king was seriously ill and there was a fear that he might not survive. With Warwick again absent from court for several weeks, Somerset was reported to be trying to win over friends and supporters. The councillors were taking sides, some favouring Somerset and others Warwick, but with so many of Warwick's adherents on the council it was unlikely that Somerset could garner sufficient support to topple him.[41] In the event, the king survived, Warwick returned to court and for nearly five months he managed to maintain good attendance at the council. His position had been strengthened during 1550 by the appointment of new councillors – Sir John Mason and Lord Clinton, who were both related by marriage to Warwick; the Earl of Huntingdon; George Brooke, Lord Cobham; and Cecil, who had found it expedient to transfer his loyalty and had been appointed secretary of state in September. Despite Somerset retaining confidence in Cecil's loyalty to him, the new secretary knew that his old master was no longer a sure way to advancement.

19

Destruction

Throughout the winter Somerset and Warwick were frequently together at council meetings, but this did little to increase the trust between them. At the beginning of 1551 Warwick was firmly in control of the government but he was unpopular, both in the country and at court where the councillors were afraid to oppose him. Scheyfve reported that even Somerset 'bows his head and endures until a better time'.[1] It would not be long, though, until Somerset became impatient and decided to take action. Meanwhile, Warwick was alert for any sign that Somerset might be plotting against him – and he had good reason to be suspicious.

Somerset's supporters were working on his behalf. In February, Richard Whalley attempted to gather support for Parliament to restore him as Lord Protector. Members of the lower house intended to raise the issue at the next session and Whalley tried to rally the lords to join them. However, after he spoke to Rutland about the matter, Rutland reported their conversation to the council, which subsequently sent Whalley to the Fleet prison for six weeks.[2] Aware that the greatest threat to his position would come from Parliament, Warwick was determined to prevent that free-minded body from meeting. The following month it was prorogued again. At the same time another of Somerset's servants was imprisoned for saying that his master was better qualified to govern than Warwick and should be preferred because he was the king's uncle. Soon afterwards, one of Somerset's supporters, Sir Ralph Vane, was sent to the Tower after a dispute with Warwick over pasture rights in his park at Posterne.[3]

Somerset took his first step against Warwick in April when he spoke to the Earl of Arundel, who was still smarting from Warwick's treatment of him the previous year. Meeting at Syon and at Somerset House, the two men discussed a plan to arrest Warwick and his closest adherents, Northampton and Herbert.

What was actually decided at their meetings is unclear and the later charges against them falsely augmented what they had discussed. Both men would later admit to having talked of arresting the three lords. However, they claimed there had been no intention to harm them, only to persuade them to improve the way they governed. Somerset probably regretted scheming with Arundel and quickly gave up any intention of carrying out the plan after the earl sent him a warning that Herbert might know of their talk. Their plotting was, though, not a complete secret. The duchess, Crane, Palmer and Stanhope, who acted as messenger, were all aware of the conspiracy.[4]

The discord within the council was common knowledge and, in an attempt to dispel such beliefs, the councillors dined together for four days at the end of April in a public display of unity and friendship.[5] Warwick, meanwhile, was doing his best to lessen Somerset's status at court. At a meeting of the Garter knights on St George's Day, 23 April, when Somerset's title had been announced, the words 'on his mother's side' were inserted before the words 'uncle to the King of England'. Warwick was making sure that no-one could misinterpret Somerset's title as meaning that he was the king's uncle through a direct relationship with Henry VIII. Just days later, at the beginning of May, on the pretext of reducing the king's expenses and because Somerset held no specific office, he was deprived of his separate table at meals and ordered to eat at the council's 'common board'. It was usual for all important office holders to have their own dining table at which they were joined by other members of the court. Henceforth Somerset would sit at other men's tables.[6] Warwick's actions may have proved to be successful. While he was at home ill for much of May, June and July, Scheyfve thought that Warwick's authority increased as Somerset's decreased.[7]

As spring moved into summer the councillors were alert for any sign of rebellion in the country. It was not unusual for the common folk to become restless as the warmer weather approached – rioting was more comfortable in good weather – but that year the risk of dissension was heightened by the problem of inflation. Earlier in the year a shortage of food, caused by poor harvests during the previous two years, had forced the council to take measures. These included controls on the sale and export of goods, setting maximum prices for the sale of animals and seizing illegally stored grain to release supplies. Then a decision both to debase and to devalue the coinage added further to people's woes, pushing up inflation even more as the shilling halved in value to 6d and the groat to 2d. The devaluation had little effect on the wealthy class who dealt in larger-value coins but the poor people, with few coins, saw their money rapidly fall in value.

Rumours of dissent had started early in April when men in London were discovered planning a riot. Meanwhile, another group in the countryside were caught planning to raise 10,000 men to kill the local gentry and then march on London to support the city men.[8] The council prepared. The Lord Mayor and aldermen were ordered to tighten security throughout the city. Commissions were quickly issued to councillors to maintain peace in the counties. Somerset was given control of Berkshire and Hampshire, and at the end of August he travelled to Wokingham to break up a conspiracy and hang the perpetrators.[9] Any activity which might encourage the spread of sedition was banned after bills were found slandering the council and encouraging people to rebel. No one was permitted to repeat rumours or speak against the king and councillors. No one was to print or sell any printed material or to perform a play without permission of the king or six privy councillors.[10] It was a far cry from the freedom of Somerset's regime.

However, this may have been an instance of fearful men over-reacting. Warwick was nervous, afraid that Somerset was scheming to raise the people against him. No doubt the quick actions taken by the council did play a part in preventing any serious outbreaks of violence. However, more effective in dissuading troublemakers congregating together was the sweating or 'hot sickness' that was first reported in London on 7 July and then swept through the country during the summer. The outbreak started at Shrewsbury in mid-April and did not finally finish in the north of England until the end of September. One source estimated that 960 people died in London during the first few days. 'A very strange kind of disease', as Simon Renard described it, it was found primarily in England and there were five major outbreaks between 1485 and 1551.[11] Little is known about the disease but it was especially virulent and could kill within a day. As its name suggests, it brought on very high temperatures accompanied by sweating, shivering, pains and vomiting. One prominent casualty of the disease was Henry Brandon, the young Duke of Suffolk, who had been suggested as a suitable match for one of Somerset's daughters. Henry and his brother Charles died within a few hours of each other after having been sent into the country from Cambridge to escape the disease.

The outbreak of sweating sickness may explain why, at the end of July, Somerset had made his will. This was a matter that men usually attended to only when they sensed that death was imminent or if they were about to go to war. On this occasion the likelihood of death may have been so high that perfectly healthy people were planning ahead. Somerset owned so much land that he no longer knew exactly how much he possessed or what it was worth. He asked Thynne to bring him any books detailing his property so they could calculate the value of his inheritance. There was a sense of urgency in the letter – Thynne was not to fail but to make all haste to reach Somerset within two days.[12]

On 11 July, as the terror-stricken inhabitants of London were flying in all directions to escape the killer disease, the king moved to Hampton Court. Three days later he received a visiting French delegation that had arrived just as the outbreak was at its height in London. The purpose of the visit was to invest Edward with the Order of St Michael and to strengthen the relationship between the two countries by finalising negotiations for a marriage between the king and Princess Elizabeth, the eldest daughter of Henri II. It was a union that Somerset opposed, perhaps because he had plans for his own daughter to wed Edward. However, the terms of the marriage were unfavourable to England and it never took place. When the visitors, headed by the Marshal of France, Jacques d'Albon, had arrived at Hampton Court, Somerset greeted d'Albon and escorted him to Edward.[13] It was to be his final official engagement for the king.

Four or five days before Somerset left court to settle the conspiracy at Wokingham in August, he had met Arundel in the garden at Somerset Place where the two men once again discussed the need for a change of government.[14] It was probably the last time they held such a meeting for, after his visit to Wokingham, Somerset was unable to return to court for a month. On his journey back to London he had stopped at Syon but during the visit a member of his household contracted the sweating sickness. Since no-one who had been in contact with a victim was allowed in the same house as the king, Somerset remained where he was. When he eventually returned to court at the beginning of October he was unaware that Warwick had become so fearful of him that he would soon launch an attack that would threaten to deprive Somerset of his liberty and his life. Warwick knew that his pre-eminent position was under threat as long as Somerset was alive and could raise support in the lower house of Parliament. He was aware, too, that if ever Somerset regained control, the deposed Protector would take his revenge against the man who had brought him down.

It was while he was sequestered at Syon during September that Somerset first realised Warwick was excluding him from council business. Thomas Hancock, a reformer with whom Somerset had earlier dealings, visited him at home to relate a strange tale. A Mrs Woodcock, one of Hancock's parishioners, had heard a voice in her head saying that the man most trusted by the king would deceive him and work treason against him. The council interviewed her but probably concluded that she was mad and sent her home. Somerset was concerned that such a matter had not been reported to him. It is possible that Warwick, fearing people might believe him to be the man referred to by the woman, wanted to keep the incident secret.[15]

Warwick felt insecure. He was aware of his unpopularity among the people and of rumours that he wanted to seize absolute control for himself. At the beginning of October, Anthony Gyller from Coventry was imprisoned for spreading rumours that Warwick had set up his own mint and was making coins bearing a ragged staff – a symbol associated with Warwick – upon one side. The inference was that Warwick sought to rule.[16]

On 30 September Somerset received a summons to court. Now there was no longer any danger of sickness at Syon the councillors believed he had no reason for being absent and should return at his 'convenient leisure'. He made no effort to return quickly and only set off for Hampton Court three days later after receiving a second summons. On 4 October he attended a council meeting at which Sir Thomas Arundell was finally granted his freedom from the Tower.[17] In light of what was to follow, the release of Arundell, a man whom Warwick suspected of being one of Somerset's supporters, suggests that he had no immediate plans to move against Somerset.

Somerset was also on hand that day to hear the announcement that Warwick was to be raised to a dukedom. Although there was the usual preamble that the number of noble houses was 'much decayed' and so the king intended to honour some of his councillors by ennobling them, in reality Warwick and his closest supporters had decided to reward themselves and the king had endorsed their proposals. Warwick was to be made Duke of Northumberland, Dorset promoted to Duke of Suffolk, Wiltshire to Marquis of Winchester and Herbert to Earl of Pembroke.

For the next few days Somerset was unaware that fate was turning against him. There had been no indication that Warwick was intending to make a move against Somerset and it is probable that he had no good reason to do so until Thomas Palmer visited Warwick at home on 7 October. Palmer accused Somerset of conspiring to assassinate both Warwick and Northampton at a banquet where their heads would be cut off. It was an extreme and fanciful allegation accompanied by the accusation that in April, on St George's Day, Somerset had intended to raise the people of London – an unlikely story since on that day Somerset had been with the king and the other Garter knights at Greenwich. Palmer named Ralph Vane, Sir Thomas Arundell, Sir Miles Partridge, Alexander Seymour (a distant relative of Somerset) and Lawrence Hammond as Somerset's accomplices who were going to take the Tower and call upon Londoners to support Somerset.[18] Palmer's dislike of Somerset had festered since the Protector's abrasive censure of him after his capture by the Scots. These charges gave him an opportunity for revenge and a means of proving his loyalty to Warwick, who had awarded him an annuity of £100 the previous November.

If Warwick had already planned to strike against Somerset, Palmer's allegations gave him the opportunity to make his move but he did not. It would be another nine days before Somerset was arrested. It seems that Palmer's accusations set the train of events in motion but Warwick needed a few days to prepare. Both Warwick and Palmer would later admit to being complicit in falsifying the charges against Somerset. Palmer would confess that he made a written accusation against Somerset at Warwick's request.[19] It is impossible to establish exactly what Palmer really said on 7 October. However, it is likely that, since he knew of Somerset's meetings with Arundel, he related this to Warwick who then saw an opportunity to elaborate the facts to incriminate Somerset further. Someone was certainly embroidering the details related to the king. William Crane later admitted that there had been a plot to arrest the lords but when Edward recorded Crane's confession in his journal he noted that they were to have 'their heads stricken off' at a banquet at Paget's house.[20]

Unaware of what had happened, on the morning of Sunday 11 October Somerset was at Hampton Court to accompany Warwick at his creation as Duke of Northumberland. After the king had invested Warwick with his sword, ducal coronet and rod, Somerset and the newly created Northumberland stood together beside the king while the other lords received their new titles. Scheyfve had already heard from a trustworthy source that Somerset was to be arrested. Somerset himself may have had no idea that, as he stood beside him, Northumberland was already plotting his downfall.[21]

Somerset's ignorance of what was to come was soon dispelled. At the council meeting following the ceremony, an enquiry was ordered into his debts to the king.[22] By 14 October he knew something was amiss. He failed to attend the council meeting that day, instead sending for Cecil, telling him that 'he suspected some ill'. Ominously, Cecil did not visit but replied by letter. The response gave Somerset no comfort. If Somerset was not guilty, he wrote, he had nothing to fear and should be of good courage but if he was guilty then Cecil 'had nothing to say but to lament him'. Somerset could do no more than to send back a 'letter of defiance'. Cecil had switched his allegiance to Northumberland, for which he had been rewarded with a knighthood the previous Sunday. Still seeking information and aware that Palmer might be involved, Somerset demanded his attendance but Palmer denied having made any accusation against him.[23]

The king was kept informed of events by Northumberland. By 15 October he probably knew what was intended with regard to Somerset when he recorded that he and the court were moving from Hampton Court to Westminster 'because it was thought this matter might easilier and surelier be dispatched there'.[24] Certainly Somerset would be closer to the Tower there.

The blow fell the next day. Somerset arrived at court, later than was usual for him, to attend the privy council meeting in the morning. With the business finished, the councillors took dinner together and then Somerset was arrested. As he was being taken to the Tower his supposed accomplices were also detained. Despite having given Northumberland the evidence to convict Somerset, Palmer was taken as he walked on the palace terrace. Others were arrested by subterfuge lest they might have warning and escape. Francis Newdigate, John Seymour (probably Somerset's solicitor) and another relation, David Seymour, were sent messages, as if from Somerset, calling them to court where they were seized. Lord Grey and Thomas Arundell, who had been released only a few days earlier, were caught. Vane, who attempted to escape, was found hiding under straw in his servant's stable. The next day Somerset's wife and William Crane were taken to the Tower. More people followed – Hertford (Somerset's son), Paget, Stanhope, Thynne, Partridge and Whalley – until, in all, forty people had been arrested.[25]

Although the Tower was not intended to be comfortable, Somerset and his wife were allowed to request 'necessary' items to be brought from their home. Somerset's list was simple and spartan and reflected the economies of a soldier, apart from a surprisingly large quantity of linen: one gown, one velvet cap, one night cap, two doublets, two pairs of hose, three shirts, two night 'kerchers', six handkerchiefs, three dozen points (tagged laces for attaching hose to a doublet), two pairs of velvet shoes, three tablecloths, four hand towels, three cupboard cloths, one dozen table napkins and £10 in money to pay for washing, cleaning and other necessaries. The duchess's requirements reflected slightly different concerns and included silk and thread for needlework together with three little books. Anne was giving thought to how she would pass her time in the Tower. The duchess also asked for a large selection of tableware including silver plates, dishes and spoons. Somerset, however, was provided with silverware sent from the royal collection by the Lord Chancellor. The presence of this and the large selection of napery demonstrate that even in the Tower they expected to maintain the formality of life at court.[26]

The conditions of their imprisonment may have been sparse compared with their recent way of life but by the standards of other prisoners they were well provided for. The Tower was especially cold and dark during winter and the duchess was allocated 20s per week to pay for wood, coal and candles to give her some comfort. She also had an allowance of 11s per day for food, sufficient for a selection of stewed mutton, boiled beef, rabbit and roast veal and capon with the occasional luxury of a dozen larks, all prepared by her own cook. For much of the time Anne was accompanied by her mother, Lady Page, and was waited on by two gentlewomen and three of the king's servants.[27]

All the prisoners were closely guarded and allowed no contact with outsiders. Somerset's four attendants permitted no-one to speak with him without council permission and when he was moved to a different lodging the servant was ordered to make up the bed beforehand so that Somerset had no contact with him. For the first few days Sir John Markham, the lieutenant of the Tower, allowed Somerset to take exercise around the grounds of the Tower and permitted David Seymour to send and receive letters, but he was quickly reprimanded and replaced for granting these liberties without council permission.[28]

Outside the Tower one of the council's first actions was to ensure that none of Somerset's belongings were removed from his houses – they may have remembered how his servants had hidden his goods two years earlier. Herbert, the newly created Earl of Pembroke, was instructed to oversee the care of Somerset's horses and stables. Other men were ordered to maintain his houses and parks.[29] No doubt Northumberland and the councillors were aware of the spoils to be distributed if Somerset was found guilty.

The council spread a story that Somerset had intended to take the Tower, with the royal treasury and military stores, and raise the people in rebellion before assassinating some of the councillors. Few men believed the tale. Scheyfve reported that many people thought Somerset had been unjustly accused and blamed Northumberland for the charges. Merchants in London went about calling Northumberland a tyrant, saying that his intention 'is to lord it over all'. Security was tightened around the city. The guard on the gates was increased and aldermen patrolled the streets at night to ensure people stayed in their own ward of the city.[30]

The council needed more evidence against Somerset. Palmer was interviewed again on 19 October and elaborated on his earlier evidence by talking of a plan whereby Vane, with 2,000 men, 100 of Somerset's horsemen and other supporters, was to attack a muster of men-at-arms in London. If the assault was unsuccessful, he said, they planned to raise the apprentices by running through London crying 'Liberty, liberty' while Somerset travelled to the Isle of Wight or Poole to raise a large force.[31]

By 24 October Northumberland was confident he had collected – or more probably fabricated – sufficient evidence to continue and arrangements were made for other witnesses to be examined.[32] Crane was questioned and named Arundel as one of Somerset's accomplices, claiming that the two men had met at Somerset's house where they discussed arresting the councillors. Arundel, he remembered, had been concerned at the legality of what they planned and wanted to call Parliament once Northumberland and Northampton had been apprehended, to seek approval for their actions. Crane made no mention of any plan to execute Northumberland, Northampton and Pembroke, only of the intention to imprison them.[33]

Ominously, at the beginning of November as the other witnesses waited to be examined, Sir Arthur Darcy, the new lieutenant of the Tower, was authorised to use torture if the examiners considered it to be 'expedient'.[34] As more witnesses were questioned, evidence of a different nature emerged when Lord Strange confessed that Somerset had asked him to encourage the king to marry Somerset's daughter, Jane.[35] It gave Northumberland another important line of attack against the duke.

The Earl of Arundel was not arrested immediately after Crane's deposition. Not until 8 November was he called before the council, ostensibly to join the discussion about how to proceed against Somerset but more probably to discover his involvement in the conspiracy. Realising the likely purpose of his presence, he asked to be excused. It was the council's business, not his, to handle such matters, he said, and reminded them that in 1550 they had excluded him for objecting to Somerset's release. His reluctance to become involved gave Northumberland an opportunity. The earl, he responded, must belong to Somerset's faction, which made him a traitor to the king. The two men became increasingly angry until Arundel retorted that neither he nor his family had ever been traitors 'but all knew who had', meaning Northumberland's father, Edmund Dudley. Northumberland was furious and ordered him straight to the Tower.[36]

As groups of councillors interrogated Somerset in the Tower, he was under no illusions about the seriousness of his situation – or of that of his friends. The questions put to him on one occasion did not directly concern what he had done but rather with whom he had acted. They appear to have been an attempt to implicate other men. The first question concerned Palmer and was an attempt to incriminate the very man who had started off this chain of events. The inquisitors wanted to know with whom Somerset had discussed his plans and who had offered him advice. He was questioned about his conversations with Sir Thomas Arundell, Stanhope, Partridge and Vane and whether he had discussed with the Earl of Arundel and Paget the need to reform the government. Significantly, there was no mention of any plan to assassinate Northumberland and the others, only to apprehend them. Disappointingly, there is no record of Somerset's replies but we do know that he admitted to meeting Arundel several times to discuss arresting the three lords.[37]

Matters were reaching a conclusion and Northumberland's next step would allow him to proceed against Somerset without the authority of the councillors. Until now all bills signed by the king had been counter-signed by at least six councillors. There had been instances when Lord Chancellor Rich had refused to use the great seal to authorise documents because they lacked sufficient signatures. The king had recently reached his 14th birthday and favoured a change of procedure; on 10 November, it was agreed that in future the king's signature alone would be sufficient since the counter-signatures were a derogation of his authority. Four days later the council sent explicit instructions ordering Rich to authorise all documents signed only by the king.[38] Henceforth, Northumberland would need the agreement of only the king and Lord Chancellor to authorise Somerset's execution. There would be no need for him and the other councillors to sign a death warrant.

Northumberland was not entirely certain of Rich's support, suspecting that he might favour Somerset's return to power. However, in just a few weeks' time Rich would relinquish the great seal, supposedly on account of illness, and Northumberland would appoint Thomas Goodrich, Bishop of Ely, to be Keeper of the Great Seal. Northumberland was preparing for what was to come and he could rely on Goodrich's support.

In the meantime, events started to move quickly once Northumberland had what he needed. On 16 November Rich issued commissions for indictments against Somerset to be heard by juries in Middlesex, London and Kent. These men were to consider whether there was sufficient evidence to put him on trial. Five charges were made against him: that on 20 April he had planned to seize the king and assume royal authority; that, with others, he planned to imprison Northumberland; that he intended to take the great seal and seize the Tower; that he planned to incite the men of London to rebellion by crying out 'Liberty, liberty'; and that on 20 May he had planned to rise against the king in open rebellion and to seize Northumberland, Northampton and Pembroke. Again, there was no mention of a plan to assassinate the three lords. However, similar indictments against Vane, Arundell, Partridge and Stanhope included the charge that with Somerset they had planned to murder Northumberland.[39]

Surprisingly these charges were agreed before either Arundel or Paget had been examined. On 23 November, the day the indictments were returned to the Lord Chancellor, the council had still not decided what questions to ask the two men.[40] It is remarkable that Arundel was not questioned early in the proceedings after being named as Somerset's accomplice by Crane. There was no evidence of Paget's involvement and his deposition became less important if Northumberland intended to drop the charge of planning to murder the lords at Paget's house. At the end of the month Northumberland and Northampton finally questioned Arundel. He was initially reluctant to implicate himself but, when it became apparent that Somerset had already confessed, Arundel finally admitted his involvement although he too denied any intention to harm the lords.[41]

The case against Somerset was weak. There may have been much talk between him and Arundel but there had been no action. Although Palmer and Crane swore before twenty-two peers and the council that their confessions were true they were unreliable witnesses.[42] Nevertheless, Northumberland was determined to proceed and preparations were made for the trial. On 30 November Somerset received a visit from Hoby, who removed his Garter pendant and warned him that his trial was to be the following day.[43] Orders were issued for the city guard to be increased to ensure that householders and their families remained at home all the following day and night.

At 5 a.m. in the cold and dark of a December morning, Somerset was taken by boat from the Tower to the landing stage at Westminster and thence into the great hall.[44] The journey had to be made early to ensure the water was sufficiently low for the boat to shoot under London Bridge. Inside the hall the recently created Marquis of Winchester, who had been appointed Lord High Steward for the occasion, sat beneath a canopy of state on a wooden platform. Sitting below him were the twenty-six peers who had been summoned as jurymen.[45] About half of all the noblemen were present but there is no evidence to suggest that the jury had been packed with Somerset's enemies. Those who were absent were largely either unable to attend or rarely visited court.[46]

Somerset was led to the bar and listened to the charges before pleading not guilty and submitting himself to the judgement of the peers. It is not entirely clear what charges were made against him at the trial but they had changed slightly since the indictments in November. He was no longer accused of intending to seize the king and assume royal authority. However, Northumberland had decided, one assumes with the consent of the council, that the accusation of planning to kill him and the other lords should be added to the list. Significantly for Somerset, the charge of gathering men with the intention of imprisoning or killing a member of the privy council had been classified as treason under the act passed by Northumberland in the previous Parliament.

After Palmer and Crane's confessions had been read out, Somerset demanded that Crane should be brought before him and accuse him to his face. Winchester, however, refused to allow it, probably aware that Somerset could undermine his evidence. Further confessions from his servants Newdigate, Hammond and Alexander Seymour were read and Lord Strange testified that Somerset had wanted one of his own daughters to marry the king. Somerset denied all the claims and prepared to defend himself against the charges. It was a matter of life and death and Somerset rose to the challenge. Scheyfve believed he had 'never given evidence of a better mind than on this occasion', and that he had won great respect for his bold defence.

Denying that there had been any plan to raise the people of London, Somerset pointed out that the witnesses had not been present. He had never sought to take the Tower, he continued, or to do anything which might endanger the king, and his assembly of men was only for his own defence. The only confession he made was that he had talked of seeking a way to bring down Northumberland; not to kill him but only to persuade him to take a different course in his government.

The trial lasted from 8 a.m. until late in the afternoon as the lords struggled to reach a decision. There was much heated discussion about whether the charges amounted to treason and whether Northumberland, Northampton and Pembroke should sit as judges since many of the charges concerned actions against them. Eventually, Northumberland conceded that planning his death was a felony, not treason, and Winchester announced that the three noblemen should remain because a peer, he believed, would always give an honest opinion.

The verdict was finally agreed, each lord answering in turn, starting with the most junior. Somerset was found not guilty of treason. However, his momentary relief at escaping execution was short-lived. Although several peers believed him to be innocent, the lords had still found him guilty of planning to raise an unlawful assembly to imprison and kill the three councillors.[47] Northumberland's last-minute decision to classify this as a felony rather than treason made little difference. Both charges carried the penalty of death by hanging. The result had probably been inevitable. Northumberland had to remove Somerset if he was to secure his own position and he knew that whether the charge was treason or felony would have no effect on the final outcome. Somerset would still be executed.

Somerset was under no illusion. He knew there would be no mercy but he thanked the lords for their open trial and begged pardon from Northumberland, Northampton and Pembroke for scheming against them. Finally, after begging the council to intercede with the king for his life and mercy for his wife and children, he was led from the hall 'without the axe of the Tower'. It was the convention for a prisoner condemned of treason to be led away with an axe carried before him, the blade turned towards him, as a symbol of his punishment. When the waiting crowd saw there was no axe they erupted with cheers of jubilation and threw their caps into the air in the belief that Somerset had been acquitted. Their shouts of 'God save the duke' rang up Whitehall to be heard at Charing Cross and word spread that he was saved. Scheyfve reported that the king heard the tumult and asked what it meant. When he was told that Somerset had been acquitted, he replied that he had never believed his uncle could be a traitor. Even when people realised the truth of the verdict, they assumed that Somerset would not be executed but that, like many men before him, he would be pardoned by the king. Some were more realistic and expected that despite Northumberland's assurance that he would seek mercy for Somerset, he would in fact work for his destruction. He dare not risk the possibility that one day Somerset might seek his revenge.

As Somerset was rowed back to the Tower, London was in darkness. A few lights flickered and he could make out the outline of his palatial house on the waterfront. He would not enter its doors again. The river had risen so that boats could not safely pass under London Bridge. At about 5 p.m. the boat drew in to the wharf alongside the crane used to unload barrels of wine at the Vintry and Somerset continued his journey through the streets of the city. Along Candlewick Street and Tower Street people stood and encouraged him with cries of 'God save the duke', many of them still believing him to be cleared of the charges, until he passed into the Tower for the final time.[48]

Northumberland had triumphed despite evidence which many people considered to be insufficient. Sir Thomas Hoby believed Somerset had 'acquitted himself very wisely' of all the charges and that Northumberland was entirely responsible for the verdict.[49] There was no proven evidence against Somerset, only hearsay from untrustworthy witnesses. His only crime was that he had talked of arresting Northumberland but he had taken no action. The other charges were concocted and when Winchester wrote details of the trial to Clinton the following day he made no mention of any intention to kill Northumberland.[50] Somerset had done nothing which should have sent him to the block. Like Thomas Cromwell, allegations which were not sufficiently serious to condemn a man had been embellished.

Eventually the truth did come out. In August 1553, shortly before Northumberland went to the block, he confessed to Somerset's sons that he had 'wrongly and falsely' procured their father's death. Soon afterwards Palmer, who was similarly condemned to die, made the confession that his written accusation had been false, invented by Northumberland and given at his request.[51]

Northumberland had achieved the verdict he sought but he still had to see it carried through. No doubt efforts were made to influence the king against Somerset and during the Christmas season he was distracted with entertainments to prevent him dwelling upon his uncle's fate and issuing a pardon. This would, after all, be the second time he had agreed to the execution of one of his uncles. After a lapse of several years a 'Lord of the Misrule' was appointed to oversee the Christmas festivities and encourage the participants to have a lively, on occasions even riotous, holiday. Banquets, masques and tournaments were organised to entertain the king until he returned to London from Greenwich on the day before his uncle's execution.

It was not a forgone conclusion that Somerset would be executed. At the end of December, Scheyfve believed that Northumberland 'is sorely puzzled at present, and does not know how all this is to end'. Somerset's future remained uncertain until 19 January amid hope that the king might grant mercy. There was no time to lose for Northumberland. Parliament had already been called for 23 January 1552 and he could not risk the possibility that its members, especially those in the lower house, might oppose the verdict and try to overthrow it. Somerset must be executed before that could happen.

On 18 January the king drew up an agenda of council business in a document of 'Certain points of weighty matters to be immediately concluded on by my council'. Notably, at the time this document was considered to be of such importance that a record was kept of what then happened to it. The following day, in the king's inner privy chamber at Greenwich and in the presence of fifteen other privy councillors, he handed the document to the Marquis of Winchester. However, in the meantime the wording of the third item had been changed. Originally written as: 'The matter for the duke of Somersetse confederates to be considered as aparteineth to our surety and quietnes of realm, that by there punishement example may be shewed to others', with the addition of a few words inserted between the lines the meaning had been changed. The final version read: 'The matter for the duke of Somersete *and his* confederates to be considered as aparteineth to our surety and quietnes of *our* realm, that by there punishement *and execution acording to the lawes*, example may be shewed to others.'[52] The original draft had made no direct reference to Somerset. It concerned only his so-called accomplices and made no mention of the death penalty. Now the council was to decide whether Somerset should be executed.

It is impossible to know by whom the interlineations were made, but the words *and his* do appear to be in Edward's hand. Allowing for the difficulty in writing between lines, it is certainly possible that some, if not all, of the additions were made by Edward. It is reasonable to assume that this list and the amendments were made under the guidance of Northumberland.

The manner in which the document was changed was strikingly similar to what happened the following year when a small insertion changed the succession as defined by Henry VIII and briefly placed Lady Jane Grey upon the throne. The addition of two small words – 'and her' – changed the succession from 'Lady Jane's heirs male' to 'Lady Jane *and her* heirs male'. Northumberland had the opportunity to be involved in amending both these documents.

The council agreed that the deposed Protector should be executed three days later. There was one final action to be taken before the deed could be authorised. That day Goodrich was made Lord Chancellor for the reason that, as Keeper of the Great Seal, 'he could execute nothing in the Parliament that should be done but only to seal ordinary things'.[53] Somerset's death warrant was no ordinary thing. Goodrich needed full authority as Lord Chancellor to use the great seal on such a document.

There was little time for Somerset to prepare. He asked for £40 that would be distributed as alms at his death.[54] On 21 January, the day before his execution, he wrote his final religious devotions in a small almanac. Prisoners in the Tower were cut off from the world outside. Throughout his imprisonment Somerset was able to lessen the sense of isolation and maintain an awareness of the daily cycle of life outside the Tower from a collection of mathematical tables. This tiny book, only 3in square and covered in red velvet, enabled him to calculate the dates of the religious festivals and saints' days, to calculate sunrise and moonrise and for how long each heavenly body would be visible in the sky. There was a table for multiplication, another for calculating high tide at various ports and one to calculate which days were good for the purpose of letting blood or taking a bath. Much of the information served little purpose for his life inside the Tower but, although he was unable to see the outside world, the book gave him a sense of what was happening there.

The devotions he wrote inside the flyleaf were taken from the Psalms and Proverbs in the Bible and show clearly his belief in the power of God.

Fear of the lord is the beginning of wisdom.
Put thy trust in the lord with all thine heart.
Be not wise in thine own conceit, but fear the lord and flee from evil.

One statement is remarkable. 'Be not wise in thine own conceit' is a warning to the reader not to assume that he always knows best. Was this finally an admission of Somerset's own failings, of his inability as Lord Protector to admit that he was wrong and of his failure to take advice? Or did he believe that he had lived by this maxim and that all his decisions had been right? His final poignant words in the little book were: 'Frome the toware, the day before my deth, 1551, E. Somerset.'[55] The year 1551 was not an error. Somerset was using the old Julian calendar in which the New Year began on 25 March.

On 22 January Edward Seymour, Duke of Somerset, and once Lord Protector of England, walked out of the Tower of London to Tower Hill where a block was set upon a scaffold. His request for mercy had not been met with a pardon. However, he was allowed execution by the axe rather than the slow death of hanging. He was well guarded, surrounded by the king's men, two city sheriffs and the Tower warders with a troop of men carrying halberds. It was 8 a.m. and although orders had been issued the previous day that all householders and their families were to remain indoors until noon, a great crowd had gathered long before Somerset arrived. He climbed the steps, knelt and, raising his hands, he commended himself to God before standing to address the crowd.[56]

Looking around with a 'cheerfulness of mind and countenance' he addressed his audience:

Dearly beloved masters and friends, I am brought hither to suffer, albeit that I never offended against the king neither by word nor deed, and have been always as faithful and true unto this realm as any man hath been. But forsomuch as I am by a law condemned to die, I do acknowledge myself, as well as others, to be subject thereunto. Wherefore, to express and testify my obedience which I owe unto the laws, I am come hither to suffer death, whereunto I willingly offer myself, giving most hearty thanks unto the divine goodness, as if I had received a most ample and great reward.

Somerset had accepted his fate. His greatest comfort, he continued, was that God had chosen not to take him suddenly but to allow him time to repent and prepare for death, the sixteenth century understanding of a 'good death'. Then he singled out the one achievement of which he was most proud, that of bringing their Christian religion closer to that of the early Church, and he encouraged the people to embrace it as a benefit from God. Suddenly there was a great noise, described by onlookers as being like 'some great storm or tempest' or an explosion of gunpowder or even a multitude of horsemen. Men panicked and ran in all directions, some of them throwing themselves upon the ground and others into the Tower ditch. The cacophony of sound grew as people shouted and cried out: 'Jesus save us, Jesus save us' but it was only the trampling of feet. The men of a certain hamlet who had been ordered to attend as guards at the execution had arrived late. Seeing Somerset already on the scaffold, they had run forward with their bills and halberds. Then Sir Anthony Browne was seen riding towards the scaffold. The people, believing that he came from the king and that Somerset was to be pardoned, raised the cry 'Pardon, pardon is come. God save the king.' But it was not so.

All this time Somerset had remained standing patiently upon the scaffold, his cap in his hand. Making a sign to the people to be quiet, he addressed them again. There was to be no pardon, he said, and he asked them to join him in praying for the king and his subjects. When he declared that he had always tried to work diligently for their benefit, shouts of agreement rose from the crowd. He asked forgiveness of God and of any man whom he had offended or injured as he forgave those who had offended him. Finally he exhorted the people to be quiet and so help him remain calm:

Lest, through your tumult, you might cause me to have some trouble … For albeit the spirit be willing and ready, the flesh is frail and wavering, and, through your quietness, I shall be much more the quieter. But if that you fall into tumult, it will be great trouble unto me.

He had witnessed executions and he must have hoped for a quick death with one clean stroke of the axe. It was a brave and calm speech given by a soldier who had many times been close to death. He was not fearful but accepted the law. His religious faith was strong and he had prepared himself to die.

Somerset knelt and Dr Cox gave him a scroll with a brief confession to God which he read and returned to Cox. Then, rising from the floor, he took the hand of each man on the scaffold as he bade them farewell before giving some gold coins to the executioner and removing his gown. Kneeling in the straw, he untied the strings of his shirt collar and the executioner bent to turn down the collar about his neck. Still outwardly calm Somerset tied a handkerchief about his eyes then raised his hands to God and laid his head upon the block showing no fear except a flush of blood to his cheeks. Then, as he knelt, ready to die, the executioner bade him rise and remove his doublet – perhaps it covered his neck. He lay himself down again and as he uttered the words 'O Lord Jesus preserve me' for the third time the axe fell. With one stroke he was dead.

His body and head were placed into a coffin and carried to the church of St Peter-ad-Vincula in the Tower where he was buried in the north side of the quire. At Tower Hill people placed their hands into his blood or dipped their handkerchiefs in it.[57] Their good duke was gone. It had been a dramatic ending for a man who had, for a short spell, been a central character on the stage of Tudor England.

Somerset was an ordinary man who was put into an extraordinary situation, not by his own merits but because his sister gave Henry VIII a son who became king while he was still only 9 years old. Somerset's assumption of the Protectorate was an idea that held merit but he failed to understand how to use the authority it gave him. He should have been well fitted for the role, with his strong sense of duty and loyalty towards Edward VI and England and his enlightened ideas on how best to govern the people. Yet his arrogance and inability to work with the privy councillors and his failure to understand when to make compromises and amend his policies made him a poor political leader. His mild character and lack of ruthlessness were inappropriate in a governor. In Northumberland, Somerset found himself facing a man who was equally ambitious but who was undeniably more ruthless.

Somerset's most enduring memorial was his religious reform. Although it was Northumberland who definitively changed the core doctrine of the Anglican church, Somerset had paved the way with his somewhat ambiguous stance on communion in the *Book of Common Prayer* and the removal of many aspects of Catholic services. But Somerset was out of step with his peers and many of his other plans were too progressive. They belonged to a later age. Much of what he worked for did eventually happen – better rights for all men, the relaxation of the treason laws, controls against enclosures, a reformed religion, action to stop religious persecution and Scotland and England being joined together under the name of Britain. Edward Seymour's achievements were constrained by the reign in which he lived. If he had served under a later monarch perhaps his legacy would have been even greater.

20

Epilogue

The king recorded his uncle's death in his diary: 'The Duke of Somerset had his head cut off upon Tower Hill between eight and nine o'clock in the morning.'[1] It was a bland epitaph with no hint of affection for the man who had steered him through the early years of his reign. Exactly what Edward was told about Somerset's supposed crimes and the extent to which he was turned against him is unknown, but his death seems to have had little impact upon the boy. In a letter to his friend Barnaby Fitzpatrick three days after the execution, Edward did not mention his uncle. Of more interest to the young king is the high tide which flooded the coast of Essex and the Christmas celebrations which were 'merrily past'. Edward was 14 years old when he signed his uncle's death warrant.[2] He could have stopped the execution and he must carry responsibility for authorising Somerset's death. He had not yet reached manhood but he had already allowed two of his uncles to be sent to the block, neither of whom had been a threat to him. They had only been a threat to other men.

The king may not have been dismayed at Somerset's death but many people were, for they 'did see in the decay of this duke, the public ruin of all England'. Three weeks after the execution Scheyfve reported that Somerset was 'deeply mourned' by the people. Calvin and other reformers lamented the passing of the man who had been their champion. There was fulsome praise from Francis Burgoyne for 'so great a man' who had been 'endowed and enriched with most excellent gifts of God both in body and mind'.[3]

Four of Somerset's alleged accomplices suffered the same fate. On 26 February Stanhope and Thomas Arundell were beheaded, and Vane and Partridge were hanged. All had denied the charge of planning to imprison and kill Northumberland, Northampton and Pembroke. In the case of Arundell, the jury only passed a verdict of guilty after being locked up overnight with no food, water, heat or light.[4] The other prisoners – Grey, Whalley, Crane, Thynne and Paget – were all released in June after paying fines and surrendering any appointments they held. Northumberland made one final attack on Paget by degrading him from the Order of the Garter 'chiefly because he was no gentleman of blood, neither of father's or mother's side', although this had not prevented his elevation in the first place.[5] The vacancy for a new Garter knight was filled by Northumberland's brother, Sir Andrew Dudley. The Earl of Arundel was never tried. He remained in the Tower until the end of the year and was eventually released in December 1552 on payment of a large fine and after signing a confession which he later retracted. Only a few months later Arundel would be one of the first to turn against Northumberland.

All indications of Somerset's eminence were being erased as his Garter hatchments were taken down in St George's Chapel and his servants were dismissed from their posts.[6] Northumberland's final act of vengeance on Somerset was still to be played out. Because Somerset had been found guilty of felony, not treason, he did not forfeit his lands and titles, but Northumberland introduced a parliamentary bill to overturn this. He intended to deprive the duke's heirs of most of his land and property and of the titles of Viscount Beauchamp, Earl of Hertford and Duke of Somerset. The bill received assent on the final day of Parliament after a lengthy and difficult passage through the lower house where it had been introduced six weeks earlier. Although it was passed on 14 April the date at the head of the act was backdated to 23 January – the day following Somerset's execution.[7] His family were not to benefit from the fruits of all Somerset's efforts and were left with just sufficient income to support them. The act did, however, benefit John, Somerset's eldest son from his marriage to Katherine Fyloll, who had been excluded from inheriting his father's property by an earlier Act of Parliament. That act was repealed and he was granted land equivalent in value to the property that had belonged to his mother. However, he never had the opportunity to enjoy his inheritance; he died late in 1552 and it was his brother, Edward, who received the land.

Parliament also passed a bill which had consequences for Somerset's son Henry. With the taint of their father's execution, Somerset's children were no longer so attractive as marriage partners. Families that had once striven for alliance with the Seymours were now more reticent and the loss of the Seymour lands made the children even less desirable. The Earl of Oxford no longer wished to uphold the marriage agreement between his daughter, Catherine, and Henry Seymour and a bill was passed annulling the agreement and preventing the transference of Oxford's lands as part of Catherine's dowry.[8]

Parliament took one further measure related to Somerset. There was enormous concern at the ease with which he had been sentenced to death and after a lengthy passage through the lower house a bill was passed to amend the act by which the Protector had been condemned. In future charges of planning to assault and kill councillors and of raising men for ill intent were to be brought within three months of the crime by two witnesses who would face the accused at trial. It is unlikely that Somerset would have been found guilty under this amended act.

In the immediate aftermath of her husband's execution, the Duchess of Somerset was allowed visits by the Bishop of Gloucester 'for the settling of her conscience'. For a while there was concern for her safety and both Jean Scheyfve and the reformer Martin Micronius thought that she would soon follow Somerset to the block for she was 'said to bear a principal part in all this mischief'.[9] It was no doubt an elaboration of the fact that she had known of the scheming between her husband and Arundel. She was not executed but Northumberland refused to release her and she remained in the Tower until 10 August 1553 when, with Queen Mary on the throne, she was released at the same time as the Duke of Norfolk. Mary had not forgotten the friendship she and Anne had shared during the years when the princess's religious beliefs caused so much controversy. In 1558 Mary granted Hanworth Manor in Middlesex to Anne and that same year the dowager duchess married Francis Newdigate, who had been a gentleman usher to Somerset. Anne needed someone to protect both herself and her property, a position for which Newdigate, already familiar with the family, was ideally suited. It was not unusual for widows of high rank to marry men who were socially beneath them; it may be that such a situation allowed Anne to maintain control of her own property. This was certainly an idea supported by Newdigate, who worked to ensure his new wife benefitted fully from her lands. At his death in 1582 he left all his property to her, acknowledging that all his preferment had come as a result of their marriage.[10]

When Anne died, five years after her husband, her extensive will was a testament to the enormous wealth she had built up following her release from the Tower. In addition to a mansion in London and a manor in Middlesex, her will inventory ran to several pages of jewellery including 'a best chain of great pearls with long beads of gold between' and a single large pearl worth about £300. Among her belongings were over fifty purses containing over £5,000 in gold coins. As well as leaving bequests for her servants, Anne also designated £10 to go to each of Oxford and Cambridge universities for the use of 'godly and poor students' and 20 marks to be distributed by preachers to poor prisoners in London.[11] Considering the size of her fortune these latter bequests might be considered somewhat trifling. Anne was buried in Westminster Abbey, not far from the grave of her daughter Jane, who had predeceased her. Anne's large and imposing monument with an effigy portraying her in a red ermine-lined robe and wearing a coronet can still be seen.

When Somerset died he left nine young children fatherless – the eldest was 16, the youngest 2. One of the privy council's first acts was to ascertain the age of the children and arrange for their care, and all except Anne were made wards of the king.[12] Edward was granted an allowance out of Somerset's estates. He and his two brothers, Henry and the younger Edward, were put into the care of William Paulet, Marquis of Winchester. Calvin was greatly perturbed by this, knowing that Winchester was considered to be a Catholic, but their tutor, Thomas Norton, set his mind at rest assuring him that the boys continued to receive instruction in the new faith. The eldest daughter, Anne, was to live with her husband. Margaret, Jane, Mary and Catherine were committed to the care of their aunt Elizabeth, widow of Gregory Cromwell, who was paid 400 marks a year for their maintenance. The youngest daughter, Elizabeth, was placed with her aunt Dorothy who had married Sir Clement Smith of Essex.[13]

The early signs of literary skill which the girls had exhibited soon faded after their father's death and their status as marriage pawns declined. Jane, Margaret and Catherine all died unmarried. Jane served as a maid of honour to both Queen Mary and Queen Elizabeth but died in 1561 at the age of 19. Her passing was marked by a grand funeral at Westminster attended by 200 members of the privy chamber and court before she was buried in the abbey.[14] Elizabeth married Sir Richard Knightley of Fausley and Mary wed Sir Andrew Rogers of Dorset and, secondly, Sir Henry Peyton. Anne, married to Northumberland's son John Dudley, was soon widowed when he was executed in 1554 after being involved in his father's plot to put Lady Jane Grey upon the throne. Her second marriage, to Edward Unton, reportedly produced seven children in ten years before she 'fell into lunacy' in 1566 and then lived on in that state until 1587.[15]

Henry Seymour finally achieved a marriage of distinction when he wed Jane Percy, daughter of the 7th Earl of Northumberland, and he won fame as one of the English admirals who defeated the Spanish Armada.[16] However, of all Somerset's children, it was Edward, Earl of Hertford, who earned the greatest notoriety. At his father's death he was deprived of his title and reduced to the rank of knight. In 1553 he was restored in blood, removing any dishonour which had attached to him as a result of his father's attainder. In 1559 Queen Elizabeth created him Earl of Hertford and restored to him the lands which his father had held by inheritance; however, within less than two years his precipitate actions ruined forever his chances of great advancement at court. Late in 1560, with the aid of his sister Jane, he secretly married Lady Katherine Grey, sister to the short-lived

Queen Jane. It was a treasonable offence to marry someone of royal blood without the sovereign's permission and especially so in the case of Katherine who was considered to be next in line to the throne after Elizabeth.

The following year, when the secret could no longer be hidden because of Katherine's growing pregnancy, the couple were imprisoned separately in the Tower. An inquiry was ordered into the validity of their marriage but no witnesses could be produced. Jane was dead and the only other participant was the priest, who could not be identified. The marriage was declared invalid and any children illegitimate. Their son, Edward, was born in September 1561 and early in 1563 a second son, Thomas, followed – to the intense annoyance of the queen since the couple were still supposed to be kept apart.

Katherine was moved to the custody of her uncle, Lord John Grey, in 1563 and for over five years she was placed with a succession of keepers. Despite her petitions for release, the queen refused and in January 1568 Katherine died. Hertford, too, was moved from the Tower in 1563 into the custody of his mother and Newdigate. Anne repeatedly petitioned for his freedom but again the queen refused. After Katherine's death, Edward married twice more and was eventually allowed to return to court but he received few rewards or appointments of consequence. In 1608 James I agreed that his heirs could inherit the title of Earl of Hertford but when he died in 1621 his sons had predeceased him and he was succeeded by his grandson, William. Just six weeks before his own death in 1660, William was restored to the Dukedom of Somerset by Charles II. However, in 1750, when the 7th Duke of Somerset died without an heir, he was succeeded by a distant cousin, Edward Seymour, who was descended from Somerset's son by Katherine Fyloll, Edward. The wheel had come full circle.

Edward VI did not long outlive his uncle and his death foreshadowed the downfall of Northumberland. Edward became ill early in 1553 and by June, probably suffering from tuberculosis, it was apparent he might not survive long. In order to prevent either of his sisters becoming queen he changed the succession. Henry VIII's will had left the crown firstly to his own children and then to the male heirs of Jane, Catherine and Mary Grey, the grand-daughters of Henry's sister, Mary. Edward was vehemently against his sister Mary taking the crown because of her Catholic faith and he still considered Elizabeth to be illegitimate. With the exclusion of his two sisters and of his Catholic cousin Mary, Queen of Scots, the Grey sisters were Edward's closest relatives. However, none of them had children.

With Northumberland's aid Edward drafted his 'Devise for the Succession'. The succession confirmed by Henry VIII had specified 'Lady Jane's heirs male'. With the addition of two small words the king and Northumberland changed the order of succession to 'Lady Jane *and her* heirs male'. The alteration was strikingly similar to that made on the document which had condemned Somerset to be executed. Altering the succession was an illegal act. As a minor Edward could not make a legal will and he ignored the fact that his father had established the succession through an Act of Parliament which could only be overturned by a further Act. Despite opposition from some of the lawyers and councillors concerning the legality of the document, the letters patent setting out Edward's plan for the succession were confirmed on 21 June.

A month earlier the 16-year-old Lady Jane Grey had married Guildford Dudley, one of Northumberland's sons. If Jane became queen, Northumberland could continue to wield power through his new daughter-in-law. Edward VI died on 6 July, never having taken the reins of power. Jane Grey was taken to the Tower and declared queen but her reign ended just nine days later. Northumberland had taken a force to East Anglia where Princess Mary had fled but, as supporters rallied to her, Northumberland admitted defeat. In London, Mary was proclaimed queen on 19 July. Northumberland was executed on 22 August 1553 and Jane and Guildford followed him to the block six months later.

Northumberland's rule had been relatively successful. Through a return to a more authoritarian regime he had preserved order throughout the country for the remainder of Edward's reign and he furthered the Edwardian Reformation which Somerset had begun. So firmly did the Protestant faith become established in England before Edward's death, that it was able to survive five years of suppression by Queen Mary before being allowed to flourish under Elizabeth. Northumberland also built a close relationship with the young king, something which Somerset had failed to do. However, he was an unpopular figure and brought about his own downfall when he over-reached himself in his ambition to govern for a second monarch.

Somerset's contemporaries and servants had seen how easily disaster could occur and were perhaps more cautious in their dealings at court. After his release from the Tower, Thynne retired to Wiltshire where he lived until 1580, having won renown for his design of Longleat House. William Cecil continued to serve Northumberland but removed himself from court during the reign of Queen Mary, knowing he would never agree with her Catholic beliefs. However, Elizabeth, on her accession, immediately reappointed him secretary of state and later Lord Treasurer, in which position he served until his death in 1598.

William Parr's marital situation continued to cause ructions at court. In 1552 his marriage to Elizabeth Brooke was legalised by Parliament, probably as a reward from Northumberland for his support against Somerset. However, the following year he made a huge error of judgement in joining Northumberland to put Lady Jane Grey upon the throne. Although accused of treason, he escaped with his life but Queen Mary stripped him of his titles and rescinded his second marriage. For five years he and his wife, Elizabeth, lived apart until Queen Elizabeth came to the throne when he was reinstated as Marquis of Northampton, appointed to the privy council and his marriage was declared valid again. However, he and Elizabeth spent only a short time together before she died in 1565. Northampton, though, had a taste for marriage and in 1571, at the age of 58, he wed the 23-year-old Helena Snakenborg from Sweden. It was a short-lived marriage for within six months he was dead.

Henry VIII's four ambitious brothers-in-law – Edward and Thomas Seymour, George Boleyn and William Parr – were all accused of treason. In a strange twist of irony, only one of them – Parr – was truly guilty of treason, but he survived and died of natural causes. Parr attempted to change the succession by putting Lady Jane Grey on the throne, an act for which he should have been executed. Like Thomas Seymour and George Boleyn, Somerset did nothing treasonable and he had no intention of committing such an act. The three men were all brought down because they had powerful enemies. The Tudor court was a dangerous place, especially for those closest to the monarch, and it was not always the king who presented the greatest danger. The secret of success and survival at the Tudor court was to cultivate friends and not actively to seek power. Parr survived by not seeking authority for himself and by making himself amenable to all men; Somerset was overly ambitious and faced a formidable foe in Northumberland. In the cauldron of court politics, that was a recipe for disaster.

Notes

Abbreviations

APC	Acts of the Privy Council
BL	British Library
Bod. Lib.	Bodleian Library
CPR	Calendar of Patent Rolls
CSP Dom. Ed.VI	Calendar of State Papers, Domestic, Edward VI
CSP For.	Calendar of State Papers, Foreign
CSP Scots	Calendar of State Papers relating to Scotland
CSP Spain	Calendar of Letters, Despatches and State Papers, Spanish
DNB	Dictionary of National Biography
HMC	Historical Manuscripts Commission
LP	Letters and Papers, Foreign and Domestic, Henry VIII
NRO	Northamptonshire Record Office
ODNB	Oxford Dictionary of National Biography
PRO	Public Record Office

Chapter 1

1   Details of Seymour ancestry from H. St. Maur, *Annals of the Seymours* (London, 1902), pp. 4–20.

2   *Calendar of Patent Rolls, Henry VII* (2 vols, London, 1914–16), I, p. 452.

3   *Calendar of Close Rolls, Henry VII* (2 vols, London, 1955–63), I, p. 345.

4   *Letters and Papers, foreign and domestic of the reign of Henry VIII*, ed. J.S. Brewer et al. (21 vols, 1965), I, 2053 (i); Appdx. 26.

5   *LP* III, 704 (p. 241); *DNB* (22 vols, London, 1998), XVII, p. 1238.

6   *ODNB*, eds H.C.G. Matthew et al. (60 vols, Oxford, 2004), vol. 49, p. 860

7   *LP* I, 3357.

8   J. Foster, *Alumni Oxonienses, 1500–1714* (4 vols, Oxford, 1892), IV, p. 1335.

9   *LP* III i, 1201; X, 1069.

10   *LP* III ii, 3516.

11   *ODNB*, vol. 49, p. 861.

12   *LP* IV i, 1512.

13   G. Cavendish, *Thomas Wolsey* (London, 1999), p. 75.

14   A mark was a unit of account worth two thirds of a pound (13*s* 4*d*) and never appeared in England as a coin.

15   *ODNB*, vol. 49, p. 861; *LP* V, 686; VI, 562.

16   *LP* XX ii, Appdx. 2 (2, iv).

17   *LP* II, 3474; IV iii, 5406 (5); *LP* IV ii, 4794 (3); IV iii, 6516 (6).

18   *LP* IX, 682.

19   M.L. Bush, 'The Lisle–Seymour Land Disputes: A Study of Power and Influence in the 1530s', *The Historical Journal*, 9 (1966), pp. 255–74; *LP* VII, 929; XI, 573; XIII i, 345;

20   *LP* XIII i, 1489; XIII ii, 898; XIII i, 1407.

21   A. Jacob, *A Complete English Peerage* (2 vols in 3 parts, London, 1766), I ii, pp. 148–9.

22   *HMC Calendar of the Manuscripts of the Marquis of Bath at Longleat House* (5 vols, London, 1904–80), IV, p. 377.

23   PRO IPM C142/46/25; PRO PROB 11/22/406; PRO C65/139.

24   *HMC Calendar of the Manuscripts of the Marquis of Salisbury Preserved at Hatfield House* (24 vols, London, 1883–1976), I, p. 60.

25   *ODNB*, vol. 49, p. 855; F. Madden, *Privy Purse Expenses of the Princess Mary* (London, 1831), p. 46. My thanks to Graham Bathe for information about the first-born Jane and Henry.

26   32 Henry VIII, c. 74.

Chapter 2

1   *LP* IX, 620.

2   *Calendar of Letters, Despatches and State Papers, Spanish*, ed. G.A. Bergenroth et al. (13 vols, London, 1862–1954),V i, p. 280.

3   Ibid.V ii, p. 39; *LP* X, 601.

4   *LP* X, 601, 752.

5   Ibid. 908.

6   *ODNB*, vol. 49, p. 861.

7   Jacob, *Complete English Peerage*, I ii, pp. 132–3.

8   *LP* X, 926, 1047.

9   C. Wriothesley, *A Chronicle of England, During the Reigns of the Tudors, from AD 1485–1559* (2 vols, London, 1875, 1877), I, p. 44.

10   *LP* X, 1069 (p. 452).

11   Ibid. 1047, 901.

12   St. Maur, *Annals of the Seymours*, p. 376.

13   *LP* X, 1256 g. 4, 5, 6.

14   *LP* V, 202.

15   Wriothesley, *Chronicle*, I, pp. 44–5.

16   *LP* XI, 202 (12); *ODNB*, vol. 56, p. 221.

17   J.E. Jackson, 'Wulfhall and the Seymours', *Wiltshire Archaeological and Natural History Magazine*, 15 (1875), pp. 167–8.

18   Wriothesley, *Chronicle*, I, pp. 59–60.

19   C. Haigh, *English Reformations: Religion, Politics and Society under the Tudors* (Oxford, 1995), p. 144.

20   *LP* XI, 5.

21   Ibid. 860.

22   Wriothesley, *Chronicle*, p. 64.

23   *The Lisle Letters: An Abridgement*, ed. M. St. Clare Byrne (London, 1983), p. 239; *LP* XII i, 483

24   *ODNB*, vol. 49, p. 861.

25   *LP* XII ii, 97; XII i, 678; XII ii, 423.

26   Jackson, 'Wulfhall and the Seymours', p. 176.

27   *LP* XII ii, 889.

28   Wriothesley, *Chronicle*, I, pp. 66–7.

29   *LP* XII ii, 911.

30   Ibid. 939, 1008 (22).

31   Ibid. 970, 977.

32 *State Papers, King Henry the Eighth*, ed. A. Strahan et al. (11 vols, London, 1830–52), VIII, 478.

33 E. Hall, *Chronicle: Containing the History of England* (London, 1809), p. 825.

34 *LP* XII ii, 1060, 1012; J. Strype, *Ecclesiastical Memorials* (3 vols, London, 1822), II i, p. 12.

Chapter 3

1   *LP* XIII ii, 732.

2   *LP* XIV i, 762, 791, 947, 835.

3   *LP* XIII i, 24, 5; *HMC Bath*, IV, p. 338.

4   *LP* XIII ii, 1280 f.17; XIV ii, 782 (p. 335); *ODNB*, vol. 51, p. 868.

5   Jackson, 'Wulfhall and the Seymours', p. 174.

6   *LP* XIII ii, 979 (5), 986 (i); XIV i, 290 (9).

7   *LP* XII i, 1207 (20).

8   *LP* XVI, 931, 932.

9   *HMC Bath*, IV, pp. 82, 93, 106–8.

10 *LP* XVI, 449, 465, 605; XIV i, 533.

11 *LP* XVI, 836.

12 *LP* XII ii, 617 (1). Rents were often fixed at 10 per cent of the annual value of the land and property. *LP* XII ii, 804.

13 *HMC Bath*, IV, pp. 90–1.

14 *LP* XII i, 806; XIII i, 223.

15 *LP* XIII i, 190 (41); St. Maur, *Annals of the Seymours*, p. 66.

16 *LP* XVI, 779 (7).

17 *LP* XII ii, 1008 (13).

18 Jackson, 'Wulfhall and the Seymours', pp. 166–7, 173; *LP* XII ii, 629.

19 Jackson, 'Wulfhall and the Seymours', pp. 145–6, 168–71.

20 *HMC Bath*, IV, p. 341; *Lisle Letters*, p. 313.

21 *LP* XIII ii, 641.

22 BL Cotton MS Vespasian F XIII, f.188.

23 *LP* XIV ii, 677.

24 BL Cotton MS Vespasian F XIII, f. 258; *LP* XV, 824; XVI, 379 (34).

25 Ibid. 1334, 1395.

Chapter 4

1 *LP* XVII, 944.
2 Ibid. 948, 956.
3 Ibid. 996.
4 Ibid. 1002.
5 Ibid. 940, 1027.
6 Ibid. 1046.
7 *HMC Bath*, IV, pp. 46–7, 55.
8 *LP* XVII, 1083, 1084, 1118, 1031.
9 Ibid. 1018.
10 Ibid. 1221.
11 Ibid. 1067, 1094, 1215.
12 Ibid. 987; XVIII i, 19.
13 C.H. Cooper, *Athenae Cantabgrigienses* (3 vols, Cambridge, 1858), I, p. 298.
14 *LP* XIX i, 139.
15 Ibid. 118, 194, 534.
16 Ibid. 297.
17 Ibid. 71, 83.
18 Ibid. 388, 290, 406, 451.
19 Ibid. 319.
20 Ibid. 533.
21 Ibid. 533.
22 Ibid. 531.
23 Ibid. 593.
24 Ibid. 601, 348.

Chapter 5

1 *LP* XVIII ii, 526.
2 *LP* XIX i, 864.
3 *Literary Remains of King Edward Sixth*, ed. J.G. Nichols (2 vols, London, 1857), I, pp. lvii–lxix; *Original Letters Relative to the English Reformation*, ed. Rev. H. Robinson (2 vols, Cambridge, 1846), II, p. 351.
4 *LP* XIX ii, 424.
5 Ibid. 546.
6 Ibid. 336.

7   Ibid. 414.
8   Ibid. 479.
9   Ibid. 492.
10   Ibid. 577, 583. De Praet was Imperial ambassador to England 1523–25.
     Granvelle was Charles V's chief minister and father of Antoine de Granvelle.
11   Ibid. 569.
12   Ibid. 654.
13   *LP* XX i, 7, 12.
14   Ibid. 170, 180.
15   Ibid. 846 (2), 723.
16   Ibid. 867, 1221; XX ii, 97.
17   *LP* XX ii, 308. Details of the campaign are taken from *LP* XX, ii, 400, 533,
     633.
18   Ibid. 96.
19   Ibid. 533.
20   *LP* XXI i, 148 (131).
21   Ibid. 431.
22   Ibid. 449, 416, 494, 489.
23   Jackson, 'Wulfhall and the Seymours', p. 173.
24   *State Papers, Henry VIII*, I, p. 780.
25   *LP* XXI i, 1108, 507, 566, 530.
26   Ibid. 636.
27   Ibid. 682, 692.
28   *LP* XXI i, 691, 687.
29   Ibid. 779.
30   Ibid. 785, 289; *CSP Span*, IX, p. 42.
31   *LP* XXI i, 864, 874, 594.
32   Ibid. 874, 892.
33   Ibid. 927, 960.
34   Ibid. 1028.
35   Ibid. 840.
36   Ibid. 1024; XXI ii, 140.
37   *LP* XIX i, 293.
38   *LP* XXI i, 1122, 1133, 1160.
39   Ibid. 1265, 1133.
40   *LP* XXI ii, 124, 140, 151.

Chapter 6

1   *Acts and Monuments of John Foxe*, ed. Rev. J. Pratt (8 vols, London, *c*.1877), V, p. 562.

2   Anne Radcliffe's religious beliefs were not shared by her husband. Held in the Tower on a charge of sorcery in 1552, Anne fled abroad after Mary's accession and was divorced by Sussex.

3   Foxe, *Acts and Monuments*, V, p. 556.

4   Ibid. p. 560.

5   *LP* XXI ii, 347.

6   ibid. 493.

7   J. Maclean, *The Life of Sir Thomas Seymour* (London, 1869), p. 4; *State Papers Henry VIII*, I, 107 (pp. 576–8).

8   *LP* XXI ii, 554.

9   Ibid. 555 (5).

10   *LP* XVIII i, 347, 351.

11   *LP* XXI ii, 541.

12   Ibid. 555 (5).

13   Ibid. 605.

14   Ibid. 697.

15   *Journals of the House of Lords, 1509–1577* (London, 1771), p. 289; *LP* XXI ii, 759, 771 (36).

16   *Acts of the Privy Council of England*, ed. J.R. Dasent (46 vols, London, 1890–1964), II, p. 10.

17   *LP* XXI ii, 605, 756.

18   *CSP Spain,* IX, pp. 19–20.

19   Foxe, *Acts and Monuments*, VI, p.163.

20   It had been enacted that the king should sign his will with his own hand.

21   *LP* XXI i, 1537 (34).

22   *LP* XXI ii, 651, 675, 684.

23   Ibid. 634, 770 (85); E.W. Ives, 'Henry VIII's Will – A Forensic Conundrum', *The Historical Journal*, 35 (1992), p. 791 (n. 57). Some historians claim that the will was stamped at a later date but that assumes the possibility that the eleven witnesses all signed a document to which no signature had been added, and then kept their action secret – an unlikely eventuality.

24   *LP* XXI ii, 770 (85).

25   *LP* XXI ii, 713.

26   *CSP Spain*, VIII, p. 556.

27   *APC,* I, p. 566; *CSP Spain*, IX, p. 341.

Chapter 7

1   Northamptonshire Record Office, F(M) c .21 – 7 July 1549.

2   A regent was responsible for protecting the realm. A Lord Protector protected both the realm and the person of the monarch.

3   *Foedera, coventiones, literae* … ed. T. Rymer and R. Sanderson (20 vols, London, 1704–35), XV, pp. 110–17.

4   Foxe, *Acts and Monuments,* V, p. 691.

5   *Calendar of State Papers: Domestic Series of the reign of Edward VI, 1547–1553,* ed. C.S. Knighton (London, 1992), 10/1/1.

6   *England under the Reigns of Edward VI and Mary,* ed. P.F. Tytler (2 vols, London, 1839), I, p. 169.

7   Ibid. I, pp. 17–18.

8   *CSP Spain,* IX, p. 100; *APC,* II, pp. 3–6.

9   J. Strype, *Ecclesiastical Memorials,* II i, pp. 22–3; *APC,* II, pp. 7–8.

10   *APC,* II, p. 8; *CSP Spain,* IX, p. 493.

11   *APC,* II, pp. 12, 14, 25.

12   D.E. Hoak, *The King's Council in the Reign of Edward VI* (Cambridge, 1976), p. 42.

13   BL MS 48126, ff, 6a–6b.

14   *APC,* II, pp. 15–22. Since the document is undated it is not clear exactly when Paget made his deposition. *CSP Spain,* IX, pp. 30–1.

15   E.W. Ives, 'Henry VIII's Will: The Protectorate Provisions of 1546–7', *The Historical Journal,* 37 (1994), p. 905.

16   *ODNB,* vol. 49, p. 897.

17   *APC,* II, pp. 41–2.

18   H. Miller, 'Henry VIII's Unwritten Will: Grants of Land and Honours in 1547', in *Wealth and Power in Tudor England,* ed. E.W. Ives (London, 1978) pp. 102–3; *HMC Bath,* IV, p. 180.

19   *Calendar of Patent Rolls for the Reign of Edward VI* (6 vols, London, 1924–29), I, pp. 118–33.

20   Ibid. II, pp. 27–9.

21   Tytler, *England under the Reigns of Edward VI and Mary,* I, pp. 171; *Collection of State Papers Relating to Affairs in the Reigns of King Henry VIII, King Edward VI, Queen Mary and Queen Elizabeth, 1542–1570, of William Cecil at Hatfield House,* ed. S. Haynes (London, 1740), p. 104.

22   *Journals of the Lords,* p. 307.

23   *CSP Dom. Ed. VI,* 10/1/17; Strype, *Ecclesiastical Memorials,* II ii, p. 298.

24   *CPR Ed. VI,* I, p. 180.

25   Bod. Lib. Rawlinson MS B. 146. f. 101.

26   *CPR Ed.VI*, I, p. 174; *CSP Dom. Ed.VI*, 10/1/14.

27   *CSP Spain*, IX, p. 48.

28   *CSP Dom. Ed.VI*, 10/1/7.

29   *APC,* II, p. 10.

30   *CSP Dom. Ed.* VI, 10/3/7.

31   *CSP Spain*, IX, p. 47; *Literary Remains*, I, pp. cclxxxvi, ccxc.

32   *CSP Dom. Ed.VI*, 10/1/7.

33   Details of coronation in *APC*, II. pp. 29–33; *Literary Remains*, I,
     pp. ccxciv–ccxcvi.

34   *APC*, II, pp. 40–1.

35   BL MS 48126, f.15a; *CSP Spain*, IX, p. 100.

36   *APC,* II, pp. 55–7, 6; A.J. Slavin, 'The Fall of Lord Chancellor
     Wriothesley: A Study in the Politics of Conspiracy', *Albion*, 7 (4), (1975),
     pp. 279–80.

37   *APC,* II, p. 58.

38   Ibid. pp. 63–4, 67–74.

39   NRO F(M) c. 21 – 7 July 1549.

40   Strype, *Ecclesiastical Memorials*, II, ii, pp. 311–12.

Chapter 8

1   J.A. Muller, *The Letters of Stephen Gardiner* (Cambridge, 1933), pp. 265–7.

2   Foxe, *Acts and Monuments,* VI, p. 36.

3   Robinson, *Original Letters*, I, p. 258.

4   *LP* XX i, 1145.

5   Robinson, *Original Letters*, I, p. 256; Foxe, *Acts and Monuments*, VI, p. 293;
     BL Stowe MS, 1066.

6   1 Edward VI, c. 12; Strype, *Ecclesiastical Memorials*, II ii, p. 311.

7   R. Needham and A. Webster, *Somerset House Past and Present* (London,
     1905), pp. 40–2.

8   J. Calvin, *Commentaries on the Epistles to Timothy, Titus and Philemon*
     (Edinburgh, 1856), pp. ix–xii.

9   *Letters of John Calvin*, ed. J. Bonnett (2 vols, Edinburgh, 1855–57), II,
     pp. 222–4.

10   Foxe, *Acts and Monuments*, VI, p. 30.

11   1 Edward VI, c. 1; *CSP Dom. Ed.VI*, 10/7/28.

12 Robinson, *Original Letters*, II, p. 439.

13 *APC,* II, pp. 25–6.

14 Foxe, *Acts and Monuments*,VI, p. 28.

15 *CSP Spain,* IX, p. 50.

16 *Tudor Royal Proclamations*, ed. P.L. Hughes and J.F. Larkin (London, 1964), I, no. 281.

17 Ibid. no. 287.

18 Foxe, *Acts and Monuments,* VI, p. 30.

19 Muller, *Letters of Stephen Gardiner*, pp. 431, 278.

20 *Victoria County History of London* (vol. I, London, 1974), p. 289; *APC*, II, p. 518.

21 Ibid. p. 140.

22 Foxe, *Acts and Monuments*,VI, p. 28.

23 *CSP Spain*, IX, p. 219; *APC*, II, pp. 139, 149–50; *Tudor Royal Proclamations*, I, no. 292.

24 *CSP Spain*, IX, pp. 219, 221.

Chapter 9

1 A.F. Pollard, *England under Protector Somerset* (New York, 1966), p.134; *CSP Spain*, IX, p. 267.

2 *LP* XIX i, 319.

3 *Calendar of State Papers relating to Scotland and Mary Queen of Scots*, ed. J. Bain et al. (13 vols, Edinburgh, 1898–1969), I, 4, 26; W.K. Jordan, *Edward VI: The Young King* (London, 1968), p. 246.

4 *APC*, II, pp. 461, 471; *CSP Dom. Ed. VI*, 10/1/36.

5 *CPR Ed. VI*, II, pp. 96–7.

6 *CSP Scots*, I, 31; W. Patten, 'The Expedition into Scotland', in *An English Garner* (8 vols, London, 1877–96), III, p. 75.

7 *CSP Dom. Ed. VI*, 10/3/22; *CSP Scots*, I, 29. It is unclear whether these estimates were for an invasion in 1547 or 1548 but the number of 18,000 and the expected length of the campaign suggest the former.

8 *A Bibliography of Royal Proclamations of the Tudor and Stuart Sovereigns*, ed. R. Steele (2 vols, Oxford, 1910), I, no. 312; *CSP Scots*, I, 34. This was a tactic Somerset had used in Scotland in 1544.

9 *APC,* II, pp. 118–19; *CSP Spain*, IX, p. 141.

10 *CSP Dom. Ed. VI*, 10/6/13.

11   Unless otherwise stated all details of the expedition are taken from Patten, 'The expedition into Scotland', pp. 51–150.

12   A harquebus was an early portable gun supported on a forked rest for firing.

13   Jordan, *The Young King*, p. 260.

14   Ibid. p. 44.

15   *CSP Spain*, IX, p. 143; *Correspondence Politique de Odet de Selve*, ed. G. Lefevre-Pontalis (Paris, 1888), no. 221.

16   R. Grafton, *Grafton's Chronicle* (2 vols, London, 1809), II, p. 504; Patten, 'The expedition into Scotland', p. 80.

17   *CPR* II, pp. 27–9.

18   *CSP Scots*, I, 50, 67.

19   *CSP Spain*, IX, p. 196.

20   *CSP Scots*, I, 56, 74, 79, 66, 72, 73.

21   Ibid. 269.

22   NRO F(M) c. 21 – 2 February 1548.

23   *CSP Spain* IX, p. 184.

24   *CSP Scots*, I, 107.

Chapter 10

1   *Literary Remains*, I, p. cxiv.

2   M.A.E. Wood, *Letters of Royal and Illustrious Ladies* (3 vols, London, 1846), III, pp. 191–2.

3   Wriothesley, *Chronicle,* I, p. 117; *LP* XVI, 41.

4   J. Hayward, *The Life and Raigne of King Edward the Sixth* (Ohio, USA, 1993), p. 97.

5   E. Dent, *Annals of Winchcombe and Sudeley* (London, 1877), p. 163.

6   Ibid. p. 193; H. Ellis, *Original Letters, illustrative of English history* (1st series, 3 vols, London, 1824), II, pp. 151–3; J. Maclean, *The Life of Sir Thomas Seymour* (London, 1869), pp. 44–5.

7   Strype, *Ecclesiastical Memorials*, II, i, pp. 208–9.

8   Ellis, *Original Letters* (1st series), II, pp. 149–51.

9   *CSP Spain*, IX, pp. 104, 123.

10   Wood, *Letters*, III, pp. 193–4; *Literary Remains*, II, p. 215.

11 N. Sander, *Rise and Growth of the Anglican Schism* (London, 1877), p. 184; *Chronicle of King Henry VIII of England*, ed. M. Hume (London, 1889), pp. 160–1.

12 *LP* XIX ii, 688 (p. 405).

13 Tytler, *England under the Reigns of Edward VI and* Mary, I, p. 145; CSP *Dom. Ed. VI*, 10/6/9.

14 Haynes, *State Papers*, p. 69.

15 Ibid. p. 61.

16 Ibid. pp. 69, 71, 73, 91.

17 Selve, *Correspondence Politique*, no. 304.

18 *CSP Spain*, IX, p. 88.

19 Haynes, *State Papers*, pp. 77–8.

20 *The Legend of Sir Nicholas Throckmorton*, ed. J.G. Nichols (London, 1874), p. 17.

21 *CSP Dom. Ed. VI*, 10/6/7; Maclean, *Life of Sir Thomas Seymour*, p. 71.

22 Haynes, *State Papers*, p. 99; *CSP Dom. Ed. VI*, 10/6/21.

23 *CSP Dom. Ed. VI*, 10/6/27.

24 Ibid. 10/6/27; Tytler, *England under the reigns of Edward VI and Mary*, I, pp. 146–8.

25 Ibid. pp. 154–5.

26 *Journals of the Lords*, p. 293.

27 Haynes, *State Papers*, p. 93.

28 J.G. Nichols, 'The Second Patent Appointing Edward Duke of Somerset Protector', *Archaeologia*, 30 (1844), pp. 478–88, 473–4.

Chapter 11

1 *CSP Spain*, IX, p. 206.

2 Jordan, *Edward VI: The Young King*, p. 168; *Journals of the House of Commons*, (55 vols, 1803), I, p. 21.

3 *Victoria County History of Wiltshire* (18 vols, London, 1953–2011), V, p. 115; S.T. Bindoff, *The House of Commons 1509–1558* (3 vols, London, 1982), III, p. 300.

4 1 Edward VI, c. 12, c. 1.

5 NRO F(M) c. 21 – 7 July 1549.

6 J. Poynet, *A short treatise of politike power* (Amsterdam, 1972, facsimile of 1556 edition), unpaginated.

7   Haynes, *State Papers*, pp. 75–6.

8   Bod. Lib. Ashmole MS 1729 f. 9.

9   1 Edward VI, c. 14; *APC*, II, p. 185.

10   1 Edward VI, c. 3.

11   1 Edward VI, c. 11.

12   NRO F(M) c. 21 – 2 February 1548.

13   *Tudor Royal Proclamations*, I, nos 300, 299, 303.

14   *CSP Dom. Ed. VI*, 10/2/32; *APC*, II, pp. 164–5.

15   Foxe, *Acts and Monuments*, V, pp. 717–18.

16   Jordan, *The Young King*, p. 440.

17   Muller, *Letters of Stephen Gardiner*, p. 420.

18   *CSP Dom. Ed. VI*, 10/4/17.

19   J. A. Muller, *Stephen Gardiner and the Tudor reaction* (London, 1926), pp. 174–80.

20   Robinson, *Original Letters*, I, p. 69.

21   'Sir Thomas Smith's Defence of his Conduct and Character, Addressed to the Duchess of Somerset', *Archaeologia*, 38 (1840), p. 126; *CSP Spain*, IX, p. 447.

22   *The Early Works of Thomas Becon*, ed. J. Ayre (Cambridge, 1843), p. 399.

23   *CSP Dom. Ed. VI*, 10/6/33; Muller, *The Letters of Stephen Gardiner*, p. 493.

24   *Literary Remains*, I, p. cccxxxiii. A painting in the National Maritime Museum of Thomas Seymour by Denisot shows that while in England he also used his skills as an artist.

25   Robinson, *Original Letters*, II, pp. 702–3.

26   P. Demers, 'The Seymour Sisters: Elegizing Female Attachment', *Sixteenth Century Journal*, 30 (2) (1999), pp. 343, 349.

27   Robinson, *Original Letters*, I, p. 2; J. N. King, 'Protector Somerset, Patron of the English Renaissance', *The Papers of the Bibliographical Society of America*, 70 (1976), p. 331; *Tottel's Miscellany*, ed. H. E. Rollins (2 vols, Cambridge, Mass., 1965), I, pp. 100–3.

28   *Writings and Translations of Myles Coverdale* (Cambridge, 1844), pp. 91–4.

29   Rollins, *Tottel's Miscellany*, I, p. 157; II, pp. 277–8.

30   King, 'Protector Somerset, Patron of the English Renaissance', pp. 329–31.

31   T. Lanquet, *An epitome of cronicles* (London, 1569), p. v.

32   King, 'Protector Somerset, Patron of the English Renaissance', p. 311.

33   *CSP Dom. Ed. VI*, 10/13/71.

34   *CSP Dom. Ed. VI*, 10/14/3(i), 10/13/70, 10/13/74. Earlier charity had primarily involved bequeathing funds to aid the poor of the local parish after the benefactor died.

Chapter 12

1 'An epistle or exhortation to unity and peace', in *The Complaynt of Scotland*, ed. J.A.H. Murray (E.E.T.S., 1872), pp. 238–46.

2 *Correspondence Politique*, nos 208, 221.

3 Ibid. nos 254, 262, 264.

4 *CSP Scots*, I, 117, 129 (1).

5 Ibid. 231.

6 *The Scottish Correspondence of Mary of Lorraine*, ed. A.I. Dunlop (Edinburgh, 1927), pp. 246–8, 304–5, 284–5.

7 *CSP Scots*, I, 330, 149.

8 Ibid. 149, 337.

9 Ibid. 248, 251.

10 Ibid. 293; *CSP Dom. Ed. VI*, 10/4/38.

11 NRO F(M) c. 21, undated but probably late July 1548; *CSP Scots*, I, 120.

12 Ibid. 320, 324; *CSP Spain*, X, p. 389.

13 *CSP Dom. Ed. VI*, 10/4/4; *CSP Scots*, I, 251.

14 *HMC Bath*, IV, p. 107.

15 *CSP Scots*, I, 274.

16 *CSP Spain*, IX, p. 322.

17 NRO F(M) c. 21 – 28 August 1549.

18 *CSP Scots*, I, 332, 338; *Scottish Correspondence of Mary of Lorraine*, p. 282.

19 Jordan, *The Young King*, pp. 292–3.

20 *CSP Spain*, IX, pp. 249, 299.

21 *CSP Scots*, I, 339.

22 *APC*, II, pp. 190–2; *Tudor Royal Proclamations*, I, no. 309.

23 J. Strype, *Ecclesiastical Memorials*, II ii, p. 482.

24 E.A. Wrigley and R.S. Schofield, *The Population History of England, 1541–1871* (London, 1981), p. 208; R.B. Outhwaite, *Inflation in Tudor and Early Stuart England* (London, 1982), p. 15.

25 *Tudor Royal Proclamations*, I, no. 309; *Four Supplications* (E.E.T.S., London, 1871), p. 100; Strype, *Ecclesiastical Memorials*, II ii, p. 482.

26 'Sir Thomas Smith's Defence of his Conduct and Character, Addressed to the Duchess of Somerset', p. 126.

27 Tytler, *England under the Reigns of Edward VI and Mary*, I, p. 116; *A Discourse of the common weal of this realm of England*, ed. E. Lamond (Cambridge, 1893), p. xl.

28 2&3 Edward VI, c. 12.

29   M.L. Bush, *The Government Policy of Protector Somerset* (London, 1975), p. 63 (note 124).

30   Jackson, 'Wulfhall and the Seymours', pp. 179–80.

Chapter 13

1   *CSP Spain*, IX, p. 19.

2   Ibid. p. 102.

3   NRO F(M) c. 21 – 25 December 1548, 7 July 1549.

4   Bush, *Government Policy of Protector Somerset*, p. 4.

5   Stow, *Annales*, p. 1015; *CSP Spain*, IX, p. 102; *APC*, II, p. 310.

6   *CSP Spain*, IX, p. 91; Hoak, *King's Council*, pp. 115–16; *CSP Spain*, X, pp. 65–6.

7   *CSP Scots*, I, 327.

8   Hoak, *King's Council*, pp. 145–6.

9   *CSP Dom. Ed. VI*, 10/1/30, 10/4/16, 10/4/13, 10/4/17.

10   NRO F(M) c. 21 - 21 March 1549.

11   BL Lansdowne MS 2, f. 34; 'Sir Thomas Smith's defence of his conduct and character, addressed to the Duchess of Somerset', p. 121.

12   BL Add. MS 48126, f. 2.

13   *CSP Spain*, IX, pp. 429, 447.

14   Stow, *Annales*, p. 1015.

15   NRO F(M) c. 21 – 7 July 1549; Sir H. Ellis, *Original Letters illustrative of English History* (3rd series, 4 vols, London, 1969), III, pp. 301–2; M.L. Bush, 'Protector Somerset and Requests', *The Historical Journal*, 17 (3), (1974), pp. 452–3.

16   Tytler, *England under the Reigns of Edward VI and Mary*, I, p. 121; Lanquet, *An epitome of cronicles*, p. i.

17   J. Loach, *Protector Somerset* (Oxford, 2001), p. 19.

18   *CSP Dom. Ed. VI*, 10/9/28; Foxe, *Acts and Monuments*, VI, p. 290 (iv); *HMC Bath*, IV, pp. 108, 111.

19   Robinson, *Original Letters*, II, p. 734.

20   *CSP Spain*, IX, p. 340.

21   *CPR Ed. VI*, I, p. 184; *HMC Bath*, IV, p. 187; L. Stone, *The Crisis of the Aristocracy, 1558–1641* (Oxford, 1965), p. 762.

22   *LP* XX i, 1032.

23   *HMC Bath*, IV, pp. 90, 101, 112, 121–2, 338; Stone, *Crisis of the Aristocracy*,
      p. 212, App. XXIII; *CPR*, I, p. 249.

24   *HMC Bath*, IV, p. 112.

25   J. Stow, *A Survey of London* (Stroud, 2005), pp. 370–1; *The A to Z of
      Elizabethan London,* ed. A. Prockter and R. Taylor (London, 1979), p. 17.

26   Stow, *Survey of London*, p. 283; Stow, *Annales*, p. 1005.

27   Needham and Webster, *Somerset House Past and Present*, pp. 46–7, 51.

28   Stow, *A Survey of London*, p. 93.

29   *Literary Remains*, I, cxi.

30   Details of property from Jackson, 'Wulfhall and the Seymours', pp. 179–86.

31   T. Fuller, *The History of the Worthies of England* (3 vols, London, 1860), II,
      p. 4.

32   Stone, *Crisis of the Aristocracy*, p. 554.

33   NRO F(M) c. 21, undated but probably late July 1548, 7 July 1549.

Chapter 14

1   *APC,* II, p. 252 no. 22.

2   Haynes, *State Papers*, p. 69; *HMC Salisbury*, I, p. 72.

3   *CSP Spain*, IX, pp. 85, 340.

4   Maclean, *Life of Sir Thomas Seymour*, pp. 66–7.

5   Ibid. p. 56.

6   Ibid. p. 67; *CSP Dom. Ed. VI*, 10/4/31.

7   Haynes, *State Papers*, pp. 77–8.

8   Ibid. p. 69.

9   *CSP Dom. Ed. VI*, 10/6/27.

10   Maclean, *Life of Sir Thomas Seymour*, p. 60.

11   Bod. Lib. Ashmole MS 1729. f. 9.

12   Haynes, *State Papers*, p. 96.

13   *CSP Dom. Ed. VI*, 10/6/16.

14   Haynes, *State Papers*, p. 98.

15   Ibid. p. 90; Wood, *Letters*, III, p. 192.

16   *APC,* II, p. 238; *CSP Dom. Ed. VI*, 10/6/14.

17   *CSP Dom. Ed. VI*, 10/6/7, 10/6/12, 10/6/16.

18   *HMC Salisbury*, I, p. 60.

19   *CSP Dom. Ed. VI*, 10/6/13.

20   Ibid. 10/6/1.

21   Ibid. 10/6/14.

22   *APC,* II, pp. 236–8.

23   *CSP Dom. Ed. VI,* 10/6/10; *CSP Spain,* IX, pp. 332–3; Robinson, *Original Letters,* II, p. 648.

24   Haynes, *State Papers,* pp. 87, 84.

25   Ibid. pp. 106–7.

26   *APC,* II, pp. 247–56.

27   Ibid. pp. 257–8.

28   'A Journall of Matters of State', in *Religion, Politics and State in Sixteenth-Century England,* ed. I. W. Archer (Cambridge, 2003), p. 57.

29   *APC* II, pp. 258–60.

30   *Lords Journals,* pp. 345–6; *APC,* II, p. 260.

31   G. Burnet, *A History of the Reformation of the Church of England* (2 vols, London, 1681, 1683), II, p. 99; *Journals of the House of Commons* (55 vols, 1803), I, p. 9; *APC,* II, p. 260.

32   Ibid. p. 261.

33   Pollard, *England under Protector Somerset,* pp. 197–8.

34   *Sermons of Hugh Latimer,* ed. G.E. Corrie (Cambridge, 1844), pp. 161–2, 164.

35   *Literary Remains,* II, pp 224.

36   Dent, *Annals of Winchcombe and Sudeley,* p. 193.

37   H. Ellis, *Original letters illustrative of English history* (2nd series, 4 vols, London, 1827), II, pp. 256–7; Hume, *Chronicle of Henry VIII,* p. 164.

38   Nichols, *Legend of Sir Nicholas Throckmorton,* pp. 17, 20.

39   Strype, *Ecclesiastical Memorials,* II, i, pp. 200–1.

Chapter 15

1   *CSP Spain,* IX, p. 408.

2   Details of these proceedings are taken from F.A. Gasquet and E. Bishop, *Edward VI and the Book of Common Prayer* (London, 1890), pp. 397–443.

3   *Lords Journals,* p. 331.

4   *CSP Dom. Ed. VI,* 10/7/28.

5   Robinson, *Original Letters,* II, 734; *The Works of John Knox,* ed. D. Laing (6 vols, Edinburgh, 1846–64) III, pp. 176–7.

6   Foxe, *Acts and Monuments*, V, pp. 746–7, 797.

7   Tytler, *England under the Reigns of Edward VI and Mary I*, I, p. 51.

8   *CSP Spain*, IX, pp. 375, 381–2.

9   Robinson, *Original Letters*, II, p. 439.

10   Hoak, *King's Council*, p. 174.

11   *CSP Spain*, IX, pp. 394–5, 406.

12   Ibid. pp. 407–8.

13   Ibid. pp. 444, 447.

14   NRO F(M) c. 21 – 12 March 1549.

15   All the letters are in NRO F(M) c. 21.

16   F.C. Dietz, *Finances of Edward VI and Mary* (Northampton, Mass., 1918), p. 81; *CSP Dom. Ed. VI*, 10/15/11.

17   2&3 Edward VI, c. 36.

18   NRO F(M) c. 21 – 25 December 1548.

19   *Tudor Royal Proclamations*, I, nos 321.

20   *Tudor Economic Documents*, ed. R.H. Tawney and E. Power (3 vols, London, 1924), II, p. 180.

21   NRO F(M) c. 21 – 2 February, 12 March, 17 April 1549.

22   *CSP Spain*, IX, p. 50.

23   NRO F(M) c. 21 – 2 Jan 1549.

24   NRO F(M) c. 21 – 25 December 1549.

25   NRO F(M) c. 21 – 2 February 1549.

26   NRO F(M) c. 21 – 8 May 1549.

27   *Tudor Royal Proclamations*, I, no. 327; Foxe, *Acts and Monuments*, VI, p. 291 (x).

28   NRO F(M) c. 21 – 7 July 1549.

29   *HMC Bath*, IV, p. 109; Lamond, *Discourse of the common weal*, p. lviii.

Chapter 16

1   *HMC Report on the Records of the city of Exeter* (London, 1916), p. 21.

2   Wriothesley, *Chronicle of England*, II, p. 13; *CSP Dom. Ed. VI*, 10/7/44, 10/8/48.

3   *CSP Dom. Ed. VI*, 10/8/41.

4   *Tudor Royal Proclamations*, I, no. 333.

5   *CSP Dom. Ed. VI*, 10/7/31.

6   *Tudor Royal Proclamations*, I. no. 334.

7   *CSP Spain,* IX, p. 395; Foxe, *Acts and Monuments,*VI, p. 291 (xv).

8   Details of the western rebellion in A. Fletcher, *Tudor Rebellions* (Harlow, 1995).

9   F.B. Rose-Troup, *The Western Rebellion of 1549* (London, 1913), pp. 433–40.

10   A.L. Rowse, *Tudor Cornwall: Portrait of a Society* (London, 1957), pp. 266, 268; CSP *Dom, Ed. VI,* 10/7/40.

11   *Tudor Royal Proclamations,* I, nos 339, 340, 341.

12   *Troubles Connected with the Prayer Book of 1549,* ed. N. Pocock (Camden Society, 1884), p. 24.

13   NRO F(M) c. 21 – 7 July 1549.

14   Foxe, *Acts and Monuments,*VI, p. 291 (x).

15   *CSP Dom. Ed. VI,* 10/8/11, 10/7/35.

16   Lamond, *Discourse of the common weal,* p. liv–lv.

17   Wriothesley, *Chronicle,* II, pp. 15–16: *Chronicle of the Grey Friars of London,* ed. J.G. Nichols (London, 1852), p. 60; *CSP Dom. Ed. VI,* 10/7/46; *APC,* II, pp. 301–2.

18   Wriothesley, *Chronicle,* II, p. 19: *Calendar of State Papers, Venetian,* ed. R. Brown et al. (38 vols, London, 1864–1947),V, p. 237.

19   Pocock, *Troubles Connected with the Prayer Book,* p. 26.

20   E.H. Shagan, 'Protector Somerset and the 1549 Rebellions: New Sources and New Perspectives', *The English Historical Review,* 114 (455), (1999), p. 58; Foxe, *Acts and Monuments,*V, p. 738.

21   Details of the East Anglia rebellion in Fletcher, *Tudor Rebellions.*

22   NRO F(M) c. 21 – 17 April 1549.

23   Shagan, 'Protector Somerset and the 1549 Rebellions', pp. 59–61, 53–5.

24   B.L. Beer, 'The Commoyson in Norfolk, 1549', *The Journal of Medieval and Renaissance Studies,* 6 (i), (1976), p. 87.

25   Tawney and Power, *Tudor Economic Documents,* III, p. 58.

26   J. Strype, *Ecclesiastical Memorials,* II, ii, p. 425.

27   B.L. Beer, *Rebellion and Riot: Popular Disorder in England During the Reign of Edward VI* (Kent, Ohio, 1982), p. 191.

28   Fletcher, *Tudor Rebellions,* pp. 120–3; Tawney and Power, *Tudor Economic Documents,* III, p. 57.

29   Strype, *Ecclesiastical Memorials,* II, ii, p. 425; Shagan, 'Protector Somerset and the 1549 Rebellions', p. 59.

30   Ibid. pp. 60, 55, 57–8.

31   Strype, *Ecclesiastical Memorials,* II, ii, p. 424.

32   Pocock, *Troubles Connected with the Prayer Book,* pp. 23, 26, 31–2, 35, 29.

33   Ibid. pp. 44–5.

34 Wriothesley, *Chronicle*, II, p. 20.

35 Pocock, *Troubles Connected with the Prayer Book*, pp. 53–4, 74.

36 F.W. Russell, *Kett's Rebellion in Norfolk* (London, 1859), pp. 109, 115, 117–18.

37 Ibid. pp. 117–18.

38 Beer, 'The commoyson in Norfolk', pp. 94–5.

39 Jordan, *Edward VI: The Young King*, pp. 492–3.

40 Russell, *Kett's Rebellion*, p. 161.

41 *Calendar of State Papers, Foreign series, of the reign of Edward VI, 1547–1553*, ed. W.B. Turnbull (London, 1861), nos 196–7.

42 *CSP Dom. Ed. VI*, 10/8/56.

Chapter 17

1 NRO F(M) c. 21 – 17 April 1549, 28 August 1549.

2 Bush, *Government Policy of Protector Somerset*, p. 14.

3 *CSP Spain*, IX, p. 454.

4 Ibid. p. 454.

5 Ibid. p. 446.

6 *HMC Bath*, IV, pp. 96–8.

7 *CSP Spain*, IX, p. 448.

8 *CSP Dom. Ed. VI*, 10/4/26.

9 BL Add. MS 48126, ff. 7v–8.

10 Pollard, *England under Protector Somerset*, p. 245.

11 *APC*, II, p. 336; *Tudor Royal Proclamations*, I, nos 352, 353.

12 *HMC Salisbury*, I, p. 75; *HMC Manuscripts of the Duke of Rutland* (4 vols, London, 1888–1905), I, p. 44.

13 *CSP Spain*, IX, pp. 445, 449; Tytler, *England under the Reigns of Edward VI and Mary*, I, p. 250.

14 R. Holinshed, *Chronicles of England, Scotland and Ireland* (6 vols, London, 1808), III, p. 1014.

15 Tytler, *England under the Reigns of Edward VI and Mary*, I, p. 205; *CSP Dom Ed. VI*, 10/9/3; 10/9/4.

16 Pocock, *Troubles Connected with the Prayer Book*, p. 78.

17 Details of coup from BL Add. MS 48126, ff. 9–15.

18 *CSP Spain*, IX, p. 457.

19 *APC,* II, p. 330.

20 Ibid. p. 332; Pocock, *Troubles Connected with the Prayer Book*, pp. 83–5.
21 *CSP Spain*, IX, p. 460.
22 Pocock, *Troubles Connected with the Prayer Book*, pp. 82–3. As part of his extended family Somerset had good cause to hope that Herbert would hurry to his aid. Sir William Herbert was married to Anne Parr, Katherine Parr's sister, and hence related to Thomas Seymour.
23 *CSP Spain*, IX, p. 457.
24 *APC,* II, pp. 333–4.
25 *CSP Dom. Ed. VI*, 10/9/16; *APC,* II, p. 334.
26 Pocock, *Troubles Connected with the Prayer Book*, pp. 86–8.
27 Foxe, *Acts and Monuments*, VI, p. 286.
28 *CSP Dom. Ed. VI*, 10/9/52.
29 Tytler, *England under the reigns of Edward VI and Mary*, I, pp. 217–19.
30 *CSP Dom. Ed. VI*, 10/9/24 (i).
31 BL Harley MS 353, ff. 76–7.
32 Tytler, *England under the Reigns of Edward VI and Mary*, I, pp. 229, 223–7.
33 J. Stow, *The annales of England until 1592* (London, 1592), p. 1009.
34 Wriothesley, *Chronicle*, II, p. 26; Pocock, *Troubles Connected with the Prayer Book*, pp. 95–100.
35 Tytler, *England under the Reigns of Edward VI and Mary*, I, pp. 208–9, 231–2.
36 NRO F(M) c. 21 – 8 October 1549.
37 *APC*, II, pp. 339, 342.
38 BL Add. MS 48126, ff. 13–13v; *CSP Spain*, IX, p. 460.
39 BL Add. MS 48126, ff. 13v–14v; Tytler, *England under the Reigns of Edward VI and Mary*, I, pp. 238–40.
40 Ibid. pp. 241–3.
41 Nichols, 'The Second Patent Appointing Edward Duke of Somerset Protector', p. 489.
42 *APC*, II, p. 344; *CSP Spain*, IX, p. 460.
43 *APC*, II, p. 343; *CSP Dom. Ed. VI*, 10/9/45; Tytler, *England under the Reigns of Edward VI and Mary*, I, pp. 272–3.

Chapter 18

1 *APC*, II, pp. 344–5.
2 Robinson, *Original Letters*, I, pp. 353–54; *Tudor Royal Proclamations*, I, no. 353.

3   Source for this and following paragraphs: BL Add. MS 48126, ff. 15–16.

4   *CSP Spain*, IX, p. 489.

5   Stow, *Annales*, pp. 1015–18.

6   'The Letters of Richard Scudamore to Sir Philip Hoby, September 1549–March 1555', ed. S. Brigden in *Camden Miscellany*, 30 (London, 1990), p. 104.

7   *Eighth Report of the Royal Commission on Historical Manuscripts* (4 vols, London, 1907–10), I (i), 87b. Yeomen Warders were distinguished from Yeomen of the Guard by not wearing a shoulder belt.

8   *Literary Remains,* II, p. 245.

9   3&4 Edward VI, c. 5.

10 3&4 Edward VI, c. 16.

11 3&4 Edward VI, c. 15, 23, 3, 10.

12 *CSP Spain*, X, p. 7.

13 *Lords Journals*, pp. 374–5; Stow, *Annales*, p. 1019; *Literary Remains*, II, p. 244.

14 *CSP Dom. Ed. VI*, 10/9/53, 10/6/28, 10/6/29.

15 Wriothesley, *Chronicle,* II, p. 33; CSP *Spain*, X, pp. 13, 28.

16 Brigden, 'Letters of Richard Scudamore', p. 118.

17 *APC*, II, pp. 384–5; Robinson, *Original Letters*, II, p. 464.

18 *Literary Remains*, II, p. 255.

19 *CSP Spain*, X, p. 43.

20 Ibid. p. 62; *APC*, II, p. 427; *Literary Remains*, II, p. 268; *APC*, III, p. 11.

21 *CPR Edward VI*, III, pp, 339–40, 430–2.

22 Brigden, 'Letters of Richard Scudamore', p. 130; *CSP Spain,* X, pp. 62, 83.

23 *Calendar of State Papers, Venetian*, ed. R. Brown et al. (38 vols, London, 1864–1947), V, p. 343; *APC*, III, pp. 104, 107; *Literary Remains*, II, pp. 255, 290, 295.

24 Ibid. pp. 478–86.

25 Ibid. p. 269.

26 Ibid. p. 255; *APC*, II, pp. 420–1.

27 Robinson, *Original Letters*, I, p. 89.

28 H. Machyn, *The Diary of Henry Machyn, Citizen and Merchant-Taylor of London*, ed. J.G. Nichols (London, 1848), pp. 4–5; *Literary Remains*, II, pp. 308–9.

29 Robinson, *Original Letters,* II, p. 410; *APC*, III, p. 43.

30 Ibid. pp. 44, 87.

31 Ibid. p. 19; *Literary Remains*, II, p. 312.

32 *APC*, III, pp. 54–5; Tytler, *England under the Reigns of Edward VI and Mary*, II, pp. 21–4.

33 *CSP Dom. Ed. VI*, 10/10/30.

34   *CSP Spain*, X, p. 109.

35   *Literary Remains*, II, pp. 272–3.

36   Ibid. pp. 273–4; *CSP Spain*, X, p. 98.

37   Demers, 'The Seymour Sisters: Elegizing Female Attachment', p. 348;
     CSP Dom. Ed. VI, 10/6/14; *CPR*, I, pp. 376–80.

38   *APC*, III, p. 35; *Literary Remains*, II, pp. 264, 280, 288–9.

39   Stow, *Annales*, p. 1021.

40   *APC*, III, pp. 142–3; Machyn, *Diary of Henry Machyn*, pp. 3–4.

41   *CSP Spain*, X, p. 186.

Chapter 19

1   *CSP Spain*, X, p. 216.

2   *APC*, III, pp. 215, 248; Strype, *Ecclesiastical Memorials*, II, i, p. 390.

3   *CSP Spain*, X, p. 262; *APC*, III, pp. 244–6.

4   *CSP Dom. Ed. VI*, 10/13/67, 10/13/65.

5   *Literary Remains*, II, p. 315.

6   *CSP Spain*, X, p. 291.

7   Ibid. p. 325.

8   Ibid. p. 279.

9   *APC*, III, pp. 256–8; *Literary Remains* II, p. 340.

10 *Tudor Proclamations*, I, nos 371, 374.

11 *CSP Spain*, X, p. 328.

12 *HMC Bath*, IV, p. 114.

13 *CSP Spain*, X, p. 227; *Literary Remains*, II, p. 331.

14 Tytler, *England under the Reigns of Edward VI and Mary*, II, p. 39.

15 J. Foxe, *Narratives of the Days of the Reformation*, ed. J.G. Nichols (London,
    1859), pp. 79–80.

16 APC, III, p. 375.

17 Ibid. pp. 374, 378–9.

18 *Literary Remains*, II, pp. 353–4.

19 *CSP Spain* XI, pp. 185, 187.

20 *Literary Remains*, II, p. 361. The source for Palmer's evidence is in the same
    work.

21 *CSP Dom. Ed. VI,* 11/4/21; *CSP Spain*, X, p. 381.

22 *APC*, III, p. 385.

23 *Literary Remains*, II, p. 354.

24   Ibid. p. 354.

25   *Literary Remains*, II, pp. 354–5; Tytler, *England under the Reigns of Edward VI and Mary*, II, p. 37.

26   Ellis, *Original Letters*, 2nd series, II, p. 215; *APC*, III, p. 424.

27   J.G. Nichols, 'Anne, Duchess of Somerset', *The Gentleman's Magazine*, 2nd series, 23 (1845), p. 373.

28   *APC*, III, pp. 390–1, 423; *Literary Remains*, II, p. 358.

29   *APC*, III, pp. 389, 392.

30   *CSP Spain*, X, pp. 386, 388, 393; Wriothesley, *Chronicle*, II, p. 58.

31   *Literary Remains*, II, p. 356. This may have referred to the muster planned for early June.

32   Ibid. p. 357; *APC*, III, p. 397.

33   Tytler, *England under the Reigns of Edward VI and Mary*, II, pp. 38–41.

34   *APC*, III, p. 407.

35   *Literary Remains*, II, p. 361.

36   *CSP Spain*, X, pp. 392–3.

37   Ellis, *Original Letters*, 2nd series, II, p. 214; *CSP Dom. Ed. VI*, 10/13/67.

38   *Literary Remains*, II, pp. 347–8; *APC*, III, pp. 411, 416.

39   *Fourth Report of the Deputy Keeper of the Public Records* (vol. 4, London, 1843) Appendix II, pp. 228–31.

40   *APC*, III, p. 426.

41   *CSP Dom. Ed. VI*, 10/13/67.

42   *Literary Remains*, II, pp. 369–70.

43   W.K. Jordan, *Edward VI: The Threshold of Power* (London, 1970), p. 94.

44   Stow, *Annales*, p. 1025.

45   Details of the trial are taken from *Literary Remains*, II, pp. 370–4; *CSP Spain*, X, pp. 405–7.

46   Jordan, *Edward VI: The Threshold of Power*, p. 94.

47   *CSP Spain*, X, p. 407; Rymer, *Foedera*, XV, p. 295.

48   Wriothesley, *Chronicle*, II, p. 63.

49   'The Travels and Life of Sir Thomas Hoby', ed. E. Powell, *Camden Miscellany*, X (London, 1902), p. 75.

50   Tytler, *England under the Reigns of Edward VI and Mary*, II, pp. 63–5.

51   *CSP Spain* XI, pp. 185, 187.

52   BL MS Cotton Vespasian FXIII ff. 273–4 (ff. 171–72; previous pagination). Allowing for changes in ink flow when the pen nib was recharged, the same nib could have been used throughout the document. However, some slight differences in letter shape do offer the possibility that the interlineations were added by both Edward and another writer.

53   *Literary Remains*, II, p. 390.

54   *APC*, III, p. 460.

55   BL Stowe MS 1066. Quotes taken from Psalms 111:10, Proverbs 3:5 and 3:7. This little book was also later used by Katherine Grey, Countess of Hertford, who was Somerset's daughter-in-law, during her stay in the Tower between 1561 and 1563.

56   Details of Somerset's execution are taken from Foxe, *Acts and Monuments*, VI, pp. 293–5; Stow, *Annales*, p. 1026; Machyn, *Diary of Henry Machyn*, p. 14.

57   Ibid. p. 14; *CSP Spain*, X, p. 453.

Chapter 20

1   *Literary Remains*, II, p. 390.

2   *Literary Remains,* I, pp. 74–5; Rymer, *Foedera*, XV, pp. 295–6.

3   Holinshed, *Chronicles*, III, p. 1035; *CSP Spain*, X, p. 452; Robinson, *Original Letters*, II, pp. 733, 736.

4   *Diary of Henry Machyn*, p. 15.

5   *Literary Remains,* II, p. 410.

6   *CSP Dom. Ed. VI*, 10/14/7, 10/14/8. Somerset's garter plate is now on display in the British Museum.

7   *CSP Dom. Ed. VI*, 10/14/20.

8   5&6 Edward VI, c. 35.

9   *APC*, IV, pp. 465–6; *CSP Spain*, X, 453; Robinson, *Original Letters*, II, p. 579.

10   Nichols, 'Anne, Duchess of Somerset', p. 375.

11   Ibid. pp. 375–7.

12   *APC*, III, p. 461.

13   Robinson, *Original Letters*, I, pp. 340–2.

14   *The Diary of Henry Machyn*, p. 254.

15   *ODNB*, vol. 49, p. 889.

16   *ODNB*, vol. 43, p. 745.

Bibliography

Primary Sources

Manuscripts

British Library

Add. MS 48126
Cotton MS Titus BI
Cotton MS Vespasian FXIII
Harley MS 353
Lansdowne MS 2
Stowe MS 1066

Bodleian Library
Ashmole MS 862
Ashmole MS 1729
Rawlinson MS B.146

Northamptonshire Record Office
Fitzwilliam (Milton) c. 21

The National Archives
IPM C142/46/25
PROB 11/22/406
C65/139

Printed

Acts and Monuments of John Foxe, ed. Rev. J. Pratt (8 vols, London, *c.*1877)

Acts of the Privy Council of England, ed. J.R. Dasent (46 vols, London, 1890–1964)

A Discourse of the common weal of this realm of England, ed. E. Lamond (Cambridge, 1893)

'A Journall of Matters of State', in *Religion, Politics and Society in Sixteenth-Century England*, ed. I.W. Archer (Cambridge, 2003)

'An epistle or exhortation to unity and peace', in *The Complaynt of Scotland*, ed. J.A.H. Murray (London, 1872)

Bibliography of Royal Proclamations of the Tudor and Stuart Sovereigns, ed. R. Steele (2 vols, Oxford, 1910)

Calendar of Close Rolls, Henry VII (2 vols, London, 1955–63)

Calendar of Letters, Despatches and State Papers, Spanish, ed. G.A. Bergenroth et al. (13 vols, London, 1862–1954)

Calendar of the Patent Rolls, Henry VII (2 vols, London, 1914–16)

Calendar of Patent Rolls for the reign of Edward VI (6 vols, London, 1924–29)

Calendar of State Papers: Domestic Series, of the reign of Edward VI, 1547–1553, ed. C.S. Knighton (London, 1992)

Calendar of State Papers, Foreign series, of the reign of Edward VI, 1547–1553, ed. W.B. Turnbull (London, 1861)

Calendar of the State Papers relating to Scotland and Mary Queen of Scots, ed. J. Bain et al. (13 vols, Edinburgh, 1898–1969)

Calendar of State Papers, Venetian, ed. R. Brown et al. (38 vols, London, 1864–1947)

Cavendish, G. *Thomas Wolsey* (London, 1962)

Chronicle of the Grey Friars of London, ed. J.G. Nichols (London, 1852)

Chronicle of Henry VIII of England, ed. M.A.S. Hume (London, 1889)

Collection of Ordinances and Regulations for the Government of the Royal Household (London, 1790)

Collection of State Papers relating to affairs in the reigns of King Henry VIII, King Edward VI, Queen Mary and Queen Elizabeth, 1542–1570, of William Cecil at Hatfield House, ed. S. Haynes (London, 1740)

Correspondence Politique de Odet de Selve, ed. G. Lefevre-Pontalis (Paris, 1888)

The Early Works of Thomas Becon, ed. J. Ayre (Cambridge, 1843)

Eighth Report of the Royal Commission on Historical Manuscripts (4 vols, London, 1907–10)

England under the reigns of Edward VI and Mary, ed. P.F. Tytler (2 vols, London, 1839)

Foedera, conventiones, literae … eds T. Rymer and R. Sanderson (20 vols, London, 1704–35)

Four Supplications, 1529–1553, ed. F.J. Furnivall (London, 1871)

Fourth Report of the Deputy Keeper of the Public Records (vol. 4, London, 1843)

Foxe, J. *Narratives of the Days of the Reformation*, ed. J.G. Nichols (London, 1859)

Grafton, R. *Grafton's Chronicle* (London, 1809)

Hall, E. *Chronicle: containing the History of England* (London, 1809)

Hayward, J. *The Life and Raigne of King Edward the Sixth* (Ohio, USA, 1993)

Historical Manuscripts Commission, Calendar of the manuscripts of the Marquis of Bath at Longleat House (5 vols, London, 1904–80)

Historical Manuscripts Commission, Calendar of the manuscripts of the Duke of Rutland (4 vols, London, 1888–1905)

Historical Manuscripts Commission, Calendar of the manuscripts of Marquis of Salisbury at Hatfield House (24 vols, London, 1883–1976)

Historical Manuscripts Commission, Report on the Records of the city of Exeter (London, 1916)

Holinshed, R. *Chronicles of England, Scotland and Ireland* (6 vols, London, 1808)

Journals of the House of Commons (55 vols, London, 1803–52)

Journals of the House of Lords, 1509–1577 (London, 1771)

The Legend of Sir Nicholas Throckmorton, ed. J.G. Nichols (London, 1874)

Letters and Papers, Foreign and Domestic of the reign of Henry VIII, ed. J.S. Brewer et al. (21 vols, 1965)

Letters of John Calvin, ed. J. Bonnett (2 vols, Edinburgh, 1855–57)

'Letters of William, Lord Paget of Beaudesert', ed. B.L. Beer, in *Camden Miscellany*, XIII (4th series, London, 1974)

'The Letters of Richard Scudamore to Sir Philip Hoby', September 1549– March 1555', ed. S. Brigden, in *Camden Miscellany*, XXX (London, 1990)

The Lisle Letters: An Abridgement, ed. M. St. Clare Byrne (London, 1983)

Literary Remains of King Edward VI, ed. J.G. Nichols (2 vols, London, 1857)

Machyn, H. *The Diary of Henry Machyn, Citizen and Merchant-Taylor of London*, ed. J.G. Nichols (London, 1848)

Madden, F. *Privy Purse Expenses of the Princess Mary* (London, 1831)

Original letters illustrative of English history, ed. H. Ellis (1st series, 3 vols, London, 1824)

Original letters illustrative of English history, ed. H. Ellis (2nd series, 4 vols, London, 1827)

Original letters illustrative of English history, ed. H. Ellis (3rd series, 4 vols, London, 1969)

Original Letters relative to the English Reformation, ed. Rev. H. Robinson (2 vols, Cambridge, 1846–47)

Patten, W. 'The expedition into Scotland of the most worthily fortunate prince Edward Duke of Somerset', in *An English Garner* (8 vols, London, 1877–96)

Ponet, J. *A short treatise of politike power* (Amsterdam, 1972, facsimile of 1556 edition)

Scottish Correspondence of Mary of Lorraine, ed. A.I. Dunlop (Edinburgh, 1927)

Sermons of Hugh Latimer, ed. G.E. Corrie (Cambridge, 1844)

State Papers: King Henry the Eighth, ed. A. Strahan et al. (11 vols, London, 1830–52)

Statutes of the Realm (10 vols, London, 1810–28)

Stow, J. *A Survey of London* (Stroud, 2005)

Stow, J. *The annales of England, until 1592* (London, 1592)

'The Travels and Life of Sir Thomas Hoby', ed. E. Powell, in *Camden Miscellany*, X (London, 1902)

Troubles connected with the Prayer Book of 1549, ed. N. Pocock (London, 1884)

Tudor Royal Proclamations, ed. P.L. Hughes and J.F. Larkin (3 vols, New York, 1964)

Wriothesley, C. *A Chronicle of England* (2 vols, London, 1875, 1877)

Secondary Sources

Beer, B.L. *Rebellion and Riot: Popular Disorder in England During the Reign of Edward VI* (Kent, Ohio, 1982)

Beer, B.L. 'The commoyson in Norfolk, 1549', *The Journal of Medieval and Renaissance Studies,* 6 (1), (1976), pp. 73–99

Beer, B.L. 'A Critique of the Protectorate: An Unpublished Letter of Sir William Paget to the Duke of Somerset', *Huntingdon Library Quarterly*, 34 (3), (1971), pp. 277–83

Bernard, G.W. 'The Downfall of Sir Thomas Seymour', *The Tudor Nobility*, ed. G.W. Bernard (Manchester, 1992)

Bindoff, S.T. *The House of Commons 1509–1558* (3 vols, London 1982)

Burnet, G. *A History of the Reformation of the Church of England* (2 vols, London, 1681, 1683)

Bush, M.L. *The Government Policy of Protector Somerset* (London, 1975)

Bush, M.L. 'Protector Somerset and Requests', *The Historical Journal*, 17 (3), (1974), pp. 451–64

Bush, M.L. 'The Lisle-Seymour Land Disputes: A Study of Power and Influence in the 1530s', *The Historical Journal*, 9 (3), (1966), pp. 255–74

Calvin, J. *Commentaries on the Epistles to Timothy, Titus and Philemon* (Edinburgh, 1856)

Cardigan, C.S. *The Wardens of Savernake Forest* (London, 1949)

Cooper, C.H. *Athenae Cantabrigienses* (3 vols, Cambridge, 1858)

Demers, P. 'The Seymour Sisters: Elegizing Female Attachment', *The Sixteenth Century Journal*, 30 (2), (1999), pp. 343–65

Dent, E. *Annals of Winchcombe and Sudeley* (London, 1877)

Dictionary of National Biography (22 vols, London, 1998)

Dietz, F.C. *Finances of Edward VI and Mary* (Northampton, Mass., 1918)

Fletcher, A. *Tudor Rebellions* (Harlow, 1995)

Foster, J. *Alumni Oxonienses: the Members of the University of Oxford, 1500–1714* (4 vols, Oxford, 1892)

Fuller, T. *The History of the Worthies of England* (3 vols, London, 1860)

Gasquet, F.A. and Bishop, E. *Edward VI and the Book of Common Prayer* (London, 1890)

Haigh, C. *English Reformations: Religion, Politics and Society under the Tudors* (Oxford, 1995)

Hoak, D.E. *The King's Council in the Reign of Edward VI* (Cambridge, 1976)

Ives, E.W. 'Henry VIII's Will: The Protectorate Provisions of 1546–7', *The Historical Journal*, 37 (4), (1994), pp. 901–14

Ives, E.W. 'Henry VIII's Will: A Forensic Conundrum', *The Historical Journal*, 35 (1992), pp. 779–804

Jackson, J. E. 'Wulfhall and the Seymours', *Wiltshire Archaeological and Natural History Magazine*', 15, (1875), pp.140–207

Jacob, A. *A Complete Peerage* (2 vols, in 3 parts, London, 1766)

James, S.E. 'A Tudor Divorce. The Marital History of William Parr, Marquess of Northampton', *Transactions of the Cumberland and Westmorland Antiquarian and Archaeological Society*, 90, (1990), pp. 199–204

Jordan, W.K. *Edward VI: The Threshold of Power* (London, 1970)

Jordan, W.K. *Edward VI: The Young King* (London, 1968)

King, J.N. 'Protector Somerset, Patron of the English Renaissance', *The Papers of the Bibliographical Society of America*, 70, (1976), pp. 307–31

Loach, J. *Protector Somerset* (Oxford, 2001)

Maclean, J. *The Life of Sir Thomas Seymour* (London, 1869)

Miller, H. 'Henry VIII's Unwritten Will: Grants of Lands and Honours in 1547', in *Wealth and Power in Tudor England,* ed. E.W. Ives (London, 1978)

Muller, J.A. *The Letters of Stephen Gardiner* (Cambridge, 1933)

Muller, J.A. Stephen *Gardiner and the Tudor Reaction* (London, 1926)

Needham, R. and Webster, A. *Somerset House Past and Present* (London, 1905)

Nichols, J.G. 'Anne, Duchess of Somerset', *The Gentleman's Magazine*, 2nd series, 23, (1845), pp. 371–81

Nichols, J.G. 'The Second Patent Appointing Edward Duke of Somerset Protector', *Archaeologia*, 30, (1844), pp. 463–89

Outhwaite, R.B. *Inflation in Tudor and Early Stuart England* (London, 1982)

Oxford Dictionary of National Biography (60 volumes, Oxford, 2004)

Pollard, A.F. *England under Protector Somerset* (New York, 1966)

Prockter, A. and Taylor, R. (eds.) *A to Z of Elizabethan London* (London, 1979)

Rose-Troup, F.B. *The Western Rebellion of 1549* (London, 1913)

Russell, F.W. *Kett's Rebellion in Norfolk* (London, 1859)

Rowse, A.L. *Tudor Cornwall: Portrait of a Society* (London, 1957)

St. Maur, H. *Annals of the Seymours* (London, 1902)

Sander, N. *Rise and Growth of the Anglican Schism* (London, 1877)

Seymour, W. *Ordeal by Ambition, An English family in the Shadow of the Tudors* (London, 1972)

Shagan, E.H. 'Protector Somerset and the 1549 Rebellions: New Sources and New Perspectives', *The English Historical Review,* 114 (Feb.), (1999), pp. 34–63

Slavin, A.J. 'The Fall of Lord Chancellor Wriothesley: A Study in the Politics of Conspiracy', *Albion*, 7 (4), (1975), pp. 265–86

Smith, L.B. 'The Last Will and Testament of Henry VIII: a Question of Perspective', *The Journal of British Studies*, 2 (1), (1962), pp. 14–27

Smith, T. 'Sir Thomas Smith's defence of his conduct and character, addressed to the Duchess of Somerset', *Archaeologia*, 38 (1860), pp. 120–7

Stone, L. *The Crisis of the Aristocracy, 1558–1641* (Oxford, 1965)

Strype, J. *Ecclesiastical Memorials* (3 vols, London, 1822)

Tottel's Miscellany, ed. H.E. Rollins (2 vols, Cambridge, Mass., 1965)

Tudor Economic Documents, ed. R.H. Tawney and E. Power (3 vols, London, 1924)

Victoria History of London (vol. I, London, 1974)

Victoria History of the County of Middlesex (13 vols, London, 1969–2009)

Victoria History of Wiltshire (18 vols, London, 1953–2011)

Wood, M.A.E. *Letters of Royal and Illustrious Ladies* (3 vols, London, 1846)

Works of John Knox, ed. D. Laing (6 vols, Edinburgh, 1846–64)

Wrigley, E.A. and Schofield, R.S. *The Population History of England, 1541–1871* (London, 1981)

Writings and Translations of Myles Coverdale, ed. G. Pearson (Cambridge, 1844)

List of Illustrations

1   Edward Seymour, Duke of Somerset, Lord Protector of England.
    © Reproduced by Permission of the Marquess of Bath, Longleat House,
    Warminster, Wiltshire, Great Britain.
2   Queen Jane Seymour. Bartolozzi engraving of Holbein drawing. Author's
    collection.
3   Henry Howard, Earl of Surrey. Author's collection.
4   Prince Edward. Author's collection.
5   William Paget. © National Portrait Gallery, London.
6   Coronation procession. Royal Collection Trust / © Her Majesty Queen
    Elizabeth II 2016.
7   William Parr, Marquis of Northampton. Author's collection.
8   John Dudley, Duke of Northumberland. © National Trust Images / John
    Hammond.
9   Thomas Cranmer, Archbishop of Canterbury by Gerlach Flicke. Bridgeman
    Images.
10 Battle of Pinkie Cleugh. The Bodleian Libraries, The University of Oxford
    (8° P. 62 Art. Seld., Sig. Gvii recto).
11 Thomas Seymour by Nicholas Denisot. © National Maritime Museum,
    Greenwich, London.
12 Queen Katherine Parr. Bridgeman Images.
13 Edward VI in Parliament from The Dethick Garter Book. Royal Collection
    Trust / © Her Majesty Queen Elizabeth II 2016.
14 King Edward VI by William Scrots. Royal Collection Trust / © Her Majesty
    Queen Elizabeth II 2016.

15 Bishop Latimer preaching. The Bodleian Libraries, The University of Oxford (Douce F. Subt. 2, p. 1353).
16 Princess Mary. Author's collection.
17 Princess Elizabeth by William Scrots. Royal Collection Trust / © Her Majesty Queen Elizabeth II 2016.
18 Sir William Sharington. Author's collection.
19 King Edward VI and the Pope. Bridgeman Images.
20 Tower of London by Wenceslaus Hollar. Royal Collection Trust / © Her Majesty Queen Elizabeth II 2016.
21 Richard Rich. Author's collection.
22 Philip Hoby. Author's collection.
23 Edward VI's council memorandum. © The British Library Board (Cotton Vespasian F. XIII f.273)
24 Somerset's final devotions. © The British Library Board (Stowe 1066, frontispiece)
25 Execution of the Duke of Somerset. Bridgeman Images.

Index